Raising Baby by the Book

Raising Baby
by the Book

The Education of

American Mothers

Julia Grant

Yale University Press

New Haven & London

Set in Adobe Garamond type by The Composing Room of Michigan, Inc.
Printed in the United States of America.

Library of Congress Cataloging-in-Publication Data

Grant, Julia, 1953–
    Raising baby by the book: The education of American mothers /
Julia Grant.
        p.   cm.
    Includes index.
    ISBN 0-300-07214-7 (cloth : alk. paper)
        1. Mothers—United States.   2. Motherhood—United States.
    3. Child rearing—United States.   4. Parenting—United States.
    I. Title.
    HQ759.G75   1998
    649'.1—dc21   97-37286
                                                                        CIP

A catalogue record for this book is available from the British Library.

The paper in this book meets the guidelines for permanence and durability of the
Committee on Production Guidelines for Book Longevity of the Council on
Library Resources.

10   9   8   7   6   5   4   3   2   1

Contents

Acknowledgments

I would not have been able to write this book had it not been for the committed teachers at the University of Massachusetts, Boston, who nurtured my passion for scholarship as an undergraduate and showed me that there was a place for me in academe. I would especially like to thank Ann Froines, Linda Gordon, Rusty Simonds, and Glenn Tinder for being inspirational teachers and scholars. As a graduate student, I was also blessed in being able to study with David Hall, Cecilia Tichi, Robert St. George, and Thomas Glick, all of whom are exemplary interdisciplinary scholars. Susan Mizruchi of Boston University and Joyce Antler of Brandeis University went beyond the bounds of generosity in mentoring me on this project when it was a dissertation. They offered simultaneous doses of criticism and support and encouraged me to submit the manuscript for publication.

Since coming to James Madison College at Michigan State University, I have received staunch support for my work from several people, including Ken Waltzer and William Allen. Several of my colleagues at Madison have also read and critiqued chapters of the dissertation. I especially want to thank Jessica Deforest, Ken Waltzer, Linda Racioppi, Colleen Tremonte, and Wallace Genser for their insightful feedback. I have also benefited from the critiques and encouragement of colleagues outside this university. Hamilton Cravens, Steven Schlossman, Barbara Beatty, Heather Munro-Prescott, Ellen Condliffe Lagemann, Virginia Vincenti, and Sarah Stage have all read parts of the manuscript and offered suggestions for improvements. During the last stages of writing, Katherine O'Sullivan See and Katherine Grant both proved to be enthusiastic and critical readers. Susan Stein-Roggenbuck was a superb research assistant, and I profited greatly from her knowledge of the history of home economics. My professorial assistant, Cara Coraluca, gave much-needed expert assistance with critical details toward the end of the project. I would also like to thank students with whom I have shared my work in progress and who have offered me suggestions about how to make my work more accessible to a diverse audience.

I have received financial assistance from the Rockefeller Archive Center, the Boston University Humanities Foundation, the Cornell College of Human Ecology, and Michigan State University, all of which made it possible for me to travel comfortably to various archives to conduct the research for this book.

There are many individuals outside of the academy to whom I am personally indebted. Every member of my family of origin has been a source of sustenance and support, including my mother and father, Kate, Sheila, Mary Ellen, Henry, Meg, and Betsy. My brother Bill, who died recently, was very proud of his academic sister, and I am saddened that he did not have a chance to see my work in published form. I have had many wonderful conversations with my lifelong friend Lisa Davis, who has worked as an early childhood educator and school social worker and has helped keep me informed about current educational practices. Deborah Swedburg taught me how to teach; she and Susan Carlisle also provided emergency lodging and emotional support during a crucial stage in the dissertation-writing process. Linda Racioppi and Jessica Deforest have been wonderful friends and colleagues; both have read and critiqued numerous drafts and whenever necessary boosted my spirits. And finally I must thank Nancy Gardner, whose love, support, and humor have enriched both my life and this project.

As I have conducted my research, I have been asked many times if I am a mother myself. Because I was not a parent when I wrote this book, I often felt compelled to remind people that you don't have to have been in the military or the presidency to write about those subjects. At the same time, I imagine it's not a total accident that as the eldest of eight children, I am fascinated by my mother's life and struggles. She not only raised eight children in the midst of difficulty and turmoil but chose to dedicate her energies as a parent educator to families in need when her own children had grown. I dedicate this book to my mother, Mary Louise O'Connor Grant.

Introduction

That calm, sure, unambivalent woman who moved through the pages of
the advice manuals I read seemed as unlike me as an astronaut.
—*Adrienne Rich,* Of Woman Born *(1976)*

Since I started researching and writing this book, my sisters have
begun having babies, occasioning many fruitful interchanges about
the ramifications of "raising baby by the book." They have shared
their thoughts about the many baby books they have consulted, from
the ubiquitous *What to Expect When You're Expecting* to those they
grab from the shelves when their toddlers have had one tantrum too
many.[1] Some of my intellectual conceptions have been modulated by
my sisters' more pragmatic views. I was chatting with my then-preg-
nant sister Meg about the propensity of today's mothers to consult
books, rather than relatives or friends, for help in rearing children,
when she objected skeptically, "Jeez, Jules, don't we consult books for
everything these days?" She reminded me that we are as likely to have
gardening, cooking, and home decorating books as we are to have
parenting books. We are indeed living in an information society.

This book charts the impact of our ever-increasing quest for information on one of the most personal and meaningful of adult activities, one with significant public ramifications. Today's American parents are besieged with advice from the medical and scientific professions on how to raise normal children. Defined primarily as "women's work" since the late eighteenth century, parents have become increasingly reliant on professional child-rearing expertise. The ideal modern mother is expected to know that two-year-olds can be "terrible," that it is important to read to small children, and that children should not be toilet-trained before they are developmentally prepared for it. But she must also be ready to change some of her child-rearing practices when the experts chance upon new findings suggesting that current practices may impede her children's development. Now more than ever, being a good parent entails accepting full responsibility for the future welfare of one's children.

The quantities of expert information available have produced considerable anxiety among parents, as they sift through competing messages about how best to care for children. This superabundance of information was apparently already a problem for some mothers by 1842, when the author of "Anxious Mothers" complained: "Everywhere we are told of the responsibilities of mothers, the great and arduous duties devolving upon them; and wherever we find a mother alive to these responsibilities, and aware of these high duties, we find also, an anxious, careworn, and dispirited woman. . . . The excessive interest awakened in behalf of education has produced in the conscientious of our sex a nervous solicitude, totally incompatible with the well discharge of their duties."[2] More than a hundred years later anthropologist Margaret Mead named anxiety as a central component of American character, and consequently of parenthood: "So long-standing and so rapid have been these processes of change that expectation of change and anxiety about change have been built into our character as a people. Our homes have been launching platforms from which our children set out on unchartered [sic] seas, and we have become correspondingly more anxious that they should be perfectly equipped before they go. . . . Walking always new roads, with hardly a map of the path before us, awareness and alertness have taken the place of custom and unconscious docility to the ways of the past."[3] Baby books and medical charts have become the maps that accompany many mothers on their journey to equip their children for adulthood.

Because adults have the ability to maintain cultural practices and traditions, they have also had the power and the responsibility to define what constitutes a good or normal child. But unlike the theoretical children found in the prescrip-

tive literature, real children have never been easy to manage, define, or systema-
tize; and parents themselves have rarely been able to conform to the ideals
described in child-care manuals. Our modern quest for scientific explanations
of children's behavior expresses our desire to manage the inherently messy
process of raising children in a complex society.

My sometimes interchangeable use of the words "mother" and "parent"
reflects the uncertainty about the gender of the caregiver that has pervaded the
advice literature on child rearing. In principle, the mother is not the only parent
of a child, and during certain periods in Western history, the father has been
regarded as the more significant parent. The emergence of our conception of
the mother as the pivotal parent, however, is inextricably entangled with the
changing character of parenthood that is the subject of this book. As the
socialization of young children became increasingly concentrated in the nuclear
family in nineteenth-century America, stricter boundary lines were drawn
around the respective responsibilities of mothers and fathers. Mothers were
invested with primary responsibility for children's well-being, and fathers with
breadwinning. With the onset of industrialization, mothers were charged with
creating and maintaining the emotional and spiritual "haven" out of which
family members, and especially children, would emerge to confront society.
The association of mothers with emotion and nurture and their role as a foil to
an ever more impersonal and contractual society have contributed to the
enduring symbolic power of the mother-child bond in American popular
literature, political rhetoric, and more recently, in the social and behavioral
sciences.[4] This book centers on mothers' organizing efforts, their education,
and their thoughts about child rearing in relation to dominant conceptions of
motherhood. Mothers' work and the meanings assigned to it have, however,
always been constructed in conjunction with definitions of fatherhood. Thus
Raising Baby by the Book also touches on the changing definitions and practices
of fatherhood, both in the prescriptive literature and in the perceptions of
mothers.

As parenting has become a more specialized occupation, it has also become
dependent on information from expert sources, not the least of which are
pediatricians, psychologists, and the baby books these professionals produce.
The association of good mothering with medical or scientific expertise con-
trasts with the notion that raising children is a matter of common sense. The
medicalization of American motherhood was a complex process, involving a
series of negotiations between mothers and the professionals—and a fair
amount of resistance all along the way. In the nineteenth century people often

sneered at those who were inept enough to raise their children "by the book," because it was assumed that common sense was a much more authoritative guide. Similarly, before the present century, few mothers would ask their family physician when they should wean or toilet-train their infants. Common sense has been defined as a "cultural system" that purports to derive its principles from the practices of everyday life. To members of a given culture, common sense is accepted uncritically as inherent in the very nature of life itself, although it is no less a cultural construct than is expertise. Common sense is, at the same time, distinctly "anti-expert," because its tenets are assumed to be within the reach of all members of the society, rather than only of individuals with specialized training.[5] What we consider to be common sense in our society clearly varies with our life experiences and the many aspects of the self—including race, class, and gender—that enter into the construction of our identities. To complicate matters, what some call common sense may have had its origins in professional expertise, an overlap that makes it difficult to distinguish between these forms of knowledge. When we talk about parenting, then, it is increasingly unclear what we mean by common sense.

Although education about motherhood had existed since the early nineteenth century, a systematic campaign for parent education emerged in the 1920s, based on the premise that scientific knowledge should displace common sense as the final determinant of effective child-rearing strategies. Grandma's theories of child rearing were deemed inadequate for a society increasingly structured according to the mandates of scientific expertise. Parent education clothed itself in the rhetoric of the behavioral, social, and medical sciences and ultimately became institutionalized in the professions of pediatrics, child psychology, and the interdisciplinary hybrid known as child development. Although child development expertise appears to be objective because of its scientific underpinnings, its content embodies the social and political tensions of our society.[6] With the media rapidly reporting medical and social-scientific research advances to a national audience, only a small time lapse exists between the generation of scientific findings about children and their dissemination. Without professional training, how do parents know how to evaluate these research findings? How does—and should—this information affect the ways in which parents interact with their children? In this book I seek to provide historical answers to these questions, by examining the experiences of mothers of the past as they processed and responded to experts' prescriptions for raising children.

Parents' responsibility for children has been at the heart of many of our most pressing cultural dilemmas. The rhetoric employed by both political parties about the need for "family values" illuminates the continual relevance of this theme. The fractured parent-child relationship has come to symbolize social discontinuity and the problems of cultural reproduction in American society. As traditional institutions for cultural transmission—such as local communities, churches, and schools—have faltered, the medical, psychological, and other helping professions have targeted the parent-child relationship as a pivotal site for the management of individual behavior. Eras marked by a rising intensity and volume of parenting prescriptions, such as the ones I concentrate on in this book, reveal uncertainty and anxiety about the survival of particular forms of civilization.[7] Thus a study of the education of mothers, both its content and its reception, can tell us much about our most pressing cultural concerns and how those concerns have been articulated in the dialogues between mothers and experts.

A rich and varied scholarship treats the rise of professional child-care advice aimed at parents, particularly mothers. Analyses of the literature have yielded many insights about the intellectual and social origins of ideas about child rearing. The early literature rarely paid attention to the audience for whom the works were written, however, and instead restricted itself to narratives in which masculine experts wrested women's authority as mothers away from them. These interpretations implied that the family was a masculine invention, and a middle-class professional one at that. Some recent analyses of motherhood, however, focus on the role women play in actively constructing their experiences in the family. According to sociologist Martha McMahon, women's behaviors and values cannot be reduced to "dependent variables" of the social structure.[8] Women undoubtedly practice mothering in the United States within the bounds of the existing social structure, but, like other marginalized groups, mothers have struggled to maintain a degree of individual choice where they are able to do so, and the choices they make can alter the larger societal institutions that govern their lives. For instance, in her study of the history of modern birthing practices, *Brought to Bed,* Judith Walzer Leavitt argues that the conjunction of women's fears about infant and maternal mortality with the desire of the medical profession to establish its authority over pregnancy and childbearing contributed to the medicalization of childbirth. Even if the medical profession ultimately gained more than women did from these changes, women, as consumers of medical expertise, have been (and continue to be) instrumental in the transformation of birthing practices.[9]

Similarly, in my study I discovered that professionals in the child sciences did not foist their findings off on unsuspecting American mothers; initially, middle-class mothers pursued knowledge about children's mental and physical development in the belief that they were specially equipped to contribute to scientific knowledge about childhood. In fact, women as a consumer group organized to demand child development expertise even before the profession was established, as they sought assistance in the increasingly complex and privatized enterprise of raising children. Unfortunately, in the process, scientists gained the upper hand, leaving mothers as consumers of knowledge about children produced mainly by those who were not themselves primary caretakers of children. But as we shall see, most mothers are discriminating consumers who evaluate professional expertise as one body of knowledge to be considered along with existing maternal practices and familial, religious, and community values.

Some scholars have postulated that dominant ideologies of motherhood reflect the experiences of white, middle-class women, but it is questionable whether these overarching ideas reflect the complexity of *any* women's lives.[10] Race, class, and ethnicity are not the only salient factors affecting a woman's approach to raising children, although they are highly significant. Even women from seemingly similar backgrounds may display striking differences in their child-rearing beliefs, an indication of the importance of such factors as age, region, religious affiliation, mother's family of origin, education, marital situation, and individual temperament. At least in the context of the twentieth-century United States, the practice of parenting is highly individualized. Yet despite the plethora of approaches to motherhood in our complex society, some common themes emerge. Perhaps most important, we find that—regardless of whether they consult professional experts—mothers consider that they have access to a considerable body of "commonsense" knowledge about children.

According to philosopher Sara Ruddick, mothers must think about how to ensure their children's survival, how to foster their development, and how to train them to be socially acceptable adults. Of course, mothers who wage a daily battle to ensure their children's survival may find it difficult to concentrate on fostering development and training their children for social acceptability. But most mothers at least understand these as aims of child rearing. The pursuit of these goals is especially complicated in a society that has no single vision of ideal childhood or adulthood but stresses the need for the specialized nurture of individual children. This concept was reinforced for me when I complimented a single mother on her calm demeanor with her two-year-old. "You have to think about it all the time," she said. "How shall I handle each problem that arises? How can I convince my child that what I think is best for her is what she needs to do?" Maternal thinking arises from the interaction between child and parent. The interaction takes place, however, within the context of particular communities that may provide important alternatives to the culture of professional expertise.[11]

In the records of mothers' study clubs and in the letters mothers wrote to child-care experts in the 1950s, I found complex thoughts about raising children and mothers' appraisals of professional expertise. I made a special effort to uncover voices of women across the spectrum—African-American, immigrant, working-class, rural, and urban women, in addition to the more commonly heard voices of literate middle-class women—as they spoke about raising children. Although the records were not as diverse as I would have wished—the most descriptive accounts were overwhelmingly those of white, native-born women—remarkable variations of opinion appear in the documents regarding numerous aspects of child raising. Interestingly, even mothers who joined mothers' study clubs were as likely to criticize as to praise expert advice, from which it can be inferred that few mothers slavishly subscribe to the precepts in the baby books.

In the course of my research on education for motherhood, I was sometimes asked whether I used oral histories. I was stunned by the vividness with which the women I encountered in various manuscript collections recorded their feelings and exchanges about children, the trials and tribulations of mothering, and memorable moments of conflict, hysteria, and humor. At the same time, in the few oral histories I conducted, I observed that many mothers whose children were now grown, with families of their own, regarded their past maternal experiences as a narrative with a satisfactory or even happy outcome and tended to discount, or perhaps failed to remember, any that did not fit easily into this narrative.

Toward the end of my writing, I contacted some of the women who had written to Dr. Spock as young mothers during the 1950s. A twenty-four-year-old second-generation Italian woman from a small village in New York had corresponded with Spock in 1957 about her troubles with two of her three preschoolers. The first paragraph of her letter explained that her five-year-old son was still periodically wetting his pants, and she was worried about his starting school without having corrected this problem. The rest of the four-page letter described the exploits of her two-year-old son, who, she claimed, was "motor-driven," "a rebel," "defiant," with a "will . . . stronger than mine." She and her husband could find no one, including the grandparents, who would babysit for the child, and they were nervous, exhausted, and at their wits' end. I wondered whether the writer had passed through these travails successfully. After explaining that I was a historian who was researching the impact of the ideas of child-care experts on American women, I asked if she remembered writing to Dr. Spock. She immediately responded that she had written of her problem with her five-year-old's toilet-training, but she was unable to remember further details of the letter. With her permission, I then read aloud from her account of her exasperating encounters with her two-year-old. She interrupted me, insisting that the child her letter described was not at all as she had depicted him. He was, she assured me, a "placid" and "quiet" child. He may have been a bit exploratory, she reminisced, but he was basically a pleasant and easy baby. As we went on to discuss her life as a mother in the ensuing years, she explained that the problematic toilet-training of her older child had resolved itself as soon as he started school. As he matured, however, he exhibited serious problems; he had been a delinquent in high school, a drug user, and he was currently taking a prescription medication for depression; she was relieved that he had not yet been in jail. Her son was now forty, but she still worried about him constantly and wondered whether his problems might have resulted from some failure in her mothering, even speculating that her ambivalence about her pregnancy might have had an adverse impact on his development.

The "rebel" two-year-old described in the letter, however, had turned into a model adult: the chief of police in his hometown, with a good marriage and lovely children. Thus, her memory of her children's babyhood was very much influenced by the path their lives had taken as adults. The difficult toilet-training of the child who had developed problems now seemed more significant than when she wrote the letter, while the rebel two-year-old's disturbing behavior had diminished in importance as he matured successfully (Telephone conversation with V. V. of Frankfort, N.Y., 23 July 1996). Oral histories undoubtedly provide the historian with crucial factual and interpretive information not easily obtained elsewhere. At the same time, rarely can they capture the immediacy of a confrontation of a young mother with a colicky infant or a rebellious toddler.[12]

My motivations in writing this book are twofold. First, I seek to document the emergence of child development expertise and educational programs for mothers from the viewpoint of the consumers and activists: the mothers themselves. Thus my analysis has much less to say about the pioneers in child development, their backgrounds, motivations, and intellectual influences, than about women who sought to transform the efforts of child scientists into a movement to benefit parents. Second, I attempt to survey the range of mothers' responses to the information being purveyed to them by the professionals and female reformers through outlets that included baby-welfare stations, mothers' study clubs, and child-care advice columns.

The focus of *Raising Baby by the Book* is on the psychological dimensions of education for motherhood: socializing, training, and disciplining children. With regard to child feeding, for instance, I am interested in the influence of the prescriptive literature on how children were fed rather than on what they were fed. Although instruction in infant health and hygiene was a central aspect of the early parent education campaign during the late nineteenth and early twentieth centuries, my preoccupation is primarily with the second phase of the campaign, beginning in the 1920s, when reformers directed their attention to the enterprise of rearing psychologically healthy and productive citizens. Unlike, perhaps, advice about children's physical care, advice about how best to raise happy, well-adjusted, and productive children is inevitably subjective and contentious; mothers are uncertain that experts should have the final say in these matters. How the science of children's bodies translated into a "science" of children's minds, with the implications of this shift for parents and families, is a major concern in this book.

I devote most substantial attention to the education of mothers in regard to the rearing of infants and preschoolers, because children at that age are most influenced by their parents and their growth is most carefully monitored. Psychologists, physicians, and educators agree that the infant and preschool years are crucial in laying the groundwork for children's social, psycho-emotional, and cognitive development. Similarly, the parents of infants and toddlers, especially new parents, are apt to be insecure about their parenting abilities and particularly eager to acquire expert assistance in rearing and managing children.

My analysis concentrates on the twentieth century, when mothering informed by medical knowledge about children became a defining feature of the American way of life. The first White House Conference on Children was held in 1909 and resulted in 1912 in the establishment of the U.S. Children's Bureau, an organization that became a primary purveyor of specialized information about children to millions of Americans. Infant-welfare stations, dispensing both information and practical assistance to mothers, flourished during the interwar years and provided the institutional setting for the development of pediatrics as a medical specialty. The shift from home to hospital births also increased mothers' exposure to scientific information about children. Child welfare institutes, which combined research, education, and activism on behalf of children, were inaugurated in several states during the 1910s and 1920s, as were state programs of parent education.[13]

These institutions advanced an understanding of childhood as a complicated and susceptible period of life requiring extensive expert intervention. Professionals established norms of child growth and behavior that defined the boundaries of normal and abnormal childhood. The medicalization of children's physical care paved the way for the intervention by experts in children's emotional health. This development was embodied in the changing concerns of the White House Children's Conference, which in 1909 revolved around the care of handicapped and dependent children, and in 1919 around the issues of children's and mothers' nutrition and health. By 1930, the primary concern of the conference was children's "mental hygiene," and the "Children's Charter" that the conference issued contended that understanding of a child's personality was "his most precious right." Children's psychological well-being took center stage at the Midcentury White House Conference on Children, as is demonstrated by its working title: "Personality in the Making."[14]

The attempt to medicalize children's psychological development reflected a pervasive faith in the ability of science to manage the social change that both parents and reformers sought. Reformers attempted to ensure that children would grow up to further our society's most valued cultural traditions in the midst of rapid transformations in information, technology, and styles of family life. Concerned that motherhood could become an anachronism among educated, middle-class women, who might choose to pursue a public life instead, educators defined motherhood as valuable work requiring extensive knowledge and training. Parent education also promised to reinscribe motherhood as a relevant occupation in the face of acute racial anxieties, which manifested themselves in campaigns for eugenics, immigration quotas, and Americanization programs. The diversity in populations of urban communities threatened to disrupt the orderly transmission of American social values to succeeding generations. By educating immigrant, working-class, and African-American mothers in modern child-rearing strategies, educators aimed both to reinforce maternal authority in the home and to speed up the assimilation processes of those families. Educators did not however anticipate the difficulties of attempting to impose homogeneous styles of child rearing on populations so diverse.

Yet science potentially stood to benefit both mothers and children by providing mothers with the tools to enhance their parenting skills. The middle-class women who orchestrated the parent education movement of the 1920s and

1930s trusted in the power of knowledge to transform motherhood into a profession worthy of the twentieth century. Twentieth-century professionals defined themselves in part by their adoption of standardized knowledge; thus, proponents of professionalized motherhood argued that mothers could adequately fulfill their duties only if they were cognizant of the principles of child development.[15] The women who championed the professionalization of motherhood sought to enhance its status as an occupation, but they overlooked the factors that differentiated it from other professions. Of greatest significance is the fact that mothers do not receive pay for their work. Motherhood is also unique in that it has been regulated by people who are not practitioners themselves. And parenting, it appears clear, has been resistant to standardization, requiring an intuition and a subjectivity that are at odds with objective science.[16]

While many women have sought up-to-date information on the rearing of children, most mothers understand that mothering is not just like any other job; in contrast to what some experts told them in the 1920s, it is not synonymous with the work of the engineer. Mothers have looked to each other as sources of knowledge and advice and have often judged the hard-earned insights of other mothers to be more practical than those of the textbook writers, many of whom were male and presumably lacking in practical experience with children. Mothers often have a degree of private power but very little public power. Thus their ability to affect the dominant discourse has been minimal, yet women's communal networks, conversations, and experiences with children have had an impact on mothers' thinking and practices that is for the most part undocumented in the mass media or in the historical literature.

The book is organized both topically and chronologically. Chapter One provides the nineteenth-century background for my treatment of parent education in the twentieth century. Chapter Two explores the role of three women's organizations that spanned the late nineteenth and the twentieth centuries—the National Congress of Mothers (PTA), the American Association of University Women, and the Child Study Association of America—in inaugurating campaigns for parent education. In Chapter Three, I examine the class, race, and ethnic anxieties that fueled the parent education campaign during the early decades of the century and investigate some of the programs aimed at educating African-American, immigrant, and working-class mothers from the 1910s through the 1940s; I highlight the sometimes congruent, sometimes colliding, agendas of reformers and their constituencies. In Chapter Four I explore some of the major institutional edifices for education for motherhood, in conjunction with child welfare institutes and the home economics extension service, and examine the tensions between research and its dissemination in key states such as New York, Iowa, and Minnesota during the 1920s and 1930s. Chapters Five and Six delve into the content of child-study clubs and women's responses to the materials they were studying, beginning in the 1920s, when the scientific utopianism of the behaviorists predominated in course materials, and continuing through the 1940s, when the democratic philosophy of family life disseminated by pediatrician Arnold Gesell and his colleagues prevailed. In the final chapter (Chapter Seven), I document the pervasive culture of the baby book in the post–World War II era as manifested in the immense popularity of Benjamin Spock's *Commonsense Book of Baby and Child Care*. Using letters written by mothers to popular child-care experts—Benjamin Spock, Louise Bates Ames, and Frances Ilg—I analyze the multifaceted postwar discourse surrounding the reception of popular child-care advice.[17]

Although little in the historical record illustrates the diverse responses of mothers to professional expertise, it seemed unlikely to me that mothers have accepted the ideas of textbook writers uncritically. After all, mothering is a subject that many women think they know something about. It is also one of the few opportunities for the powerless and culturally marginalized to exert power; therefore, mothers may show substantial resistance to efforts to thwart that power. To quote again from Adrienne Rich's penetrating analysis of motherhood as experience and institution, *Of Woman Born,* "Powerless women have always used mothering as a channel—narrow but deep—for their own human will to power." I sought to uncover the ongoing dialogue between mothers and the experts, to reveal the complex process of negotiation between the producers of professional expertise and the consumers. Most of all, in this book I aim to enter women's conceptions of child rearing and motherhood into the historical record.[18]

Chapter 1 Fitting Their Nurture to Their Nature: The Emergence of Education for Motherhood

Diverse children have their different natures; some are like flesh which nothing but salt will keep from putrefaction, some again like tender fruits that are best preserved with sugar. . . . Those parents are wise that can fit their nurture according to their nature.
—*Anne Bradstreet, "In Anne's Hand" (1664)*

The words of Anne Bradstreet, the mother of seven children and the first published American woman writer, remind us that concerns about appropriate disciplinary strategies are not unique to contemporary parents. In Bradstreet's time as in our own, parents have been responsible for training children to carry on the cultural values and traditions of their society. While parents in traditional societies learn informally about how to raise children, parents in modern Western societies are inclined to seek "expert" advice on child rearing, often from professional or written sources.

Clearly, some aspects of the relationship between parents and children are timeless; yet this relationship also reflects values specific to the culture and historical period, as well as broad social changes, pressures, and tensions. During the past several centuries the period of life defined as childhood has lengthened, and adults have paid increasing attention to the special needs and requirements of children. At the same time, scientific prescriptions for meeting children's special needs have proliferated. To what extent are parents able or willing to heed those prescriptions? The question lies at the heart of this book.

The late eighteenth and nineteenth centuries played a pivotal role in fashioning our contemporary ideal of family life, although the modern child-centered family had been in the making for hundreds of years. The relatively small, close-knit nuclear family organized around the needs of children, with the mother as the primary caregiver, has furnished the prototype for American "family values."[1] A glance at nineteenth-century images of childhood—the whimsically illustrated children's books, the toy-stocked nurseries, the fussy clothing in which the children of the genteel were dressed—suggests that children had begun to acquire a distinct and privileged status in many American homes.

By the early 1800s middle-class parents were experiencing such an intensified sense of responsibility for the proper upbringing of their children that many described parental responsibilities as "awful." In a letter to her brother in 1833, Abigail Alcott fretted: "It seems to me at times as if the weight of responsibility connected with these mortal beings would prove too much for me—Am I doing what is right? Am I doing enough? Am I not doing too much? is my earnest inquiry."[2] The rearing of children, because it entails the transmission of cultural values, is among the most crucial of societal undertakings. While caring for children has often been a collective enterprise, in the nineteenth century the awesome responsibility for producing virtuous and civilized adults was increasingly placed on mothers.

Educators, physicians, and clerics issued a torrent of books, pamphlets, and magazine articles on child rearing, which were consumed by the growing middle class. Women in Protestant evangelical churches founded maternal associations where they read about and discussed both biblical and secular theories of child rearing. Sunday schools, infant schools, and kindergartens were organized to attend to the educational needs of young children. Physicians became family advisers, counseling young mothers on the best ways to supervise their babies' health and behavior. Toward the end of the century, scientists undertook to delineate the normal behaviors and developmental processes of young children. Determining the progress of normal development and promoting the healthy physical and mental growth of young people would become a project of the mass media and the numerous professions and institutions that emerged to assist parents in rearing children.

THE TRANSITION TO "INTENSIVE" MOTHERHOOD

For sixteenth- and seventeenth-century colonial American women, child rearing was only one of a multitude of tasks shared by neighbors and kin. With the help of older children, mothers supervised numerous offspring—their own and those of neighbors and relatives—while attending to household needs—sewing, washing, preparing food, and caring for the sick. Historian Laurel Ulrich defines seventeenth-century mothering as "extensive," explaining that "mothering meant generalized responsibility for an assembly of youngsters rather than concentrated devotion to a few." (She uses the terms "extensive" and "intensive" to differentiate between two forms of mothering.)[3] During the colonial period mothers raised an average of seven or eight children to adulthood, but during the nineteenth century women's fertility rates declined dramatically. By midcentury most women were having five or six children, and by 1900 the average woman had three or four children at close intervals and ended her childbearing at an earlier age than her grandmother had.[4] With fewer children to share their resources of care and affection, middle-class mothers of the nineteenth and twentieth centuries increasingly engaged in "intensive" parenting—that is, they concentrated their attention on the physical and emotional nurture of individual children. Certain mothers, however, continued to engage in extensive mothering: those who were living in slavery, raising large numbers of children, struggling to make ends meet, caring for children alone, or working for wages inside or outside the home.

Evidence for the shift from extensive to intensive mothering comes in part from the increase in published advice to parents.[5] The growing popularity of advice manuals was related to the rising rate of literacy, particularly among women, and the greater availability of printed materials, especially in the urban North. Only a sprinkling of child-rearing advice had made its way to America during colonial times, but by the early 1800s the supply was growing. Geographic and social mobility were on the rise, especially in New England, where "the stranger became not the exception but the rule." Acquiring information about rearing children could be difficult when word-of-mouth advice from relatives and lifelong friends was not accessible.[6] Literacy afforded parents access to information substantially different from the face-to-face communications that had characterized earlier eras.[7]

As the market economy evolved, distinctions between home and work led to more highly differentiated roles for men and women. Increasingly, fathers were working outside the home, and as a consequence many urban mothers took over child-rearing functions they had previously shared with their spouses. And women had more time to devote to child rearing as their economically productive activities and the number of their offspring declined. The increasing disjuncture between home and work also contributed to a more systematic differentiation of childhood from adulthood, because middle-class children were less likely to engage in productive labor.[8] Increasingly, the home was romanticized as a warm, safe enclave in an ever more impersonal, competitive, market-driven society. Women, who presided over the home, were expected to maintain spiritual and emotional values that were absent from an industrializing society, while simultaneously preparing male children to compete in the marketplace.[9] The new publications about the care and management of children helped women fulfill their practical, moral, and psychological functions as the family became more privatized.

These publications presented diverse approaches to rearing children that set the framework for future debates about the nature of the child. In their texts early nineteenth-century American authors generally combined both romantic and rationalist approaches to rearing children. The late seventeenth-century liberal John Locke, a physician as well as a philosopher, had been one of the most influential proponents of the rationalist approach, that infants must be systematically disciplined and educated if they are to become civilized adults. The eighteenth-century Romantic Jean-Jacques Rousseau had opposed routinization in the lives of the young. While rationalists sought to tame children and prepare them for their future role as adults, Romantics hoped to preserve children's innocence and natural virtue, which they saw as threatened by industrial society. Romantic and rationalist writers, however, shared a heightened consciousness of the processes of growth and development and expressed the fear that "normal" childhood was not to be easily achieved.

Since colonial days Calvinist beliefs had exercised a pervasive influence on American family life. While Calvinists did not disregard the need for moral training, they believed that human beings were inherently depraved and that grace was necessary for salvation. The new theorists downplayed those ideas and placed greater emphasis on the role of parental nurture in the child's attainment of salvation, an emphasis that middle-class parents apparently shared. According to Linda Pollock, eighteenth- and nineteenth-century American and English diarists, quite unlike their sixteenth- and seventeenth-century counterparts, commonly wrote about their responsibility to train their children to become morally upstanding adults.[10]

Changes in children's physical surroundings and care began to reflect the heightened attention to childhood as a special stage of life. During previous centuries, children often slept in the same rooms as their parents and participated in many adult activities. By the mid-1800s, most upper-class families had nurseries, and prescriptive literature advocated special living spaces for children. Parents began to acquire child-size furnishings, such as high chairs, and toys became a regular feature of many homes. Children had always played, of course, but usually with normal household objects; children had fit into their parents' households, rather than households' being shaped to meet the needs of children.[11]

Although pediatrics did not become a specialty within medicine until the late nineteenth century, physicians had been producing child-rearing texts for parents since the seventeenth century. Given the high mortality rates of infants and young children, physicians often voiced frustration that mothers, who were responsible for the physical care of their offspring, were not equipped with proper information.[12] Medical practitioners, though themselves still uncertain about which practices best preserved the children's health, nevertheless blamed mothers' child-rearing practices for the children's illnesses. The famous English pediatrician William Buchan, whose child-rearing texts were more influential in America than in England, displayed this attitude in his popular *Advice to Mothers* (1804), where he appealed to mothers' fears for their infants' health and promised to provide remedies that would ensure their children's well-being: "What a train of ills seem to await the precious charge, the moment it [the infant] is taken out of the hands of nature! But as the most of these calamities are the consequence of mismanagement or neglect, I shall endeavour to show how they may be prevented by tender and rational attention." Once the child had left the hands of nature, it was open to the damaging influences of civilization, primarily through the mother. According to Buchan's conception, the mother's responsibilities included a knowledge of the principles of child health. He defined a mother as "not . . . the woman who merely brings a child into the world, but [she] who faithfully discharges the duties of a parent. . . . No subsequent endeavours can remedy or correct the evils occasioned by a mother's negligence."[13] Buchan's writings were part of the growing tendency to trace the physical, emotional, and spiritual ills of childhood to maternal "negligence."

With fewer children, parents became anxious about ensuring the physical survival of their children, and physicians gained an enhanced role as family advisers. The supervision of the children's health became one of the most essential functions of the family.[14] Mothers were expected to monitor the mental, physical, and spiritual growth of their children, with the assistance of physicians, clergymen, educators, and the soon-to-be-professional social workers and child psychologists.

Still, no public agreement existed about the extent to which women could or should be educated; leaving children's care and socialization up to them was therefore a questionable enterprise. In his popular treatise on child care published in 1825, physician William Dewees was quite forthright about his misgivings regarding the responsibilities assigned to mothers: "Is it not both unfortunate, and unjust, that the responsibility and care of early education should so exclusively devolve upon the mother?" He suggested that the father, because of his educational background, was more qualified for this undertaking.[15] It is hardly surprising that a voluminous literature emerged to educate women to undertake the "awful" responsibility of parenting or that the middle-class mothers who sought to live up to that responsibility began to feel a creeping sense of anxiety.

THE ARRIVAL OF THE BABY BOOK

In the introduction to *Some Thoughts Concerning Education* (1699), John Locke claimed that his motivation in writing the book derived from parents' befuddlement over the proper way to rear children: "I myself have been consulted of late by so many, who profess themselves at a loss how to breed their children . . . that he cannot be thought wholly impertinent, who brings the consideration of this matter on the stage." Clearly, even seventeenth-century parents were confused about the right methods for raising children. Locke's remarks shed light on the subtle and gradual process through which the modern child-centered family emerged. The book, in which Locke articulates a secular and rational approach to child rearing, went through at least thirty-five English editions before the end of the nineteenth century. It is most famous for its metaphor of the child's mind as a blank slate for parents to write upon. By this Locke meant that children are not born with concepts or attitudes but instead garner them through experience; thus education must begin at birth, when children's minds are most pliant. Locke's theory implicitly countered the Calvinist notion that infants were by nature depraved prior to conversion. He was not a complete believer in the primacy of nurture over nature, however; rather, he stressed that parents must design child-rearing methods according to their child's "natural genius and constitution." In keeping with religious thought, Locke maintained that parents must demand complete obedience from the young child, but he argued that compliance should be achieved through reason, as opposed to beating and chiding, whenever possible.[16] To determine the correct procedures for guiding particular children, parents should "study their [offspring's] natures and aptitudes, and see, by often trials, what turn they easily take, and what becomes them," Locke advised. Around the same time, as we have seen, Anne Bradstreet characterized children as possessing different natures (either "tender fruits" or "flesh") and thus requiring different types of nurture for their moral development.[17]

Eighteenth-century diarist Susan Huntington, like Locke, advocated that parents gain an understanding of their children's minds before attempting to mold them: "The person who undertakes to form the infant mind, to cut off the distorted shoots, and direct and fashion those which may, in due time, become fruitful and lovely branches, ought to possess a deep and accurate knowledge of human nature."[18] Huntington's image of parents as a gardeners with pruning sheers is revealing; once they have gained an "accurate knowledge of human nature," it is permissible for parents to snip and shape children's minds.

Rousseau was not as confident as Locke or Huntington about the beneficial effects of parental training. In his educational treatise *Emile* (1762) he proposed a much more romantic vision of the child's nature than Locke had. Whereas Locke began his book with the famous line, "All the men we meet with, nine parts of ten, or perhaps ninety nine of one hundred, are what they are, good or evil, useful or not, by their education," Rousseau commenced with, "Everything is good as it leaves the hands of the Author of things; everything degenerates in the hands of man." Rousseau diverged from the widespread view that human institutions were necessary to counter the vagaries of human nature; instead, he insisted, nature itself was the source of goodness.[19] Rousseau viewed the prevailing tendency to rush children into adulthood as problematic. He saw childhood as a stage of development worth prolonging and protecting, as opposed to merely a necessary if disagreeable passage along the road to adulthood. Although Rousseau believed that the proper place for an infant was at its mother's breast, he was not sanguine about the effect mothers might have on growing children, because he thought mothers were less concerned with assisting the development of young children than with civilizing them.[20]

The English physician William Cadogan's *Essay on Nursing* (1749) addressed not only the feeding, but also the clothing and management of infants. Like

Dewees and Rousseau, Cadogan displayed contempt for mothers and their ineptitude, an attitude that would permeate the medical establishment for many years. With regard to nursing he claimed, "In my Opinion, this Business has been too long left to the Management of Women, who cannot be supposed to have proper Knowledge to fit them for such a Task, notwithstanding they look upon it to be their own Province." Cadogan shared with Rousseau a disdain for women who chose to give their children to a wet nurse rather than breast-feed them themselves, a tendency which he considered to be a sign of the increasing "unnaturalness" of women. According to Cadogan: "The Treatment of children in general is wrong, unreasonable, and unnatural." He claimed that mothers' practices were grounded neither in reasoning nor in nature but in customs learned from their great-grandmothers, "who were taught by the Physicians of their unenlighten'd Days." Expert treatment of children would be based on both nature and reason, in proportions that presumably only the most up-to-date physicians could correctly gauge. It is impossible to know whether parents were indeed as influenced by physicians' advice as Cadogan suggests, but it is notable that he dates physicians' influence on parental practices at least to the seventeenth century. Indisputably, though, the "expert" advice of a given period may, as Cadogan observed, later become "common sense," which may then be overturned by a new round of expertise.[21]

As we have seen, William Buchan in his *Advice to Mothers* (1804) exhibited similar fears about the dangers that mothers could pose to their young children. He warned mothers that they might endanger their children's health even at the time of conception: feelings of fear, melancholy, and most especially anger must be avoided, for they might harm the fetus. Under the obvious influence of Rousseau, Buchan believed that "nature" was the child's best physician, advocated that mothers breast-feed their own babies, and disparaged the use of medicines for children. Buchan anticipated educational thinkers of a later period in insisting also that early learning was dangerous for children's nervous constitutions. Children were to be left to develop naturally, but mothers would require their physician's advice in order to determine the nature of nature.[22]

The innocent, "natural" child idealized by these physicians was a response to the model of the systematically disciplined and regulated child that was also emerging in the child-rearing literature. Romantics were disturbed by the increasing regimentation of everyday life and sought to protect children from the adult world, rather than to prepare them for it. The "natural" child and the "regulated" child would be the two poles around which conceptions of children's nature would revolve in the following century. By the early 1800s, then, numerous philosophical justifications accompanied these diverse approaches to parenting.[23]

"THE HAND THAT ROCKS THE CRADLE": MOTHERS AND DOMESTIC EDUCATION

Although they had their differences, the advice writers of the early nineteenth century were unanimous in the view that the rearing of children was a responsibility of great magnitude. In the United States, rhetoric linking patriotism and motherhood, designated "republican motherhood" by Linda Kerber, first emerged during the revolutionary era. Kerber argues that in the premodern era motherhood was regarded as a private function, distinctly unrelated to public affairs. In justifying women's exclusion from the privileges of citizenship, however, eighteenth-century American republican ideology defined female citizenship in terms of women's roles as mothers. The language of republican motherhood allotted women the political responsibility of bearing and rearing citizens for the new nation. In a democratic society, individuals could not merely inherit status but must be educated and equipped to maintain or improve it through their own merit and industry. Women as child rearers would take on this crucial task of cultural reproduction—and they would need to acquire sufficient education to fulfill their newly defined responsibilities. That necessity eventually became a justification for women's higher education.[24]

During the nineteenth century, parenting was both valorized and viewed as a uniquely feminine responsibility, whereas previously the boundary lines between mothers' and fathers' obligations, particularly toward older children, had not been so strictly drawn. In earlier centuries, women were primarily responsible for the care and feeding of infants, but fathers, because they were thought to possess the reason and authority that mothers lacked, were regarded as the principal educators of older children. Child-rearing manuals were therefore initially addressed primarily to fathers, but once mothers were charged with the primary socialization and education of children, published advice was almost invariably directed toward women.[25]

In the nineteenth century, good mothering—as defined by the white middle class—became a paradigm for the maintenance of society in general. T. S. Arthur, author of *The Mother* (1846), argued, "Upon the character of the mother depends, almost entirely, the future character and position of the child." Writer and reformer Lydia Sigourney (1838) expressed an even more ambitious vision of motherhood: "No universal agent of civilization exists, but through mothers. . . . In proportion as it prevails, national enmities will disappear, prejudices become extinguished, civilization spread far and wide,—one great people cover the earth, and the reign of God be established." In the literature on domestic education, evangelical Christian teachings converged with more secular theories of child rearing. According to Arthur, mothers, regardless of their circumstances, bore responsibility for their offspring's salvation. Describing the mother of a wayward son, he intoned, "If she had truly loved her child, she could have brought an influence to bear upon him that would have saved him."[26] Maternal nurture was rapidly replacing grace as the central factor in children's moral development.

Motherhood was women's greatest task, according to the prescriptive literature, and in the antebellum era mothers began to assert their expertise as practitioners—in writing. In *The Maternal Physician* (1811) a mother of eight chastised male physicians for telling mothers how to nurse and feed their babies: "These gentlemen must pardon me if I think, after all, that a mother is her child's best physician . . . and that none but a mother can tell how to *nurse* an infant as it ought to be nursed." She took particular issue with physicians who claimed that it was fatiguing for women to nurse and who advocated scheduled feedings for infants.[27] Challenging the intrusion of physicians into women's work of nursing and caring for infants, the author sought to maintain women's authority over the care of small children. As the anonymous publication of her work suggests, women, especially married women, confronted social barriers when attempting to enter public discourse.

The maternal physician was not alone in her belief that women's work with children gave them access to special knowledge about childhood. Mrs. Barwell, an English mother, wrote a remarkably insightful child-rearing text, published in the United States in 1844. Barwell too asserted that women were better able than men to comment on certain matters: "We have several able and judicious treatises on Infancy by medical men; but they are inevitably deficient on many points, to which a woman alone is competent to do justice." Barwell departed from the conventional understanding of childhood, not least of all in her benign interpretation of infant crying, which was commonly viewed as an expression of the will that needed to be eradicated: "As the violence of this period of childhood [infancy] arises so much from want of language, pains should be taken by the mother to establish between herself and her child some means of communication that will smooth the difficulty." Barwell anticipated later psychological thinking in the recognition that mothers' visual communication with their babies through facial expressions has a significant effect on infant development.[28] A work of considerable imagination, Barwell's book contains a body of experiential knowledge about mothering that compares favorably with the findings of twentieth-century experts on child development.

An article in *Ladies' Magazine* (1829), echoing the theme that mothers possessed important empirical information, even suggested that a mother would be the guiding light of modern psychology: "We have often thought, that if the philosophy of mind was ever perfectly developed, it would be the work of some highly intelligent, affectionate, attentive and indefatigable mother. . . . She has done more than see ideas unfold; she has implanted them—she has watched the beginnings of reason—she has assisted the first efforts of thought." This seems a bold depiction of women's potential, especially since women were to be flagrantly excluded from the scientific community in the later decades of the century. Evidence is emerging, however, that girls in the 1830s and 1840s were more likely than boys to study scientific subjects in secondary school, in part because the traditional classical curriculum of boys' schools often left no room for the addition of such subjects as anatomy and natural science. Young women's scientific studies were perceived as useful preparation for their work as mothers. The Reverend J. S. C. Abbott recommended in *The Mother at Home* (1833) that women keep records of their children's development for their own edification and for the benefit of the scientific community.[29]

Both male physicians and mothers who wrote child-rearing manuals agreed that raising children was a discipline that had to be learned. In *The Mother's Book,* the writer and reformer Lydia Maria Child contended that the maternal instinct was not infallible: "You may say, perhaps, that a mother's instinct teaches fondness, and there is no need of urging that point; but the difficulty is, mothers are sometimes fond by fits and starts—they follow impulse, not principle." The pioneering female educator Catherine Beecher reminded the readers of her *Treatise on Domestic Economy* that mothers should not be blamed for mistakes made in child rearing, for they "have never had the knowledge which they have needed"; she insisted that all women should receive domestic education.[30]

The advice-givers urged that instead of alternating between affectionate indulgence and vengeful punishment, parents should rationally discipline their children. This advice was somewhat at odds with the characterization of women as tender, affectionate, and emotional. Some women were alienated by the notion that reason rather than sentiment should guide them in rearing children. One indignant mother confronted Lydia Maria Child: "Well, I should be ashamed of myself if I *could* punish a child when I was not angry. Anybody must be very hardhearted who could do it."[31] This brief outburst is an indication of the reluctance that some women must have felt to implement standardized child-rearing practices. Yet whether they were sympathetic to the views being touted by a growing array of writers or not, women were becoming more aware of the part they played in their children's emotional and moral growth.

If, as Warren Susman says, "one of the things that make the modern world 'modern' is the development of consciousness of self," then a modern approach to parenthood was distinctly in evidence by the late eighteenth century. Parents' diary entries from that period reveal much greater introspectiveness and understanding about themselves as molders of children's characters than in previous eras. Through reading, mothers were seeking to supplement the knowledge about children that they could acquire through their everyday activities. Lydia Sigourney advised mothers to increase their scientific knowledge of infants, declaring, "Intercourse with infancy is improving, as well as delightful. . . . Let us study night and day, the science that promotes the welfare of our infant." Whereas understanding of human nature had previously been the province of theology and philosophy, by the mid-nineteenth century increasing numbers of educated middle-class mothers wished not only to acquire the knowledge to understand children but to contribute to it.[32]

HELP FOR ANXIOUS MOTHERS: THE EMERGENCE OF MOTHERS' ORGANIZATIONS

During the antebellum era, Northern women outnumbered men among churchgoers. The emergence of women as the mainstay of Protestant congregations coincided with the explosion of associational activity in the early 1800s. In addition to organizing missionary, abolitionist, temperance, and moral-reform societies, women formed maternal associations—most often as adjuncts to evangelical Congregational, Presbyterian, or Baptist churches—where they talked about and prayed for their children. Commonplace in the Northeast, maternal associations were important arenas for the transmission of new theories of child rearing.[33]

Historian Mary Ryan has used Oneida County, New York, as a case study to document the explosion of associational activity in the early 1800s. She offers as evidence for this trend an issue of the *Sabbath School Visitant and Juvenile Magazine* (1829) that depicted a child questioning her mother, "Mother, . . . I longed for you this afternoon when I came home from school, and they told me you were gone to the Maternal Society: You go very often. Mother, what is a Maternal Society?" The organizations flourished in New England and eventually in New York, where the evangelical movement known as the Second Great Awakening had inspired reform work by female believers. In 1836, two rural counties in New Hampshire alone reported thirty-eight maternal associations, with a total membership of more than one thousand women.[34]

The first maternal association on record was founded by Mrs. Payson in Portland, Maine, in 1815. The group stated its purpose as that of "combining the practical experience of a community of mothers and adding thereto all the information which they can obtain from reading, as to the best methods of training up children in the way they should go." Payson was purportedly encouraged in her efforts by her husband, the Reverend Doctor Payson, who was concerned that his wife had no other outlet for her talents than her family, which "occupied nearly all her time, and greatly exhausted her spirits."[35] This was a recurring theme: mothers sought relief from the stress of child rearing and their isolation from other adults by forming maternal associations and, later, child-study clubs. These groups gave women a respite from their maternal responsibilities, while simultaneously validating their work as mothers.

The origins of a New Hampshire group founded in 1817 exemplifies this trend: "One of the members, the mother of a numerous family had, for some time previous, been borne down under the weight of her responsibility, which she felt inadequate to sustain. The thought often occurred to her, 'Cannot the anxious mothers among us band together, so that by uniting in familiar conversation and prayer, they may labor more successfully for the spiritual good of their children?'" Feeling overwhelmed and "anxious" about their maternal responsibilities, nineteenth-century mothers discussed "family government and discipline," "parental qualifications," "errors of parents," and "speaking the truth."[36] Although at the end of the nineteenth century child-study groups discarded the religious framework of the earlier associations, they continued to emphasize mothers' responsibility for children's character and behavior.

Despite the greater availability of published literature during this period, relatively few people owned books. To supply their members with background material, some maternal associations established small libraries. The Baptist Maternal Association of Utica went further than this in 1833, when they arranged for the director of a local female academy, Abigail G. Whittelsey, to edit a monthly journal for maternal associations, *The Mother's Magazine*. Soon other maternal associations began publishing similar journals, with titles such as *The Mother's Assistant and Young Ladies' Friend* and *The Mothers' Journal*. Many of the articles were written by Christian clerics, although there were also contributions by mothers and educators and reprints of the writings of Locke,

Rousseau, Dewees, and the educational theorist Johann Pestalozzi, among others.[37]

The maternal associations appear to have drawn their members primarily from the growing lower middle class, contrary to the assumption of many historians that progressive child-rearing advice reached only the upper classes. The Utica Maternal Association, for instance, was composed primarily of the wives of artisans and mechanics, and a Boston association claimed that its members had few educational opportunities because of their pressing household responsibilities. Some argue that these women sought to join groups to facilitate their children's entry into the middle class, but it is just as likely that they joined for the more obvious reasons already discussed—to gain information and support.[38]

At first glance the maternal associations seem quaint offshoots of evangelical culture, yet the groups had therapeutic features that anticipated the "talking cures" and self-help of later periods. Self-disclosure was valued as a means of both solving problems and assuaging anxieties. The author of *Newcomb's Manual for Maternal Associations* (1840) recognized the practical worth of group discussions: "It is important that the members should express themselves freely in regard to their own trials, that they may sympathize together, and receive the aid of each other's experience in difficult cases. Truth is elicited by facts and experiments; and the mother, who has reared a family of children, may be able to give information more important to the young mother, than any thing that can be found in books." Group members believed that mothers' own experiences represented an invaluable source of knowledge. The constitution of the Utica Maternal Association (1824) stated that each mother should "suggest to her sister members such hints as her own experience may furnish, or circumstances seem to render necessary."[39] Interestingly, it was assumed that without an organizational forum mothers might not have access to such knowledge. At least within some segments of society, then, the traditional kinship networks that supplied child-rearing knowledge may no longer have been fully functional.

The literature of domestic education disseminated at the clubs reflected a significant softening of traditional Calvinist child-rearing prescriptions, which had focused primarily on enforcing rigorous discipline in order to "break the will" of the young child and instill unquestioning obedience to parents and other authorities. Advice writers continued to uphold the necessity of children's submission to parental will but counseled parents to use gentler methods of gaining compliance. Mothers were encouraged to be calm and reasonable with their children, to explain the reasons for punishment whenever possible, to refrain from excessive prohibitions, to resist finding fault with children, and to comfort them in their disappointments. Instead of stringent adherence to the old adage, Spare the rod and spoil the child, the new advice stressed the importance of maintaining the bond of affection between mother and child— meanwhile gently steering the child in the right direction.[40]

Drawing on the traditions of mutual benefit societies, the early associations offered practical, spiritual, and emotional support systems to their members, who celebrated births and other significant events in their family lives together. Members also cared for one another through childbirth, sickness, and death. They further entrusted one another with responsibility for the moral and spiritual welfare of their children in case of a mother's death. The possibility of untimely death—their own or their children's—was a central reality of motherhood during this period and a unifying theme in the clubs. The secretary of the Maternal Association of High Street Church, of Providence, Rhode Island, reported in 1855, its nineteenth year of existence, "This year, in the history of the Association, has been an unprecedented one, from the fact that none of its members, either mothers or children, have been removed by death."[41]

Unlike in Britain, where the first mothers' meetings were conducted in the 1870s by upper-class women who sought to reform the rural and urban poor, the first American maternal associations were organized by mothers for their own benefit, decades earlier.[42] American female "home missionaries" did conduct similar meetings for the poor, however, at a later period. Hannah Root Hubbard, a well-off New England widow, organized a series of mothers' meetings in association with Chicago's Protestant Congregational Church between 1864 and 1882. The purpose of the meetings was to convert poor mothers as a means of improving the spiritual welfare of their families. Hubbard believed that the spiritual transformation of the mother was a crucial first step in eliminating the drunkenness, delinquency, and violence that plagued many poverty-stricken families. Hubbard recruited working-class and immigrant women and even persuaded some Catholic mothers to attend her Protestant gatherings. Visiting in the home, offering prayer, consolation, and practical assistance, Hubbard extended a sense of community to these women—many of them newcomers to the city. She did intend to instill a sense of maternal responsibility in her recruits, but her primary objective was obtaining their salvation.

Nevertheless, Hubbard's meetings, which initially drew only a few mothers, then more than a hundred, served primarily as a source of solace. These mothers had difficult lives, and in the mothers' club their suffering was recognized. Hubbard told of one poor Norwegian mother who walked eight miles with her children to attend a meeting: "She was almost heartbroken from trouble with her intemperate husband—I kept her all night, tried to cheer and comfort her." An Irish Catholic mother who attended the meetings had a more tragic story: "With anguish and weeping she told me how her two little children had been suffocated to death by smoke from her burning house—while she was away to work." About another meeting, at which a mother described her seventeen-year-old daughter's suicide, Hubbard wrote: "In view of all these and other trials—I felt that we needed to speak of ourselves as well as of our children today. . . . We could tell each other our sorrow—and help bear each others' burden." Mothers would speak of their afflictions and longings and receive healing through their talk. And after they had all spent one session comforting bereaved mothers, Hubbard remarked: "They seemed like a band of mourning mothers together."[43]

Literary critic Ann Douglas has commented that nineteenth-century women used group mourning as a form of "therapeutic self-indulgence." According to this interpretation, women's sentimentalization of grief detracted from their ability to alter the conditions of their lives in a more purposeful way. Yet indigent mothers in the middle of the nineteenth century had few opportunities to take control of their lives. These poor women—who came from a wide range of ethnic backgrounds—found in the maternal associations a common language that articulated and gave meaning to their pain; the associations created a sense of community that helped women to withstand, if not overcome, the harsh conditions of their lives.[44]

Hubbard's minutes of the meetings also provide a record of the advice she imparted. She stressed that prayer should form the basis for family life and that mothers furnish a positive moral example to their children and spouses. The home should be "pleasant" and "spiritual . . . so that our children can grow in grace."[45] Although they could not control the household income or the prejudices or environmental hazards that confronted them, mothers were expected to sustain a positive spiritual atmosphere under the most trying of circumstances. Hubbard insisted that mothers must be models of virtue, even when their husbands undermined their efforts through intemperance and other disruptive behavior.

Perhaps the predominant subject of discussion in the meetings was the ever-present problem of parental impatience with small children. Hubbard urged mothers to have patience with their children and to refrain from getting angry with them. She embellished one lecture by recounting a mother's vision "of the angel coming and taking her child away—because she was fretful with it," a tale likely to play on maternal guilt feelings in connection with the death of small children. One mother approached Hubbard after a meeting to admit, "My greatest fault is getting out of patience with my children—I never felt before how wrong it is—till you talked about it in the Mothers' meeting."[46] Mothers should show forbearance not only because they served as "moral examples" but because impatience had an adverse effect on children's moral and psychic development. Women were learning that their emotional behavior could have significant effects on the spiritual welfare of their families.

Hubbard affirmed the value of reason in dealings with children, suggesting that "mothers of young children [undertake] to correct them not under excitement—but to talk and pray with them first—as doing far more good than a whipping alone."[47] Hubbard's attitude toward discipline appears to have been fairly representative for the period. Horace Bushnell's influential *Views of Christian Nurture* (1847) articulated a philosophy of child rearing similar to hers. Without rejecting the notion of infant depravity, Bushnell placed greater emphasis than earlier clerics had on the tender loving care of a mother, who could help to "weed out" sin at an early age. Like Bushnell, Hubbard was not opposed to corporal punishment but insisted that it be administered in a reasonable and calm manner. Along with many secular writers on child care, Hubbard stressed that mothers should substitute rationality for impulse in caring for their children.[48]

The associations invested mothers with a responsibility that could at times be onerous. Surely some mothers were put off by Hubbard's preachiness, her desire to convert them to her brand of evangelical Protestantism, and her insistence that mothers were accountable for their family's spiritual well-being. Yet the associations provided women with a venue where they could articulate their private concerns in a public setting.

"SHARPENING EACH OTHER'S WITS": THE MOTHERS' CLUB OF CAMBRIDGE

The Mothers' Club of Cambridge began its meetings in 1878, during the final years of Hubbard's maternal association. Yet more dissimilar groups could not be imagined. Meeting in suburban Boston, the Cambridge mothers were well-off young wives of academics and professionals who sought to advance their own education and create a community where they could socialize and share their experiences. The group quickly grew to forty members; a cap was then set on the membership. Eventually the daughters, aunts, and friends of the original forty women formed three spin-off mothers' clubs. Occasionally over the course of the next fifty years, the four groups held joint meetings to share speakers and celebrate anniversaries and other festive occasions.[49]

Although the first-generation group was Protestant in origin, the topics selected for deliberation were largely secular and provided an opportunity for women without the benefit of a college education to discuss serious literature on child rearing. The group, which combined educational and social functions, displayed the prejudices and beliefs of a privileged class, selecting new members at least partially on the basis of their respectability. During consideration of one potential member, for example, the dismaying fact was revealed that she wore imitation lace on her collars.[50]

Initially, club meetings centered on discussions of books by such well-known authors as Harriet Martineau and John Locke. After some members raised the objection that certain authors, such as Martineau, had never reared children, the group decided to focus more on their own experiences in group discussions. Stella Scott Gilman had her account of the group's activities published pseudonymously because members thought it "unseemly" to have their names appear in print. Entitled *Mothers in Council* (1884), the book described the group's growing disenchantment with the advice-givers: "In some cases they were not disappointed, but in others they found that common-sense contradicted the author, and it was felt that there were those in the growing club who were capable of treating practical subjects more to the edification of the others than any writer whose circumstances were likely to be far different from those of the club."[51] When common sense contradicted the printed material, then, mothers were likely to challenge the validity of the textbooks on the basis of their own experience.

This discontent with the textbook writers' expertise led to the decision to base group meetings on papers written by individual members on jointly chosen topics, such as the differences in the education of women and men, obedience and discipline, rudeness in children, and the management of the household.[52] After hearing a talk by "Mr. Hall," for instance (perhaps psychologist G. Stanley Hall, with whom they were familiar), who instructed mothers to neglect some of their household duties, if necessary, to spend more time with their children, one woman suggested that if "Mr. Hall were not a bachelor, if he were married and had eight children, he might have a different sermon for us." Another wondered which of her duties *could* be neglected.[53] At both nineteenth-century and twentieth-century clubs, women expressed doubts about the ability of male professionals to understand the practical difficulties of simultaneously caring for children and managing the home.

The women were equally opinionated when it came to the views of other mothers, although they could not claim in that case that their antagonists had no experience. A discussion of obedience, held during the group's second session, reveals the range of opinions. Club members had read Jacob Abbott's *Gentle Measures in the Management and Training of the Young* (1871), an immensely influential book, which attempted a compromise between religious and scientific thinking about children. Abbott was quite clear about the need for obedience but argued that it was to be gained by systematic and reasonable discipline rather than severe punishments. One member said, "What is known as 'blind' obedience should never be demanded of children, because it banishes all originality and spirit." Stella Gilman quickly replied, "It is just this sort of obedience that we must insist upon." Some mothers agreed that blind obedience "furnishes the child a definite principle of action," and that children must be prepared to follow the rule of law and God as adults. But others wondered whether children should obey all adults—such as their nurses or relatives—or only their parents. According to Gilman: "Thus we talked on, coming no nearer to a single opinion than we had been when we began, but we were all the time getting what we came for. We were sharpening each other's wits, and becoming acquainted with more views and ways than our own."[54]

These mothers were consumed with concern for their children's physical, emotional, and spiritual well-being. In a historical account of the club from 1904, one member ventured that the group had "passed through the time when the temperature of baby's bath was debated with all the heat, if not the acrimony, of the Philippine question, and when the degree of moral enlightenment to be expected at the age of twelve months caused anxious thought."[55]

The members worried about the diet and posture of their children, in keeping with the medical concerns of the period; looking back, though, they thought that "however distracting it was for us to hurry from breakfast food to posture classes, it was less terrifying than the exclusive attention of our daughters to Psychology."[56] The first generation of club members believed that their daughters, who by the early decades of the twentieth century were forming their own club chapters, had less confidence in their ability to be good mothers. The second-generation Cambridge mothers were more likely to have received a college education and to have tried their talents in an arena other than motherhood. They were also trained to regard scientific expertise as their guide to everyday life, including child rearing. Remembering the group's early days,

Mrs. Crothers speculated: "There were no haunting doubts as to the desirability of the job [of mothering] and not many as to our ability to do it."[57] Crothers's claim is perhaps exaggerated, given that in some of her other writings she discussed the vigilance with which her group attended to their children's bodies and spirits, but the doubts and fears of the early Cambridge mothers seem comparatively innocuous in retrospect.

The founding members were able to debate their views freely, knowing they were on an equal footing with mothers with similar experiences and education. It was easier for them to be skeptical of expert prescriptions for child rearing than it would be for women of their class and position in a later period, for during the late nineteenth and early twentieth centuries most works on child rearing, by clergymen, philosophers, and pedagogues, did not have the persuasive appeal that science would have for their educated daughters.

SCHOOLS FOR CHILDREN AND THEIR PARENTS: INFANT SCHOOLS AND THE KINDERGARTEN MOVEMENT

The infant school movement in the United States arose at the same time as the maternal associations and similarly sought to bolster the traditional family through education. Like the maternal associations, infant schools appear to have been largely a Northern phenomenon.[58] The first American infant school societies were established in the late 1820s in New York, Philadelphia, and Boston. The schools enjoyed a brief heyday in the 1830s before losing public appeal by the 1840s, primarily because of changing beliefs about the value of early schooling.

Infant schools provided a full day of instruction for working-class children between eighteen months and legal school age (which varied by geographical area). The new community of educational reformers targeted two seasons of life largely neglected in previous educational schemas: early childhood and adulthood.[59] One proponent of infant schools explained: "In the nursery—that retired and scarce heeded place of instruction, but which, nevertheless, shapes more minds than all the public schools on earth—these experiments on the infant mind will operate with a power that must cause a great and rapid change. Lyceums, too, are becoming the fashion, partly, no doubt, in consequence of finding that man is susceptible of improvement in every season of life."[60]

Schemes of early childhood education have always had as a secondary motive the reformation and education of parents. Early infant schools were more blatant in their evangelical zeal, however, than later efforts to educate young children. The schools advertised their intention to provide moral training for poor children, who would then be charged with saving their parents from moral degradation. According to William Russell, the editor of the fledgling *American Journal of Education,* "In well authenticated instances, the obdurate heart of a vicious parent has been touched by the innocence of his child, or pierced by an unexpected word of gentle admonition." But if proponents of the infant schools hoped that children might save their unenlightened parents, opponents argued that parents would be relieved of responsibilities that were properly theirs, and that it was "unnatural" to attenuate the relationship between mothers and their young children.[61]

Advocates of infant schools included both educational reformers convinced of the importance of developing new pedagogies and religious women who considered their purpose to be the salvation of the poor. Both groups maintained that infant schools would benefit poor mothers overwhelmed with household duties and wage work, by providing their younger children with a protective and improving environment. Like advocates of the common school movement, proponents of infant schools contended that the education of young children should be a public mandate.[62]

Under the influence of Johann Pestalozzi, who stressed the importance of teaching perceptual skills to young children, reformers aimed to cultivate an educational institution that was both rational and affectionate and provided a healthy, recreational environment for poor children. A few viewed such schools as a positive alternative to primary schools, which they denounced because their routinization did not allow children enough physical movement or opportunity to express themselves creatively. Indeed, progressive educators such as Russell and Robert Owen hoped that the primary school would follow the example of the infant school and promote perceptual training and positive interaction between children and educators. But instead many infant schools adopted both the content and the routines of primary schools, by requiring small children to sit passively through instruction in reading, writing, and arithmetic.[63]

The infant schools succeeded initially because early instruction was considered beneficial for children's intellectual development. Although few hard data exist on the age of school attendance in the early nineteenth century, it was not unusual for children as young as three or four to attend primary school. By the 1830s, however, the notion became widespread that "precocity" could endanger the development of children's minds and even lead to insanity. This belief, combined with the continued romanticization of the mother-child relation-

ship, contributed to growing public skepticism about infant schools. But the
idea of early education was soon resuscitated in the form of the kindergarten,
which gained American adherents in the 1860s and became the basis for a
popular social movement by the 1880s.[64]

Kindergartens left infants to the care of mothers and thus were not as
threatening to family life as the infant schools. The new system offered a
supplement rather than an alternative to familial education, in short three- to
four-hour sessions. But kindergartens resembled infant schools in their attempt
to improve family life through an educational venture directed at both mothers
and children. Mothers' meetings and home visits by kindergarten teachers were
considered critical components of the schools at their inception. Kindergartens
were greeted with unexpected enthusiasm by the American public. Proponents
argued that kindergartens could help meet the challenge of socializing the poor
and immigrant children who were increasingly crowding American cities. Also,
women found in kindergarten teaching a paid occupation that allowed them to
fulfill the traditional female role of caring for the young. The new "child-
gardens" were also popular because they clearly constituted "a new environment appropriate for children, not a school," as Barbara Beatty succinctly
argues. The first kindergarten was established by Elizabeth Peabody in Boston
in 1860; by the turn of the century, most large educational systems included
kindergartens.[65]

The kindergarten movement furthered the ideology of the child-centered
family in significant ways. Kindergarten advocates promoted the romantic view
of children as innocent creatures who needed guidance and protection. The
kindergarten also brought play, previously deemed an insignificant, childish
activity, to the forefront of educational thinking about young children. In
developing his kindergarten "gifts" or "occupations," Friedrich Froebel used
pedagogical strategies that built on children's imaginative play. Later kindergarten theorists would regard Froebel's activities for children as developmentally inappropriate, overly rigid, and old-fashioned, but play has remained
central to the kindergarten experience and has become a defining characteristic
of our modern understanding of childhood. The kindergarten, with its child-
size furnishings, colorful toys, and natural ambience, was the model child-
centered space.[66]

Froebel and his followers believed that women should play an integral part in
the project of child-gardening, both in the home as mothers and in the schools
as educators. Although he at first promoted the notion of "scientific motherhood," for Froebel "scientific" meant spiritual rather than empirical. He in-

sisted that children's education should conform to the natural laws of human growth, but he believed that the laws of nature and the laws of God were one and the same, and he relied on divine insight rather than the scientific method to perceive those laws.[67]

Kindergarten proponents claimed that women were naturally endowed with special spiritual attributes important in the care and cultivation of the young, which could be strengthened and enhanced through the study of kindergarten philosophy. According to Elizabeth Harrison, a prominent American kindergarten supporter, "The mother's loving guidance can be changed from uncertain instinct into unhesitating insight." By "instinct" she referred to a human propensity that could be focused in either a positive or a negative direction. One of the chief functions of the kindergarten was to guide the instincts of both mothers and children along the path intended by nature and God.[68]

Clubwomen avidly adopted kindergartens as a major platform of their reform movement during the 1880s, when scores of them read kindergarten child-rearing texts, participated in kindergarten mothers' meetings, and lobbied to make kindergartens a part of the public school system. The kindergarten movement mediated between an understanding of motherhood as natural and sacred and the emerging philosophy of scientific motherhood. Its theorists claimed that "the nurture element . . . lies within the breast of every woman" but also insisted that the mere act of bearing a child did not make a woman "motherly." Their intention was to maintain the value of "mother love," while "rationalizing" it.[69] That is, the first advocates of kindergartens believed that they were drawing on a base of instinctual maternal knowledge to formulate sound pedagogical principles.

The Chicago Conference of Mothers, held in 1894 by kindergarten representatives, reflected the mix of expert and "inexpert" voices that marked the movement in its beginnings.[70] Mrs. Chappel read a paper on motherhood "from an unscientific standpoint," which elicited "cordial applause" from the audience. A Dr. Bridge, however, was met with a "great buzz of disapproval from the large audience of thinking mothers" when he argued that mothers should eliminate all fruit from their children's diet and substitute small quantities of alcohol instead.[71] Mothers had been feeding their children fruit for years without negative consequences, and many of them undoubtedly were also opposed to alcohol in principle. The boundary lines between medical practitioners and mothers were not yet as firmly drawn as they would be in later decades.

The audience of mothers and educators gave a more favorable reception to the ideas of progressive educator John Dewey, who urged his listeners (in a succinct statement of the evolving philosophy of child-centered parenting) to be "psychologists"—to take their cues from "the child's nature and not make the child follow the parent's nature." At the same time, Dewey warned mothers against relying on books for their child-rearing practices; he asserted that "it is not necessary to know a text-book in order to study a child."[72] But how were mothers to determine the nature of the child? This was the question that the pioneering child psychologist G. Stanley Hall would try to elucidate.

G. STANLEY HALL AND THE CHILD-STUDY MOVEMENT

Controversial in his own lifetime, G. Stanley Hall is now recognized as a central figure in the history of the child sciences in general and child psychology in particular. A psychologist who spoke in a language lay audiences responded to, Hall contributed to forging a fruitful alliance between education and psychology and generating enthusiasm among parents and teachers for the scientific study of children.[73] Hall was one of the founders of the academic discipline of psychology in the United States. Beginning in 1889, he served as the first president of Clark University, which set the pattern for university-based scientific research. He also gained considerable recognition when he arranged to bring Sigmund Freud to this country for the first time in 1909.

Hall applied evolutionary concepts to child development, even postulating that the development of children recapitulated the history of the human race. According to Hall, parents and educators should not interfere with the natural process of child development, which was triggered by genetic signals.[74] In his autobiography, Hall spoke to the impact of this line of thinking: "It sometimes seemed as if parents regarded the nascent stages of childhood as a necessary evil which must be accepted with what grace they could. Therefore the gradual realization of what infancy and childhood really were, and the new appreciation of the fact that children's nature and needs should be normative and determine their treatment in both the home and school, came almost like a new gospel."[75]

In 1891, Hall founded the journal *Pedagogical Seminary* to help disseminate his ideas to the educational and psychological community and provide information about the burgeoning child-study movement. He also organized a child-study exhibit for the World's Columbian Exposition of 1893 in Chicago that attracted widespread attention and led to the founding of the Illinois Society for Child Study. The popularity of his message helped spark the formation of child-study societies—at least twenty-three sprang up during the 1890s. One of the most influential was the Illinois Society, whose annual conferences attracted up to 3,000 teachers and parents. The child-study societies were oriented primarily toward gathering data to reform education so that it would meet the developmental needs of children at different ages. For the Illinois Society, "the desire to change that which violates the child's life in the school of the present was the predominant motive."[76] Thus proponents of child study envisioned their task as both discovering the true "nature" of the child through research and reforming the school and the home to foster the child's development.

But the methods Hall devised to acquire his data were controversial from the outset. Through questionnaires distributed to children by teachers, parents, and clubwomen, Hall garnered information about his young subjects' fears, punishments, lies, and play activities. Hall's project gave women with no scientific training the sense that they were participants in the emerging science of the child. The natural and social sciences were still in their infancy, and distinctions between amateurs and experts were not yet firmly in place. But to the extent that Hall ignored the demarcation between the two groups, he angered those researchers who wished to establish the differentiation. Although Hall alienated certain of his colleagues because of his subjective research methods, some of his findings have been corroborated in recent times by scholars using conventional research techniques.[77]

The permeability of the boundaries between amateur and professional analyses is apparent in Sara Wiltse's survey for *Pedagogical Seminary* in 1894 of the most significant research studies in child development. Wiltse acknowledged the importance of Hall's pioneering works and of biologist Wilhelm Preyer's *Mind of the Child*, published in 1881. She gave a nonscientist, Millicent Shinn, the same prominence as these two scholars, however. Shinn, an active member of the American Association of University Women, was instrumental in urging educated mothers to compile information about their children's development in the service of science. Wiltse praised Shinn's observations of her infant niece (later published in her *Biography of a Baby*) as "the best records of an individual child yet published in this country." Wiltse also complimented the studies of children carried out under the auspices of the Women's Anthropological Society of Washington. Discussing the potential of this research, Wiltse observed, "The sympathy and tact of educated women ought to produce the best possible results." Both Wiltse and Hall believed that the subjective observations of mothers and teachers should be joined with the more objective methods of the scientists to guarantee the fullest and most accurate knowledge about children.[78]

Hall's practice of employing nonprofessionals to observe children was controversial, like his use of the questionnaire to gather data. Critiques of Hall's work as unscientific and unobjective, offered by such renowned psychologists as Hugo Munsterberg and James Mark Baldwin at the turn of the century, contributed to the decline of child study as Hall had conceived it.[79] Yet his impact on scores of middle-class mothers and teachers during the late nineteenth and early twentieth centuries was immeasurable.

Like the kindergarten philosophy, Hall's ideas appealed to literate middle-class mothers who were trying to retain the traditional maternal role while simultaneously incorporating scientific knowledge into their child-rearing practices. The notion that the proper practice of motherhood demanded esoteric knowledge allowed women to reconcile their intellectual interests with their everyday lives in the home. Hall's belief that women would have a part to play in the emerging science of child psychology was immensely appealing to these middle-class mothers, who felt themselves uniquely suited to understand children's psyches. By the early twentieth century, however, it was clear that mothers would be barred from contributing in any meaningful way to formal expertise on child development. As consumers of child development expertise, however, mothers were influential in determining the extent to which abstract ideas about children would be put into practice.

Undoubtedly, scores of mothers were so overwhelmed by wage work and housework that definitions of good motherhood constructed by professionals had little meaning for them. Realizing that this was the case, during the Progressive Era many reformers—both male and female—would focus on the environmental factors that inhibited poor mothers' ability to ensure their children's well-being. Whether the reformers were intent on improving a mother's disciplinary strategies or the housing where she raised her child, most agreed that science should play a pivotal role in efforts to improve both the home and the overall social environment.

Chapter 2 Divine Motherhood Versus Intelligent Parenthood: Women's Organizations and the Child-Study Campaign

In an article for the *Ladies' Home Journal* (1923), F. Scott Fitzgerald decried the reverence for traditional motherhood: "Motherhood, as a blind, unreasoning habit, is something we have inherited from our ancestors in the cave. This abandonment to the maternal instinct was universal, so we made it sacred."[1] Like many intellectuals of the 1920s, Fitzgerald sought to wrest motherhood from the strictures of tradition and religiosity and reconfigure it for the modern era. Perhaps some hoped that the "objectivity" of modern science would undercut the sentimentality with which Americans treated mothers.

By the nineteenth century, the valorization of motherhood had reached its pinnacle. Clubwomen, as we have seen, used the reverence for motherhood as a rationale for women's education and organizational work. In the early part of the nineteenth century, middle-class women formed evangelical maternal and moral-reform societies, which were predicated on the need for motherly virtue both at home and in public. In the latter part of the century, the proliferation of women's study and civic clubs eventuated in the formation of the politically activist General Federation of Women's Clubs in 1890.

Clubwomen fought for legislation to benefit children and families and lent their support to such maternalist institutions as the U.S. Children's Bureau. Lobbying for legislation to provide mothers' pensions, separate systems of juvenile justice, and state regulation of housing, sanitation, and food, women's organizations of the late nineteenth and early twentieth centuries engaged in what they termed municipal housekeeping—that is, they made women's traditional maternal concerns for the well-being of children and families their springboard for social reform. During the suffrage campaign, leaders of the women's club movement argued that the special qualities associated with women's maternal nature necessitated their participation in the body politic.[2]

By the 1920s, however, many women's organizations were characterizing motherhood itself as an outdated institution in need of reform and modernization. The consumer ethos and preoccupation with individual self-fulfillment that pervaded the era detracted from the club members' reformist preoccupations. During the post-suffrage era, domesticity and maternity lost many of their nineteenth-century moral connotations.[3] Clubwomen continued to lobby for legislation that embodied traditional female concerns; simultaneously, they focused on transforming domestic life itself by bringing scientific principles to bear on mothers' work in the home, an undertaking that would eventually undermine the legislative agenda.

As historian Paula Baker has remarked, "By the 1920s, domesticity was reduced to a private occupation, not a collection of admirable cultural traits."[4] Women increasingly encountered doctrines that—far from emphasizing female superiority in the domestic sphere—represented them as sadly inadequate to the task of reforming the home. As a result, mothering came under increasing scrutiny from experts in psychology, medicine, and education, and organized women themselves, which culminated in a national movement for child study and parent education.

The campaign for parent education was conducted on several fronts, including in the mass media, the schoolhouse, the day nursery, the women's club, and the health clinic. Education for mothers included lectures, clubs, and classes, many of them conducted by women who were professional reformers. Like the social workers, nurses, and home economists who disseminated information to mothers, numerous women's organizations, inspired by the popular and intellectual appeal of child psychology and by the demands of current and potential constituencies, were impelled to educate mothers.

The histories of three national women's organizations—the National Congress of Mothers, the Child Study Association of America, and the American

Association of University Women (AAUW)—all of which span the late nine-teenth and early twentieth centuries—reveal the changing preoccupations of organized women during this period. All three organizations supported the cause of child study and parent education during the 1920s as a means of addressing the uncertainties that accompanied modern motherhood. Yet the organizations differed in the extent to which their members subscribed to the ideology of scientific motherhood. Despite these differences, the organizations' leaders were united in the wish that their constituencies should have the benefits of modern science in the rearing of children.[5]

THE EMERGENCE OF POPULAR CHILD PSYCHOLOGY

The transformation of parent education into a full-fledged campaign in the 1920s was buttressed by developments in psychology, which increasingly de-fined itself as a "science" of the human psyche. The behaviorist approach to psychology, particularly as espoused by John Broadus Watson, had much to do with investing child psychology with scientific credentials. Parent educators also culled ideas from the work of psychologists Edward Thorndike and William James, educator John Dewey, and the founder of psychoanalysis, Sigmund Freud. For the most part, however, less renowned educators, psychologists, and pediatricians reconfigured ideas that were circulating among professionals for a popular audience.[6]

Theories of early childhood have embodied a tension between the Romanti-cism of G. Stanley Hall's work—the Rousseauian idea of designing education according to the child's "innate nature"—and the Lockean concept expressed by Watson that children need to be trained to fit into adult society and that so-called child nature must be suppressed to prepare children for the world they must inhabit as adults.[7] During the 1920s, both conceptions existed, although the rationalist paradigm predominated.[8]

As we have seen, G. Stanley Hall's developmental psychology had significant ramifications for education, which he thought should be constructed to allow children to express their inherent qualities. By the 1920s, Hall's research had fallen out of favor, but the theory that education and child rearing should be molded to the child's nature persisted, for it formalized an existing middle-class propensity toward child-centered parenting.[9] In the ideal middle-class family, children's needs occupied center stage. Yet, smaller family size and the inten-sified mother-child relationship, experts such as Watson and his behaviorist followers hypothesized, could easily lead to maternal overindulgence and "spoiling."

Paula Fass suggests that the receptivity to behaviorist principles of child rearing in the 1920s was a reaction to the affectionate, overprotective family, which was doing little to prepare children for the impersonal world they must enter as adults. Far from being a "haven," the family was often characterized by 1920s cultural critics as plagued by too much intimacy. Watson warned against "too much mother love," and F. Scott Fitzgerald complained: "The home is not so much insufficient as it is oversufficient. It is cloying."[10] The sacrificial mother, who had been sanctified in the nineteenth century for her willingness to devote herself to her family without recompense, was chided and ridiculed, if not vilified, by twentieth-century cultural critics.

Watson conducted a campaign against maternal indulgence and the conception of childhood proposed by the developmental psychologists. He sought to prove that psychology had the potential to be as "scientific" as the natural and physical sciences. Unlike psychoanalysts, who assumed that the wellsprings of human conduct were unconscious and thus not easily verifiable or quantifiable, Watson believed that behavior was shaped primarily by external stimuli and was therefore easily controllable once it was clear which stimuli elicited desirable forms of behavior.[11] He portrayed children as human "machines" whose behavior could be programmed by maternal technicians. Departing from developmentalists such as Hall who focused on the unfolding of the nature of the child, Watson proclaimed, "The behaviorists believe that there is nothing from within to develop." He boasted: "Give me a dozen healthy infants, well-formed, and my own specified world to bring them up in and I'll guarantee to take any one at random and train him to become any type of specialist I might select—doctor, lawyer, artist, merchant-chief, and yes, even beggar-man and thief, regardless of his talents, penchants, tendencies, abilities, vocations, and race of his ancestors."[12] Watson's claim was an extreme version of the environmentalism that had been undergirding the parental-advice industry since the nineteenth century. The Watson model child would have been recognizable to nineteenth-century clerics; she was polite, neat, and self-controlled. But such traditional notions of children's conduct were to be achieved by the up-to-date conditioning methods of the behaviorists. Thus behaviorist theories of child rearing married techniques of modern social science with older Protestant dictates on discipline.[13]

Watson's theories were promulgated in popular magazines and the *Infant Care* bulletins published by the Children's Bureau in the 1920s and 1930s. Through these publications, the ideas of the behaviorists entered millions of homes and were adopted in some form by scores of American parents. But these ideas were tempered by the more child-centered theories of John Dewey and G. Stanley Hall, who insisted that home life and education must shape themselves to the individual child.[14] And progressive educators and psychoanalysts upheld a notion of "personality development" as the goal of child rearing, in contrast to the behaviorists' single-minded emphasis on the child's acquisition of appropriate behaviors.

The popular and professional fascination with behaviorism epitomizes the "scientific utopianism" of the period: the belief that the application of scientific engineering could eliminate the sources of social problems. The language of scientific utopianism was used in very different spheres, from industrial management to housekeeping and child training. In *Child Welfare Magazine* the author of an article entitled "Formulae and Technique in Behavior" claimed, "If the daily conduct of men and women could be guided by a technique as effective as that of the dentist or engineer, the age-long battle against ignorance, superstition, and prejudice would have been won."[15] Presumably, women's traditional homemaking and mothering practices fell into the category of ignorance and superstition, which would ideally be transformed through scientific expertise.

Aiming at efficiency and predictability of outcome, behaviorists designed their child-rearing prescriptions around schedules and routines for young children. This strategy was congruent with the Protestant work ethic and seemed more "scientific" than Freud's troubling theories of the unconscious. But Freud and Watson shared the conviction that the early years were a critical stage of life, and both stressed the effects of parental behavior on children's adult lives.[16] The conviction that inadequate early nurture might have dire consequences was a constant refrain in the popular literature. A writer for *Child Welfare Magazine* told the story of a nurse who was asked to take care of a three-day-old baby and replied, "I don't know about taking it. A baby has formed so many bad habits in three days." Some parents must have felt insecure about raising children in the fanatical child-rearing climate of the 1920s. Social change appeared to be accelerating at a breakneck speed. The promise of the new psychology of child nurture was that if child training was adapted to modern conditions, social change could be contained on an individual and familial level.[17]

The average women who flocked to mothers' study clubs during the 1920s and early 1930s were attracted to the practical slant of behaviorist child-rearing principles. Parent educators, however, found ways to combine behaviorism with developmental theories. They upheld the behaviorist emphasis on routine and regularity in young children's upbringing but also sought to delineate the stages of behavior that children were expected to go through as they developed—and advised that parents seek to understand rather than merely correct children's misbehavior. The most obvious legacy of 1920s child-rearing advice is behavioral conditioning; however, there was often a countervailing focus on reacting to the age-specific needs of children.

In constructing popular study courses for mothers, parent educators were treading already tilled ground. Public health workers, magazines such as *Good Housekeeping* and *Woman's Home Companion,* and the pamphlets on child care issued by the U.S. Children's Bureau and various state agencies had been urging that mothers impose appropriate health habits on their children for some time. L. Emmett Holt's *The Care and Feeding of Infants* (1896), which went through several editions and was on the bookshelves of many American homes, stressed regularity in habits of eating, sleeping, and feeding for young children and described the appropriate foods for each age group. The behaviorists appropriated Holt's attention to physical habits and added the concept of "psychological habits"; the inculcation of physical and psychological routines in young children came to be known as habit training.[18]

The concept of habit was a scientific formulation of a term that had previously carried moral significance. Eighteenth- and nineteenth-century clerics and educators had underscored the importance of instilling good habits of behavior in children beginning at birth. The new psychology drew on William James's chapter "Habit" in *Principles of Psychology* (1890). First published in *Popular Science Monthly* in 1887, the chapter was so popular that it was distributed in pamphlet form. James stressed the urgency of correct habit formation and proposed that human personality was a compilation of habits: "Could the young but realize how soon they will become mere walking bundles of habits, they would give more heed to their conduct while in the plastic state."[19] If human personality was, in large part, a bundle of socialized patterns, then the key to social control lay in learning how to foster good habits and eliminate bad ones.

The work of educational psychologist Edward T. Thorndike mediated between instinct and habit. Unlike G. Stanley Hall, who claimed that the expression of instinctual impulses was an integral aspect of children's development, Thorndike underscored the value of habit in transforming impulses into civilized behavior. In an apparent rebuttal to Hall, Thorndike contended, "What development *is* can never tell us what it ought to be." His insistence that habit formation occurs with constant repetition was taken literally by educators and educated parents nationwide.[20] Watson further characterized emotions as "ways of behavior that had to be learned like other sets of habits." Countless books and pamphlets on habit training were perused by child-study groups nationwide, and "habit clinics," precursors to child-guidance clinics, sprang up throughout the 1920s. Habit training for children in their formative years promised easy answers to the dilemmas of child rearing that troubled American mothers.[21]

Habit training was oriented toward the instillation of "good" habits of eating, sleeping, elimination, and behavior and the eradication of "bad" or "undesirable" habits. According to psychoanalyst Martha Wolfenstein, who analyzed the U.S. Children's Bureau *Infant Care* bulletins from 1914 to 1945, professionals and parents alike during the 1910s and 1920s viewed the infant as being endowed with "strong and dangerous impulses" that must be eradicated, especially such autoerotic activities as thumb-sucking and masturbation and also temper tantrums, dawdling, and stammering. Wolfenstein observed that the infant's wants and needs were clearly distinguished during this period, with wants being defined as "illegitimate pleasure strivings." Thus mothers should beware of overly indulging their young ones, lest they mature into little tyrants. This emphasis would change quite dramatically during the 1940s and 1950s, when professionals would insist that mothers should gratify rather than regulate children's early desires.[22]

Mothers of the 1920s were also enjoined to allow their infants to "cry it out," to avert the "spoiling" and unruly behavior that might follow if babies were picked up whenever they cried. Informed parents were to approach problems of eating, sleeping, and elimination with impersonal objectivity. The capstone to the philosophy was warnings against excessive displays of affection toward children, which might subvert discipline. In his chapter "The Dangers of Too Much Mother Love" in *Psychological Care of Infant and Child,* Watson criticized mothers' propensity to kiss and hug their children, recommending instead that parents communicate their affection through a sturdy handshake.[23]

Many middle-class families apparently adopted behaviorist child-rearing strategies during this period. In her autobiography, Sidonie Matsner Gruenberg, director of the Child Study Association, described the preferred child-rearing practices of the 1920s: "This was the time when rigid training on all fronts was the sign of the superior and informed parent. The child must not be indulged. If he cried when put down to sleep, the mother was supposed to turn a deaf ear and let him shriek until exhausted. Feeding on time was like a religion. Parents watched the clock instead of the baby, even waking it in the middle of a peaceful nap for food right on the dot."[24] The language of habit training pervaded middle-class mothers' discussions of child rearing. Mothers boasted about toilet-training their babies before the age of one and about their success in placing their children on a strict sleeping schedule.

Some mothers were of course uncomfortable with the behaviorists' mandates. Watson reported an encounter immediately following a lecture in which he had inveighed against the dangers of parental sentimentality. An elderly woman approached him and exclaimed: "Thank God, my children are grown—and that I had a chance to enjoy them before I met you."[25] This kind of indignation at extreme forms of advice was not unusual. Yet while many women clearly had reservations about the wisdom of particular child-rearing prescriptions, clubwomen and professional women continued to press for the dissemination of scientific knowledge that would help them raise happy and healthy children.

MATERNALISM AND THE RHETORIC OF SCIENTIFIC MOTHERHOOD

The National Congress of Mothers, the American Association of University Women, and the Child Study Association of America were major proponents of the ideology of scientific motherhood during the 1920s. The National Congress of Mothers and the American Association of University Women also played a significant role in the maternalist politics of the late nineteenth and early twentieth centuries.[26] Maternalist politics derived from the conception that women had unique personal *and* civic responsibilities to children and families that were based on their reproductive capacities. Molly Ladd-Taylor defines maternalist activists as those who believed that women shared a "feminine value system based on care and nurture," which united them across race and class backgrounds. According to some historians, maternalists emphasized women's duties to their families, whereas feminists advocated women's individual self-fulfillment. The two camps of activists were not always readily distinguishable, however: many so-called maternalists supported feminist aims and vice versa. In fact, only one of the organizations I discuss—the National Congress of Mothers—falls neatly within this definition of maternalism.[27] All three groups, though, adhered to a philosophy of scientific motherhood, which combined the maternalist view of women as uniquely equipped to care for children with a more modern conception of motherhood as requiring acquaintance with expert knowledge. This latter philosophy ultimately contributed to an alteration in, and in some cases the demise of, the more politicized version of maternalism promulgated by the women's progressive reform organizations at the turn of the century.

The Child Study Association and the Congress of Mothers were maternalistic in the sense that their aims and purposes derived from their members' identities as mothers. The congress stressed the social and political power women could wield if they drew on maternity, the traditional source of female authority. The Child Study Association was more narrowly educational in focus than the congress and had a less lofty notion of the possibilities inherent in motherhood. Although Child Study Association leaders were zealous in their belief that private domestic reform could have public ramifications, their maternalist vision was essentially private. The American Association of University Women, by contrast, was an organization whose purpose was to promote higher education and professional employment opportunities for women. Its ideology was characterized by both a conception of women as individuals with the same rights and responsibilities as men and a traditional maternalist concern with the ways in which educated women might put their uniquely feminine characteristics to use.[28] Even though the American Association of University Women's early agenda highlighted the importance of a college education for women modeled on the classical education offered men at elite institutions such as Harvard and Yale, during the 1920s the AAUW united with the Child Study Association and the National Congress of Mothers in a national campaign to educate women for motherhood.

Central to this cooperative effort was the Laura Spelman Rockefeller Memorial, under the astute leadership of economist Lawrence K. Frank. Frank, who had worked with the poor on New York's Lower East Side, was influenced in his work by Lucy Sprague Mitchell, an educator whose Bank Street Nursery School combined a program of progressive education with research on young children. In 1923, at the request of Beardsley Ruml, director of the memorial, Frank constructed a plan to subsidize research on children that would search for the underlying causes of such social problems as delinquency, maladjustment, and even poverty and disseminate the findings to parents.[29] Ultimately, as a result of Frank's efforts, the memorial granted approximately $12 million to research, teaching, and dissemination of research in child development, thus providing a solid foundation for the construction of the new science. Frank believed that research was pointless, however, if it was not placed in the service of reform; he noted in a memo that he intended to "guard against the usual divorce between scientific discovery and dissemination." Women's associations, Frank concluded, could play a vital role in promulgating principles of child development to mothers, and his assistance ensured that women's groups would occupy a prominent place in the parent education movement and that the movement would reach a broad spectrum of mothers.[30]

DISSEMINATING THE "GOSPEL OF CHILD DEVELOPMENT":
THE CHILD STUDY ASSOCIATION OF AMERICA

Both a forerunner of and a major participant in the parent education movement of the 1920s, the Child Study Association of America (CSA) began as a small child-study circle in 1888, when three mothers started meeting in New York City at the urging of Felix Adler, a prominent progressive educator. The mothers, who included Adler's wife Helen, all belonged to the Ethical Culture Society, which Adler formed to promote the "religion of humanism"—a form of secularism combining science and reform—after he became disenchanted with traditional Judaism. Adler was interested in using the kindergarten to reform child-rearing practices; thus the Mothers' Society to Study Child Nature (as it was initially called) met with a trained kindergarten teacher while the members' children attended a cooperative kindergarten.[31]

As the society gained in numbers, its members expanded their readings and activities beyond the kindergarten. Perhaps the wish to avoid the many texts whose authors assumed a Christian readership led to the use of more secular philosophical treatises, such as Rousseau's *Emile,* Plato's *Republic,* and Locke's *On Human Understanding.*[32] In 1890, after the membership had expanded to thirty, the group was renamed the Society for the Study of Child Nature. Debate about a new name for the club centered on whether to incorporate the word "mother" in the title. The decision not to do so may have reflected the club's inclusion of nonmothers and the wish to avoid being lumped together with mothers' clubs whose purposes were less academic. The society decided to limit its aims to academic ones; philanthropy and social reform were considered to be "extraneous to the objects of the Society." When a member suggested that the group become involved in the reform of the public schools, another woman pronounced: "Politics was at the root of this evil, the responsibility for which rests with the Fathers, and that politics should be kept separate and distinct from educational matters." Keeping politics separate from education was not always an easy matter, however, and as the group gained in numbers and confidence, the women, indeed entering the arenas of education and politics, eventually established a committee to investigate the sanitary conditions in the public schools and founded vacation schools for the children of the poor.[33]

Some members hoped to become more than dilettantes in their study of the child. As we have seen, some individuals, such as psychologist G. Stanley Hall, thought that mothers—by virtue of their interactions with children—might be charged with collecting scientific data about children. Amateurs were encouraged to participate in the evolving science of child development by keeping "baby biographies," painstaking records of the growth and development of infants. Such record-keeping became a popular avocation of scientists and parents alike during the late nineteenth and early twentieth centuries. Anthropologist Margaret Mead, born in 1901, claimed that her mother had kept thirteen notebooks on her behavior and development as a child.[34] Charles Darwin inaugurated the trend with the publication of his journal of his infant daughter's first three months of life. In *The Mind of the Child* psychologist William Preyer exhorted fathers to keep accurate records of their infants' development, as a means of aiding scientists to learn about childhood.[35] In 1891 Helen Adler read a paper before the society arguing that mothers rather than fathers should be responsible for chronicling the child's growth and development. She contended that women were best fitted to observe and describe the phases of children's development. The minutes of the meeting contained this report: "She recalled in glowing terms the devotion of the *Mother* to the child, the time given to its physical welfare, the pains taken to soothe it in sickness, to sympathize with it in its grief, to absorb self in the child. And should not that person, who can do and be all this for the child, be the one to understand its nature best, and be the proper person to observe it correctly? If she is not yet fitted for scientific observations, why should she not fit herself for them?"[36] According to Adler, with the aid of scientific training, mothers could call on their experiences with children to compile scientific data about childhood. The notion that the child sciences must be based on objective observation would, however, shortly undermine mothers' efforts to add their voices to the discourse of child development.

As Theodora Martin has pointed out, even the seemingly innocuous study club, in spite of its avoidance of political controversy, aroused public criticism. Women were accused of neglecting their families to attend the gatherings. Early members asked themselves: "Can a woman of family take courses of study and join classes for different purposes, and at the same time do her duty to her family?" Members also valued their own intellectual growth but did "the time devoted to young children stunt the mental growth of the mother?"[37] The child-study group itself offered a resolution to this perceived conflict. Members could further their intellectual growth by studying children; at the same time, they would be pursuing ends perceived as beneficial to their families.

The association's members did not conceive of women's education as limited to education for motherhood, however. In the 1910s group members embarked on the study of G. Stanley Hall's works on adolescence and education for women. Hall theorized that the higher education of women negatively affected their procreative capabilities and maternal inclinations. The members of the group shared his concern but remained committed to education for women: "Conceded during discussion that the Higher Education creates dissatisfaction with the narrow home life, but that without it there would be no progress, and that the larger experience of college life makes for a better preparation for the larger life."[38] This passage suggests that group members were aware of the disjuncture between their "narrow" home lives as wives and mothers and the "larger experience of college life," which many of their daughters were experiencing. Hall's opinions notwithstanding, the members were not willing to forsake the benefits of higher education merely so that women would be more satisfied with their roles as wives and mothers.

At the same time as they championed higher education for women, the group insisted that the care of children was women's domain. Motherhood was not only a central aspect of their identities as women but their undisputed province within the family. At a group meeting in the mid-1910s, "It was conceded that as a rule, fathers play no part in the lives of children." And as late as 1922 in a discussion of eugenics, a group acknowledged that it was important to choose a father as "half of the ancestry for the child" but that "after impregnation the father has a small part in the child's life." The association members appeared to accept as a matter of fact that the designation "father" had little to do with caring for children and that women played the crucial parental role. Another recurring topic concerned mothers who worked outside the home. The consensus within the groups seemed to be that a woman's primary responsibility should be to home and family, although members admitted that work outside the home might be possible for some women and necessary for others.[39]

A woman's sphere of activity could be broadened only if her childbearing and child-rearing duties permitted; but this did not mean that the clubwomen entirely ignored issues of gender. Members were quite concerned about how to raise girl children in an era of fluctuating gender roles. A discussion in 1890 about whether members should raise their daughters to seek the vote suggests that at least some of the members perceived that as a laudable goal. During a conversation about how to inculcate female virtue, some questioned whether the association of women with purity was not a social invention. Physical exercise and new standards of dress for women were also advocated, in the interests of both preserving their physical health and enhancing their freedom.[40] The minutes suggest that the group discussions served the purpose of stretching the boundaries of acceptable behavior for women, yet still allowed them to discharge their maternal duties with respectability.

Even while voicing the conviction that women were primarily responsible for children, association members consistently encouraged mothers to engage in activities outside of the home. During the 1920s, this recommendation became almost an injunction, as educators and psychologists analyzed the phenomenon of the "overprotected child," suffering from the excessive attention of a self-sacrificing mother. Child-study work became an avocation, and in some cases a vocation, for the powerful leaders who emerged from the organization's study groups, such as Bird Stein Gans, Cecile Pilpel, and Sidonie Matsner Gruenberg. As paid staff members for a voluntary organization, these women managed to achieve a degree of autonomy while simultaneously embracing maternal values by promoting child-rearing education for women.[41]

The members of the original chapters struggled to formulate their own philosophy of child growth and development in relation to professional expertise. Sidonie Matsner Gruenberg, the organization's leading spokesperson in the 1920s and 1930s, described the early meetings: "They were fumbling their way by practical experiment and group discussion, as well as by the study of theoretical material, to a new grasp of the nature of children."[42] Gruenberg supplemented her participation in the group with classes in psychology at Teachers College, where, she noted in retrospect, they studied the behavior of dogs, chickens, and other animals, but never children. In 1911 she began writing articles for *Good Housekeeping* on strategies of child rearing and then accepted a commission to write a manuscript, which was published in 1912 as *Your Child, Today and Tomorrow*. Discussing the manuscript with her, Edward Thorndike expressed disbelief that a book containing psychologically sound information could be made accessible to mothers or that they would want to read a book on child behavior.[43] Gruenberg's book was followed by many others that successfully translated the findings of child psychology for a popular audience. What was distinctive about her work, however, was that the author was a self-educated mother rather than a trained professional.

According to Gruenberg, parents needed to modernize their child-rearing practices by gaining an understanding of what children's needs were at different ages. A 1913 pamphlet published by the organization attributed parents' problems to their inability to adapt their disciplinary techniques to changing times: "The widespread lack of respect of children for their parents is due, in large measure, to the fact that the tendency of the parent is to become more and more conservative."[44] Educators stressed that traditional authoritarian discipline was likely to be ineffectual in the modern era. The organization advocated that parents seek to understand the causes of their children's misbehavior rather than merely punish them and that they attempt to place children in situations where they would be less likely to misbehave. In 1916, the members of Chapter 13 of the association unanimously agreed that "too much censure" was a far greater danger than "too much spoiling." With their endorsement of permissive, child-centered households and their intellectual approach to child rearing, these clubs were subject to parody and public criticism. Members were accused of being "freaks and faddists who were spoiling their children through the application of new-fangled notions." Magazine articles ridiculed mothers who, heeding the dictates of child study, allowed children to turn their houses upside down. Even members' children had fun with their mothers' preoccupation. A joke popular among the children of child-study mothers was that "Child Study means we children have to study our parents." As the culture in general became more permissive in the 1920s, the group found itself trying to modify its child-centered position. In 1930 one leader spoke of the need to "find a middle road between the 'old puritanism' and the absolutely uncontrolled freedom of today."[45]

The organization was in the vanguard of the parent education movement, by virtue of both its early genesis and its intellectual breadth. At a time when most child-study clubs focused on the practical recommendations of behaviorists, the New York members were exposed to a wide spectrum of psychological thinking, including psychoanalysis. During the 1910s the organization sponsored a series of lectures by the noted psychoanalyst A. A. Brill, which provoked argument and discussion but engaged the members' interest. It may have been the influence of psychoanalysis that led to protracted discussions on such topics as sex education, nudity in the home, and the dangers of same-sex friendships.

While early members had studied and debated the merits of a range of child-rearing prescriptions, as the group grew and developed powerful leaders, the ideas discussed eventually rigidified into a dogma of sorts. The group was influenced by the increasingly authoritative presence of clinical experts on the child, who were rapidly assuming the role that had been occupied by clerical authorities in the nineteenth century. In the early years, every member of each club took a share in its leadership, but as the organization expanded, group leaders were recruited from among long-term members, with a resulting separation between the leadership and the membership. Leaders now served the purpose of instilling in club members the philosophy of child rearing that the organization stood for. A question-and-answer format provided the structure for most meetings. Commenting on the work of the CSA, sociologist W. I. Thomas claimed that the association should be considered a "propaganda organization," because it focused on conveying basic and accepted principles of child study to its members.[46] Although the association did not endorse any particular psychological school, it presented its own progressive child-centered philosophy as the final word in child-study work.

A benchmark for the group as a nationally recognized organization for parents was the launching of its journal *Child Study* in 1923. The association was brought to the forefront of the parent education movement when it was recognized by Lawrence Frank of the Laura Spelman Rockefeller Memorial as furthering the kind of work he wished to promote. Frank believed that transmitting principles of child psychology to parents could effect sweeping social change. He was attracted by the intimacy of the association's child-study groups, by the organizational structure, which ensured that each group was under centralized leadership, and by the high intellectual quality of the work. He initiated talks with Bird Stein Gans and Sidonie Matsner Gruenberg about the possibility of their providing leadership for the parent education movement as a whole.[47]

But most social scientists were less enthusiastic than Frank about investing leadership in a group of women without academic credentials. Edward Thorndike advised Frank that although the association was the "best of the amateurs in the matter of child training," the possibilities for expansion of the work were not great. The work of the association, he insisted, "can be neither so popular as semi-psychological articles in a household magazine nor so valuable as an extension course at a university." Even more insidious was the feeling among several of Frank's associates that the association's organizers could never lead the campaign for parent education because they were predominantly Jewish.[48]

Frank seems to have been influenced by the comments of his advisers, and while he provided the association with funding, the Laura Spelman Rockefeller Memorial's support fell short of what would have been required to place the organization at the center of the movement. In 1924 the memorial awarded the organization a three-year grant of $30,000, with the condition that it rename itself the Child Study Association of America, presumably so that the group would be identified with a national constituency, rather than with New York Jewish intellectuals. The funds allowed the organization to continue its study club activities and to expand its work into African-American communities in New York and other Northeastern cities. The association also sponsored a number of influential conferences for parent educators, the first of which took place in 1925 and "put parent education on the nation's intellectual map."[49]

Although the membership did continue to expand throughout the twenties and thirties, the association never attracted the broad constituency Frank had hoped for. This failure may have been due in part to the association's commitment to academic rigor; it even withdrew its sponsorship from groups that did not live up to the CSA's high intellectual standards. It also refused Frank's offer to participate in publishing the mainstream *Parents' Magazine,* choosing instead to continue issuing its own journal, *Child Study,* which had a limited readership.[50]

Notwithstanding its intellectual stance, which limited its national impact, the association did exert its influence in arenas other than its study clubs. Several of the organization's leaders published a number of influential texts on child study, which would be consulted by parents, educators, and child-study clubs. The organization's outreach activities also included a speakers' bureau, nationwide conferences on parent education, and radio programs. In 1917, the group initiated its Summer Play School program in New York City settlements, which provided a summer experience for inner-city youth and provided educational programs for the children's parents.[51] In the late 1920s and 1930s, the organization engaged in outreach efforts to immigrant and urban African-American communities of the Northeast.

The Child Study Association did much to popularize child study through its outreach activities, but it was less successful in organizing study groups outside the class of educated middle-class women from which it drew its membership. Begun by a small cadre of mothers seeking answers to the dilemmas of child rearing, the organization transformed itself into a nationally recognized organization committed to delivering the "gospel of child development."[52]

MEDIATING BETWEEN TRADITIONAL MOTHERHOOD AND SCIENTIFIC EXPERTISE: THE NATIONAL CONGRESS OF MOTHERS (PTA)

Unlike the Child Study Association, the PTA, originally called the National Congress of Mothers, attracted 2,000 women to its first meeting in 1897. The key organizer for the event was Alice Birney, a widowed mother of three who had studied the works of G. Stanley Hall and Friedrich Froebel but still felt the need for more information.[53] Her studies, combined with her participation in the mothers' meetings sponsored by kindergarten advocates, persuaded her that mothers must band together in the service of the child. Her concerns were both for the individual mother, in need of education, and society as a whole, in need of social and political reform. She wondered: "How can mothers be educated and the nation be made to recognize the supreme importance of the child?"[54] In 1895 at the Chautauqua Summer School, Birney discussed her vision with a group of mothers whose ardent response to the idea matched her own feelings. She elicited the support of the wealthy and socially prominent Phoebe Apperson Hearst, who lent both financial resources and prestige to the undertaking. The two women then solicited the interest of one "woman of position" in each of several regions of the country, whom they invited to attend the initial conference and to organize other women in her area. The meeting, which took place two years later, exceeded their expectations, both for the numbers of women attending and for the enthusiasm with which the gathering was received by the public and the media.[55]

The program for the conference quoted the kindergarten theorist Friedrich Froebel: "The destiny of nations lies far more in the hands of women—the mothers—than in the possessors of power."[56] The organizers of the congress believed that both social problems and social reform originated in the home; with such a conception they assigned culpability to mothers for the ills of society, but they also proposed a primary role for women in the reconstruction of society. Prominent kindergarten spokespersons such as Lucy Wheelock and clubwoman Ellen Henrotin shared the platform at the congress with educator of the deaf E. M. Gallaudet and moral crusader Anthony Comstock. The titles of the talks—"Reading Courses for Mothers," "The Afro-American Mother," "Playgrounds in Cities," "Mother's Relation to the Sound Physical Development of Her Child," "Day Nurseries," "Mothers of the Submerged World," and "Parental Reverence as Taught in the Hebrew Home"—give some idea of the range of individual and social concerns of congress members. The maternalists' platform, to modern eyes an interesting combination of progressive and conservative causes, projected women's traditional concerns into the public sphere. Molly Ladd-Taylor explains that the organization provided a bridge "between mothers and experts, grassroots activists and political reformers, and between traditional and modern concepts of child care."[57]

Conference speakers exhorted women to draw on their moral authority as mothers to effect a social and political transformation by advancing the welfare of children and families. Articulating a program of "women's *duties* and *obligations* rather than *rights*," the organization supported women's activism for family issues and avoided feminist causes unrelated to motherhood, such as suffrage. Because they considered the mother-child bond to be of inordinate importance to both children's development and the maintenance of society, congress members were indignant at social policies—such as child custody laws favoring fathers—that failed to take into account mothers' centrality in the socialization process.[58]

Congress members were equally concerned about the abysmal conditions of poor and immigrant children and the sickly, spoiled children of the rich. The poor child, suffering from inadequate housing and improper nutrition, and the rich child, whose pampered existence was inadequate preparation for adult life, seemed to these women to be the most visible symbols of the changes wrought by industrialization and urbanization.[59]

In the influential *The Century of the Child*, Swedish theorist Ellen Key exhorted women to concern themselves with the "holiness of generation."[60] In 1905, President Theodore Roosevelt, a pivotal figure in the eugenics movement, addressed the annual meeting, where he was enthusiastically applauded for declaring that women should remain in the home and continue to propagate. The keynote speaker at the early meetings was G. Stanley Hall. When Hall complained at the 1905 convention about unmarried educated women, the members indicated their approval through vigorous applause.[61] Congress members, however, put the rhetoric of eugenics in the service of educational and environmental reform. They deplored "the unpropitious conditions which environ much of the childhood of the race, and from which only a dwarfed humanity can come forth" and pledged to enlist "the divine function of maternity" in the effort to correct those environmental conditions. Linking nineteenth-century conceptions of the power of motherhood with both social reform and the emerging behavioral sciences, the congress organizers proposed "the study of the little child as the key to the many problems which confront and daunt the human race."[62]

That motherhood was at the same time women's "divine" and "natural" function was unquestioned by most nineteenth-century women; however, the somewhat contradictory proposition that women must learn to be good mothers had been gaining credence throughout the nineteenth century and subtly encroaching on ideologies of divine and natural motherhood. These ideologies were also undermined by the significant minority of women who chose careers over marriage and motherhood and by working-class mothers who were forced into paid employment. In addition, the increase in the numbers of middle-class women receiving a college education generated widespread concern that academic training would detract from women's child-rearing responsibilities.[63] According to both expert and popular opinion, the American family was increasingly unstable, a conception buttressed by the steady rise in divorce rates. Social scientists theorized that the family's instability was due to "cultural lag," meaning that the traditional structure of the family was failing to keep pace with the technological advances altering society as a whole.[64] Thus the conference-goers believed that modernized motherhood might help ease the family safely into the twentieth century.

Congress leaders theorized that an educated motherhood, mediating between modernity and tradition, would enable the family to sustain itself in the face of rapid social change. The group heartily endorsed the home economics movement, which promised simultaneously to modernize and to reinforce traditional gender roles. The organization also advocated informal education for motherhood, in the form of child-study clubs. Mary Lowe Dickinson, a speaker at the first convention, entreated mothers to "become students of childhood and students of every system, scheme, plan, and practice for the development of body, mind, character of the child." Both Dickinson and G. Stanley Hall envisioned a child-study movement that would comprise teams of mothers, teachers, and scientists cooperating in the enterprise of gathering accurate data on child life, and the congress gave its fervent approval to such a movement.[65]

The congress's valorization of motherhood encompassed inherently conservative elements; however, in the organization's approach lay a nascent feminism. PTA members aspired to extend the principles of motherhood as they understood them—nurturing and caretaking—to the social organism as a whole and believed that the designation "mother"—which any woman could adopt—implied a responsibility to improve the welfare of all women and children. Thus, in seeking to remake the world according to traditional feminine values, Congress members enlisted women's power in the service of various social reforms to improve the lot of needy women and children.[66]

These organized mothers assumed that it was women's responsibility to contribute to the creation of favorable environmental conditions for mothers and children from all walks of life. During the early decades of the twentieth century, therefore, they lobbied for mothers' pensions (the genesis of contemporary welfare), a juvenile justice system, child labor laws, the U.S. Children's

Bureau, the Sheppard-Towner Infancy and Maternity Protection Act, and educational provisions for the disabled, to name a few of the many reforms championed by the PTA. It was intensely active in campaigns to promote children's health, and thanks to its Summer Round-Up, begun in 1925, hundreds of thousands of school-age children received health examinations and treatment for physical problems. Many of the reforms sponsored by congress members were eventually adopted as governmental responsibilities, such as school health clinics, playgrounds, and hot lunch programs for school children.[67]

Although child welfare was a persistent concern of the PTA, the organization modified its definition of child welfare throughout its history. At the turn of the century, reform took precedence over educational work, in keeping with the progressive fervor of the period. In 1924 the congress began the process of transforming itself from a maternalist organization that both valorized and politicized the concept of motherhood into a purportedly scientific professional organization, which was seemingly less gender-based. Changing its name to the National Congress of Parents and Teachers, the group approved the participation of fathers in the organization and acknowledged the need for increased cooperation between parents and schools. The change reflected the increasing desire for the organization to distance itself from "sentimental motherhood" and to focus instead on more gender-neutral "parenting." The inclusion of "teachers" in the title was a sign of the increasing concern with children's education. As the public schools continued to broaden their areas of oversight to include the health and overall welfare of the child, parents countered by extending their influence into the schools. School officials' perception of the PTA as intrusive made them reluctant to work with the organization at first, but PTA leaders, who hoped to engender a closer cooperation between home and school, managed to gain a surprising degree of influence in the public schools.[68]

By the late 1920s the broad-based conception of child welfare that had characterized the earlier PTA was undermined by a growing emphasis on cooperation between home and school. The organization continued to lobby for child labor laws and an adequate system of juvenile justice, but it focused increasingly on more middle-class concerns. PTA leaders saw in parent-teacher work "the most fundamental and far-reaching benefit to childhood."[69] The attempt to extend the principles of motherhood to society as a whole was undermined by the effort to inject expertise into parenthood, which, as it was now defined to extend the gender boundaries of parenting, also detracted from a politicized vision of motherhood.

In part as a result of the greatly amplified role of the public school in American society during the early twentieth century, the PTA underwent an unparalleled period of expansion during the 1910s and 1920s. The organization increased its paying membership from 60,000 in 1915 to 500,000 in 1930. Movement leaders worried that in the process of expansion the organization's purposes had become unclear. PTAs had acquired a reputation for being interested primarily in purchasing equipment and sponsoring social events, rather than for sponsoring a broad platform of social and educational reform.[70]

In the aftermath of World War I, however, substantial attention was directed toward both children's health and parent education programs. For the first time, army recruits were given I.Q. tests and psychological and physical examinations. The results were alarming: half the recruits were judged to have below-normal intelligence. According to the studies, the average army recruit had a developmental age of less than fourteen. Although shrewd scientists recognized that the examinations were probably inherently flawed, the uproar sufficed to galvanize reformers to try to ensure that Americans were raising their children to healthy adulthood. Scientific parent education thus emerged as an urgent priority within the PTA.[71]

At the same time, the organization's position on motherhood was reformulated, as can be traced in its journal, *Child Welfare Magazine*. Until the 1920s, the articles in the journal were written primarily by women, many of whom were mothers without advanced degrees. Books on child psychology were only occasionally reviewed, and articles on child rearing generally recognized the importance of motherly experience and expertise. A 1919 review of *Mental Hygiene of Childhood* by William A. White is indicative of the tone of the journal in those years: "Few mothers will agree with many statements of the author. It is not a book that shows real experience with child-life. Causes of children's actions are not understood. Many of the conclusions are an injustice to childhood." The implication is that a mother's own experience is the standard for judging the expertise of child psychologists, a perspective that would be superseded within the PTA by reliance on the authority of experts. The congress was regarded with some disdain by others in the parent education movement, who considered it to be sentimental, amateurish, and moralistic, qualities that were anathema to the objectivistic ideals of child psychologists.[72]

On the basis of the belief that women by nature had a unique capacity to understand and care for the young, the early PTA, as we have seen, attached great significance to the role of mothers in gathering and disseminating information about children. But during the 1910s and 1920s a dramatic change took place, which was reflected in the pages of *Child Welfare Magazine*. Articles by experts—child psychologists, pediatricians, and educators—proliferated in the journal. Many of the authors no longer regarded mothers' experiences as a valid touchstone for correct principles of child guidance. Indeed, mother love was actually considered dangerous to the child. According to Douglas Thom, a well-known child psychiatrist, "The very love of the mother for her child may be the 'stumbling block' that prevents her from fulfilling the obligations of her parenthood." Other articles chastised parents for their ignorance and enjoined them to heed expert advice. Educational psychologist Michael Vincent O'Shea contended, "Much of what passes under the name of 'common sense' in the training of children is just superstition, ignorance, and prejudice."[73] Scientists and educators questioned the reliability of the "maternal instinct" in the rearing of children, and some even doubted whether it existed. Many of the authors argued that although women were designed to bear children, they were ignorant of the best methods of raising them.

The commitment to scientific expertise in parenting was confirmed by a reinvigorated campaign within the PTA for parent education. Child-study groups and mothers' circles had been a component of the organization for some time, but scientific authorities in child training and development lent new legitimacy to the enterprise. Preschool circles, in particular, flourished, in part because of the claims of Sigmund Freud and the behaviorist John B. Watson that the first three years of a child's life determined its adult development. The organization elevated parent education to a prominent place, and in order to be designated "superior," state branches had to demonstrate their effectiveness in this arena.[74] Many organizations competed in the parent education marketplace in the 1920s, but the PTA, by situating itself in the context of the public schools, gained access to a huge constituency. In 1932, PTA branches received reports from a total of 3,055 study clubs in thirty-four states; study groups were the most popular activity sponsored by parent-teacher associations during this time.[75]

Despite the PTA's prominence in the national parent education movement and its attempts to cultivate a more professional image, it was criticized by more academic proponents of child study for its lack of educational rigor and the informal style of its "mothers' circles." It may have been these very factors that enabled the PTA to maintain its traditional appeal to women, however. The new emphasis on scientific expertise of *Child Welfare Magazine* was not all-encompassing. The term "parents" in the title of the organization still referred almost exclusively to mothers, and the reverence toward professional expertise coexisted with an attitude that mothers' study clubs should not be overly formal or academic. In her column on PTA study clubs, Grace Crum, urging untrained mothers to lead study groups, insisted: "A mother's own experience is the basic foundation in working with children." She encouraged leaders to structure meetings in accordance with mothers' interests rather than follow a set outline of study.[76] This line of thought suggests that some members were ambivalent about substituting expertise for experience. In practice, then, the PTA mediated between traditional motherhood and scientific expertise.

The PTA's expansion and increasing alliance with the social sciences contributed to the de-emphasizing of its maternalist reform agenda. Nonetheless, the organization continued to back social-welfare legislation throughout the 1930s, although its support was no longer couched in the lofty language of motherhood. The organization gradually adopted a view of motherhood as requiring professional assistance for its proper performance, yet maternalism continued to permeate the child-study clubs, where mothers' actual experiences with children were regarded as a departure point for any consideration of professional expertise. With the diminishing emphasis on motherhood as a public activity, however, the voices of mothers themselves were increasingly marginalized in the professional discourse of child development.

WHAT'S AN EDUCATED MOTHER TO DO? THE AMERICAN ASSOCIATION OF UNIVERSITY WOMEN (AAUW)

At first glance, the American Association of University Women seems a very different type of women's organization from the PTA or the Child Study Association. Championing the higher education of women was the preeminent purpose of the association, which was founded in 1882 by Marion Talbot and Alice Hayes with the help of Talbot's teacher, chemist Ellen Richards of the Massachusetts Institute of Technology. The three arranged for the first official meeting of the Association of Collegiate Alumnae in 1882. In 1884 the Western Association of Collegiate Alumnae was founded, followed by the Southern Association of College Women in 1903. All three organizations were finally subsumed under the rubric of the American Association of University Women in 1921.[77]

Since its origins the association had promulgated competing notions about the purpose of women's education. The founders of the organization were determined to expand the range of women's opportunities in higher education and in professional careers. Talbot and Richards were also interested, however, in the application of science to domestic life, and together they helped develop the new discipline of home economics. All three founders assumed positions of leadership in women's education; at the same time, they espoused conservative ideas about women. In 1910 Marion Talbot admitted, "So far that as the social and economic arrangements of society allot to men and women different tasks, so far must the educational machinery be developed differently for the two sexes."[78] Although ostensibly the organization encouraged women to pursue educational opportunities equal to those afforded men, it wavered over the meaning of that equality. Aligned with those who recommended that women's education be "feminine" were proponents of child study for college women. The inspiration for the organization had come from Marion Talbot's mother, Emily Talbot, who had persisted fiercely in her efforts to ensure that her daughter received a high-caliber education. Emily Talbot was a self-educated woman who had raised four children, in addition to devoting herself to philanthropic and educational work. She was appointed secretary of the educational division of the American Social Science Association, where in 1881 she initiated one of the first systematic efforts to engage mothers in the task of collecting information about their infants' development. Talbot's conviction that mothers should be involved in the development of the new child science was shared by Charles Darwin, with whom she met and discussed her project.[79]

Association member Millicent Shinn was instrumental in the organization's early child-study efforts and would later gain a certain renown for her book *Biography of a Baby* (1900), based on her careful observations of her infant niece. Shinn established a committee on child development as early as 1890 and distributed a schedule on which members could record their observations of infants. She hoped these would generate articles on child development.[80] The project never took off, for the social sciences, as we have seen, increasingly discouraged amateur contributions. As a result, the fledgling child-study committee of the association went into retreat, though it would be revived as a parent education program during the child-centered 1920s.

In 1898 some members of the association had recommended that college courses relating to homemaking and motherhood be developed for the benefit of the students who, unlike most earlier college alumnae, would go on to become wives and mothers. President M. Carey Thomas of Bryn Mawr is said to have quipped that "our failures only marry," but many teachers and administrators at elite women's colleges were concerned that in fact educated women would not put their education to use except in child rearing.[81] Although many early female college graduates had remained unmarried, the increasing numbers of women attending college meant that more would marry and have children.

In an article entitled "Shall the College Curriculum Be Modified for Women?" educator Mary Roberts Smith commented, "We do not expect a man to become a distinguished engineer or professor of Latin by studying a little literature, history, music, and language, yet we expect a woman to undertake an occupation for which, in this age at least, some definite kind of training should be necessary." At that time, 28 percent of the association's members were married, and it was estimated that approximately 40–60 percent of college women would ultimately marry. Smith joined the chorus of late nineteenth-century observers dismayed by the increasing proclivity of middle-class women to have fewer children, for she believed that "the possibility of motherhood is the primary consideration to which the aims of self-culture and self-support must forever be subordinated." Because careers outside the home were still frowned on for married women, many educators proposed that making a career of marriage and motherhood provided a solution to the predicament of the college-educated wife and mother.[82]

In most cases, members of the organization who championed a college education to address the needs of future mothers did not endorse a narrow focus on technical activities such as cooking and sewing. Instead, they argued for a redirection of academic subjects such as economics, sociology, psychology, and biology toward the problems of everyday home life. In the 1910s, for instance, a New York chapter recommended a curriculum for women that included courses in personal hygiene, environmental hygiene, child hygiene, and the family, along with law, political science, and the status of women in industry as a means of introducing "the scientific method into the vocation which most needs it, that of directing household and family life."[83] Education for motherhood was a fairly minor theme in the organization until the 1920s, when the quest for expansion led the group to capitulate to social pressures for women to put their education in the service of domesticity.

After the unification of the three regional associations in 1921, the organization hired its first staff person, Frances Fenton Bernard, as educational secretary. Bernard was directed to canvass the membership and propose a project related to education that would attract new members, including educated women whose primary occupation was child rearing. Until 1921, not a single member of the association's educational committee had advocated for preschool and elementary school education. That changed when Helen Thompson Woolley was appointed to the committee. She was not only an accomplished child psychologist but the assistant director of Merrill-Palmer School, an institution founded to train middle-class women for motherhood and preschool education. Woolley was a dynamic speaker and fluent writer, well-suited to promoting the cause of child study. She would serve as vice-president of the AAUW from 1923 to 1925.[84] That such major players in the organization as Bernard, Woolley, and soon-to-be president Aurelia Reinhardt were mothers who were active in the national PTA was emblematic of the changing status of college-educated women and surely helped push the group in the new direction.

In 1922 the educational committee proposed that the study of preschool children might fit the bill as the organization's new educational project, although the authors of the report acknowledged that child study might seem "like a radical departure from previous interests of this association." Members of the committee criticized women's higher education that made no provisions for training mothers in the management of children. "The college-trained woman," they contended, "approaches the task of providing a wise educational environment for her young children with no more specific preparation for it than the mother whose education ended with elementary school." They envisioned careers in parent education as a promising vocation for college-educated women. Some members, attempting to deflect criticisms that the project had little to offer women employed outside the home, argued that it would offer college graduates new fields of professional endeavor.[85]

Bernard encouraged members to study preschool children because of the growing popular and scholarly interest in children and the potential for university alumnae to make a genuine scientific contribution. She announced to the 1923 convention that the development of a parent education program would become a major focus of the organization. According to Lois Meek Stolz, educational secretary of the organization from 1924 to 1929, this speech was "shocking" to some women in the association, especially those who had been classics majors and had fought to have access to the same curriculum as men. President Virginia Gildersleeve of Barnard and President Ellen Pendleton of Wellesley were said to have remarked privately that child study represented a step backward for college women. Many who opposed the association's new direction had, by not having children, sidestepped the traditional perception that higher education detracted from women's maternal duties. Yet they rarely voiced their misgivings publicly, perhaps because Freudian theory, which was increasingly influential, characterized the lives of unmarried women as abnormal.[86]

The obsessive interest Americans displayed in child psychology during the 1920s, fears about the disintegration of family life, and uneasiness about the plight of educated women with children all converged to enlist the leaders of the association in the campaign for child study and parent education. The results of a 1928 survey of Radcliffe alumnae hinted at a significant potential constituency for the new program. Respondents were asked how university women could best serve their communities. The largest number replied that women could be of most service in their roles as mothers and teachers of the next generation. Some critics accused women of "forgetting their primary function: the continuation of the human race." This sentiment was reflected in a 1923 conference resolution recommending that all colleges develop courses in parent education. Yet because participants disagreed about whether only women should be urged to take such courses, the resolution does not stipulate for whom these courses were to be created.[87]

In 1927, Ada Comstock, president of Radcliffe, explained the AAUW decision to adopt the cause of child study: "As new members were brought in by our drive, many were found to be young mothers, interested in the education of little children and glad to be directed in studying it. And so the sails filled, and the ship made off on the new tack." Comstock neglected to note, however, that the ship was fully launched only with funding from the Laura Spelman Rockefeller Memorial. In 1923 Lawrence Frank met with President Aurelia Reinhardt to discuss the matter of funding the organization's child-study work. He stressed that child study was valuable not only for the children's sake, but because "women are prone to 'return to the blanket'" and may "relinquish or lose all interest in further learning."[88] Child study promised to integrate the academic and personal interests of homebound women and provide them with an intellectual connection often lacking in their day-to-day lives.

Frank had another agenda as well. He hoped that association members, trained in the methods and content of child study, would become leaders of the parent education movement he hoped to create. His vision of the organization fitted in with the members' conception of themselves as an elite group of women who, although many of them had chosen marriage and motherhood, intended to enlist their talents and education in the service of the community. In 1924 the Laura Spelman Rockefeller Memorial provided the American Association of University Women with $79,000 for the salary of a director of child study and parent education, training for study-group leaders, a traveling library, and expenses for the organization's journal, one third of which would now be devoted to child study. The grant, paid over seven years, provided a solid foundation for the organization's work in parent education.[89]

Frank initially proposed that a married woman with children should direct the group's parent education campaign. But few women had Ph.D.'s in child psychology at the time, so the childless Lois Meek was recruited. Meek was to have a long and distinguished career in child development. At Teachers College, she studied child psychology with John Dewey and Edward Thorndike. Under her tenure as educational secretary, the organization played a prominent leadership role in the parent education movement. Child study held center stage in the work of the organization until 1930, when Meek left the group to become director of the Institute for Child Welfare at Teachers College.[90]

During its early years under Meek's leadership, the association inaugurated a two-pronged program of child study and international relations, both of which became mainstays at state and local branches. As was characteristic of child study in the 1920s, the groups began with the study of preschool and elementary school children. Frank was insistent that child study was not to be confused with social welfare but was "primarily an enterprise in education and research wherein the members develop a greater knowledge of the development of the child." This pronouncement, however, did not prevent individual chapters from initiating reform projects based on their studies. Many groups established cooperative nursery schools for their members and worked for playgrounds, school health clinics, and day nurseries in their local communities. Thus the American Association of University Women child-study groups helped college-educated mothers extend their influence into the public arena.[91]

The campaign to educate mothers was, by the organization's own account, a successful one. The organization, although it never had the popular appeal that the PTA enjoyed, sponsored 432 child-study groups nationwide in 1928. The association's intellectual approach to child study may have alienated the very groups of women and organizations that Frank had hoped its members would lead. Unlike the informal child-study clubs associated with home economics extension programs and the PTA, AAUW child-study groups were exhorted by association leaders never to degenerate into "experience meetings" but to rely on "facts and known principles." The leaders wished their parent education program to be identified with a strictly scientific point of view.[92]

The association's intellectual approach to child study did, however, have some appeal for its own constituency. Following an annual convention in 1927, an exultant Meek reported to Frank: "I never dreamed that in three years we could convince this Association that a study of children was an important part of the work of college women. Even presidents and deans were interested, asking questions and buying literature." In 1931 Marion Talbot recognized the success of the campaign, calling the study groups "the center of [the American Association of University Women's] life and the reason for its existence." The organization, which had 20,000 members in 1924, attained a paid membership of over 45,000 by 1935.[93]

The American Association of University Women did not live up to Frank's hopes, in the sense that it never attracted substantial numbers from outside the organization to its groups and did not play a key role in the dissemination of child development expertise outside of its own constituency. Child study may not have continued to hold appeal for the masses of women within the association, though. As of 1948, a little less than half of the members were married with children.[94] Educated mothers may have felt that it was redundant to focus their intellectual interests on child rearing instead of expanding their horizons outside the family circle.

The PTA, the Child Study Association, and the American Association of University Women all promoted the notion that mothering must be made scientific. By advocating an educated motherhood, the leaders of these organizations hoped to raise the status of mothers. The organizations differed, though, in the extent to which they actually valued expertise versus maternal experience. The American Association of University Women, whose members were educated middle- to upper-class women, explicitly sided with expertise as opposed to experience. During training sessions for study-group leaders, they discussed "how to obviate the difficulty encountered in the study groups with mothers who ask personal questions and tell personal experiences which do not bear directly on the subject of study."[95] By holding its sessions in a classroom atmosphere and making them as objective and scientific as possible, the group tried to professionalize mothering and bring child study up to the standard of traditional academic work. At the same time, the association was divided in its advocacy of scientific motherhood. Some members may have found that "science" was valued over motherhood, but others were displeased with the emphasis on motherhood in an organization ostensibly designed to help educated women advance in academia and the professions. The competing values and agendas portended that parent education could not continue for long to occupy the premier place in the association.

These contradictions did not plague the Child Study Association, which had been founded on the premise that mothers should be educated in the principles of child development. While maintaining that mother's place was in the home, the group agreed that expert knowledge was essential to the proper discharge of maternal responsibilities. Although rather eclectic, this approach to parent education was nonetheless highly standardized. Club leaders clearly saw it as their mandate to instill precepts of child development in their members. The organization did, however, provide its primarily middle-class members with the opportunity to expand their intellects and to develop a consciousness of themselves as women and as mothers.

Despite the PTA's commitment to science and to professionalizing motherhood, its child-study groups remained organized around the needs and interests of mothers rather than the requirements of academic subject material. This model proved most successful in attracting thousands of small-town and rural mothers to participate in the study of children. Although the political impact of its maternalist message had been tempered by the emphasis on professional expertise, the PTA continued to offer mothers a common ground for their interests in their children and their schools. Interestingly, it may have been the PTA's "sentimental" focus on women's unique role as mothers that appealed to the largest constituency.[96] Although membership in the PTA posed few challenges to traditional gender roles, it did serve to reinforce women's values and provided women with a safe entry into public activism.

The work of these three organizations during the early decades of the twentieth century illuminates the transformation of maternalist ideology through its encounter with a progressive vision of the social sciences during that period. As these group histories indicate, maternalism did not survive unscathed.[97] The notion that women were divinely and naturally ordained to be mothers was complicated by the idea that expertise supplied by clinicians and social scientists was needed in order to be a good mother. Maternalism was undermined as a source of female authority, but few substitutes were provided. Perhaps some people suspected that the professionalization of motherhood might subvert conventional understandings of child rearing as solely a woman's activity. But this indirect approach to changing parenting could not succeed without a full-fledged attack on the prevailing division of labor by sex.

Parent education promised to accommodate women's demands for meaningful work by endowing motherhood with the rhetoric of professionalism. But the rhetoric proved misleading, because professionals, unlike mothers, generally have responsibility for the research, literature, and regulation of their fields of expertise. In fact, parenting is not a likely candidate for professionalization; the parent-child relationship is highly individualized in our society, and the nuances and complexities that characterize this most dynamic human interaction do not lend themselves to standardization.

Many of the mothers in child-study groups recognized that prescribing their interactions with their children was problematic. They wrestled with the textbook prescriptions, demanded that their voices be heard and their experience with children recognized. They were ready neither to abandon the traditional mother's role nor to embrace wholeheartedly the ideology of scientific motherhood. Although it was often women themselves who orchestrated this movement, the attempt to transform motherhood into a standardized occupation was met with considerable resistance, as we shall see in the following chapters.[98]

Chapter 3 "What Is the Matter with Our Children Today?": Race, Class, and Ethnicity in the Parent Education Movement

From every home, from city and country, from rich and poor, comes the call, "What is the matter with our children today? What has come over them? Why are they so different from us? Why is it so difficult to have them do and think as we did and thought as children?"
—*Bird Stein Gans, Child Study Association, 1923*

A torrent of radio and print journalism during the 1920s alternately railed against and praised the unconventionality of contemporary youth. Although the term "generation gap" was not yet in use, some applauded young people's independence, verve, and style, and others bemoaned their deviations from traditional morals and values. Perhaps most startling was the lack of reverence for their elders that some of the young exhibited and their willingness to question the cultural traditions with which they had been raised. A writer for the *New Republic* in 1924 complained that youth now seemed to have the upper hand: "A parent nowadays needs to be thick-skinned as a dinosaur! . . . The frank criticism they make of their parents' ideas, religion, even of their own training as children!"[1]

Bird Stein Gans, a parent educator with the Child Study Association, did not have to go far to find evidence that parents from various class backgrounds were experiencing generational difficulties.[2] An African-American mother from Cincinnati claimed that before she joined a child-study group "there seemed to be such a gulf between herself and her children." In Robert and Helen Lynd's classic study of Middletown, the generation gap emerged as a ubiquitous problem: "Middletown parents are wont to speak of many of their 'problems' as new to this generation, situations for which the formulae of their parents are inadequate."[3] Parents could not help wondering about the efficacy of traditional child-rearing strategies in a modern era.

Some of the tensions between parents and children arose because of children's rising educational attainments in comparison to their parents' and the enhanced role of the school in everyday life. Once charged with transmitting traditional wisdom, schools now also served to inculcate new scientific and technical knowledge in students. Middletown mothers protested that their daughters, influenced by their home economics classes, ridiculed their mothers' "rule-of-thumb practices" as old-fashioned. And the Lynds cited a bemused father who exclaimed, "Why, even my youngster in kindergarten is telling us where to get off. . . . He won't eat white bread because he says they tell him at kindergarten that brown is more healthful!" The family sociologist Ernest Groves hypothesized that the American child "feels more keenly than he used to feel the difference between family life and life outside the family. Life is more traditional within the family than outside, and the child, going back and forth between the two environments, may feel that the family represents a suppressing or even a backward influence." Parent educators sought to transform the "backward" family into a unit more fully capable of preparing its children for modernity.[4]

This gap between parent and child was magnified in immigrant families, where many children felt superior to their parents because of their greater familiarity with the language and mores of America. The fear of immigrant parents that the school would undermine their parental authority was, in some cases, realistic. One Italian immigrant mother chided her son's teacher, who was also Italian: "You will even probably tell him that he does not have to listen to his mother. You have different customs here; and if I let Tony do as you tell him, I cannot control him. You, Mr. Teacher, are an Italian yourself, and you know what bad ideas are being put into our children."[5] Children's increasing educational attainments and an information explosion created new and more diverse sources of social authority that competed with parental authority. Educators argued that if parents were to keep pace with their children, they needed to take advantage of the new education for parenthood.

THE "PROBLEM" OF THE IMMIGRANT MOTHER

During the late nineteenth and early twentieth centuries, Americanization campaigns were conducted by middle-class, largely Protestant reformers to usher immigrants into mainstream society by teaching them the English language and American principles of citizenship. The reformers also strove to disseminate American "family values" to ensure the acculturation of seemingly unassimilable southeast European immigrants. From the parent educators' perspective, some of the problems exhibited by immigrant families were unique to their situation, and others were similar to those of native-born families. Like poor and working-class families of American origin, many immigrant families were unable to put into practice child-care prescriptions that assumed an adequate standard of living. The generational difficulties experienced by other Americans were compounded in immigrant homes by the divergence between the experiences of parents and those of their children.

Social workers and educators postulated that the effects of generational differences must be especially severe for immigrant women, who were sometimes confined to the home and who lacked familiarity with the language and customs of America.[6] A leader of the League of Mothers' Clubs, an organization composed primarily of immigrant women in New York City, contended, "The mother in the home is left far behind her husband and children in opportunity. Her influence is lost and she becomes ineffectual when the other members of the family understand the newer attitudes of America." Some commentators speculated that the predicament of immigrant mothers was merely a more extreme version of the problems experienced by American-born mothers struggling to keep pace with their more up-to-date children. The feeling expressed by the leader of the largely immigrant Henry Street Mothers' Club in New York City would have been recognizable to many middle-class mothers: "Each mother with a grown-up daughter is bemoaning the ways of the younger generation and wondering what this world is coming to."[7]

Generational difficulties were, however, complicated by the process of acculturation to American life. Immigrant mothers complained about their bossy children, and social casework reports of the period abound with examples of friction between parents and children that stemmed from the children's Americanization. Studies of juvenile delinquency invariably commented on the loss of parental authority in immigrant families. Immigrant parents who tried to impart traditional cultural values to their children found themselves thwarted by their adopted country, which employed visiting teachers, child protection agencies, and probation officers to monitor parents' child-rearing practices. An Italian father of seven stated: "I came to learn that I have almost no power over my own children. . . . Oh, how often I know too well, that a good spanking can cure the bad habits of my children. Yet I must think twice before I do this. Here in America I may be taken to court for having administered punishment on my own son."[8] Reformers, though they may have underestimated the strength of kinship ties between first- and second-generation immigrants and overstated the extent of this generational gap, did not invent the problem.

A special rhetoric evolved in the education of immigrant mothers that linked the adoption of American child-rearing methods to citizenship. The Baby Hygiene Association of Boston, which sponsored mothers' meetings, claimed in its 1917 annual report: "With the baby as a starting point the mother learns how to care for herself and the home. . . . She begins to see the importance of citizenship and education." And a Children's Bureau project in Waterbury, Connecticut, which trained Lithuanian and Italian mothers in the feeding and care of children, maintained that its courses strengthened "the mother's grasp of her country's ways, preventing the break in the family ties which comes when the children grow up Americanized and the parents fail to understand their children's new ways and interests."[9] Many immigrant mothers did not have access to the socializing institutions of work and school that their spouses and children participated in. Americanizers hypothesized that immigrant women, because of their failure to participate in those institutions, were more attached to their ethnic communities than the rest of their families and were in danger both of losing authority over their children and of keeping them from assimilating. Nevertheless, reformers envisioned the *educated* immigrant mother as the critical binding agent who could simultaneously hold the immigrant family together and integrate it into the larger American culture. From the point of view of parent educators, immigrant mothers desperately needed to be brought in touch with modern society.[10]

When World War I broke out, the patriotism of immigrants who did not support the U.S. military involvement in Europe was thrown into question. The involvement of disproportionate numbers of immigrants in trade union, anarchist, and other political activities also aroused skepticism about the patriotism of recent arrivals. By teaching immigrants the fundamentals of American language, life, and citizenship, reformers hoped to ensure the newcomers' assimilation and patriotism.[11]

The progressive women's movement, including the General Federation of Women's Clubs and the National Congress of Mothers, adopted the Americanization of immigrants as one of their major reform goals during the 1910s and 1920s. A 1920 article in *Woman's Home Companion* voiced the theme: "Everywhere in America women are trying to break down the barrier between the foreign-born and the American-born. The war proved that it could be done, and the labor unrest, based many times on insufficient understanding of American ideals and institutions, is daily showing that it must be done." Frances Kellor, director of the national Americanization Committee, saw as one of the most frustrating obstacles to Americanization the "old-world physical and psychological characteristics" that "persisted under American clothes" in the native-born children of immigrants to this country.[12] A twofold educational strategy, aimed at both immigrant children and their mothers, was initiated to eradicate the "foreignness" of the immigrant family.

As nurturers and socializers par excellence, middle-class women considered themselves especially qualified to assist in the efforts to transform the parenting practices of immigrant women. Female reform leaders believed that all women, even if they were not actually mothers, possessed maternal qualities that enabled them to identify with other women across the entire spectrum of class and ethnic backgrounds. Gwendolyn Mink illuminates the ideological underpinnings of this viewpoint: "As natural educators, mothers held the key to the rehabilitation of republican citizenship. Since all women were given this natural vocation, they shared a common identity that counterbalanced rigid social distinctions of race and ethnicity."[13]

The discourse of Americanization embodied assumptions about the power of nurture over nature in producing upstanding American citizens. It found a logical home in the parent education movement, which similarly emphasized the role of nurture. By insisting that motherhood was central to the experience of women from all cultures, though, the Americanization and parent education movements also underscored that the purpose of a woman's life was to bear and rear children. In fact, in both campaigns, such essentialist views—those which attributed group traits, whether ethnic, racial, or gender, to biology, or nature—vied with positions that emphasized the role of environment. Many Americanizers, despite their optimistic stance, still believed that inherent differences in character and intelligence existed between nationalities, and between racial groups as well. Parent educators were struck by dissimilarities between the population groups with whom they worked and were not always sanguine about the possibility of educating all groups equally.

New developments in the social and behavioral sciences were, however, undermining the concept that intelligence and character were predetermined by group identity. In the early 1910s studies conducted using Binet's intelligence tests indicated that the majority of juvenile delinquents were "feeble-minded." The results were countered by Augusta Bronner and William Healy, who insisted in their study of juvenile delinquency *The Individual Delinquent* (1915) that delinquency was due to "bad social conditions created by socially unfit parents, the effects of which are not those of biological inheritance." Evidence about the heritability of group characteristics was still scanty, but many social scientists in the 1920s shared reformist convictions that the influence of the environment came foremost.[14]

While reformers concentrated on improving the external environment within which immigrants functioned, they also viewed the family as the most essential agent in the socialization of children, the future citizens of America. The immigrants who clustered in northern urban settings during this period— including East European Jews, Poles, and Italians—retained familial patterns that diverged from the prevailing vision of the ideal American family. Children of immigrant parents were more likely to work and less likely to be singled out for special treatment in the family than American middle-class children. Some immigrant cultures also favored different emotional styles than that associated with European-American Protestants; Italians, for instance, were known for their open displays of anger and affection. Grace Caldwell, a nursery school teacher in Boston in the 1920s, complained that the Italian children she worked with were subjected to too much noise, not enough reason and rationality in their discipline, and "too much knowledge of intimate family life."[15]

Reformers generally also regarded the traditional patriarchal structure of many immigrant families with disapproval. According to social worker Sopho-nisba Breckinridge, "Almost all the foreign-born groups hold to the dominion of man over woman, and of parents over children." Parent educators sought to instill the concept of individualism in mothers and to weaken the traditional authority of fathers in the immigrant family.[16] Both immigrant mothers and their children were to be introduced to the American concept of individuality, which conflicted with the collectivism that motivated many immigrant groups. Reformers wished to teach mothers that their children were unique individuals with distinctive needs and that it was parents' responsibility to raise children who would pursue their own best interests, rather than devote their lives to fulfilling their obligations to their parents. Female reformers, who were being encouraged to extend their own talents into the public arena, also tried to convince immigrant mothers that they were individuals and should learn to express themselves outside the confines of the home.[17]

As they attempted to alter immigrants' family structures, parent educators enjoined the mothers to gain a scientific understanding of children's nature and needs, both psychological and physical. The home should accord with those needs and provide special spaces and furnishings for children, as the child-rearing literature mandated. This was an impossible requirement for both working-class and most immigrant families, who had limited space to begin with and often shared their meager living space with lodgers and kin. The educators undermined the immigrants' traditional parenting practices by insisting that children should be subjected to discipline from infancy and that scheduled feedings, strictly observed, were the prerequisite for physically and emotionally healthy babies. If the infant had already been fed and diapered, parents who picked her up when she cried were spoiling her. Many immigrant mothers, by contrast, allowed the baby to dictate the feedings and tended to initiate discipline at a later age.[18]

Educators who developed Americanization programs for immigrant mothers regarded home economics—which encompassed cooking, sewing, child care, and other issues of household management—as the mainstay of the curriculum. Some immigrant women welcomed such assistance in homemaking; Russian immigrant Mary Antin described the woman who helped her mother to use her new cookstove as an "angel of deliverance." Others felt acutely the condescension that sometimes accompanied these efforts. Some historians have postulated that education for immigrant women neglected their development as individuals capable of intelligent thought and concentrated solely on their roles as housewives and mothers.[19] Some reformers undoubtedly held biased views of the intellectual capacities of immigrant women, yet as we have seen in previous chapters, the campaign to educate mothers was not limited to immigrant women. In addition, the reformers' emphasis on motherhood was pragmatic as well as ideological. Because ethnic traditions often discouraged married women's participation in public activities, many immigrant mothers rarely ventured beyond their homes and neighborhoods. Reformers observed that it was "practically impossible to enlist the attention of mothers except through service offered through their babies and younger children." In most immigrant communities, however, women's roles as mothers were socially validated; therefore, sometimes by invoking maternal duty, parent educators could persuade women to attend their classes.[20]

Parent education was thus part of a larger reform agenda urged by many female settlement-house workers, who sought to imbue immigrant women with the ideals of municipal housekeeping and encouraged them to extend their homemaking activities to the community at large through political activism. The educators also aspired to create community among immigrant mothers, to model the ideals of democratic society in the mothers' club. This dual purpose is evidenced in the description of a kindergarten teacher, who was seen as both an instructor and a community organizer:

> The kindergarten teacher is welcomed by the shy foreign mother because of their common interest in the little child, and the mother finds in this bright-faced teacher a friend and advisor, whose calls are a source of real pleasure and profit, for she comes to her not with a patronizing air, but in the spirit of a sister, and soon persuades the mother to attend the monthly mother's meetings, where she meets many other women of different nationalities, all trying to bring their children up in the way they should go and finding it a difficult matter in our crowded city streets.[21]

Americanization, in this context, involved building a community of mothers from diverse ethnic backgrounds, on the basis of the common experience of raising children in an alien culture. The quotation also suggests some reformers' awareness of their own class biases and their efforts to avoid condescension.

At least some educators were aware that they must approach immigrant women with respect for their culture and accomplishments if they were to successfully engage them in programs. Hannah Kent Schoff, president of the PTA, alluded to this issue at a conference in 1919: "The women feel that in their own countries they have brought up children successfully and that they do not need to be told everything. By learning the good things our foreign-born people know, and showing them that they have some things to teach us, their attitude is entirely changed."[22] Consequently, in many immigrant mothers' clubs and classes time was set aside for sharing ethnic crafts, songs, history, and costumes. At the same time, reformers continued to underscore the importance of altering traditional child-rearing practices to correspond to the "modern" American methods of raising children.

SAVAGE VERSUS CIVILIZED PARENTS: THE ROLE OF CLASS IN PARENT EDUCATION

Accommodating to an age when "tradition" was often a pejorative term and new knowledge was continually challenging the old posed parenting problems for mothers from many different backgrounds. In the early decades of the century, as the responsibility of child rearing loomed ever larger, the burden came ineluctably to rest on the shoulders of mothers, who often lacked the communal support for parenting that mothers in earlier eras and different cultural milieus had enjoyed. As Molly Ladd-Taylor notes, in general, native-born white women were most subject to the dictates of scientific motherhood. Because of their educational attainments and identification with the professional classes, such women were more susceptible to and interested in the findings of the child sciences. Many middle-class mothers had grown up in smaller families than immigrant and working-class mothers, had had little prior experience with young children, and lacked an extensive network of kin to provide assistance and reassurance. Most important, they were able to ensure their children's economic survival and could thus afford to worry about their children's emotional well-being.[23]

The role of class differences in family styles underlay many of the discussions of parent education. In a collection of essays representing the views of the radical wing of the parent education movement, John Langdon-Davies divided parents into the "savage" and the "civilized." Savage parents emulated the child-rearing strategies of their parents and grandparents and produced children like themselves. Civilized parents used "every available device and ingenuity to prevent their children's being like themselves."[24] Langdon-Davies did not specifically adduce a class factor in his analysis, but social welfare workers agreed that poor and immigrant parents were more reluctant to relinquish family child-rearing traditions than were middle-class families.

Mothers often turned to child-rearing texts to assuage their insecurities, but there were clear class differences in their use of these resources. A 1930 study found that 79.4 percent of white parents of the highest socioeconomic status had read at least one book on child rearing in the previous year, in contrast to 26.7 percent of parents from the lowest socioeconomic group. Among African-American parents, 71 percent from the higher socioeconomic group had read at least one book on child rearing and 46.1 percent from the lower group (interestingly, a higher percentage than among lower-class whites). More members of all groups read newspaper and magazine articles on child rearing than read books, however, with 88.2 percent of the white population and 78.1 percent of the African-American population claiming to have read at least one article.[25]

Clearly, women's propensity to call on expert advice when rearing children was rapidly extending beyond the middle class. This tendency was generated in part by the shift from home to hospital births (home births dropped from 50 percent to 15 percent between 1915 and 1930), for hospitals played an important role in inculcating the precepts of scientific child care.[26] It was only a short step from consulting pediatricians about the care of sick children to consulting them about normal children. Immigrant women, especially Jewish women, who had initially turned to clinics for the health needs of their infants often employed private doctors once they had the means, an enviable sign of advances in both Americanization and economic status.[27]

Historians Neil Cowan and Ruth Schwartz Cowan have demonstrated the tendency of first- and second-generation Jewish immigrants who became parents between 1920 and 1945 to adopt the child-care practices recommended by the local experts they encountered in the baby-welfare clinics, schools, and social settlement houses, and in their books and pamphlets on children. Jacquelyn Litt explains that Jewish mothers viewed "medicalized mothering" as a "distinctly American practice," which served to differentiate them from less acculturated immigrants and facilitated their entry into the middle class. They were aided in their transformation by the relatively large number of Jewish physicians and networks of Jewish women who compared notes about the clinics and physicians they consulted.[28] Medicalized mothering had its pitfalls, however, according to one immigrant mother:

> I remember Stanley [her firstborn], we then went by the books, and I remember the saying, "You don't touch the baby. You feed the baby regularly and you don't touch the baby in between." And that baby cried for a very, very long time. We had a sick baby and a baby who really needed to be loved and held. And I remember the first time I really held him because he was sick. . . . And that is the first I remember rocking him. And after that we walked him at night and we paid much closer attention. It took that much time to relate to this child. We were trapped in the book.[29]

Although this Jewish mother described herself as "trapped in the book" as a new mother, she soon recognized that she was the best judge of what her child needed. Nonetheless, there is no doubt that medical practitioners were monitoring mothering, thereby laying the groundwork for a much more scientifically informed motherhood.

Child-rearing expertise was available to women in differing degrees, depending on their class, geographic location, level of literacy, and access to medical care. Information about "scientific" methods of training children was more accessible to middle-class and urban mothers. Margaret Jarman Hagood found, in the study she conducted of Tennessee tenant farm mothers in the 1930s, that mothers only rarely nursed their babies on a schedule, even though most middle-class women were aware that the experts wanted them to schedule infants' feeding. Hagood claimed, "The notion was new to some and incomprehensible to a few."[30] Some mothers chose to disregard professional expertise and in rearing their children relied primarily on knowledge dispensed by family and friends. Women with strong ethnic traditions and from marginalized groups, such as African-Americans, were more inclined to perceive educators' attempts to modify their child-rearing practices as an imposition of "foreign" values.

In a study of Nashville mothers conducted in 1933, 75 percent of the white women Cora Trawick Court interviewed claimed to be interested in parent education, while only 35 percent of the African-American women surveyed voiced interest in the topic. One mother commented, "I don't need nobody to tell me anything. All I need is a place to leave my William when I go to work. I used to go to that Mothers' Club, but shucks, it ain't nothing. White folks just naturally can't tell you nothing about raising children."[31] This mother was well aware that the leaders of parent education were usually white and were likely to have little understanding of the predicament of women of her class and race. Indeed, several of the mothers in the study complained that the parent education classes in their neighborhood were run by white women, most of whom were childless.[32] Some working-class mothers were also vexed by the intrusive queries of educators, social workers, and researchers, who presumed that they had the luxury to concentrate on their children's psychic development. In her eloquent novella "I Stand Here Ironing," Tillie Olsen recounts the reactions of a Depression-era working-class mother who is asked by a teacher to discuss the origins of her teenage daughter's emotional problems: "And when is there time to remember, to sift, to weigh, to estimate, to total? I will start and there will be an interruption and I will have to gather it all together again. Or I will become engulfed with all I did or did not do, with what should have been and what cannot be helped." Poor mothers were expected to assume responsibility for their children's well-being in accordance with standards set by middle-class society; the time and resources required for particular methods of child rearing were taken for granted. Another mother, ground down by the daily demands of motherhood, responded to a question about whether she was having interesting experiences with her children: "It may be that I am having interesting experiences with children, but I cannot tell you what they are. I do not see them, I am too busy with their care to see their development."[33] This was a recurring theme in the statements of poor and working-class mothers: that the questions posed by experts were irrelevant to the dilemmas they faced.

BETTER BABIES, BETTER MOTHERS: PARENT EDUCATION FOR THE POOR

During the late nineteenth and early twentieth centuries the mothers' meetings conducted at day nurseries, kindergartens, and settlement houses frequently combined discussions about child care and feeding with practical lessons about cooking, sewing, and home furnishings.[34] The scientific nursery school surfaced as an even more systematic enterprise for training parents in the child-rearing strategies advocated by experts in the 1920s. Like nineteenth-century infant schools, nursery schools were designed to reshape rather than supplement family life. According to the sponsors of a Boston nursery school for immigrant and working-class children, "If the nursery school movement does not result ultimately in better mothers and better homes, it will of course be a failure." Only about 20 percent of the nursery schools founded during the 1920s engaged in outreach efforts to the poor, but the child training techniques employed in them were often adopted by day nurseries and kindergartens serving working-class families. The nursery school provided its young charges with a nutritious diet, regular exercise, and plenty of sleep, taught personal hygiene, and sought to train children in the "sound mental habits" of behavior that were considered an essential part of middle-class decorum.[35]

Perhaps the predominant opportunity for parent education among the poor during the 1910s and 1920s arose in conjunction with the child health movement, which focused on reducing rates of infant mortality. Infant health was a major rallying cry for the women's club movement, whose lobbying efforts had helped to establish the U.S. Children's Bureau. The bureau was responsible for numerous studies documenting the lamentable state of children's health and for the publication and dissemination of information on child care to millions of American mothers. The combined efforts of the women's club movement, the Children's Bureau, and the Women's Committee of the National Council of Defense resulted in an extensive campaign for children's health during and after World War I. The campaign promoted birth registrations, well-baby health examinations, maternal instruction in infant care, and the dispensation of bacteria-free milk at milk stations. The promotion of breast-feeding and the provision of clean milk were perhaps the most significant undertakings, because many infant deaths in poorer communities were attributed to milk contaminated owing to inadequate refrigeration. With the designation of 1918 as Children's Year, reformers made preschoolers the target of their efforts. The data gathered at the scores of clinics where toddlers were examined were utilized by the Children's Bureau to lobby for the Sheppard-Towner bill, which provided funds for the prevention of health problems among mothers and children.[36]

The children's health movement achieved a significant victory with the establishment of several thousand infant-welfare (meaning health and well-being) clinics during the interwar period. These became centers for the diffusion of child-rearing advice to poor mothers and helped to spur the development of the profession of pediatrics. Sydney Halpern argues that physicians involved in the infant-welfare movement made use of government and philanthropic funding to begin their work with children of the poor before extending their services to the middle class in the form of the lucrative pediatrics profession.[37]

At the infant-welfare clinics, public health nurses disseminated information about the advantages of breast-feeding and hygienic practices in the home and encouraged women to seek medical advice when their babies displayed disturbing ailments or disabilities. Scores of immigrant and poor women lined up at infant-welfare clinics to have their babies weighed, examined, and medicated and to bring home the bacteria-free milk that was sometimes distributed. They also participated avidly in the "better baby" contests sponsored by clinics and settlement houses to reward women for producing healthy babies. The clinics and nurses undoubtedly contributed to the physical well-being of babies and mothers; meanwhile, however, the focus on maternal education shifted attention away from environmental factors that mothers could not control, such as poverty, inadequate housing, and poor sanitation and nutrition.[38]

One of the most significant attempts at parent education for poor immigrant women was directed not at mothers but at the older sisters in immigrant families who cared for their siblings. Sara Josephine Baker, head of New York's Bureau of Child Hygiene and a leading child welfare advocate, organized the Little Mothers' Leagues to teach school-age girls the essentials of feeding, bathing, and clothing infants. In 1911 the leagues attracted approximately 20,000 girls in New York City. Baker hoped that her students would in turn instruct their mothers in healthy child-rearing practices. In addition to the leagues' efforts to educate girls, New York's infant-health campaign included birth registrations and home visits by nurses to new mothers to instruct them in caring for their infants. The city's many efforts to improve babies' health appear to have had an effect, so that by 1914 New York had the lowest rate of infant mortality of any major city in the United States or in Europe.[39]

Although Baker's accomplishments in the area of child health were formidable, she tended to categorize immigrant mothers' child-care techniques in general as pathological rather than single out particular unhygienic practices. In her "Talks with Mothers" (1913), she warned that many traditional child-rearing practices could lead to infants' death: "Our grandmothers used to believe in rocking babies, walking with them, jumping up or down, clothing them too warmly, feeding them all sorts of things when they were very little, letting them taste of everything, giving them comforters to suck and keep them quiet, etc., and a great many babies die." In fact, the list of practices aforementioned did not jeopardize children's health. The primary causes of infant mortality were unclean milk, unsanitary and dangerous housing conditions, and lack of adequate medical care. In her study of poor London mothers at the turn of the century, Ellen Ross observed that it was difficult or even impossible for most to implement the most basic sanitary measures: "Even such modest and effective methods as hand washing around babies and more thorough cleaning of their utensils would have demanded, in many households, different quarters, more fuel, and better plumbing."[40]

Baker admonished immigrant mothers who tended to consult their relatives or friends about problems with their children rather than follow the advice of visiting nurses: "My first caution is, don't ask your neighbors to tell you what you had better do with your own baby. If you do that, I might just as well not give these little talks, for anything I might teach you may be undone by the guess work of some foolish woman next door." She then told the story of a woman who had been advised by her neighbors to bathe her feverish infant in cold water or give it a medicine to bring down the fever. When the mother brought the infant to the Milk Station it was found that the baby was merely overdressed. The lesson, according to Baker, was "If the mother had taken the advice of any one of her honest neighbors her baby might have died."[41]

This threat, though extreme, was sometimes effective in persuading mothers to replace traditional child-rearing practices with those advocated by experts, for if there was one thing that mothers from different classes and ethnic backgrounds shared, it was the desire to ensure their infants' survival. Yet some mothers felt a sense of loss in relinquishing their autonomy. An Armenian mother in Boston complained that her infant belonged "to the doctor and the nurse more than to me." She added: "And they say to me always, 'This is a free country.' What does it mean? It is not free for the mother and child."[42]

Not all public health reformers were as unreflective as Baker in their work with immigrant mothers. Physician Alice Hamilton, who cared for immigrant women and their babies in Chicago, noted in retrospect, "Those Italian women knew what a baby needed far better than my Ann Arbor professor did," especially in regard to her teacher's advice that children should consume nothing but milk until they developed teeth. Hamilton was humbled by her observation that some of the maternal practices she fought most diligently to eradicate were later endorsed by experts. She wryly remarked, "I cannot feel I did any harm, . . . for my teachings had no effect."[43]

Like the doctors and nurses who assumed that poor mothers must be instructed in the essentials of infant care, parent educators felt they had a mission to inform less educated women about the principles of child psychology and development. One educator charged: "A large proportion of the children of the country are in the care of parents having a minimum of education . . . the problem of parental education is therefore largely concerned with this group." This assertion was bolstered by the findings of a study by Harold Anderson published in 1936, which revealed that lower-class mothers were less likely to practice recommended child-rearing strategies than were mothers from the upper classes. According to the study, 46.5 percent of mothers from the lowest class as opposed to 29.1 percent of the highest class "relied on their own experience" in child rearing. These figures might imply that working-class women had more confidence in their work as mothers because they had not been trained to believe that doctors' expertise in that sphere was superior but trusted instead that raising children was a matter of common sense. Class differences may also have contributed to working-class mothers' resistance to experts' attempts to dictate the terms of their family lives, the primary arena in which the economically disempowered can exert control. Anderson, however, read the statistics to mean that lower-class women needed more expert training to rear their children.[44]

Poor mothers also were more likely than middle-class women to defer to the advice of their mothers and grandmothers in deciding how to care for their children. Margaret Quilliard, a field worker for the Child Study Association, noted the "unquestioning acceptance of former methods of child training" among settlement-house mothers; in working with them, she found their "loyalty to parents and grandparents" one of the most serious obstacles. Poor parents also tended to cling to interpretations of child behavior that differed from those of child development professionals. They were likely to view their children as either "good" or "bad" by nature and were resistant to the notion that parental disciplinary techniques were the key to producing well-behaved offspring. In a study of African-American mothers in Tennessee, Ophelia Settle observed: "These parents have no idea of the modern methods of child training; they use the methods of their parents and grandparents, and when they fail they do not question the efficacy of the methods; they are rather confirmed in their beliefs that the child is naturally bad."[45] It is not surprising that in a societal milieu where a host of external factors could adversely affect children's development, parents would resist accepting responsibility for children's misbehavior. As this quotation suggests, however, some failed to blame the environment outside the home as well. Perhaps the religious framework within which many African-American mothers lived, with its emphasis on original sin and the ubiquity of evil, was an explanation for their children's problems easier to accept than parental or societal wrongdoing.

The criticisms of working-class mothers as too traditional and uninformed lent weight to assertions that parent education should be largely geared toward this group. But some educators were unconvinced that the upper classes were better equipped than the poor to raise their children. In response to an allegation that poor families' maladjustment precluded their participation in parent education classes, educator Ruth Andrus asked, "Do we have any *evidence* that the families of settlement children are less well adjusted than those in other walks of life?" Conversely, privileged mothers sometimes complained that they did not have access to the education available to poor women. A young mother protested, "There were motherhood clinics and baby stations aplenty in the districts of the 'poor' women; why not for me? Why was it taken for granted that because I was 'intelligent' and 'educated,' I did not need this training?"[46]

As this well-off mother suggested, the common perception was that the problems of raising children in modern society were universal ones. Nineteenth-century literature had popularized the idea that mothers from all classes and racial backgrounds had a special bond with their children and were prepared to sacrifice for them. Later, universal motherhood took on a new meaning: it was the problems of child rearing, rather than the sentimental bond between mother and child, that were posited as universal. Sidonie Matsner Gruenberg observed that settlement-house mothers and the Ivy League mothers cited the same difficulties with their children: sibling rivalry and sleeping, eating, and disciplinary problems. The only difference was "the vocabulary in which these matters were revealed."[47] In the nineteenth century the link between mother and child had seemed to symbolize the bonds that held society together; by the 1920s, that bond appeared to be fragile, uncertain, and of questionable desirability.[48] For many parent educators, however, the bonds between mothers and children, no matter how imperfect, united women of diverse class and ethnic origins in a common experience of maternity.

But many organizations devoted to parent education, including the Child Study Association, were implicitly, if not explicitly, segregated by class and race. Most organizers argued that homogeneity of educational and social status, because it allowed members to identify with each other, was essential to the success of a child-study group. New York State coordinator of parent education May Peabody, however, maintained, "Emphasis on *the child* should overcome differences in intelligence, abilities, experiences, social adjustments, and class, so called."[49] Notwithstanding her democratic claims, Peabody's listing of differences suggests that, like many of her colleagues, she may have associated differences in intelligence with class. Although educators tended to believe that problems of behavior and temperament crossed class lines and could be remedied by altering the environment, most continued to view intelligence as unevenly distributed across classes. Nursery school educator Abigail Eliot organized two mothers' groups—one comprising upper-middle-class Anglo-American women from Cambridge, and another poor Jewish, Italian, and African-American women from Boston. "The Cambridge parents," Eliot remarked, "being highly intelligent, are a wholly different problem from the ones here but no less of a problem and there seems to be no less need of instruction in child care."[50] Eliot's equation of intelligence with class was a symptom of the class prejudices inherent in the movement. While most parent educators believed quite firmly in the power of nurture to produce well-adjusted and law-abiding citizens, they were much less certain about the role of nurture in determining intelligence.

The question was far from resolved in the 1920s, when researchers began to study the relation between environment and intelligence. Eliot articulated the prevailing view among parent educators that while heredity might be a factor in a child's development, little could be done about it, and that it was essential to focus on improving the child's environment: "We do not know, for instance, how far heredity and how far environment makes the children in the Cambridge school better developed linguistically and in general intellectually than the children at Ruggles Street." But Eliot also contended that educators did know that children were very "plastic"; therefore, it was crucial to emphasize environmental factors in work with young children.[51]

Adults were not so plastic and therefore represented a more perplexing dilemma for social reformers. The publication of Edward Thorndike's *Adult Learning* in 1928, however, which postulated that adults from twenty-five to forty-five learned at the same rate as teenagers, inspired hope in parent educators.[52] The characterization of adults as learners excited educators and reformers, who perceived adult education as a potential vehicle for significant social change. In their work with diverse groups of adults, educators were struck by the differences in individuals from diverse racial, ethnic, and class backgrounds. Educators were motivated to mold education according to individuals' varying needs and capabilities, whether inborn, as intelligence was often assumed to be, or learned, through contact with the environment.[53]

Accordingly, parent educators attempted to devise classes tailored to fit the needs of poor and immigrant parents. Reading, for example, had always been a central component of the child-study group, but the rural and small-town members of child-study clubs were less willing and occasionally less able to read than their counterparts in American Association of University Women and Child Study Association groups. Immigrant and African-American mothers who belonged to groups in urban areas such as Boston, New York, and Cincinnati also balked at digesting extensive written material. In describing rural mothers in Georgia, organizers claimed, "They do not want to have to study or read. . . . They say that they are too busy to read, and that it has been so long since they have been accustomed to reading books that it would be too much a burden for them."[54] Thus the reading and study that attracted intellectual women to child-study groups might keep less educated women away; the "study" aspect of the groups was not often what drew them. Reading had to be limited to bulletins and short articles. And for most poor women, not only were the time and sometimes the skills to read books wanting, but also the money to buy them.

Organizers repeatedly emphasized that they had to include a social component to attract poor and working-class parents to their programs. Poor mothers' lives were too hard, their work days too long, for them to take an evening to attend an event that did not include a sip of tea or a chance to chat with neighbors. In structuring meetings for poor women, organizers also had to consider the mothers' fatigue and their child-care needs. Parent educators sometimes postulated that poor mothers must be given "something to do" during meetings, such as sewing bibs or making playthings for their children, to make the meetings worth their time.[55] These plans could backfire, however, if the mothers involved were unable to purchase the materials because they lacked funds. Educators encountered a similar hurdle in poor mothers' financial inability to put into practice the advice their leaders offered. A leader of child-study groups for parents of children in the New City Public Schools confessed: "Many [poor parents] are so burdened by heavy work that they have little time to study children . . . realizing that desirable adjustments which should be made in the home to give the children privacy and individual attention are quite impractical."[56] The traditional child-study advice that children needed toys and a play area of their own was especially problematic. Not only were many poor and immigrant parents uninformed about the importance of toys for children's development, but they could not afford them. In a story in *Children* (1929), it was theorized that the reason a child stole continually was that his mother was unable to supply him with toys. Once the parent educator provided the child with toys, the problem was eradicated.[57] The moral of the story was that treating children like "children" could prevent them from entering a life of crime.

The most sensitive parent educators recognized that it was difficult if not impossible to impose child-centered family styles on immigrant and poor populations. The leader of a study group at a settlement house composed of Italian immigrant women protested: "It strikes me as almost futile to use this material among people who are so handicapped that they haven't the equipment of the most humble American home. . . . [It seems] almost ridiculous to talk about sleeping habits to a woman who hasn't even a crib for her baby to sleep in."[58] Educators had to be creative in order to adapt their materials to the exigencies of working-class life.

Much of the material to which poor and immigrant mothers were exposed in mothers' meetings was didactic—lectures on child hygiene, feeding, and the like—but organizers found that they could not keep the mothers' interest long with this approach. It was much more effective to start from the women's own experience, drawing on their questions about problems with their own children. Margaret Quilliard recommended that in working with mothers from poor neighborhoods, leaders adopt "a friendly informal procedure that releases the mental activity and emotions of the members," and that "encourages freedom of expression and indicates respect for the individual." No less than her fellow educators, Quilliard felt that the purpose of parent education was to instill mothers with the "correct" principles of child development, but the method she suggested at least provided poor mothers with an opportunity to assert their own opinions about the materials.[59]

While many parent educators tried to tailor their materials to the needs of poor women, some carefully orchestrated child-study meetings were subverted by the mothers themselves. At the Trinity Settlement House in Albany, New York, the teachers intended to conduct discussions about child training for kindergarten mothers, but the mothers preferred to play athletic games during meeting time. The director of a kindergarten in Cincinnati complained that the African-American mothers did not arrive at meetings on time and often fell asleep during lectures. Educators in New York City criticized mothers who attended meetings to enjoy a "comfortable," relaxing time, and resisted the emphasis on study and academic discussion.[60]

The different ethnic groups had no unified response to the professional expertise offered. Jewish, Italian, African-American, and Polish mothers often chose to take advantage of the educational opportunities offered them in settlement houses, kindergartens, day nurseries, and infant-health clinics. Because most programs were voluntary, participants could often change or influence the agenda to bring their particular needs to the forefront. When the interests of reformers and participants collided, the organizations were short-lived; for organizing efforts to take hold, some balance had to be struck between the objectives of reformers and those of participants.

One might argue that parent educators were engaged in the task of nation building, in the attempt to construct a core set of "family values" that could unite the country in spite of the diverse national origins of its citizens. Thus parent education programs for immigrants and African-Americans served as a locus for the transmission of scientifically informed, middle-class child-rearing values to those who were considered ignorant of fundamental American social values. In practice, however, educational programs needed to be devised to combine presentation of new information with recognition and appreciation for cultural differences. After all, adults already had well-established cultural traditions, which they would not readily trade in for a new set of values. In encounters between educators and their constituencies, then, some, though not all, values were subject to negotiation.

EDUCATION TO FIT LIFE'S NEEDS: THE LEAGUE OF MOTHERS' CLUBS

Betty Trager, a member of the Rose Wasserman Mothers' Club and of New York's umbrella organization the League of Mothers' Clubs, described her evolution as a clubwoman from the late 1920s through the 1940s: "I was a young wife and mother with an active, three year-old son who sometimes was more than I could cope with. One day I was having an especially trying time with him when a neighbor seeing my difficulties, said to me, 'I go to a child study class at the Henry Street Settlement and it has helped me in handling my child. Why don't you come with me and get a few pointers on how to train yours.' That day I went along with her was a lucky one for me for I got a great deal more from the Settlement besides Child Psychology." Besides learning about children, Trager took classes at the settlement in home nursing and entertaining. She made new friends, with whom she relaxed every Tuesday night and listened to speakers on a wide range of topics. As her children grew older and became more independent, Trager became involved in more settlement activities: "I found I had more time for myself so I looked beyond my own narrow horizons and became interested in community and civic problems." She participated in the league's lobbying efforts for public housing and studied consumer problems. She joined a parent-teacher organization to work for higher appropriations for schools. Trager was the model "municipal housekeeper" and an exemplary member of the League of Mothers' Clubs.[61]

The League of Mothers' Clubs was formed with a view to uniting the mothers' clubs that had multiplied in New York City during the early decades of the century to provide increased educational and social opportunities and political power. The local mothers' clubs were associated with settlement houses, day nurseries, churches, and kindergartens and were primarily conducted by middle-class female reformers for first- and second-generation immigrant mothers. John L. Elliot, president of New York's Association of Neighborhood Workers, proposed in 1912 that a citywide association of mothers might help to improve the situation of these immigrant women and their families. The leadership of the clubs initially comprised professional reformers and was later supplemented by leaders drawn from the rank and file. By 1926 the organization had a membership of approximately 5,000 mothers, belonging to eighty-five clubs dispersed throughout New York City, with an average local mothers' club membership of from fifty to sixty mothers.[62]

Most of the members of the league were either first- or second-generation Jewish and Italian mothers who became involved in the clubs through their children's activities at settlement houses. A 1928 study of fifty-nine New York mothers' clubs found that seventeen held their meetings in either Yiddish, Italian, Spanish, or Greek, and another twenty-two clubs conducted the meetings in more than one language. Most of the members were not yet naturalized, although the clubs encouraged women to become citizens by offering classes in English and citizenship. League organizers prided themselves on their ability to unite women of diverse ethnic origins, although individual clubs tended to be composed primarily of a single ethnic group. At the 1939 annual dinner, a league mother pronounced: "Many of us were born on the other side of the Atlantic. Nearly all of the rest are daughters of immigrants. . . . Nearly every nationality under the sun is represented here in this room full of American women."[63]

Mothers' clubs—which combined educational, recreational, philanthropic, and legislative activities—provided a link between immigrant mothers and American urban society. League mothers simultaneously embraced Americanization, ethnic identification, and political activism. Members appear to have been selective about the causes they espoused and the classes they attended. Organizers often had preconceived ideas about what the members' activities should be, but the continuation of such activities depended on the participation of league mothers.

Immigrant mothers were steeped in the ideology of municipal housekeeping by the settlement-house workers who managed the organization. The primary purpose of the league was "to make the immeasurable force, the 'mother power' of the community of value to it by educating the individual. . . . They were taught to recognize first, their responsibilities in the home, next, their obligation to the neighborhood and the community." In this context, municipal housekeeping was tied to a philosophy of progressive education, which suggested that the education of the individual should lead to social activism. Mothers would learn to care for their home and families properly first before moving on to reforming the larger urban landscape, and it was hoped that those reform efforts, both inside and outside the home, would instill in them a desire for a broader education. They would "learn by doing," in the popular parlance of progressive education.[64]

The league's educational and social activities were always central to its membership, but it was in the context of its political work that the group attracted the most notoriety. During the late 1920s and 1930s, league mothers lobbied to gain better housing for themselves; busloads of mothers were transported to Albany in 1935, where they spoke before the state legislature about the dire consequences inadequate housing had on children's well-being. Their efforts were central to the enactment of legislation for public housing. By conducting a survey in 1933 which showed that poor families were unable to afford adequate supplies of milk to nourish their children, league mothers were also instrumental in New York City's campaign to regulate the price of milk. These legislative activities provided much publicity for the league, including the regular appearance in both local and national newspapers of photographs of immigrant mothers at City Hall, the Albany State House, and even on a few occasions the White House. These political activities complemented by educational activities related to home economics and child rearing.[65]

While the programs and activities of local mothers' clubs were diverse, the league leadership maintained a fairly coherent ideology. The organizers of the league combined a vision of the need for political and economic change with a worldview that attributed social and economic ills to emotional disturbances. During the 1920s, this therapeutic orientation was especially significant in shaping reformers' conception of the impact mothers had on their children's future lives as citizens. Homemaking and child care were at the center of the organization's work, and the group had access to a wide range of experts who were attracted by the opportunity to disseminate their knowledge of the child sciences to immigrant mothers. The league's Committee on Education and Child Welfare was chaired by Elizabeth Fitchandler, a member of the Child Study Association. The committee also included Elizabeth Irwin, who was a prominent progressive educator, and representatives of the Mental Hygiene Association and the Vocational Association for Juniors, in addition to three league mothers. One account of the committee's view of its mission stated: "The mother will be shown the necessity of maintaining the same principles and standards in the home that are taught the child by the schools and social service organization."[66] This was a clear statement of the reformers' desire to bring immigrant child-rearing practices into accord with those advocated by professional experts.

The organizers, who were also concerned about the potential dangers of juvenile delinquency and family disorganization in immigrant families, proposed education as the key to resolving these problems. The league's bulletin advised mothers: "Education is to fit life's needs. With widespread divorce and juvenile delinquency, with disintegration of the home on all sides, experts agree that this is the greatest need which our civilization faces, better homes through homemaking education." This message fell short of what many immigrant mothers needed, though. Following a session where a judge addressed a group of mothers on the problems of juvenile delinquency at the Henry Street Settlement, a mother complained of her inability to protect her son from the dangers on the street, especially when she must go out to work. Speaking of her son, she told the judge, "It's not that my son is bad; it's just that he's not a hero."[67] The resignation implicit in this woman's testimony suggests her recognition that a mere alteration in her practices as a mother could not protect her child from the dangers of the urban environment.

In their appeals to immigrant mothers, league leaders both incorporated the popular language of parent education and modified it to suit their audience. Touching on the association's favored concept of generational difference, the league stressed that it sought to "level the barriers between the mother and the growing girl." In this case the barriers were to be dissolved by providing children with special objects and furnishings: "What little girl would not like to have a little box in which to keep her possessions? What boy would not like to have a desk at which to study his lessons?" In their local clubs, mothers took advantage of classes that helped them "make do" with their limited living spaces and finances; some club meetings were devoted to creating homemade toys and others to lessons suggesting ways for women to arrange their homes more artfully. League organizers were attempting to indoctrinate their members in the ideology of the child-centered family, while simultaneously taking into account the concrete realities with which mothers lived and worked.[68]

The league also sought to obtain quality education for its members through the establishment in 1923 of a speakers' bureau that provided services to all the member clubs. Settlement-house workers were proud of their efforts to obtain prestigious speakers on mental hygiene and child rearing, but they soon realized that professional prominence meant little to mothers who judged the speakers on their own cultural terms. In general, members were enthusiastic about speakers from their own ethnic communities, especially about those who spoke in Yiddish or Italian. They also were receptive to religious representatives from their communities, so rabbis and priests alike sometimes addressed league meetings. The Stuyvesant mothers' club, whose program was deemed the best of the year (1925 or 1926) by league members, included a talk on birth control given in Yiddish, a discussion of menopause, and a lecture on Americanization by New York's Mayor Walker.[69] Such an eclectic approach to education in the clubs was not unusual, although it is unlikely that most groups would have entertained discussions of such provocative subject matter.

Mothers' clubs had always included a variety of discussions and lectures on children's health and well-being as a critical component of their educational programs. But in 1924, the league leadership determined that members should take a more academic approach to their studies, which consciously furthered a therapeutic perspective on children. Child Study Association representative Elizabeth Fitchandler advertised new child-study groups for mothers with children under four "to explain the very newest and best way to take care of little children." From complaints about the attendance at these new groups' sessions, however, it can be inferred that the studious approach of the association held little attraction for league members. As usual, the message of child guidance had more appeal, however, when it was delivered in a familiar language. League members' less than enthusiastic response to the association's version of child study was counterbalanced by their approval for speakers from their own ethnic and class backgrounds. A talk given in Italian on child training by Miss Concistre "was just wonderful and the mothers loved her as they always do" (though generally mothers were dubious about the child-care recommendations offered by single women). They also responded with delight to the lecture "Mother's Responsibility for Racial Tolerance." By contrast, a talk on child training by Mrs. Feldman of the Child Study Association was less well received. Given the preponderance of Jewish women within both the League of Mothers' Clubs and the Child Study Association, it is noteworthy that the league mothers were unresponsive to the German-Jewish women of the Child Study Association. This can probably be attributed to the divergence between the experience of the earlier German-Jewish immigrants, often women of some education and wealth, and that of the poorer East European Jews who came to the settlement houses in the early twentieth century.[70]

In 1930 the league devised a new tactic for instilling in club members a more psychological orientation toward rearing children. The Child Welfare Committee recommended that the league appoint "parental advisers" with whom league mothers could "discuss behavior problems of their children before they get too serious that the advice of a psychiatrist is needed." A trained parent education worker, backed up by a psychiatrist, would deliver speeches to local mothers' clubs and then make herself available for consultation following the talks. At the first lecture at the Grand Street Settlement the turnout was good, "but the questions were not many of them Child Study questions," according to Feldman. Furthermore, only two appointments for consultations were made following the lecture. Judging by the attendance at various league activities, mothers were more receptive to information and discussions about children's health than to those about behavior and training, which they may have viewed as both more intrusive into their personal belief systems and more threatening to traditional values. Although league mothers displayed an interest in the physical aspects of child care, such as nutrition and child health, they were uncomfortable with the emphasis on mental hygiene, or mental health, and with the notion that some children might be mentally "abnormal."[71]

League mothers were more inclined to attend parent education classes when they could acquire tangible benefits from them for their children. For instance, the child-study clubs arranged in conjunction with the Summer Playschools that the Child Study Association organized at New York's settlement houses in 1925 maintained regular enrollments. On the immensely popular summer boat trips up the Hudson for mothers and their children, sponsored by the league, free milk was dispensed, and public health nurses had an opportunity to instruct mothers in the proper feeding and care of children. According to the league's 1938–39 annual report, four times weekly during the summer months the "S.S. Colonel Clayton [became] a floating settlement house" for approximately four hundred mothers and children.[72]

Unlike the middle-class mothers who made up the National Congress of Mothers, the American Association of University Women, and the Child Study Association, league mothers did not have the luxury of concentrating their energies on the psychic dimensions of motherhood. At a time when middle- and upper-class women were turning their reformist zeal toward the private problems of mothers in the home, the members of the league found that they could not isolate concern for their children from the larger public issues confronting them. In the words of league member Josephine Schain: "The minute we start to clean up the house we come in contact with such problems as street cleaning, garbage collection, tenement house inspection and whatnot. . . . The broom alone will not do the work. The good housewife soon finds that there is another phase of housekeeping that is her responsibility also—namely, municipal housekeeping."[73]

"THE CHILD WAS MINE": AFRICAN-AMERICAN MOTHERS AND CHILD STUDY

The pressing urban issues that confronted the immigrant mothers in the league were undoubtedly even more daunting for the African-American mothers who participated in the Child Study Association's Inter-Community Child Study Committee, whose headquarters were in Harlem. The large network of settlement houses that catered primarily to European immigrants paid scant attention to the harsh conditions that many African-American women faced upon moving to Northern cities, however. To survive in their new Northern setting, African-Americans had to rely largely on traditions of self-help and mutual aid.[74]

Educational work, including issues of child care and homemaking, was an important component of the platform of the National Association of Colored

Women, formed in 1896. These activist African-American women aspired both to "uplift" their own race and to achieve identification with the goals of the white women's club movement. Josephine Ruffin stated the group's aims in 1895: "It is 'meet, right, and our bounden duty' to stand forth and declare ourselves and our principles, to teach an ignorant and suspicious world that our aims and interests are identical with those of all good aspiring women." Thus clubwomen adopted the rhetoric of maternalism as a means of enhancing the status of African-American women and engaging in reform efforts aimed at improving the lot of their families. Black women's organizations combined the goals of racial integration and racial identification; however, they did not clearly distinguish between their educational and social-reform efforts and civil rights, which differentiated them from most white female reformers.[75]

In keeping with its maternalist vision, the National Association of Colored Women lobbied for and established kindergartens, day nurseries, and mothers' clubs. African-American teachers had organized mothers' clubs in tandem with the local public schools in Baltimore as early as 1898. The Colored Women's League of Washington founded kindergartens for young children, mothers' meetings for women, and domestic science classes for youth. In 1913, educated African-American women in Georgia set up mothers' clubs affiliated with the public schools, to study housekeeping, cooking, gardening, manual training, and child care. A constitution linking the clubs identified their objectives as "the betterment of home life, the training of children, and the improvement of the community in every way possible." Organized women were a major force in seeking to ameliorate the problems that beset African-American families.[76]

The institutionalization of the National Congress of Colored Parents and Teachers in 1926 was another focal point for child welfare educational work in the African-American community. The organization came into being because of the segregationist practices of Southern PTA chapters, and it remained underfunded and lacked sufficient backing from the white PTA throughout its existence; nevertheless, it served an important function within the context of the African-American community. A study conducted in the 1930s revealed that African-American parents were more likely to attend PTA meetings than were white parents.[77] The parents and professionals who participated in parent-teacher and child-study work expressed concern about the perilous state of African-American children's health and well-being.

Harlem also was the home of several significant reform efforts by African-American women. In 1921 they established the Utopia Children's House, which provided a full day of supervision for preschool children and an after-school program for the children of working mothers. A group of African-American women had also founded the Hope Day Nursery for Colored Children in 1901. Women were extremely active in the many African-American churches that flourished in Harlem during the 1920s and 1930s and housed a range of educational and charitable programs and services for church and community members.[78]

Parent education thus became established in Harlem within the existing network of services and programs for children and parents. Inaugurated in 1929, the Inter-Community Child Study Committee evolved from child-study groups conducted in the Harlem public schools in association with the Child Study Association. The committee was formed by white fieldworker Margaret Quilliard and Alonzo deGrate Smith, an African-American pediatrician on the staff of Harlem Hospital, with the aim of promoting child-study work, first in Harlem and eventually in a number of urban African-American communities in the Northeast. The work was subsidized by the Laura Spelman Rockefeller Memorial, which had provided funds for the association's outreach efforts into poor and immigrant neighborhoods.

Although the Child Study Association lent financial resources and the leadership of Margaret Quilliard to the committee, the work was carried out primarily by African-American women, who were already active in a number of community organizations.[79] Yet there appear to have been some discrepancies between the motivations of African-American clubwomen and those of the association organizers. Seeking to "Americanize" African-American family life, white reformers clearly viewed African-Americans as less than full-fledged Americans, because of their race and culture. Some African-American female activists sought to incorporate Anglo-American values and standards of behavior into their family lives, but that did not mean that they assumed that they were inadequate as parents or attributed the racial problems to the problems of the family.[80]

African-American family life drew the attention of educators and reformers who sought a resolution to the racial and ethnic conflicts which plagued early twentieth-century America. Social scientists observed that African-American families had higher rates of divorce, separation, illegitimacy, and juvenile delinquency than did white families. Sociologists detailed the disorganization which accompanied the African-American family's migration to the urban industrial milieu of the Northeast. The increasing numbers of African-Americans migrating to Northern cities challenged the thinking of urban educators who tried to reconcile their own racial prejudices with their reformist convictions.[81]

Despite the ostensible emphasis in parent education on the role of the environment in shaping character, deeply entrenched theories of biological inferiority, and a concomitant belief in the inability of African-Americans to assimilate, prohibited reformers from directing their attention toward this community in any significant way. There were, however, some exceptional programs, although these also maintained racial biases. Many educators believed that African-Americans were intellectually inferior to whites. For instance, Margaret Quilliard commented that in her child-study groups for African-American mothers she was unlikely to use Harrison Elliot's "democratic process," for it was not suited to "persons of limited intellectual ability."[82] If parent educators were skeptical that intelligence could be improved through education, however, they were more sanguine about the possible benefits of education in reshaping family life.

Quilliard's correspondence reveals that her work was prompted by what she perceived to be the "potential menace" that both African-American and immigrant populations posed to white middle-class culture: "I feel the foreign born groups and the Negroes both present situations which hold many potential difficulties for the American people if they are not handled wisely. I know of no better way to establish relationships between the ideals which we are trying to work out in America today and the foreign born and Negro groups than through the medium of child study activities." Quilliard described the work as a "shortcut" for presenting the child-study movement to African-American parents, considerable numbers of whom would probably not receive much benefit from it "unless we work *directly* and *specifically* with their racial group." Harlem, as a "strategic center of Negro life in America," seemed an ideal site for the promulgation of child-study ideals in the African-American community.[83] While white reformers do not appear to have been overly optimistic about the potential of African-Americans to be integrated into American society, they clearly sought to contribute to the construction of an African-American family life that would be less jarring to the sensibilities of middle-class whites. African-American mothers who engaged in child study did not share these objectives; they sought educational, economic, and social "progress" for their children and families. Rarely able to confine themselves to discussions of the private activities of discipline and training that absorbed white, middle-class mothers, in their groups they were forced to confront the social barriers that limited the possibilities of African-American children in the United States.

Educators hoped to inculcate in mothers of all racial and ethnic backgrounds their progressive philosophy of child rearing, which substituted an understanding of the nature and needs of children at various stages of development for traditional authoritarian disciplinary techniques. This approach was distinct from that of many mothers, whose primary concern was to teach children to be obedient and respectful of parental authority. This was an especially critical component of African-American mothers' child-rearing philosophies, however, for historically they had demanded their children's compliance as a means of ensuring their safe passage through the shoals of white society. Parent educators sought to supplant such "commonsense" philosophies of raising children with scientific methods; science—the province of white middle-class professionals—should, they argued, play a vital role in determining effective child-rearing practices.[84]

At the time of the committee's first endeavors, there were already several child-study groups in Harlem, two of which were affiliated with the Child Study Association and had been in operation for several years.[85] A critical catalyst was Dr. Alonzo deGrate Smith, an activist in the child health movement and member of the Harlem Adult Education Committee, who became interested in the work of the Child Study Association and went to its headquarters to join. A native of New Jersey, Smith was a graduate of Howard University, who would later join Howard's medical school faculty. He was so convinced of the significance of child-study work that he immediately contacted Quilliard about the possibility of expanding the opportunities for parent education in Harlem.[86] After an apparently fruitful conversation, Quilliard and Smith organized a series of meetings in 1928 and 1929, which were attended by Harlem professionals, child-study mothers, and Child Study Association leaders, to gauge the level of interest in Harlem in parent education. Eventually, the Harlem group spawned a larger organization, which included representatives from Baltimore, Washington, D.C., and several urban communities in New Jersey.[87]

The speeches given at two mass meetings held in 1928 and 1929 indicate some of the divergent assumptions held by Child Study Association organizers and Harlem representatives. At the opening meeting, director of the association Sidonie Gruenberg gave an address emphasizing the universality of parental perplexity, buttressing her thesis with essentially similar examples of problems experienced by parents in Switzerland and by a rural group in Iowa. She reiterated the theme of generational difficulties, stating: "Not only people in every walk of life, but of every nation, are facing a conflict between the traditional concept of their relationship with their children and the conditions they are actually facing." These universal generational difficulties were to be dealt with at the most basic level, beginning with a change in the interactions between mothers and children.[88]

As a representative of Harlem and of the medical profession, Smith did not echo the theme of universality from Gruenberg's speech but argued that some of Harlem's unique problems could be alleviated through an understanding of child psychology. Smith offered examples from his practice of behavioral and medical problems that were psychological in nature. His primary example concerned the feeding problems a child had developed in the wake of his father's departure from the family, a situation that may have been representative of the nearly one fourth of New York's African-American families headed by women.[89] The doctor admitted that his psychological orientation was met with skepticism by some of his patients, who remarked, "Dr. Smith is all right except he just comes in and plays with the baby and doesn't give any medicine." Sharing with many social and behavioral scientists of his day a reluctance to explain human behavior on the basis of genetics, Smith questioned the existence of the maternal instinct: "It is questionable as to whether there is such a thing as mother instinct. I sometimes doubt it from the way mothers treat their children." He acknowledged, however, that most of his patients resisted the notion that parenting was something that must be learned—they believed that mothering came "naturally" to women.[90]

In his speech, Dr. Jacob Ross, principal of Public School 139, drew attention to the "environmental handicaps" that the Harlem child faced, particularly the child who lacked supervision because of the parents' long working hours. Ross, Smith, and Marion Pettiford, a visiting nurse, all alluded to a study indicating that 75 percent of Harlem children had mothers who worked outside the home and that their absence contributed to problems of juvenile delinquency.[91] The comments of these Harlem professionals undermined somewhat the message of the association, which focused solely on issues of interaction between parents and children. But while the Harlem professionals had a broader vision of the meaning of "child study" than did the association, they nevertheless at least paid lip-service to the progressivism implicit in applying the child sciences to everyday life.[92]

In their speeches to the audience, club mothers upheld the basic message of the Child Study Association, insisting that too many mothers embarked on the serious task of parenting without adequate preparation. Irene Smith conceded that before participating in child-study work, she was unaware of just how much she did not know about children. She went "out of curiosity" to her first meeting, "feeling that there was nothing for me to know because the child was mine." That other African-Americans also claimed ownership of their children suggests the extent to which these women maintained their right to govern them and resisted encroachments on their authority in this realm. Many of their own grandmothers had not had access to that authority, since legally the children of slaves belonged to their owners and *not* their parents. But Smith's sense of herself as an authority was shattered at the first meeting, which she described as a "rude awakening" that left her feeling "mighty small" and vowing to be a better mother. But while both Smith and Aspinall were convinced of the significance of child study, they admitted that it was difficult to interest other mothers in the community, who felt that they were "interfering."[93] Many African-American women were reluctant to allow doctors, educators, or even middle-class clubwomen of their own race to intrude on a relationship that they greatly valued and in which *they* were the authorities.

Yet clearly women such as Smith and Aspinall were persuaded that their learning about children would benefit their families. This gain was to be achieved primarily through a shift to a child-centered philosophy of child rearing. In conceptual terms, this meant recognizing that children had rights and needs that could compete with traditional parental authority, an idea reflected in the comment of Josephine Dawson that "my children are friends and companions instead of my feeling I am an authority over them."[94]

African-American members of Child Study Association study groups were absorbing ideas about childhood that contradicted deep-rooted conceptions within their own communities. Admittedly, education is meant to force students to examine their preconceptions. In child-study groups, mothers were asked to examine whether parenthood was something that they were equipped for by nature, whether their children's behavior was shaped by genetic or environmental factors, and what kind of relationship they should have with their children—all questions worth asking. But the association failed to address the environmental and social conditions under which mothers and children from diverse class and ethnic backgrounds lived and worked. And in all too many cases, the answers to the questions educators posed were ready-made and their child-rearing prescriptions did not integrate mothers' real-life experiences.

During the next few years, the committee expanded its work in Harlem and initiated chapters in Brooklyn, in Montclair and Englewood, New Jersey, in Baltimore, and in Washington, D.C. The few statistics available suggest that the average member was better off than many of her African-American counterparts. In an Englewood, New Jersey, group with forty-six members, thirty-one described themselves as "housewives." Their husbands' occupations ranged from coal man, Pullman porter, gardener, and mechanic to dentist and minister, the majority being nonprofessional. Those members who did work were in occupations traditionally relegated to African-American women: most were laundresses and domestics; one was a nursery school director and one a dressmaker. According to a poll, ten members of a sixteen-member Montclair, New Jersey, group believed that women with children should not work outside the home unless it was economically necessary. The leader of a mothers' group at the Henry Street Settlement Nursing Center described the members as well educated, and indeed a few had studied to become teachers.[95] Although the African-American mothers who participated in study groups may have been better educated or more financially solvent than many, there is no doubt that poverty was an omnipresent factor in their lives. Most African-American women in Harlem lived on the edge, and when the Depression came, many were pushed from the edge into the abyss.[96]

The committee adapted its outreach efforts to the African-American community, modifying child-study literature to attract that constituency. Using traditional African-American occupations in their examples, committee leaders emphasized parenting as a profession and the need to modernize child-rearing methods, focusing on "speaking points" such as these:

> Do you light your homes as your grandmother did? Do you heat your house as your grandmother did? Do you feed your family as your grandmother did? Do you bring up your children as your grandmother did? Can people do better work if they are trained for their job?

> A Pullman porter must have two weeks of training for his job. A beauty specialist must have three to six months of training for her job. A first-class barber must have from five to six months training for his job. A teacher must have at least three years of training for her job. How much training do you have for your job as a parent?[97]

As they did with white parents, educators stressed that changes in technology must be accompanied by changes in parenting and that parents, like those in other occupations, must have access to training.

Organizers contacted and lectured at day nurseries and social service agencies and appointed a special church committee. In their outreach efforts, however, they inevitably ran up against the problem that African-American churchwomen were already "overorganized": women often contended that they belonged to too many organizations. Quilliard complained that Harlem community leaders regarded child study as "insignificant" compared to the other causes competing for their attention.[98] During a period when many struggled to put food in their children's mouths, it is not surprising that the association's educational program did not attract large numbers of parents.

Yet the popularity of child study in Baltimore during a similar period suggests that the approach to parent education in New York was at least partly responsible for its limited success. Baltimore had a long-standing history of African-American activism on education. It was also the home of an active white Child Study Association chapter that claimed to be unable to foster African-American child-study work because of the segregation of its public facilities. A core of African-American educators, however, working with key organizers from the white group, dedicated themselves to delivering the message about child development to a large audience. The most crucial figure in the crusade was Baltimore public school principal Estella Carr, who was the daughter of Mrs. Eddie Aspinall, a member of Harlem's first child-study club and an active member of the committee, the PTA, and New York's United Parents Association.[99] Aspinall recruited Carr to the committee's first meeting, and Carr then returned to Baltimore to form a committee of teachers, social workers, and health-care workers, all interested in both the private and the public dimensions of child welfare.

They organized fifteen parents' groups, but recognizing that many mothers would have neither the time nor the inclination to join such a group, committee members were not content to work only in that arena. To supplement those efforts, they organized a series of mass meetings sponsored by the public schools. Each of these gatherings, which were inspirational as well as educational, attracted anywhere from eight hundred to twelve hundred parents. The large attendance was due to the concerted efforts of Carr who, with the cooperation of the Baltimore director of schools, Dr. Francis Wood, distributed circulars to all the African-American school children in Baltimore to take home to their parents. The meetings included orchestral music, singing of spirituals, and an opening invocation by a local minister, along with informational addresses by teachers, child development professionals, and child-study mothers. By incorporating elements integral to African-American traditions, they were able to speak about child development in a framework that was familiar to the parents attending the meetings, who came from a wide range of class backgrounds.

The Baltimore committee differed from the larger organization not only in the structure of its programs but in the issues that it placed at the top of the agenda. Two of their most pressing concerns were how to provide adequate day care and how to reduce the rate of juvenile delinquency, issues rarely discussed by the national association in other than psychological language. The committee was disturbed both by the paucity of orphanages for dependent children, many of whom were being sent to reform schools instead, and by the economic conditions that forced mothers to work. One group speaker provocatively insisted that "the city and state have not done their job towards the Negro. . . . A decent set-up for the delinquent colored child would include an institution for the feeble-minded, a mother's pension relief, for colored as well as white, that she may stay at home and care for her children." The group asserted its sense of racial identification and of self-reliance by maintaining that institutions for African-American children should be staffed solely by African-American personnel. The group's preference for mothers' pensions over day nurseries as a means of providing for child care suggests that it shared the maternalist values of white female reformers who thought that the best place for a mother was in the home.[100] Unlike the association leaders, however, the Baltimore educators could not address the private dilemmas of parents and children without considering the larger political context.

In New Jersey and New York, which were close to headquarters and heavily influenced by the national leadership, the traditional study group was at the center of the committee's programs. African-American mothers' reasons for joining study groups appear to be somewhat dissimilar to the reasons that white middle-class women offered for participating. White women were likely to say that they joined the clubs because of problems with their children or for reasons of sociability. The majority of African-American mothers, however, claimed that they joined because they were interested in education, broadly defined, for both themselves and their children. Members explained that they would "like to learn more to teach" their children, that they would "like to send them through school and college," and that they hoped to do more to help them. The mothers in the Montclair, New Jersey, study group repeatedly expressed their hope that their children would be "intelligent." The white leader of this group expressed little enthusiasm for this goal, however, and urged mothers to remember that intelligence was a matter of "capacity," thus implying that they could do little to influence their child's level of intelligence. Like white mothers, African-American members were concerned about learning the "proper" methods of raising children so they would not get "undesired results"—and they hoped that professional expertise would help eliminate the uncertainties of child rearing.[101]

The fact that the problems discussed in African-American child-study groups were often similar to those discussed in white middle-class child-study groups reinforced parent educators' assumption that the problems of parent-hood were universal. Mothers worried about how much obedience to expect from their children and what kinds of punishment were appropriate. Children's lying, quarreling, sibling rivalry, and thumb-sucking were discussed. Sex educa-tion, a topic that loomed large in the minds of white middle-class parents, was also of concern to African-American mothers. Often, however, African-Ameri-can mothers articulated needs specific to their community. In 1931 a Brooklyn group led by physician Isabella Granger discussed the problem of boys' playing football on city streets and resolved to work for playgrounds and parks for their children. The realities of racism for both children and their parents may have been broached, particularly in groups with an African-American leader, but such discussions did not make their way into the records of the clubs. That independent African-American groups did discuss racial prejudice is suggested by a topic covered in Granger's group: "Teaching Children Race Pride."[102]

Regardless of why African-American women joined groups, the issues of economics and disadvantage that shaped their lives often intruded into their child-study activities. Mrs. Keron Battle, a study group leader, regretfully re-vealed that she would not be able to devote much energy to the movement during the 1930s because she would need to work outside the home; she confided to Quilliard that her inability to continue had "been a sickening disappointment." An enthusiastic school teacher, Charlotte Atwood, organized a group of teachers from Washington, D.C., to engage in child study. The group failed to take hold, not from lack of interest, as she pointed out to Quilliard, but because "they are simply driven to exhaustion within the sys-tem. It is not that they need convincing—what they need is time and energy and a chance to lift their eyes from the road along which they let themselves be driven."[103] A Harlem group formed in the early 1930s decided it would disband as a child-study club and consolidate its efforts as a civic league, which would attempt to locate jobs for the unemployed and aid widows and children. Chronic health problems plagued group members and their families and con-tributed to frequent absences from meetings and loss of members. Quilliard was moved by the efforts of African-American mothers to attend study groups in spite of the demands placed on them: "When I realize the handicaps under which these Negro women live and work, I am amazed that they attend any meetings at all. It is just one more proof to me that they, like many other mothers, are concerned over the welfare of their children and are willing to make a good many sacrifices and efforts on their behalf."[104] Thus Quilliard recognized the universality of mothers' experience, while simultaneously acknowledging the "handicaps" complicating that experience in the African-American community.

It is difficult to assess the meaning of child study for the African-American mothers who participated in the study groups, because the evaluations that the committee used, by asking only what mothers gained from the group—never what could have been improved—elicited a heavily biased sample of mostly flattering testimony. A Harlem mother testified that "my entire life seems to be changed. The home is agreeable and I haven't got quite so much worry with the children. When disturbances crop up, I can ward them off calmly, instead of flaring up as before." Josephine Dawson maintained that five years of group work "helped us to understand not only our children but ourselves. Many times we were going at the children and the children were all right. All the difficulty was in ourselves." A New Jersey member revealed that participation in the group had made her "less nervous," "less fearful of things," and more able to speak at public gatherings and meetings. Perhaps it was the opportunity for self-reflection—time to talk about themselves and their children—that took the edge off many mothers' "nerves." For the mothers who advanced from study-group membership to leadership and who became active in the organizing efforts of the committee, participation offered a chance to develop both their intellects and their leadership abilities. Unfortunately, when the Child Study Association did not provide the financial resources to train all the women who exhibited talent and dedication to child study, the development of the movement from within the African-American community was thwarted.[105]

Throughout the history of the committee, African-American members accused the association of being segregationist because the groups affiliated with the committee were not integrated into the larger activities of the association. Quilliard denied such allegations although she admitted that "we have been careful not to impose too large a proportion of Negroes upon the work of the association as a whole, until we had paved the way for it," and that the committee's Harlem activities had not been advertised in the organization's bulletin because they held "little interest for members of the Association."[106] Despite repeated invocations about the universality of the problems of motherhood, the association's actual activities reinforced the separation of African-American mothers from their white counterparts.

Association organizers also contended that the African-American community lacked leadership from within. Quilliard complained about the difficulties of finding African-Americans with "sufficient educational backing, profes-

sional training and leadership ability" to warrant instruction in parent education. She also bemoaned the committee's failure to attract the most influential
African-Americans in Harlem to its ranks: "The work seems too insignificant to
them to deserve their interest and cooperation." The lack of finances and the
inability of many mothers to pay even modest dues also frustrated the work, for
the association did not have access to extensive funding.[107]

In the Harlem committee, problems of social class within the membership
also hindered the group's progress. Although the clubs attracted women of
varying means, several mothers active in the child-study committee complained about the "high hat" attitude of certain "intellectuals" on the committee. Like their middle-class white counterparts, many bourgeois African-American activists set themselves apart from their poorer counterparts and viewed
their reform task as one of "uplifting" the misinformed masses. In speaking of
the attitude of the more educated African-American committee members toward the less educated, one member said: "There is one thing college hasn't
taught them, and that is how to be tolerant toward the rest of us."[108]

As the Depression advanced during the 1930s, the work was increasingly held
up by financial setbacks and the elimination of foundation monies for the
Child Study Association. Several study groups were forced to disband, either
because they could not afford to pay their instructor or because the community
agencies that had sponsored the group were no longer able to do so. The
resignation in 1935 of Margaret Quilliard, who was highly esteemed by committee participants and intensely active on behalf of the group, ushered in the
decline of the activities of the Inter-Community Child Study Committee.[109]

The School of Household Administration at the University of Cincinnati
also received funding from the Laura Spelman Rockefeller Memorial for its
outreach into the African-American community. The stance taken by Lawrence
Frank, a representative of the philanthropy, toward African-Americans resembled that of many other reformers: he combined an emphasis on meeting the
educational needs of African-Americans both as "individuals and as members
of an inevitably separate social grouping" with a concern that a "more satisfactory basis of living side by side may be created and disseminated among both
whites and blacks."[110] The funding for the Cincinnati program probably did
more to address the needs of mothers as individuals and members of a "separate" social group than it did to enable them to live with their white neighbors.
Although an ideology of racial separatism surely was at work in this and other
programs for African-Americans, the fact that the leadership of the Cincinnati
program was in the hands of community members contributed to its vitality.

The School of Household Administration initiated its work by training African-American women at the university with the assistance of fellowships in child study and parent education from the Laura Spelman Rockefeller Memorial. The program benefited in particular from the organizational talents of Lillian Watson Foster, an African-American mother of two who held a degree from the University of Cincinnati and had previously been a grade school teacher. Granted one of the Memorial fellowships, Foster proved to be particularly adept at working with both mothers and social service professionals and helped make this educational program of real service to the community.[111]

The Cincinnati organizers began their work in the most obvious of places: the African-American church. Even though church mothers did already belong to too many organizations, ministers were usually willing to announce that a child-study meeting would be held following the service. Some study groups begun as a result of such an initial meeting thrived; at other times groups foundered for lack of interest. After a year of effort, only eight study groups had been founded, with approximately one hundred mothers participating.[112]

Written reports submitted to the Laura Spelman Rockefeller Memorial reveal the organizers' efforts to discern the techniques and strategies that might attract mothers to their groups. The failure of a group, formed in conjunction with the Calvary Methodist Episcopal church group, to maintain its enrollment elicited a suggestion from the social worker who led the group: "I feel you cannot hold the mothers' attention by merely lecturing and discussing. It is necessary to have some handiwork in connection with the meeting. We started a project of the mothers making dresses for their children, but this plan did not materialize because of the low economic status of the members and lack of funds with which to buy supplies." Organizers observed that African-American women were so tired from their long day of work that an enjoyable social hour was a necessary part of any successful meeting. The mothers became more invested in the clubs if they elected officers and planned their own recreation. Pivotal to the success of the meetings, as well, was an emphasis on mothers' questions and the leader's use of everyday language.[113] Despite a slow start, within a few years the Cincinnati program had made substantial progress. Foster had an instant constituency in the recipients of mothers' pensions, who were required to attend classes in child study, but she discovered that the mothers were enthusiastic about these mandatory meetings. The mothers insisted on having elected officers and appointed a committee to plan the social hour following the meeting. According to the organizer, these mothers were "extremely interested and entered into the discussion by asking most intelligent questions." Observing the mothers' distrust of doctors and their reluctance to obtain regular physical examinations for their children, the club leader addressed the problem by bringing a doctor and a nurse in to do a sample physical examination and answer questions. Although members had to travel considerable distances to attend meetings, their enthusiasm "did not slacken."[114]

The Cincinnati educators also organized groups in conjunction with the city's women's clubs, day nurseries, kindergartens, and health centers. A speech before the local Federation of Negro Women's Clubs resulted in the formation of a study group whose members found the work "splendid" and continued meeting for at least two years. The Shoemaker Welfare Center Club for Mothers, organized in 1929, was an especially spirited group, enrolling 160 mothers in 1929–30 and maintaining an average attendance of 69. Committees of up to 20 mothers were charged with putting together the weekly program. The group was supervised by a trained parent educator, who consulted with specialists in nutrition and child health. Each meeting included a demonstration of the preparation of inexpensive foods and well-balanced menus, a discussion of some phase of child care, and a recreation period. During the mothers' meetings, a nursery school demonstration session was conducted for preschool children by an African-American teacher.[115]

Lillian Foster was determined to involve the African-American social workers at the Shoemaker Welfare Center in the school's parent education programs. At first social workers were dubious about the benefits of parent education; however, by 1930–1931, a report noted, "The work is now taken as a matter of course and not looked upon with suspicion or fear." Perhaps it was organizers' consultations with social workers about how they could more adequately address the needs of the mothers who attended the center that lessened the suspicion with which the workers had initially greeted the overtures of parent educators. The social workers were soon convinced of the urgency of the work and in designing the program for the following year, they entitled it "How the Home and the Parent Influence the Health and Development of the Child."[116]

When the Cincinnati parent educators reflected on their achievements and failures, they noted that African-American mothers tended to have lower attendance rates than white mothers because of poor health and economic conditions. Most of the mothers in the Cincinnati groups worked outside the home. One organizer admitted that, as an "inexperienced worker," she had made mistakes. She had tried to reach too many people and in so doing had neglected the groups that were most enthusiastic about the work. She also noted that her light skin color and her youth had made it difficult for the mothers to accept her as a leader. According to the program's research assistant Janet Arnold, "There is a strong resentment among the negroes of lower social status against one of a higher social status lecturing to them. Yet a negro leader, after the first contacts are made, is more successful than a white leader." Despite these reservations, Arnold believed that a "great good has been done."[117]

In 1930 Arlitt was pleased to inform Beardsley Ruml of the memorial that in two years of work, more than eleven hundred African-American women had become involved in the School of Household Administration child-study groups. She also reported that African-American parent education workers were being trained in integrated classes at the university.[118] Attendance continued to increase even during the Depression, when in order to attend meetings, many of the women had to make special arrangements to leave whatever jobs they could obtain.

Foster's 1933 report to the memorial details the benefits of study-group participation and cites the acquisition of a taste for reading as one of the most concrete developments. Some mothers made scrapbooks compiled of articles about child welfare; others brought in articles and books for the class to read. One parent volunteered to pay the director because her child's behavior had shown such improvement. As a result of child-study classes, many parents were less fearful of the doctor and more attuned to their children's medical needs. Leaders also reported that parents showed more discrimination about using corporal punishment. A day nursery mother had begun the class by saying, "I beat him and I want you teachers to beat him and make him mind. I have no time to fool with him trying to train him"; but she finished the program with at least a verbal recognition that there might be other ways of disciplining a child. In the closing words of Foster's report, "So much impressed are some we have helped that they plan to continue as an organized group next year to read and discuss articles on child welfare even without the leader."[119]

With the cessation of memorial funding in 1933, many of the study groups for African-American mothers continued meeting. A few nursery school groups were funded by the Methodist Church, and other groups continued to be led by volunteers who had been trained during the five years of funding. Still other groups met on their own, without a leader, to continue their social gatherings and their discussions about children.

Although the School of Household Administration was appreciative of Foster's excellent work, racism pervaded its evaluations of her work. In a letter to Beardsley Ruml, Ada Hart Arlitt confided: "We have found it necessary to have the Negro project supervised by a white worker inasmuch as this both adds to the esteem in which the project is regarded by the Negro people and assures that the classes will be met on time and conducted for the required period."[120] Yet it was undoubtedly Foster's identification with the mothers in her groups and her contacts with African-American social workers, health professionals, and ministers that made possible her accomplishments. The concerns about segregation that plagued the Child Study Association's efforts are not discernible in the records of the Cincinnati project, possibly because the largely African-American leadership of the project retained a high degree of autonomy. Notwithstanding the controls apparently imposed by the white organization, whites remained relatively invisible in the program.

But despite the inherent success of the project, its external relations with the University of Cincinnati were marked by racism. After four years of working with African-Americans, Arlitt reported that these mothers appeared to assimilate information on child training "as readily as the members of white groups of corresponding social level."[121] In an important essay published in 1921, "On the Need for Caution in Establishing Race Norms," Arlitt had warned psychologists about the dangers of attributing I.Q. differences among children to race. In a comparative study of native white, African-American, and Italian immigrant children, she found that class was a much more salient factor than race in predicting I.Q. Apparently, she drew similar conclusions from her work with African-American mothers. Having discarded the concept that lower-class African-American mothers were less intelligent than lower-class white mothers, she accepted class rather than race as the criterion for determining the intellectual capacities of mothers in child-study groups.[122]

The notion of class is central to discussion of the social composition of child-study groups. I have already discussed the extent to which child-study groups affiliated with the American Association of University Women and the Child Study Association tended to be narrowly academic and to rely much less heavily on experience than did the groups associated with the less socioeconomically privileged members of the PTA. In forming study groups for mothers from less privileged backgrounds, organizers repeatedly emphasized the importance of beginning with the mother's experience, rather than from a text. Poor mothers, they argued, did not respond well to dry textbook theories. Rural mothers and mothers from small towns were also inclined to privilege experience over book learning, and the records of rural meetings disclose passionate debates over child behavior and development.

Ironically, women from privileged backgrounds appear to have been beguiled by the power of science and hence readier to bow to professional expertise than their less privileged counterparts were. Poor mothers, by contrast, often resisted the notion that their gaining expertise in child development would solve familial and social problems, and only with difficulty were they persuaded to rely on experts' advice. These parents, too, may have recognized the shortcomings in their child-rearing strategies, but they were less confident in the experts' power to transform their lives.

Parent educators offered a modernized motherhood as a solution to the problems created by the generation gap, and also as a vehicle for consolidating diverse American family styles into a homogenous whole. Parent educators' platform reflected white middle-class assumptions about both preferred modes of child rearing and the inferior intellectual abilities of working-class mothers and their children. The parent education programs for poor, immigrant, and African-American mothers that were designed and led by middle-class white organizers suffered from those latent assumptions and had difficulty maintaining their enrollments.

Programs conceived and carried out by immigrant and African-American women themselves, such as the Baltimore project, the Cincinnati School of Household Administration program, and to some extent the League of Mothers' Clubs, held greater appeal for their constituencies. In designing their educational programs, these organizations took seriously the needs and interests of poor mothers, rather than imposing a model of education that had been developed with highly educated middle-class women in mind. As we have seen, these successful groups concerned themselves less, on the whole, with abstract theory and more with an eclectic range of topics than did the typical middle-class group. They discussed a variety of issues related to the well-being of children, including immunization, housing conditions, nutrition, and juvenile delinquency; some confronted political issues of relevance to mothers. The format of these programs often incorporated elements from other culturally specific community organizations with which mothers were familiar, such as the African-American church and ethnic voluntary associations. Thus, although it was true that women from diverse backgrounds had their role as mothers in common, motherhood was so deeply embedded in the particularities of differing cultural experiences and traditions that reformers could not possibly succeed in establishing a universal design for parent education.

Chapter 4 Bringing Science to the People: Delivering the Message of Scientific Motherhood

In 1929 the National Society for the Study of Education devoted its twenty-eighth yearbook to preschool and parental education. In an introductory essay the editors wrote, "If one were to inquire of any student of social progress, 'What is the newest development in the educational world?' the answer would surely be, 'Schools for infants and a constructive program of education for parents.'"[1] The book then documented an astounding proliferation of parent education programs, from those of small women's clubs to classes offered by public health clinics and agricultural extension services. According to the influential adult educator Eduard Lindeman, "Parent education, considered as a part of the total adult education movement, arrives as a completion of the genetic educational ladder; all age-groups of the population are soon to be included in the educational scheme, beginning with preschool children and ending with their mature parents."[2] Nursery schools were expensive to operate, however, and many parents lacked the funds for this type of education for their children. Moreover, a clear and pressing demand for parent education existed, as demonstrated by the numerous women's organizations and clubs that clamored for scientific information on children. Parent education could also be organized in various settings, from the formal to the informal, and when volunteers could be trained to lead groups, parents could be educated relatively inexpensively.

As we saw in Chapter Two, women established organizations and institutions dedicated to both fostering scientific research on children and disseminating that research. The Children's Bureau, founded in 1912 by female settlement-house workers, was the first and most visible manifestation of women's public activism on behalf of women and children. The bureau was, however, only one item in a multifaceted reform agenda designed to improve the care of the nation's children. In addition to child health stations designed to educate poor women and the numerous programs associated with settlement houses, during the interwar years a far-reaching network of educational services was available to rural women in conjunction with child welfare institutes and the home economics extension service.

Organized women lobbied in the 1910s and 1920s for child welfare institutes, interdisciplinary academic units charged with generating as well as disseminating information about children. With the financial support of the Laura Spelman Rockefeller Memorial and state and federal tax monies, the child welfare institutes inaugurated at Columbia's Teachers College, Yale University, the University of Minnesota, the University of Iowa, and the University of California at Berkeley provided institutional spaces for furthering the new science of child development. With investments of approximately $12 million in child development, the memorial funds were critical to the establishment of the profession. The memorial's generous provisions to child welfare institutes were, however, contingent on the institutes' commitment to parent education. Thus Lawrence Frank chose to fund major land-grant universities, in large part because he foresaw that the home economics extension service could be used to provide educational opportunities for homemakers in child development. Unlike many scientists involved in the creation of the institutes, Frank saw a distinct role for home economists in the distribution of knowledge about children to American mothers. Home economics extension workers (or home demonstration agents, as they were also called) appealed to broad constituencies and extended the land-grant tradition of bringing science to the nation's farmers to bring science to the nation's mothers. An investigation of the institution of child welfare institutes, the home economics extension service, and their relation to education for motherhood again illuminates the central role that both stay-at-home mothers and professional women played in educating mothers—and the tensions that characterized their endeavor to interject science into women's traditional domain: the home.[3]

COMBINING RESEARCH AND REFORM: CHILD WELFARE RESEARCH INSTITUTES AND STATE PROGRAMS OF PARENT EDUCATION

During the 1920s, a burgeoning number of child welfare institutes focused on the development and dissemination of research on the "normal" child.[4] These institutes united academic and social aims. The social motivations are revealed in their original designation as "welfare" institutions, a word suggestive of the organizations' reformist bent and their concern with the well-being of children and their communities. These interdisciplinary spaces brought psychologists, physicians, sociologists, and home economists together to obtain an empirical base of knowledge about children. Although these institutes have generally been discussed in terms of their research contributions, especially in Hamilton Cravens's intriguing account of the Iowa Child Welfare Research Station, *Before Head Start,* some of the most prominent child welfare research institutes—in Iowa, Minnesota, and California—were also significant for their forays into parent education.[5]

Child welfare research institutes were the product of both popular and professional agitation.[6] Professionals had a vested interest in pursuing specialized types of research and building institutional homes for themselves and often were more interested in their individual projects than in parent education. The women's groups that agitated for child welfare institutes, however, did so in the belief that the findings they could produce would be rapidly put to use to improve children's health and well-being. Reformers such as Frank viewed research not as an aim in itself but as a means of furthering the education of parents and thereby fueling social change. An inherent conflict was thus built into the structure of the institutes. The researchers were expected to discover the best means of conserving normal childhood, but their constituencies were demanding information before the researchers had time to generate reliable research data. Still, initially women's organizations, educators, child psychologists, and pediatricians consolidated their efforts to make child welfare research institutes a reality.

A prime example of the link between women activists and researchers in the creation of a child welfare institute was the campaign for the Iowa Child Welfare Research Station, founded in 1917. The station owed its existence to political agitation by women, and by one woman in particular, Cora Bussey

Hillis, a prominent Iowa clubwoman, whose husband had served as mayor of Des Moines. Hillis had been actively involved in the women's and child-study club movement; she was the founder of the Des Moines Women's Club in 1886, was a member of the Iowa Child Study Society (founded in 1897), and was one of the organizers of the Iowa branch of the National Congress of Mothers in 1899. Hillis was also responsible for the establishment of Iowa's first hospital children's ward and instrumental in reforming the state's juvenile justice system.[7]

Hillis's public ventures were motivated by her personal traumas as a mother and caretaker. As a young child, she had assumed responsibility for a younger sister who had a serious spinal condition, and as an adult Hillis had watched three of her own children die of various ailments. She concluded that her children's deaths might have been prevented had she known more about child care. She described her attempts as a young mother to discover trustworthy information about child rearing: "I waded through oceans of stale textbook theory written largely, I fancy, by bachelor professors or elderly teachers with no actual personal contact with youth. I discovered there was no well-defined science of child rearing, no standards on which all might agree."[8]

Hillis assumed that her quest for reliable advice mirrored the plight of countless other mothers who sought help in the rearing of children. Although a prominent member of Iowa's elite, Hillis defined herself in her lobbying efforts primarily as a mother: "I, a mother, voicing the inarticulate cry of countless other mothers for some dependable source of guidance in the rearing of children, dare speak."[9] Hillis's upper-class background undoubtedly made her experience as a mother quite different from that of less privileged women. Yet it was true that mothers from all classes experienced high rates of infant and maternal mortality during the early decades of the century; 10 percent of all infants died before the age of one.[10]

Ultimately, Hillis's frustration with the lack of information on raising children culminated in a plan to establish a child welfare research laboratory to purvey scientific information about children to parents. She initiated discussions with the administration of the Iowa State College of Agriculture and Mechanical Arts in 1901, which went nowhere. Her next overture was to the State University of Iowa (later to be called the University of Iowa), where psychologist and dean of the graduate school Carl Emil Seashore objected to Hillis's proposed venture because of his own desire to establish a clinic for abnormal children, at the medical school. With the appointment of Thomas MacBride as president of the university, however, a compromise between the two was reached. MacBride offered to help Seashore establish a psychopathic hospital in conjunction with the medical school if Seashore would assist Hillis in her efforts.[11] Seashore and Hillis formed a child welfare committee composed of the presidents of the state's major women's organizations, including chapters of the National Congress of Parents and Teachers, the Women's Christian Temperance Union, the Federation of Women's Clubs, the Equal Suffrage Council, and various religious groups.[12] The diversity of this constituency suggests that female activists of various ideological commitments found the child-study campaign a congenial platform on which to stand. Members of the various organizations differed in the stands they took on suffrage and in their notions of what a child welfare institute should consist of, yet they were eventually able to arrive at a legislative proposal that all could agree on. In 1915, the committee introduced a bill in the state legislature calling for the inauguration of a child welfare research station at the University of Iowa. Initially defeated (some congressmen argued that the "God-given love of the mother" should suffice for rearing healthy children and that children's place was in the home and not in a laboratory), the bill was reintroduced just as the United States was entering World War I. Some congressmen argued that money for the station should be used for military purposes, but others pointed to the dismaying results of the newly instituted psychological and intelligence tests for enlisted men. Proponents argued that a child welfare station might have averted such a situation. The legislature appropriated $50,000 for the new station, whose purpose was research into the "best scientific methods of conserving and developing the normal child, the dissemination of the information acquired by such investigation, and the training of students for work in such fields." In 1919 the Women's Christian Temperance Union appropriated $10,000 annually for five years to the station for the study of eugenics. Social and behavioral scientists, however, were increasingly rejecting eugenics as either a fruitful line of inquiry or a means of reform. Therefore, the institute used the grant instead for research on child growth, intelligence, and nutrition.[13]

Psychologist Bird Baldwin, who had been instrumental in the development of intelligence testing for World War I army recruits, was appointed the director, and the station initiated its interdisciplinary research on the child, drawing staff from the fields of pediatrics, psychiatry, nutrition, education, psychology, and anthropology. Despite the public demand that the institute disseminate its findings to parents, little was accomplished in this arena in the early days. Hillis was dismayed that research was preempting education at the station and wrote to Baldwin: "It has been my hope ever since the conception of the idea for the

Iowa Child Welfare Research Station that ultimately its findings might be made available to parents and teachers everywhere. . . . To substitute an enlightened parenthood for ignorance, sympathetic understanding for indifference, and intelligent direction for haphazard drifting, would be a great service to the child-life of the Nation."[14] Hillis, who shared with many of her generation a messianic view of the possibilities inherent in the scientific method, seemed oblivious to the fact that accurate findings might take years to produce. Baldwin, however, must have felt some sympathy with Hillis's aims, for in 1924 he approached the memorial for funds to support the station's work in parent education.[15]

In 1924 the Laura Spelman Rockefeller Memorial awarded the station a grant to train May Pardee Youtz to organize parent education in conjunction with the university extension service. Frank envisioned the institute as a focal point for parent education, which would be carried out in a variety of locales with the cooperation of Iowa State College and the State Teachers' College. Frank's vision of a decentralized program was anathema to Baldwin, who was not optimistic about the consequences of decentralizing knowledge. In particular, Baldwin was troubled by Frank's insistence that the Iowa State College's School of Home Economics should have an important role in the venture, because home economists had neither the prestige nor the training that Baldwin thought necessary for such an endeavor. Baldwin was more confident about the possibilities of the laboratory nursery schools, housed at the institute itself, where infants under two were given regular physical and mental examinations and parents were instructed on the best means of conserving their children's health and well-being. The utopian attitude prevalent during the early days of child study is suggested by this 1925 report on the activities of the nursery school: "New interests can be awakened, undesirable temperaments changed, fear complexes eliminated, social aversion and extreme shyness overcome, language habits completely modified, motor control improved, and physical growth accelerated or retarded." If the Iowa researchers were dubious that serious parent education could be carried out through the decentralized network of the extension service, they were more confident that expert nursery schools, under the auspices of a research laboratory, could achieve the goals that Iowa citizens had set for them.[16]

The nursery schools housed at the institute would not be the only locus of parent education in Iowa, however, because the constituencies that could benefit from the facilities were inherently limited and both Frank and women's lobbying organizations had a broad vision of the purposes of parent education in Iowa. Frank was willing to provide significant sums of money for the station's research work only if it displayed a strong commitment to the kind of decentralized program of parent education that he envisioned. Frank was already working closely with Anna Richardson in the parent education project of the American Home Economics Association, whose connections with Iowa ensured that home economists would be involved in the new venture. In 1925, therefore, three demonstration centers for parent education were established in Des Moines, Council Bluffs, and Mason City, with participation of the state's three major academic institutions. The Iowa State Council on Child Study and Parent Education was founded in 1926 to assist in the development of a statewide plan. The council included representatives from the PTA, the American Association of University Women, and the Women's Division of the Iowa Farm Bureau. And in 1926 Baldwin succumbed to the public demand for popularization by instituting radio broadcasts from the station on child care. With the talented May Pardee Youtz as director of parent education and the cooperation of state colleges and home economists, child-study groups flourished throughout the state, in both rural and urban areas.[17]

The Iowa station was unique in its success and longevity, perhaps in part because it received backing from the state and the university, in addition to philanthropic monies. California also relied on a vigorous child welfare community to help initiate and sustain the University of California at Berkeley Child Welfare Institute. The state had one of the country's most active PTAs, which by 1916 had enrolled more than four thousand members in study groups. The association promoted the notion that study should lead to action, and this propensity led in 1923 to the organization's lobbying on behalf of a state-sponsored child welfare institute and a program of parent education.[18] The California legislature offered its support to such an institute in 1925, contending, "There is at this time, through Parent-Teacher Associations, Mothers' Clubs, and other child welfare organizations and individuals, a nation-wide desire and insistent *demand* for dependable authority on which to base the training of the child." The legislation was passed, however, before the university agreed to actually sponsor the institute. Because of the state's solid support for the institute, Frank was especially interested in funding the program, for he anticipated that government funds would eventually underwrite his ventures. Initial discussions with the faculty were less than auspicious, though, because of academics' traditional wariness toward interdisciplinary enterprises and the reluctance some psychologists felt at being associated with the low-prestige specialty of child psychology. With the promise of substantial funds for research, however, the faculty relented and the institute finally came into being in 1927.[19]

As with all his projects in this area, Frank sought to tie research institutions to more pragmatic programs of education. In the case of California, Frank attempted to involve the state's department of education. The state supervisor of education, William C. Woods, was enthusiastic about including a parent education component in the public schools. There were numerous justifications for the memorial's funding of the California Department of Education. California had the largest number of individual PTA chapters of any state and hosted an extensive program of adult education, which included five hundred child welfare classes for mothers and a division dedicated to the education of immigrants. In addition, an organizational structure for Smith-Hughes and Smith-Lever specialists in home economics was already in place. California educators and state officials were yet more favorably disposed toward parent education once several research studies came out suggesting that faulty parenting was the cause of delinquency.[20]

In 1925 California inaugurated a parent education division within its Department of Public Instruction. Proponents of the new division argued: "The home has failed to keep up with the demands made upon it by twentieth century civilization. In consequence, the home shows signs of disintegration, and children coming from modern homes show increasing signs of delinquency. We should endeavor to enable parents to rehabilitate the home and make it a more modern, efficient institution." Alarmed by the social dislocations that were changing the context of the modern family, educators, legislators, and social scientists saw parent education as a tool to enable the family to adjust to contemporary life. Ethel Richardson, the head of adult education in California, appointed physician Herbert Stolz to direct parent education in the state. When the plans for the University of California Institute of Child Welfare were completed in 1927, Stolz was simultaneously appointed as director of the institute, thus "uniting parent education and child study."[21]

Frank and the various individuals associated with parent education in California conceived of a state program which relied on the united efforts of the institute and the Department of Education. Conflicts arose, however, between those oriented toward providing parent education and those primarily interested in child research, and as in many such cases, the individuals involved sought a mediator in Frank. While the scientists at the university were most interested in conducting "extensive research with the view to setting up norms," Frank's more reformist vision involved "studying optimum conditions of growth and development in children, demonstrating to mothers and teachers, both in the home and the school, the necessary adjustments to be made in securing more intelligent ways of living."[22] The experimental attitude of many of the institute's personnel troubled Ethel Richardson, who wrote to Frank: "It happens that the Deans and President are also concerned with the exact sciences and would, therefore, not be likely to recognize the difficulties and necessary adaptations which must be made in studying children. In discussing the plans for the institute, the committee on the budget quite clearly thought of children as they would have thought of plants or white rats."[23] Richardson, an educator, stressed the "welfare" aspect of the work, while the scientists' emphasis was on "research." Although Frank was generally hospitable to those who were more interested in dissemination of knowledge than in research, he constantly had to reconcile the diverse parties to secure his ends.

The PTA's ongoing activism helped to ensure the continuation of parent education in California. The organization paid to house the California institute's nursery school until 1933 and consistently pressured the institute to disseminate its research findings to the public at large, an attempt that both enlarged and systematized California's child-study movement. As it had in several other states, the PTA organized women into groups, which then had access to information and trained personnel provided by the institute. The organizers stressed that the study groups should provide parents with opportunities to develop critical thinking skills. Leaders were urged to be on their guard "constantly against the tendency to distribute authoritative opinion to persons incapable of criticizing it" and to avoid directing the discussion "toward preconceived conclusions." Some leaders discovered that when members read the texts on a particular subject before a meeting, they were less likely to be spontaneous in their responses; therefore, they reconfigured the meetings so that members would discuss a subject such as discipline before specific readings on the subject were recommended. The California program was remarkably effective at reaching a broad range of parents through the public schools, the PTA, and the home demonstration extension service. In 1941, the program hosted 1,891 study groups throughout the state, with an enrollment of 48,739 parents.[24] The connections between the highly regarded research institute and the classes themselves were hard to discern. Still, parent education as a social movement flourished in California throughout the interwar years.

With the establishment of the University of Minnesota Institute of Child Welfare, Minnesota also became a mainstay of both child development research and parent education. The institute was the brainchild of Frank, who initiated discussions in 1923 with his former classmate, president of the university Lotus D. Coffman. The students and faculty were enthusiastic about the plan, although there was some opposition from the psychology department, which feared competition from the interdisciplinary enterprise. Coffman's insistence that the institute be incorporated as a department within the university and his provision of incentives to faculty who participated in the activities of the institute ensured its longevity.[25]

In 1925 the memorial awarded the University of Minnesota a grant to fund the institute for five years, which allowed them to hire director John E. Anderson, a comparative psychologist; an anatomist; a pediatrician; and a researcher in mental testing. The university's initial proposal to the memorial barely mentioned work with parents, and Frank insisted that a revised proposal be submitted with increased provisions for parent education. Faculty members from the agricultural extension division of the university suggested that effective extension work in parent education might be accomplished through the combined efforts of the division and the institute. The agricultural extension program, with its home demonstration bureaus, provided a valuable network that fostered local leadership in parent education throughout the state. Such a structure appealed to Frank, but it was less enticing to Anderson, who, like Baldwin, wanted to have more control over the process. Combined lobbying by Frank and the agricultural extension division paid off, however, and in 1929 a child development specialist was placed on the state staff of the Home Economics Extension Service.[26]

The institute's first ventures into parent education included a free correspondence course in child care and training, in which more than six thousand parents were enlisted, and a study group program. The institute faculty engaged in few promotional efforts, but the PTA helped organize groups of parents by mandating that to fulfill its criteria for standard and superior work, local chapters must sponsor study groups. The institute contributed leadership and study materials to the groups, and soon the demand for leaders was greater than the institute could meet. Intensive work in parent education was carried out by the institute in Duluth and in the Twin Cities, where groups were sponsored by PTAs, college clubs, churches, and the evening division of the Board of Education.[27]

The Home Demonstration Office of the Agricultural Extension took over a large measure of the institute's work in parent education, beginning in 1929. The office could rely on groups of women already organized by local home demonstration agents into Home Bureau clubs. The organizers enlisted women in five-week group sessions in child care and training. Some of the groups received lessons in Finnish and Norwegian; the English-speaking children of Scandinavian parents often translated reading materials for their mothers. The leaders were primarily laywomen from the community with very little training, so that "the subject matter had to be very simple and explicit." The groups organized by the Agricultural Extension Division represented a broader cross-section of the community and were better attended than other groups sponsored by the institute, which tended to represent the upper occupational levels of the population.

The groups sponsored by the Home Demonstration Office were the most enthusiastically received, perhaps, educators speculated, because these women were already well organized as active members of the Home Bureau. The philosophy of the extension program was ultimately one of self-help. A 1937 report on the project indicated that the goal of the project was to "lead women to think through their problems and find solutions." When querying participants about the advantages of the groups, one member spoke of the "contact and exchange of ideas, with earnest-minded women whose desire is to make life a little better for those who follow after." Organizers were able to report some more concrete results as well. Home economics extension workers claimed that as a result of participation in child-study clubs, some mothers had "put the strap away," were more likely to bring their children to physicians and dentists for checkups, and were increasingly cognizant of children's needs for "constructive play materials."[28] Minnesota's parent education program benefited from the organizational skills rural women had honed elsewhere first and which contributed to the viability of the projects.[29]

Child welfare research institutes and state programs of parent education responded to several perceived needs in their constituencies. Women sought assistance in raising children and lobbied, especially through such organizations as the PTA, for reliable research on parents and children. Educators regarded parent education both as an essential preventive measure and as an intriguing experiment in progressive adult education. Child psychologists, pediatricians, and social scientists shared educators' concern with parent education as a preventive measure but also had an investment in pursuing their careers as researchers. The establishment of child welfare research institutes lent increased legitimacy to the child-saving professions and provided institutional homes for researchers. Child welfare research institutes thus appealed to both producers and consumers of information.

The Home Bureau study groups sponsored by the agricultural extension divisions were effective educational vehicles for transmitting child-rearing information to rural and small-town mothers. Parent education leaders were constantly complaining that they could not begin to meet the demand of mothers' groups for leaders, speakers, and reading materials. But while both home economics extension workers and child welfare institute personnel could agree on the need to develop and disseminate information about children, inevitably tensions arose between researchers and disseminators and between producers and consumers of knowledge. As the field of child development became increasingly professionalized, a division of labor emerged along gender lines: the scientists, who were mainly men, increasingly gained both the upper hand over those applying the knowledge, who were mainly women, and the funding. For scientists seeking to make a name for themselves in this new study of the child, the decentralization of knowledge advocated by Frank and the extension educators was somewhat problematic, given that they were not yet on sure ground in their knowledge and that it was intrinsically difficult to ensure that the nonscientists were imparting the "correct" child-rearing advice. Parent education progressed meanwhile as well, although its actual benefits were not very closely tied to the research work being carried on at the various institutes. Because the extension service was decentralized and lacked sufficient trained personnel, parents were responsible for organizing and directing most groups. As a result, women developed their leadership skills, and groups assessed, rather than merely disseminated, expert advice. Thus in practice parent education did not achieve what it had initially promised—the transformation of parenting according to definitive scientific principles—but it achieved successes that had not been foreseen.

Popular interest in child development helped ensure that researchers' findings would find a wide audience, but the pressure to produce and popularize findings of benefit to women and children often resulted in the oversimplification of child development research and in circumvention of the scientific method that the experts touted. Parents were in a hurry to find solutions to the problems of child rearing and demanded that researchers swiftly produce information that would alleviate some of the problems of twentieth-century family life. These demands posed problems for researchers, such as George Stoddard, who directed the Iowa station after Bird Baldwin died in 1928. He described the dilemma in an interview: "If you want to go into a reform movement, you shouldn't get in just by jumping in front of barricades, but have a solid pyramidal base in research, development, experience, and support."[30]

Historian of the child development movement and child psychologist Robert R. Sears instructed contemporary practitioners that the field "grew out of *relevance*" and that "child development is a product of social needs that had little to do with science qua science."[31] According to Sears, practitioners should not seek to evade social responsibility, which is inherent in their work. Despite this injunction, however, the demands of establishing a new academic discipline did not always mesh neatly with the needs of those who had helped establish the discipline.

MODERNIZING MOTHERHOOD: HOME ECONOMICS AND PARENT EDUCATION

Like the genesis of child welfare institutes, the emergence of home economics as an academic discipline was very much a product of social forces. The establishment of the home economics curriculum in universities and secondary schools was one response to the tensions generated by women's increasing levels of education and virtual exclusion of married women from the labor market. Home economics provided socially legitimated career opportunities for women while reinforcing their traditional roles as wives and mothers, though it employed the language of modernity and science. Pioneer home economist Ellen Richards contended, "Home Economics stands for the ideal home life for today unhampered by the traditions of the past; the utilization of all the resources of modern science to improve the home life." Richards affirmed that applying science to the problems of everyday life would "shape the new education to bring all science to the people," especially women, many of whom had been denied the benefits of scientific education. Home economists are often thought of as champions of traditional womanhood; their efforts to modernize women's roles have only recently begun to receive attention.[32]

Home economists sought greater access for women to the expertise that was redefining women's work. Richards argued that women must become household engineers, evoking a popular icon of the 1910s, signifying efficiency, inventiveness, and expertise. Home economists aimed to diminish the differences between the old-fashioned mother in the home and a masculine, technological society by supplying mothers with the tools of modern science. Parent education was a logical extension of the home economics agenda. Mothers were urged to rely on the behavioral sciences for their child-rearing strategies rather than on their natural instincts.[33] The new emphasis also provided vocational opportunities for home economists as experts in child development and parent education.

During the early years of home economics, the physical sciences dominated

the educational agenda, and child care occupied a minor place in the curriculum. At the early meetings of the American Home Economics Association,
conference sessions on nutrition, clothing, and household management and
technology held sway. The few public school home economics programs that
included child care in the curriculum were geared primarily toward the poor,
who, it was assumed, had much to learn about hygienic methods of caring for
children. Sporadic efforts were made to educate girls and young women in the
physical care of infants; but a sample syllabus produced by the association in
1913 completely omitted mention of the care of children.[34] In ensuing years,
however, child development occupied a more central place in the home economics curriculum, as the behavioral sciences became increasingly legitimate
and home economists recognized the advantages of addressing a topic that had
widespread societal appeal.

Home economists were also increasingly aware of the gaps in the standard
curriculum, which had initially catered primarily to women who planned to
pursue careers. In a 1917 study of college-educated women, 80 percent of the
respondents urged that home economics programs include child study. Home
economics courses focused on cooking and sewing, but American women were
less likely to bake their own bread and make their own clothes. By contrast,
middle-class mothers were increasingly focusing attention on the care of children. One woman said, "If I were planning home economics courses, I would
omit much of textiles, etc., and get right at the child business. . . . Women do
not know how to care for themselves or their babies after the babies arrive—
and they do not know how to train children from a physical or ethical standpoint." In her 1926 presidential address to the association, Katherine Blunt
suggested that home economists continue to develop courses of study in areas
such as child training that directly impinged on adult homemakers' lives.[35]

The organization finally lent wholehearted support to the parent education
movement at the 1924 convention, where it resolved to place the development
of a curriculum in child care and training at the top of its educational agenda.
Home economists bolstered their case for the inclusion of child care in the
curriculum by insisting that the study of children be granted the same attention
and resources as agriculture. Dean Anna Richardson of Iowa State College
proclaimed in 1926: "The newer Home Economics . . . must include child
development and parent education if it is to function as training for the great
vocation of homemaking or anything like the same breadth of lines as is
modern agriculture." Similarly, an editorial in the *Cedar Rapids Gazette* (1915),
calling for state funding to establish a child welfare institute at the University of

Iowa, excoriated the public propensity to support "research on hogs but not on children." The comparison with agriculture underscored the scientific component of child development work and threw into question the disparity in public funding for the two fields. In 1925, home economists lobbied successfully to have the Land Grant College Association recognize child care as a key element in the home economics curriculum.[36]

Proponents of integrating child rearing into the home economics curriculum found a useful ally in Lawrence Frank, whose vision of parent education encompassed an auspicious combination of researchers and practitioners, professionals and laypeople. Frank proposed a plan that included research funds for child welfare institutes; fellowships designed exclusively for women in child development and parent education; funds to support women's club work in parent education; and a central role for home economists in disseminating the insights of the child development movement to the American public.[37] Clearly he believed that women—as professionals, clubwomen, and homemakers—should be at the forefront of what he perceived to be a social movement of the greatest magnitude.

In 1925 Frank met with Dean Anna Richardson, Katherine Blunt, and Agnes Fay Morgan, chair of the Home Economics Department at the University of California, to discuss potential funding for the association's work in parent education. Frank foresaw the possibility of applying the federal funds provided by the Smith-Lever (1914) and Smith-Hughes (1917) acts for extension work in home economics to disseminate child development expertise to American families. The legislation mandated that educational funds that had traditionally been earmarked to educate primarily male farmers would also be used to educate rural women. Frank was especially intrigued by the possibility of making use of the rapidly growing network of home demonstration agents working in rural areas with the Agricultural Extension Service. The agents, working in Home Bureau offices, were engaged in organizing and educating local homemakers and dispensing information about a variety of women's enterprises, from sewing to gardening. With proper training, Frank reasoned, the agents could also function as parent educators. By providing seed money for child development projects in states with major land-grant universities and established extension services, the memorial might ensure parent education's future sponsorship by state educational institutions.[38] Such a plan provided obvious benefits for home economists, who envisioned greater professional possibilities and societal influence for themselves as leaders in parent education.

As a result of the meeting, home economists won a four-year grant from the memorial to provide for the employment of Anna Richardson as a parent education specialist.[39] Richardson faced a daunting task, for she and her colleagues needed to persuade university administrators to allow them to extend the boundaries of home economics beyond chemistry and nutrition and their practical applications and into the social sciences. Genevieve Fisher, Richardson's successor as dean of home economics at Iowa State College, expressed this concern in a memo to the president of the college, Raymond Hughes: "I appreciate," she admitted, "that it is difficult for us to live down the well established tradition that we are primarily interested in cooking and sewing." Frank, pleased to note that many home economists were willing to expand their scientific agenda to include parenting, which he viewed as the homemaker's most important subject matter, suggested in a memo that home economists had a "conviction of sin" but were willing to "remedy their mistakes as soon as possible."[40] Frank's equation of the narrowness of home economics with "sin" is representative of the combination of science and reform that informed his vision. Home economists' sin lay in not linking their educational projects with any larger project of social reform.

Advocates believed that enlarging the scope of home economics to include the care of children would ultimately ensure that the discipline appealed to adults as well as high school students, men as well as women. One home economist elaborated on the expanded role of home economics work: "Home economics, which in the past has too often been a narrow and sometimes rather sterile specialty, is now undergoing a remarkable evolution toward meeting its requirements more fully. Most of its contents must soon find a place in every institution that pretends to fit its students anywhere except in a classroom."[41] The expansion of the subject matter of home economics into the arena of family life suited many who, like Frank, embraced the progressive educational tenet that education should contribute toward the betterment of human relationships.

This conception of home economics fit nicely with the popular credo of the progressive education movement. But home economists anticipated an added benefit from the association of home economics with child development: an alliance with the increasingly respectable disciplines of psychology and sociology. Frank projected that home economists would work closely with the child welfare research institutes funded by the memorial and associated with several major universities in disseminating the ideas developed by child psychologists to a broad public.

Home economists' growing interest in child development was, however, met with skepticism by male academics who were reluctant to ally themselves with such an undeniably female discipline. Frank wrote to Richardson: "I have heard criticism that the association is engaged in promoting interest and activity among its members for work in child study and parent education and that this promotion is causing some embarrassment to the educational people. . . . I imagine they are as usual rather disturbed and worried by signs of activity and determination on the part of the feminine members of staffs." Some of the male psychologists who staffed the child research institutes feared that the association of parent education with home economics would subvert their efforts to elevate the prestige of child development research. Bird Baldwin, director of the Iowa Child Welfare Research Station, was said to have complained to his colleagues, "Why are the Home Economics people trying to break into this field of child study and parent education?" And Harold Jones, an important behavioral psychologist at the California Institute of Child Welfare, complained to Frank that they were "getting a little too much cooperation from Household Science."[42]

Child developmentalists were still struggling to be recognized as legitimate scientists within the disciplines of psychology and medicine, and they feared that connections with a "women's" discipline such as home economics would taint their efforts. Home economists, by contrast, stood to gain prestige by affiliating themselves with disciplines dominated by men. Nonetheless, recognizing the fears of their male colleagues in the social sciences, they underscored in their exchanges with them that home economists would be primarily disseminators rather than producers of information in the behavioral sciences. Flora Rose, who jointly directed Cornell's College of Home Economics with Martha Van Renssalaer, addressed the concerns of social and behavioral scientists that home economists might be trespassing on their professional turf: "Just as physics, chemistry or economics are taught in other departments at the university and application made in home economics, so also application is made in the College of Home Economics with reference to environmental conditions in the governing of family life with special reference to children."[43] Thus, as a tactic to ensure themselves a place in the child development movement, home economists yielded to the growing division of labor between the producers of knowledge and those who applied it.

Even though home economics was almost exclusively a women's field, home economists' involvement in the movement for parent education during the 1920s and 1930s tended to diminish rather than enhance their belief in the strict division of labor according to sex. As parent education classes became more common in secondary schools, universities, and adult extension programs, many home economists came to believe that the classes should not be limited to women. In a 1931 text for public school administrators, Cora Winchell observed: "With the changing order has come an increase in activities of women outside the home, and now men and boys are sharing more fully in homemaking. Harmonious relationships among family members cannot be realized if education in home management and family relationships is sex-limited. . . . To both men and women falls the responsibility of child rearing."[44] A home economist at the University of Minnesota, Alma Binzel, warned of the limitations of discussing only mother-child relationships: "The great danger at present is that parenthood shall be narrowly conceived in terms of mother-craft and motherhood, that father-craft and fatherhood will thus be ignored." During the early years of parent education, home economists participated in a balancing act, trying to meet the needs of mothers as the primary caretakers of children, while simultaneously aiming to transform child rearing into an enterprise worthy of the skills and talents of men as well as women.[45]

But in the end, home economists were discouraged in their efforts to involve men in active parenting. Reporting on a conference on household engineering held in 1927, a commentator remarked on the "universal dissatisfaction of the women with the authoritarian basis of family life and . . . the universal satisfaction of the men with it." This reporter also noted women's "insistent demand" that men accept some responsibility for child rearing. Another attendee commented that the "usual easy acceptance of differentiation of function—the woman as housekeeper, the man as wage-earner—was sharply challenged."[46] In seeking to make the home more professional, many home economists— professional women themselves—began to challenge the boundaries that separated men's work from women's work. The 1920s and 1930s were a transitional era in the social and behavioral sciences that opened the door for questioning the accepted constructions of family life with regard to gender. From calling the maternal instinct itself into question and proposing knowledge as the key to expert parenting it was not much of a leap to wondering whether men weren't equally able to care for children. Unfortunately, the "insistent demands" of vocal home economists during the 1920s and 1930s for a more equitable division of labor in the home became increasingly muted during the more complacent 1940s and 1950s. During those decades, psychoanalysts would impose a more comprehensive explanation for relegating women to the work of mothering and would reinstate the maternal instinct with a vengeance.

Although home economists were largely excluded from the privileged arena of the production of scientific knowledge of the child, they approached their role as disseminators with vigor. Child welfare institutes established at the University of California, the University of Minnesota, and the University of Iowa cooperated with home economists in moving education beyond the confines of academia and into America's rural villages and small towns. Other institutions, such as Cornell University, Georgia State College, and the University of Cincinnati, combined state and federal funding with support from the Laura Spelman Rockefeller Memorial to implement curricula in child development, organize nursery schools, and train extension workers in parent education. In these and many other states, such as Massachusetts, Michigan, and Oklahoma, home demonstration agents were key participants in the transmission of knowledge about children to American homemakers. A case study of one of the most extensive programs, that associated with Cornell University's College of Home Economics, demonstrates the progressive potential of a decentralized system of education for homemakers.

"CHILD GUIDANCE WAS THE TURNING POINT FOR ME": THE CORNELL CHILD-STUDY CLUBS

From the 1920s through the 1940s, New York State was home to an active and ambitious program of parent education conducted by home economists. The state boasted both a Bureau of Parent Education and a popular program of extension education sponsored by the Cornell University Agricultural Extension Service, which the College of Home Economics used to develop a multifaceted program of parent education in 1925. For the next twenty years, Cornell's Child Study Program would engage thousands of New York homemakers in a dynamic program of adult education, focused on discussing and dissecting theories of child rearing, women's roles, and the family.

Home economics began auspiciously at Cornell in 1900 with one staff person, pioneer Martha Van Rensselaer, and a reading course for farm women on household problems that aimed to lessen the drudgery of farmwork and the isolation that homemakers experienced, especially in the years before most families had access to automobiles. The courses encouraged farm women to read as a means of improving their domestic lives and stimulating their intellects. According to one of Cornell's bulletins, "The very practical nature of the farmer's wife's occupation makes it desirable to base that occupation on scientific principles as well as to relieve it with a thought of poetry, history, or fiction." The course provided women with readings on typical home economics topics, such as home sanitation, decoration, gardening, and child care, in addition to those related to the arts and humanities. One rural woman wrote to the college to express her gratitude: "I cannot tell you what it means to me to think that somebody cares. My life is made up of men, men, men, and mud, mud, mud. Send me the bulletins and remember me in your prayers." Another woman vividly conveyed the importance of the reading material Cornell sent her: "We live in the country and I read a great deal. If I get out of reading matter when there is a blizzard in force it would be next to getting out of food." In 1901 Van Rensselaer initiated a study program called Saving Steps, designed to help farm women manage their household chores more efficiently. Saving Steps eventually had an enrollment of 70,000 women, many of them in study groups.[47] These popular courses paved the way for Cornell's later efforts to establish child-study clubs for mothers.

The care of children was incorporated into home economics at Cornell in 1919 with the establishment of a "practice house" where undergraduates could apply their home-management and child-rearing skills. The practice house included a "resident child," usually a foster child, on whom the home economics majors could practice their lessons in child development. In 1925 Cornell received a four-year grant from the memorial to institute its Department of Child Development and Parent Education (which would later be called the Department of Family Life), with an affiliated nursery school for research and parent education.[48] From the beginning, the department sponsored a wide range of graduate, undergraduate, and extension courses in child development and family life, using its nursery school as a training ground and laboratory for researchers, students, and preschool and home economics teachers.

Shortly after the establishment of the new department, Margaret Wylie, extension specialist in child study, instituted the Cornell Child Study Club Program as a component of the Agricultural Extension Service. Wylie had received her Ph.D. in psychology from the University of Michigan and done postdoctoral work at the Illinois Institute of Juvenile Research, where she studied preschool children. Wylie was a superb educator of adults, in part because she empathized with the problems of ordinary mothers and respected the insights and experiences they had garnered while caring for children.[49]

Wylie and her colleagues made use of home demonstration agents, trained by specialists in child development, to create educational opportunities for mothers throughout the state. The agents sponsored local lectures and discussions designed to arouse interest in child-study clubs and then trained local mothers to lead groups. Once such a group had been organized, Cornell contributed syllabi, pamphlets, and a lending library, with the sole stipulation that the groups send the college detailed meeting minutes. The college also sponsored annual conferences at the Ithaca campus to instruct home demonstration agents and study group mothers in methods of leading discussion groups and in the latest theories of child development and family life. The early history of the program thus supports Marilyn Irvin Holt's analysis of educational programs for rural women: "In the early years of farm women's education, professionals coexisted with those who based their work on firsthand knowledge, thus providing a venue where much negotiation between professional expertise and women's everyday practices in the home occurred."[50]

Cornell organized groups in some fifty New York counties, for a range of mothers, from farm women to middle- and upper-middle-class urban women. Child-study groups drew on both the rural and urban constituencies of the Home Bureau. Many groups were clustered around Buffalo and Rochester, while others were centered in rural villages scattered throughout the state, such as DeKalb Junction in St. Lawrence County and Sandy Creek in Oswego County. During the interwar years, an influx of New York urban dwellers into rural areas coincided with the development of central school districts in agricultural regions. Rural migration and the central school system contributed to the breakdown of urban-rural distinctions.[51] Thus even child-study groups in rural areas were likely to comprise women who lived both on farms and in small towns and villages, and the groups provided a milieu where traditional ideas of child rearing customary in an agricultural environment competed with the modern "child-centered" ideas advanced by professionals and some urbanized parents.

Whether women who participated in the Cornell study groups came from agricultural or nonagricultural families, they resembled one another in their level of educational achievements and involvement in the community. Home Bureau and study group mothers tended to be "joiners" who were often members of the Grange (a rural organization), the PTA, or a local church, in addition to the Home Bureau. Child-study mothers were better educated than their non–study group counterparts; most had some high school education, and sometimes a year or two of college, whereas the average length of education for most rural New York women was between eight and ten years. Educated women may have felt isolated in rural settings, far from the cultural opportunities they had experienced in their youth. One rural woman who attended a series of child-study lectures sponsored by the local Home Bureau testified, "We have little opportunity to hear of the latest movements in child training in

Suffolk County. As one who has spent her college days studying psychology . . . I have therefore especially enjoyed these lectures."[52]

Home Bureau mothers were from the solid middle class of the nation's rural population and were likely to be white, native-born, and relatively comfortable economically, with intact, medium-sized families of two to four children. Study group mothers were by no means uniformly well-off, however; many were unable to afford even the smallest course materials fees and found it difficult to make time or secure transportation to attend meetings. Although few of the mothers worked at full-time paid employment before World War II, throughout this period many rural women were a key factor in their family's economic survival, working within the home, cultivating large gardens, participating in dairy work, or selling handicrafts. In addition to being a wife and a mother, the typical farm woman was her husband's business partner, and child rearing was only one of the many responsibilities that required her attention.[53]

Child-study work was most appealing to mothers who could provide their children with the basics—nutritious food, suitable clothing, and health care—and could afford to think about their psychic development. In 1936, a poor mother from Oswego County angrily wrote to her home demonstration agent in response to the letters on child development that had been sent to rural women, "When you are so interested in our children—please tell us of some way out of these difficulties? No work. No money. Children undernourished. Lack of proper clothing. Both should have tonsil operations. Please state of what benefit your foolish letters are in such a case."[54] Writing during the dark days of the Depression, characterized by an upsurge in the activities of the home economics extension service, this woman evidently craved relief and assistance rather than expertise.

For homemakers who could afford to attend to both their own and their children's psychic needs, the clubs provided a community setting where mothers' concerns were accorded special significance. The clubs reflected the philosophy of the "decentralization of knowledge" that was at the root of extension education. According to a Cornell memo: "Extension education is safe when the power of knowledge is decentralized and there goes to the county leader, thence to the local leader and to the individual citizen a corresponding power to acquire knowledge, understanding and effectiveness. Extension education is . . . not a system by which nuggets of truth are done up in a safe package at the central office and delivered by a messenger and carried by her to the individual group. . . . The thinking must be shared all along the way."[55] Given that the competing philosophy of scientific expertise was often privi-

leged in educational programs, it is unlikely that the philosophy of decentralization was put into practice on a regular basis. That there were not enough
trained personnel to meet the demand for mothers' groups meant, however,
that members were often left to process reading materials on their own, a
situation that made the ideal of the decentralization of knowledge a reality in
many groups.

Beginning with the study of texts on the physical and psychological care of
infants and preschool children, the groups combined analyses of academic
subject material with discussions of maternal experiences, problems, and frustrations. Wylie and her staff at Cornell assumed that adult homemakers must
have an opportunity to connect learning with living and encouraged group
members to integrate their experiences as mothers with the course materials.
The staff accorded the groups substantial autonomy and believed the processes
of group education to be more important than the mastery of specific subject
matter. The meeting minutes of these clubs, duly provided to Cornell, include
lengthy records of debates about child-rearing techniques, which we will read
about in the next few chapters.

Initially, home economists were concerned with imparting generally accepted principles of child development to mothers, but within a few years
dissension from within the ranks of child psychologists over the scientifically
"correct" methods of child rearing contributed to an increasing emphasis on
critical reading and thinking in child-study groups. Although membership in a
child-study group was an indication of members' willingness to acquaint themselves with scientific expertise, the structure of the groups encouraged mothers
to read works critically, measuring the theories against the realities of everyday
life in the home and prevalent alternative value systems.

The participants frequently expressed their gratitude for the opportunity to
apply their intellects in a setting where women's work was taken seriously and
where critical reflection was encouraged. As Lilian Diane Madigan, a member
of the long-lasting Bennett Study Club, phrased it: "The greatest benefit to me
has been through the knowledge that every two weeks I would meet and be able
to *discuss*. . . problems which were pertinent to my job!" Members also relished
the respite from their daily chores. A leader of a group from Hilton County,
New York, wrote to Wylie at Cornell: "My furniture never was so shabby, my
wardrobe so nearly exhausted nor I so happy as I am now. At one time I felt as
though I was stagnating. All I seemed able to talk about was housework and
babies. Child guidance was the turning point for me. Studying and reading
books on psychology has given me an entirely different slant on life. My time is

so occupied with worthwhile things that I don't have time to be small and petty. Things which used to make me fume and rage don't even sink under my new armor plate."[56] The volunteers who led the groups repeatedly expressed their appreciation for the training they received in leadership, the contact with other women, and the chance to do extensive reading and studying.

The mothers' groups organized by home economists nationwide represent one of the earliest attempts to educate large numbers of homemakers and should be considered a significant effort at adult education. The child-study clubs sponsored by home economists, in fact, bore some resemblance to the modern discipline of women's studies. Although mothers' groups lacked an overarching feminist agenda and their members on the whole accepted the division of labor by sex, like women's studies the groups served to validate and legitimate women's experiences by making them a crucial part of the curriculum.

Yet this potentially liberating educational experience was ultimately held in check by the ideology of scientific motherhood, which ensured that women would maintain their place as wives and mothers in the home. During the 1920s it was debatable as to whether the working mother would have a place in contemporary society, but the explosion of information on the complexity and magnitude of parental responsibility provided new rationalizations for keeping mothers in the home. Nevertheless, the modernization of mothering was pursued by scores of women, who viewed that aim as a means of buttressing their roles within the existing division of labor and who could not yet imagine combining motherhood with a career outside the home.

Although the aims of parent educators may seem modest by contemporary standards, child-study mothers had to struggle to acquire the benefits of modern motherhood. Spouses were reluctant to participate in child rearing; children were resentful of their mothers' outside activities. Child-study participants protested about family members' propensity to stifle the mothers' efforts to improve themselves and their families. Child psychologists were reluctant to admit home economists to what was perceived to be a masculine domain. Still, to those women who were struggling to improve their situations from within the restricted sphere of traditional motherhood, child-study groups provided a setting where mothers' concerns occupied center stage. In helping create these uniquely female educational institutions, which mediated between nineteenth-century maternalism and twentieth-century scientific motherhood, home economists made it possible for mothers to interject their voices into the discourse of child development, voices that we will be hearing in the chapters to come.

Chapter 5 Caught Between Common Sense and Science: Mothers' Responses to Child Development Expertise

Who can guide and govern a steam-car, unless he be acquainted with the handles to the several parts of the machine? and who can guide a child, unless he know the various *handles* of the mind? Some parents and instructors seize the first within their reach, which is almost sure to be the wrong one. Others seem to think that the moral machine has but one handle.
—*Reverend Edward N. Kirk, "Use the Best Motives,"* The Mother's Assistant, *1 (January 1845)*

Kirk's analogy of the child's mind as a machine was a striking anticipation of the theories of the behaviorists in the 1920s, who postulated that children's behavior could be controlled through a knowledge of the scientific mechanisms by which the mind functioned. Falling infant mortality rates both promised that science could lead to recognizable improvements in children's behavior and provided middle-class women with additional time and energy to concern themselves with their children's psychic well-being.[1] By the 1920s child training and psychology had become a national obsession.

We know relatively little, though, about mothers' responses to child development expertise; some scholars assume that mothers submissively put expert advice into practice, and others assume that there is no intrinsic relation between advice books and parents' practices.[2] In fact, mothers' responses to child development expertise were not predictable or monolithic. The communities in which mothers lived and worked helped to shape their responses to expert advice, as we have seen in previous chapters. Mothers whose communities were not particularly hospitable to professional values were better able to maintain traditional values than mothers whose communities endorsed the superiority of expert prescriptions. Regardless of their circumstances, however, most women applied expert prescriptions selectively, after testing them in the real-life laboratory of the home.

The records of several child-study groups of the 1920s and 1930s provide us with a window into the thinking of a group of mothers as they read about and discussed popular child-care literature. The records are drawn primarily from the Cornell College of Home Economics extension service, the University of Minnesota Institute for Child Welfare (in conjunction with the state's extension service), and the Child Study Association of America. The Cornell Home Bureau child-study clubs, of which hundreds were active from the late 1920s through 1945, left richly detailed records of their meetings that reveal a good deal of negotiation between traditional child-rearing practices and the advice being offered by the professionals.[3] The detailed minutes of Child Study Association meetings, whose leaders apparently saw it as their role to steer group members toward accepting recommended child-rearing practices, rarely diverge from summaries of expert advice. By comparison, the Cornell club members were much more critical of textbook prescriptions, and their reported discussions reveal a great diversity of opinions about the applicability of expert advice to everyday practices in the home. These differences in the records of the two groups reflect distinctions in the way meetings were conducted—the Home Bureau study clubs characteristically had a much more freewheeling style, and the Child Study Association groups favored more structured, leader-driven meetings; but some of the difference may stem from the extent to which secretaries allowed controversy to enter the recorded minutes. The scanty records of the meetings of African-American and immigrant mothers are rather sparse outlines that yield only limited information about the mothers' concerns. This fuller discussion of mothers' thinking about child development expertise will therefore pertain primarily to the experiences of native-born white women of the northern and midwestern United States.

Reception theorist Paul Lichterman's characterization of readers of self-help books could also be used to describe child-study club mothers: "They read the books ambivalently, and in ongoing relation to other frameworks for situating personal selfhood in a social context."[4] These frameworks might include a woman's religious background, her own upbringing as a child, her age, and the region she lives in, in addition to the more commonly discussed factors of race, class, and ethnicity. For those belonging to study groups, another framework for understanding the self was the group itself. In many cases, as we have seen, child-study clubs formalized, strengthened, and in some cases provided the maternal networks of advice and assistance that had long been a component of women's lives. The study groups functioned as what literary critics Stanley Fish and Janice Radway have termed "interpretive communities," communities of readers that evaluate prescriptive texts against group norms, expectations, and practices.[5] The paradox of these programs was that in the process of seeking to acquire scientific knowledge about child rearing, mothers often more securely identified themselves as being in possession of useful knowledge that might be juxtaposed or combined with the more socially legitimated knowledge of experts.

During the 1920s, the curricula of child-study groups reflected the public absorption with the care and training of infants and toddlers, and young mothers nervous about their parenting skills were more likely than experienced mothers to join groups. As parent education and club mothers themselves matured during the 1930s, the curriculum expanded to a wider range of issues: adolescence, the family, and women's roles in the modern world. The vast majority of child-study clubs read similar materials, such as government child-care bulletins; articles from such magazines as *Parents', Child Welfare Magazine,* and *Child Study;* and books on child training written for a popular audience. The more elite groups sponsored by the Child Study Association and the American Association of University Women, however, consumed denser reading materials, including books written by psychologists for other professionals and books written from a psychoanalytic perspective.

"WE CAN'T ACCEPT ALL THE FINDINGS OF PSYCHOLOGY": MOTHERS DEBATE THE EXPERTS

Although they might take as their starting point a syllabus highlighting such topics as infants' feeding, sleeping, and toilet training, child-study clubs often departed from their outlines of study; mothers would share anecdotes and advice about their children's misbehavior and amusing antics, and confessions about their own misgivings about themselves and their family lives. Many groups lasted for a lifetime and became important sources of community for their members, holding birthday parties, anniversary celebrations, and showers. Indeed, some mothers' clubs formed in the 1930s and 1940s continue to meet to this day, but now the members are helping each other meet the challenges of old age. Having bonded with each other around the experience of motherhood, they have shared their experiences as women for a lifetime.[6]

Many new mothers who joined groups shared concerns about infants and toddlers common to twentieth-century mothers: children who didn't eat enough, who wouldn't sleep "on schedule," who resisted toilet training, or who cried too much. Habit training, with its concrete rules and mandates for rearing the young, was posed by parent educators as the solution to these seemingly universal dilemmas. It met with a mixed response from study group mothers, however. Young mothers were often eager to believe that they could control their children's behavior through educating them in correct habits, but older mothers tended to doubt that the many parental practices deemed dangerous by the behaviorists were as problematic as the experts made them out to be. After all, many of them had been engaging in these practices for years and had observed no negative consequences.

The child-centered approach to parenting, which had been promoted by the Child Study Association, was in conflict with much of the behaviorist agenda of the 1920s. The association, in keeping with its academic spirit, investigated the tenets of both behaviorism and psychoanalysis during this period. In 1926, an association leader theorized that the behaviorist routine was an improvement over past methods of child care: "Though the routinized child has many disadvantages, the child of an earlier age had to cope with constant attention and irregular hours of sleeping and eating." The association had a tradition of deferring to experts, but its members found themselves in a dilemma when it came to behaviorism. By the early 1930s progressive educators and some child psychologists were beginning to reject the behaviorist dogma, and the association followed their lead. In 1931, an association leader would inform her group: "The scientifically trained child, i.e., the see nothing, hear nothing, but routine feeding, dressing, etc. is not the perfectly brought up child."[7] As the vanguard of the child-study movement, the association would always align itself with the critical edge of progressive education and child psychology.

Yet initially, behaviorist methods of child rearing attracted mothers from both the Child Study Association and Home Bureau groups, perhaps because they promised clear-cut answers to the messy problems of child rearing. An association member expressed what may have been a common response to Watson's ideas: "I swallow Watson whole because I want to believe that I can do something about fears, not because I am convinced that he is sound." Watson and his followers promised that conditioning was the answer to alleviating such amorphous problems as fears, dawdling, and stammering in children. Psychoanalytic popularizers had stressed the repercussions of children's fears for their future lives as adults, but behaviorists offered means for banishing fears from the child's psyche. In *Psychological Care of Infant and Child,* for instance, Watson demonstrated how a child's fear of rabbits might be "unconditioned," by placing a rabbit in a cage at the end of a room where the child ate and bringing the cage closer to the child at mealtime. This approach was not always easy to put into practice, observed a mother in a Cornell study club who wanted to "uncondition" the child's fear of her grandmother, "it being impossible to put a grandmother in a cage at the end of a forty-foot room during the child's lunch, as Watson suggests with the rabbit."[8]

Some mothers had more success in applying behaviorist techniques, however. Through the use of conditioning techniques, a Child Study Association member helped her child overcome her fear of the radio. Her three-and-a-half-year-old daughter had been frightened into vomiting by a loud noise that the radio emitted and had been afraid of the radio thereafter. Following the incident, the mother played soft music on the radio and encouraged adults to dance to the music in the presence of the child, a strategy that had the desired effect. Trying out suggested training strategies at home could have a range of results; however, mothers were unlikely to repeat a recommended child-rearing technique if it didn't work. As the leader of one group stated, "All we can do as parents is to work on what seems sensible and try it out experimentally. We can't accept all the findings of psychology."[9]

One of the central issues for educators and mothers alike was putting the baby to sleep, a challenge behaviorists proposed to solve by strict and unyielding scheduling. Children were not to be given inducements to sleep, such as rocking, because they would become accustomed to the inducements rather than learn the good habit of sleeping on schedule. Abundant anecdotes and evidence attest that many mothers of this period strove to put children on regular sleeping schedules, but some were more flexible in their approach than the behaviorists recommended. At the Oakfield Home Bureau Child Study Club in New York, the members discussed Watson's admonition to mothers to ignore crying children and put them to bed without the usual bedtime rituals, to prevent the development of "bad habits." One mother admitted, "I just can't stand it to hear Johnny cry and it only takes 10–15 minutes to rock him to sleep so we do it." While this mother was defensive about her tendency to rock her baby to sleep, in opposition to standard expert advice, another mother had a more positive assessment of rocking: "Some babies need that human contact and the comfort of the adult's presence."[10] It is impossible to know whether this woman acquired her confidently held idea from a book, a relative, her own experience, or several of these, but she clearly had a handle on a concept that was not in vogue in the 1920s.

The members of the Child Study Association study groups were similarly unconvinced that mothers should abandon soothing, singing, and rocking as a means of helping their babies to sleep. A columnist for the organization's bulletin defended the practices, noting: "Mothers use such to bridge abrupt transition." This eminently sensible explanation for the practice, however, was confined to a publication produced by amateur mothers. Despite the fact that psychologists, and even the U.S. Children's Bureau in its *Infant Care* pamphlets, advised giving up the common maternal practice of soothing a child to sleep, many mothers were unwilling to relinquish a remedy that undoubtedly gave comfort to both mother and child.[11]

Some study group mothers also displayed flexibility about picking up the baby when it cried, in opposition to the recommendations of many experts. A Home Bureau agent reporting to Cornell was indignant at one mother's ideas, expressed at a county meeting: "One woman ruined meeting by insisting on giving her ideas about kindness to children, which were thoroughly sentimental and selfish. . . . Her main idea was that if a baby cried it needed picking up, that it was lonely!"[12] Proponents of behaviorism argued that if mothers "gave in" to baby's demands, children would inevitably gain the upper hand and become spoiled little tyrants. Of course, mothers who spoke in favor of responsiveness toward children were vindicated by child development professionals in the 1940s and 1950s, who were to characterize behaviorist child-rearing techniques as pathological.

Parent educators were as worried that mothers would dominate their children as they were that children would dominate their mothers. At a parent education conference in 1926, child psychologist Helen Woolley said of the mother who stayed at home with her child: "Either she dominates, makes the child too dependent on her; or she is oversolicitous and fearful and communicates her fear to the child." Other speakers at the conference alluded to the need for mothers to wean children psychologically at an early age; in keeping with this agenda, they encouraged mothers to develop interests outside of the home. Some experts were even less sanguine about the potential of maternal love. A writer for *Child Welfare Magazine* proclaimed, "How many young things do you know who are in revolt, parent-ridden? How many almost at the end of their ropes—nearly done in, in fact, by the over-bearing love of their progenitors?"[13] Underlying these passages may be a certain discomfort with the intimacy and intensity of the mother-child bond, as families became smaller and more isolated from each other. With all the passion that these and numerous other authors of the period spent inveighing against mother love, it seems surprising that few offered alternatives to exclusively female child rearing. Mother was the one who had to change, instead of the family structure.

Many group members were themselves uncomfortable with the portrait that was being painted in the popular literature of mothers who cared for their children with tyrannical devotion. In reaction to an author who claimed that mothers were so obsessed with their children that they were reluctant to allow others to participate in their children's care, a New York Home Bureau study group reacted defensively: "There might be a few like this but all felt mothers were glad to have others share in the care of [the] child and could not think of any mothers of the type mentioned in the book."[14] Indeed, defending the position of the homemaker *against* critical experts appeared to be one of the primary functions of the Home Bureau study groups.

One of the paradoxes inherent in the child-study philosophy is that the mother's extra efforts were intended to encourage the independence of both child and mother. Mothers in child-study groups occasionally reflected on their propensity to obsess about their children. A settlement-house mother admitted: "I have one fault—I give him too much affection. I yearn over him. That is because I have no baby. But I am learning to suppress my emotions. I am gradually withdrawing because I want him to be independent." A Minnesota Home Bureau mother admitted to the same problem: "I now realize under the guise of too personal interest that I have made my children over-dependent on me. I should read more about 'mental weaning.'"[15]

The literature on the dangers of excessive maternal attention was tinged with obvious misogyny as well as with discomfort at the exclusivity of the mother-child relationship. Although emphasizing the dangers that "too much mother love" could hold for children's psyches, it surely did not pose positive alternatives to the existing sexual division of labor. Still, it offered the possibility that mothers could relax some of their controls on their children; less dependent children could mean more independence for mothers. In the context of their group discussions, mothers encouraged each other to be less fearful about their children's activities. According to a Minnesota Home Bureau leader, "One mother can watch her youngsters climb a tree now with almost no fear that they are due to break a leg or an arm." Mothers commonly conceded that their new relaxed attitude was beneficial to their children. In one group the mothers said that the "relaxed attitude when applied had worked wonders." Numerous group members congratulated themselves when their children became more self-reliant and they themselves more relaxed about their child-rearing responsibilities.[16]

At the same time, mothers for the most part rejected Watson's injunction that mothers should not hug, kiss, or caress their children, for fear of spoiling them. Sidonie Gruenberg claimed: "John Watson, the behaviorist, caused no little stir and discussion in the group when he spelled out his conviction that overly sentimental treatment of children was damaging." After discussing Watson's denunciation of maternal coddling, the secretary of a Cornell club observed, "Most mothers agreed that while it could be overdone the child who was not given much affection always suffered."[17] Child-study mothers were reluctant to let science invade every aspect of child rearing, and indeed many believed that nurturance and affection should take precedence over the strict routines and impersonal discipline advocated by the behaviorists.

Although marked skepticism was expressed about rigid behaviorist child-rearing prescriptions, some groups appeared to accept the precepts with few or no reservations. In the rural villages of Perry and Castile in Wyoming County, New York, the Mary Jemison study club ostensibly adhered to the scheduling that Watson and the authors of the *Infant Care* pamphlets had advocated. As part of a series of skits put on to share their new knowledge with their husbands, they dramatized the predicament of the parents whose child require long ceremony before going to bed at night. The parents handle the situation successfully after the mother reads to the father from a child-care text: "A well-regulated, routine life for a child is absolutely essential to his physical and mental welfare. Regular habits can be formed only if the child learns from experience that he is to do the *same thing* every day at the *same hour*."[18] The skit, which is performed for the benefit of *fathers*, shows a mother using expert advice to bolster her position as a child-rearing authority. Such perfect implementation of expert advice, however, is only didactic; generally, the women speak much more spontaneously about the difficulty of putting expert prescriptions into practice. The before-mentioned script, for example, was not accompanied by a discussion of the actual exigencies of everyday child care but supposedly represented the ideal.

Educators assumed the sleeping and eating problems of infants and young children to be ubiquitous, but those working with rural women found out otherwise. A leader tried to deliver a lesson on "sleeping behavior" to a group of farm women from East Concord, New York, but the questions she posed to the mothers were met with by perplexity. The leader reported to Cornell: "In the country it seems they eat everything—have schedules—go to bed early and the children have to help out a great deal as the mothers are so busy—many outdoors a better part of the day. The whole family is so busy from hard work that they retire very early."[19] In the traditional farm family, children went to bed at the same time as other family members, tired from a long day of work, and consequently put up little resistance. The increasing segregation of children from adults in the modern family may have been the primary cause of the sleeping problems that bedeviled so many mothers.

Modern mothers were also preoccupied with their children's eating habits, which involved issues of parental control and childish rebellion. Parent educators sought to transform what were often stormy battles of will between parents and children into calm and rational activities. A young adoptive mother wrote to Gruenberg to say that acquiring an impartial attitude toward baby's eating was her key to success: "In all the time she [her adopted baby] has been with me I have never let myself get nervous or tired so that I was able to feed her as if I had all the time in the world and at least gave her the impression that it did not matter to me whether she ate anything or not, none of this 'finish your spinach.'"[20] Advice that mothers attempt to gain some distance from their children's eating and sleeping problems could be soothing to mothers who were tired of cajoling their children to eat and sleep. Perhaps the cultivation of impartiality was a corrective to the concern that mothers were lavishing on their children's most mundane activities and behaviors.

In another play the Mary Jemison group enacted for their spouses the family ordeal of suppertime disrupted by a toddler who refuses to eat what is put before her. The wife convinces her husband that they must employ the techniques she has been learning in the child-study club: "Let's be *modern* for once. Oh, I know you like implicit obedience and all that, but what good is obedience, if you only gain it by slapping?" The parents purchase a baby-size table and chairs. Both parents avoid saying "don't" to the child and try to reinforce positive behavior rather than correct negative behavior. Putting the new ideas into practice produces an amiable baby at mealtime, and the father concludes that the modern methods are the key to success: "I guess we'll both go modern and give these up-to-date ideas a chance, seeing our children are of the modern variety."[21] According to the ideology, modern strategies of child rearing were needed to coax modern children into eating and sleeping properly.

Mothers were irritated, however, at the disagreements among advice-givers. The authors of some publications, for instance, insisted that baby should eat the right kind of food, while others directed mothers to display indifference toward their children's eating habits. A Cornell group from Webster County reacted with outrage to an author who claimed that mothers were not properly nourishing their children: "Of course this raised an uproar. As we do think we are giving our children proper food and enough. . . . Still, our eminent psychologists say we should not force or insist on child eating."[22] Once again, mothers reacted defensively when authors challenged their maternal capabilities but also exhibited resentment at the competing messages with which they must contend.

Along with feeding and sleeping, toilet-training was at the top of the list of concerns for mothers with toddlers. Mothers were intrigued by reports that with proper handling, babies could be toilet-trained by an early age, even before they were six months old, a highly desirable possibility for mothers tired of changing and washing dirty diapers.[23] The literature advised placing infants over chamber pots and giving them enemas to instill the "habit of elimination." A woman in a child-study club from Monroe County, New York, excitedly reported to her group that a specialist in Rochester was able to toilet-train infants at the age of three weeks, with the assurance that the child would wet no more than two diapers in its life.[24] Early toilet-training depended on strict schedules, which included waking infants and toddlers in the night to go to the bathroom. Although early toilet-training appeared advantageous for the mother, eventually mothers themselves began to question the efficacy of toilet-training at a young age, observing that children subject to such training often reverted to their "bad habits" at a later date.[25]

At times it seemed that mothers were most passionate about extinguishing undesirable habits. In particular, early study groups invested a great deal of time in discussion of the apparently omnipresent thumb-sucking habit. A group of California mothers listed thumb-sucking, along with obedience, as their most pressing concern about their young children. The intense anxiety about the "sucking habit" seems to have stemmed both from exaggerated attention to issues of cleanliness due to the new awareness of the role of bacteria in disease and from the psychoanalytic inclination to view "sucking" as an implicitly sexual activity. Mothers inundated the Children's Bureau, pediatricians, nurses, and parent educators with questions about how to eliminate the troublesome habit. Experts such as Children's Bureau pamphlet writer physician Douglas Thom advocated using mechanical devices to "cure" thumb-sucking, such as a disagreeable-tasting ointment to be placed on the thumb, or alternatively a special cuff, which would be positioned on the elbow so that the child could not bring her thumb to her face.[26]

Concern about thumb-sucking appears to have been widespread, and even the most progressive thinkers shared it. Myrtle McGraw, a friend of Lawrence Frank and a prominent child psychologist, chose to do a "home study" on the Frank family as part of a child development course she was taking in the 1920s. Frank was a friend of the psychoanalytically inclined anthropologist Margaret Mead and was acquainted with the developmentalist approach of such progressive educators as Caroline Zachary and Lucy Sprague Mitchell, yet even he was not immune to behaviorist ideas. McGraw described her visit to the Frank home: "In those days [of] behaviorism rigidities of management was [sic] in vogue, and along with a pediatrician's antiseptic attitudes, thumbsucking was very bad. . . . The first thing I saw was these braces on the thumb, and those tongue depressors on the elbow, so the baby couldn't get her thumb to her mouth and she was blissfully sucking away on her great toe."[27]

The following passage from the minutes of a rural New York study group shows that the concern about thumb-sucking was not restricted to the educational elite: "Donald Herrick—nearly 5—sucks two fingers. Everything has been tried the mother has heard of. If his hands are covered he doesn't do it, but if someone else puts him to bed and forgets to cover his hands—he is sucking his fingers for all he is worth. His hands may be covered for two months and then if they are not covered he is at it again. He doesn't want to do it—has been shamed, offered rewards but nothing proves successful. . . . His fingers he sucks are calloused and nails not good and his mouth is getting deformed."[28] Unfortunately, the vigilance with which parents attacked the problems of "sucking" could backfire, producing an anxious child who sucked even more vigorously. In such cases, the advice of popular experts, which many parents followed, often served merely to exacerbate the problem.

Groups did not limit themselves to such concrete issues as thumb-sucking and toilet-training but undertook discussions of a more philosophical nature as well. Perhaps the most compelling topic was the relative impact of nature and nurture on children's temperaments. According to Watson's schema, children were made, not born. Watson's theories undermined geneticist understandings of child behavior, which had played a part in the thinking of earlier child-study groups. Early groups had held parents responsible for providing correct training, but they could always blame heredity if things didn't turn out quite as planned. The 1890 minutes of the Child Study Association contained an amusing reference to this ploy: "In case of *BAD* results of *careful* training, the parent must not feel that result is due to her own shortcomings (by that we mean, individual traits are very often inherited from the father's family!)." The parent education movement was explicitly environmentalist, although its conception of environment was limited to the impact of the parents—and especially the mother—on the child's temperament.[29] Behaviorists claimed to have access to knowledge that would enable mothers to shape their children's character at will. But when mothers encountered the recalcitrant behavior of their children, they were loath to accept the total responsibility for their children's deportment that the experts bestowed on them.

Whenever the question of heredity versus environment (what we now call the nature-nurture debate) was addressed in child-study clubs, lively discussions were likely to erupt, despite the groups' ostensible environmental bias. Leaders might align themselves with the environmental point of view but they seldom went unchallenged by participants. A Child Study Association leader claimed, "It is no longer possible to blame a child's disposition on Uncle John or Aunt Sue." But as they noted the temperamental differences between their own children, members rejected the idea that *training* was solely responsible for a child's disposition. Remembering World War I, the mothers observed that some of their children had been notably disturbed by the war's events, while others had maintained their composure. Members of a St. Lawrence County Home Bureau group disagreed over whether a child's temper was inherited: although some believed that it was inborn, the majority accepted the behaviorist contention that "a child is born with a neutral brain and learns about his temper later." Many of the reading materials attributed children's temperaments to their training, but some women were more influenced by eugenics arguments, such as the members of a Sandy Creek Home Bureau group who maintained that adopted children placed in "good" families often exhibited "undesirable characteristics."[30]

The environmentalist explanation of child behavior could place excessive blame on mothers, even if the explanations generally referred to "parents." In a PTA study guide, Grace Crum pointed out that groups were shifting their attention from the "problem child" to the "problem parent."[31] Mothers were undoubtedly absorbing the notion that they bore some responsibility for their children's difficulties, yet in early study group meetings a fair amount of controversy arose over whether mothers should accept total responsibility for children's shortcomings. According to the secretary of a Syracuse Home Bureau study group, "War was almost declared during the discussion of: 'The product that comes out of the home is the test.'" And another group from Hamilton, New York, rejected out of hand the leader's notion that neat housewives produce neat children.[32]

The discussions about the relative impact of nurture and nature touched the core of members' beliefs about their work as mothers. On the one hand, mothers were resisting and, in some cases, reacting defensively to the tremendous responsibility for determining a child's fate that experts were assigning to them. But the discussions also exhibit philosophical concerns. Was it the job of the mother to encourage the development of a unique individual or to shape a child in her own image? For many, their experience as mothers and common sense suggested that children's temperaments were not solely a product of nurture. Mothers of more than one child were struck by the individual differences between their children. Parent educators pointed to the *place* of the individual child in the family as an environmental factor, but many mothers remained convinced that individual character was not as malleable as the behaviorists made it out to be. In 1924, one of the Cambridge Mothers' Clubs had been meeting for nearly twenty-five years. By that time, members had relinquished some of their conceptions about the plasticity of childhood: "We have had our turn of thinking that childhood is a plastic period and the child a bit of clay to be moulded according to the wisdom imbibed once in two weeks at the Mothers' Club. We have found that such clay has curious and baffling elasticity, a way of springing back into the original form when the shaping hand is removed."[33] Sara Ruddick defines "humility" as a valued maternal virtue, one that entails accepting "the facts of the independent and uncontrollable, developing and increasingly separate existences of the lives it seeks to preserve." The experience and practice of motherhood could certainly generate such humility and helped to counter textbook notions about the malleability of children.[34]

By the 1930s, many child-study groups embraced a more complex conception of the heredity versus environment issue, one that mirrored a growing sophistication within the psychological community itself. The Child Study Association was dominated by the environmentalist approach to children in the 1920s. By 1930, though, leaders conceded, "Now it is admitted that children are born with certain predispositions, though this is unwillingly admitted, lest heredity should once more be blamed, to the detriment of the child's well-being."[35] Parent educators worried that considerations of heredity would detract from parental responsibility for their children's well-being and that accepting a genetic influence on children's personality meant that parents would be required to label children as either good or bad. Children may perhaps have benefited from educators' insistence that parents refrain from such labeling; however, parent educators hardly refrained from labeling parents as good or bad.

One of the hallmarks of a "good" parent was using appropriate punishment methods. Experts recommended reasoning, isolating the child, and putting the child in a chair in a corner as better disciplinary methods than scolding and spanking, and some educators frowned on the concept of punishment altogether.[36] Discipline and punishment headed the list of parental concerns and provided the subject matter for intense conversation in study groups. The Child Study Association was most stringently opposed to traditional punishment techniques. A leader, for instance, informed her chapter: "Punishment is often a sign of weakness on the part of parents." Sidonie Gruenberg, in fact, attributed children's disobedience to excessive prohibitions on the part of parents. The permissive style of parenting advocated by the association could backfire, however, as the group members themselves would later admit. In 1930, Cecile Pilpel explained to her group, "At first, in the reaction against the rigidity of authority, parents began to set youth on a pedestal—and to worship it. They threw off any semblance of authority and strove to meet their children as 'pals.'" Mothers often found fault with the child-centered philosophy backed by parent educators. In 1937, the secretary of a Cornell group recorded the club's consensus: "Present day discipline is too lax—that modern methods are not the right ones—that ideals of young people are not high enough!" Intriguingly, a group ostensibly formed to learn modern methods of child rearing concluded instead that a reversion to traditional methods of child rearing was preferable.[37]

Mothers in most child-study groups agreed that discipline had to be practiced. The question was: What kind of punishment was appropriate? Child-study groups allowed mothers the opportunity to examine their disciplinary strategies, to explore alternative methods of disciplining children, and to share the frustration and anger that accompanied children's problem behavior. Evidence suggests that as a result of participation in child study, mothers modified the extent to which they applied corporal punishment. Corporal punishment was a routine form of discipline in many families throughout the interwar period. In her study of family violence in Boston, Linda Gordon observes that corporal punishment was often used by poor families as a means of ensuring children's survival. Working-class mothers commonly admitted that they had resorted to drastic disciplinary measures but were changing their tactics as a result of club participation. A working mother from Rochester admitted, "I have learned that my boy doesn't do things just to devil me. I have found there are other ways to deal with him than slamming him around." In another Rochester group, the members jointly agreed to modify their disciplinary strategies. According to the secretary, "Our children are 'flabbergasted' when we use a quiet tone in correcting the act which formerly meant shrieking or spanking." The new techniques had some new consequences, however. The secretary admitted, "I do think though that they have less manners and much more backtalk and smartiness since."[38] Regardless of their class background, mothers sought compliance from their children and were initially unconvinced that the new methods would have the desired results.

Most child-study group members were loath to rule out corporal punishment altogether as an appropriate disciplinary measure. Contending that infants were too young for reasoning, many mothers argued that spanking was the only way to get their point across. Even Sidonie Gruenberg, an advocate of the child-centered approach, did not reject the possibility of physical punishment. When asked whether a mother could slap her child, she responded, "You say, 'May I slap a child,' and then immediately you have to ask, 'Which child, and who are you?'" One group considered the case of a one-year-old child having a tantrum. The text they were reading recommended putting the child alone in a room to "cry it out." Some of the mothers, however, protested that their child would cry for hours and that spanking was the only way to stop it.[39] But even if members agreed that corporal punishment was sometimes necessary, they always conceded that it should be used sparingly and never arbitrarily.

Mothers in rural New York commonly used punishments that had been disparaged by child-care experts since the mid-nineteenth century, some of which entailed frightening or shaming children into good behavior (for example, by tying them up in the front yard). By the 1920s, considerable attention was paid in the prescriptive literature to eliminating, or at least averting, the development of fears in children. In the case of the Cornell groups, meeting minutes were sent to Margaret Wylie, head of the extension division at the school's headquarters. Although Wylie apparently read the minutes, she rarely responded to them, perhaps because she appreciated the importance of group autonomy. The only exception seems to have been when she saw that punishments were being recommended that might be abusive or damaging. In discussing a disobedient child, several mothers in one of the Cornell clubs recommended shutting the child up in a dark closet, and the secretary of the group duly recorded the suggestion in the minutes. Margaret Wylie wrote to the group advising them that such a punishment was liable to make the child needlessly fearful. The group discussions almost certainly made mothers think twice about customary disciplinary tactics. A mother, for example, who considered telling her son that a mouse was in the cupboard to prevent him from opening it thought better of it when she remembered the admonition in her child-study class that mothers should avoid frightening children.[40]

Discussions about discipline could be cathartic for individual mothers, who could experience considerable anguish over their responses to children's misbehavior. A group of Cornell mothers conceded that they all spanked and scolded their children too much. One mother confessed that the situation had gotten so out of hand that her children dodged her for fear of being struck. She seemed to have gained some relief from talking about her frustrations and a week later reported that "her children thought she was sick because she was so quiet even her husband noticed it. . . . She said she felt much better and that the *kids* are really good." A mother in a Hilton, New York, group, who was described by the leader as being "nervous and in very poor health," also admitted to spanking and scolding her intelligent, high-strung toddler continually. She claimed that the discussions had helped her to be calmer and more pleasant with her son. In the context of these discussions, women were apt to be introspective about their own behavior as parents. A mother from Ontario County, New York, wanted to know what to do with a child who, when angered, shook and threw things. Another member asked whether the child had ever seen any grown person act that way, and the mother laughed and covered her face.[41] As mothers delved into their responses to children's behavior, they began to develop a therapeutic understanding of the interactions between themselves and their children.

ALL MOTHERS HAVE PROBLEMS: SETTING THE STANDARD FOR NORMALCY

Perhaps most helpful about these discussions was the reassurance mothers received that the egregious behavior they observed in their children was not particularly abnormal. A mother who complained that her child bit and slapped other children was counseled by another mother whose son had behaved similarly to refrain from whipping her child, lest his spirit be hurt. "Don't worry," she told her troubled companion, "he will soon outgrow his behavior."[42] Judging a child's behavioral normalcy could be difficult, especially as conceptions about appropriate child behavior and parental discipline were shifting rapidly. The groups afforded a collective—if inexpert—forum for gauging standards of normalcy.

In setting their own standards for normal behavior, mothers, though not uninfluenced by professional judgments, commonly questioned the basis for the experts' conclusions. A lively Cornell group was most explicit about its distrust of experts. According to the group secretary: "The comment oftenest voiced is 'Have these writers had experience with children?' The methods are so different from our former knowledge of dealing with children that some are slow to accept them."[43] Instead of discussing the textbook methods, one group of mothers spoke candidly of their own strategies for dealing with such problems. According to the group secretary, "I'm afraid it's one subject we each had our own opinions on and that we each had met the situation in the best way possible, whether or not it conformed with the text." The language of this sentence, which stresses that mothers met their problems "in the best way possible" implies that groups could serve the function of reinforcing mothers' decisions, regardless of whether they conformed to expert advice.[44]

Another topic about which study group mothers displayed decided opinions was that of the nursery school. Experts were excited about the prospects the scientific nursery school might afford for teaching mothers optimal child-rearing strategies. Many of the institutions involved in parent education sponsored nursery schools, which combined research on young children with education for them and their parents. Programs for parents often included readings on the benefits of the nursery school, and mothers were encouraged to visit nursery schools and to observe the calm, impersonal training techniques and their outcome: quiet, composed children, eating and sleeping on schedule. In fact, children may be more likely to "behave" in a nursery school situation than at home. Educators concluded that if mothers would only duplicate the child-rearing strategies practiced by nursery school teachers, they would be much happier with their children's behavior.[45]

Educated mothers from middle- to upper-middle-class homes were more likely to be positive about the benefits of the nursery school. They usually had time and resources to devote to developing nursery schools for their children, and they also tended to be predisposed in favor of scientific expertise in child rearing. Members of the Chicago Women's Club exclaimed in 1926: "Think what it would mean to us as parents if we had the benefit of that kind of expert objective all round advice when our children were from two to four years old." A Child Study Association chapter agreed on the need for nursery schools because "very few homes could be normal in this complicated age in which we are living."[46]

Rural mothers, by contrast, were inclined to feel that nursery schools were themselves abnormal. One group rejected out of hand the idea that they should read about nursery schools: they all lived on farms and considered that nursery schools would probably never be a part of their experience. In another group, the mothers complained that the nursery school situation was entirely different from the home and that it was inaccurate to draw comparisons between the two. Children in large groups, they argued, were more likely to behave than individual children in the home. Another mother felt that it was unfair to compare their situation with that of the nursery school teacher who has "nothing to do all the time but guide and supervise the child. In the home the mother has so many other things to do that are equally important that a child can't possibly get more than a portion of the same help and training." Mothers resented the implicit comparison between their own child-rearing strategies and nursery school techniques and accomplishments. In addition to the fact that mothers were busy with household duties besides child care, the intensity of the mother-child relationship is often absent from children's relationships with paid caretakers. A study of contemporary family day-care providers sheds light on the change in children's behavior outside of the home setting. In the words of one of the providers: "All the developmental hurdles—moving from bottle to cup, giving up the pacifier, becoming toilet-trained, eating a variety of foods, learning to cooperate, accepting discipline—are relatively easy to accomplish in day-care, because these are not my children. We are not engaged in a life-or-death power struggle, which I believe mothering entails. Because I'm not their mother, they don't have to relinquish any power to me in the process of toilet-training, nor do I 'win' anything. It is just my job."[47] These mothers may not have had the vocabulary of the thoughtful day-care worker, but they did understand that important factors distinguished their work from that of the nursery school teacher.

The premise of the nursery school was that to develop properly, children required special environments. The literature advised mothers to provide a special nursery or play area for children, both to encourage self-reliance and to acknowledge children's unique status in the home. But small-town and farm mothers did not always acquiesce to sequestering their children in nurseries, perhaps because it was an impossibility in their busy homes. A group of farm women disputed the notion that children needed to play separately from adults: "Our group believed that a child should have some privacy but should not be completely isolated as was stated in the book. Most of the mothers agreed that they would rather have their children near them so they could work and watch them too."[48]

The mothers were generally receptive, however, to lessons on the value of toys in nurturing children's development. Leaders pointed out that toys had educational and developmental functions, a concept new to many working-class and rural mothers who had not gone out of their way to provide their children with toys. Creating home-made play materials proved to be a favorite activity of mothers in the Home Bureau groups. In a Minnesota Home Bureau group the members constructed both play equipment and children's furniture, neither of which they could have afforded to purchase.[49] After a session constructing a home-made doll or colorful building blocks mothers would have something concrete to offer their children.

Another topic that seems to have elicited widespread enthusiasm from study group women was sex education. Reports of meetings of African-American, rural, and urban mothers alike testify to the appeal of this subject (immigrant women appear to have been an exception, although I do not have sufficient data to corroborate this impression). Mothers were eager to learn the best way to inform their children about sexuality, even if doing so was a future undertaking. The vast majority of women reported that their knowledge of sexuality was "abysmal" and that they lacked the ability to discuss it with their children. Some admitted that what they learned in classes were "things we should have learned many years ago." As women who came of age during the 1910s and 1920s, when sex was becoming a topic of public discourse, they were acutely aware of the shortcomings of parental reticence on the subject. Few mentions of the content of sex education made their way into meeting minutes, and it is likely that the discussions would seem absurdly rudimentary by contemporary standards, yet they evidently fulfilled a felt need. A Minnesota Home Bureau leader reported in 1933: "I think we had our most interesting meeting as there was more discussion than ever before. The subject seemed to be a most vital one to everyone present. . . . Mrs. Vaadeland walked all the way in, more than six miles, facing the wind, and part of the way back." Another Minnesota mother said that the classes made it much easier for her to answer her four-and-a-half-year-old boy's questions about sex. Others proclaimed that the lessons had helped them to have both a "happier sex life" and a "happier home." Members were pleasantly surprised to be able to calmly absorb information that might have shocked them in the past. Some groups discussed the topic of birth control, although this theme could apparently generate disapproval. After a visitor attended a child-study meeting in Monroe County, New York, on the topic of birth control, rumors circulated that the group was a "rotten mess"; and a study club leader was actually fired by Cornell for preaching birth control to a group of Catholic mothers.[50] For the most part, however, classes on sex education contributed to members increased comfort in discussing controversial subjects related to sexuality, such as birth control, premarital sex, and divorce.

Few groups outside of the Child Study Association, however, moved beyond basic sex education to use the language of sexuality associated with such thinkers as Sigmund Freud and the sexologist Havelock Ellis. Eventually, the word "repression" would make its way into the language, but by the time it entered common parlance, it was divorced from many of its sexual connotations. Historians of psychoanalysis have spoken of the ways in which Americans domesticated Freudian terminology. "Repression" and "sublimation" were often used interchangeably in child-study groups, usually in the context that a certain amount of repression was necessary and that youth must learn to channel sexual impulses into socially acceptable activities. A Child Study Association group leader explained, "Repression has been overadvertized as the source of terrible consequences. Repression is an essentially normal necessity."[51] In the process of introducing psychoanalytic terminology, group leaders distorted Freud's concept of repression and divested it of the negative psychic consequences attributed to repression by psychoanalysts.

The popularization of psychoanalysis contributed to a heightened awareness of the role of sexuality in human relationships. Perhaps in part because of their acquaintance with psychoanalysis, Child Study Association members became more sensitive to the sexual dangers lurking behind seemingly harmless interactions between parents and children, and between children of both the same and different sexes. Members worried about the psychological impact of excessive affection between opposite-sex siblings and same-sex friends and discussed the possible pitfalls of same-sex education in terms of its purported contribution to the development of homosexuality. Awareness of sexuality among clubwomen closed as many avenues for the expression of sexuality as it opened. The emphasis on the importance of a "normal" sex life for women, which could be liberating for some mothers and their children, proved problematic and troubling for others.[52]

The opportunity to speak about sexuality, however euphemistically, was valued by club members, but the growing understanding of childhood as a special stage of life was most significant for members' thinking and practices. Mothers often indicated that child-study groups had taught them that their children were individuals with personalities of their own. This was a new concept for some. One mother was said to remark after a series of meetings, "Do you mean that a young child has a personality? Why I never thought of such a thing!" Study groups instructed mothers to become attuned to the unique personalities of their children and to search for the *causes* of children's actions rather than to label behavior as either good or bad. A mother from New York City spoke of the shift in her own thinking about children: "I used to think they were just naturally naughty for the love of it, but I believe now that they are struggling in an unfamiliar world trying to do the best they know, even as you and I."[53] For those who had previously held to the notion that children should be seen and not heard, the idea that parents must take into account the children's individual needs and personalities was a novel concept.

Mothers' private problems, seemingly insignificant to their family doctors, perhaps even to their husbands, received recognition in this public arena. A mother in a Rochester group confided that it was a relief to her to know that she had not been singled out for "especial martyrdom." As a member of a Sandy Creek, New York, group phrased it: "We all certainly have been helped much in Study Club and these little things which seem small to others does [*sic*] mean a lot to us, to be able to see why child acts as he does and remedy the situation."[54] The successful group was not necessarily one whose members stringently followed the guidelines set by the sponsoring institution. Leaders often admitted that some of the most productive meetings had diverged from the outline of study. In a letter to Cornell, Mrs. Ralph White, a member of a Niagara County club, confessed, "We get lots of discussion but first thing we know, we have gotten off the track. We all enjoy our study group very much."[55] The most successful groups placed the mothers' concerns at the center of the curriculum.

As they developed their understanding of children's care and development, mothers could acquire a more serious interest in the social and behavioral sciences. At the very least, it caused women to think about what made their children tick. The content of child-study groups provided a backdrop for mothers' comparison of their own ideas. Rhoda Denison, a member of a Rochester, New York, group, wrote to Margaret Wylie, director of extension courses for Cornell: "We have received new ideas, of course, and had an opportunity to pick them apart and put them together again, but we also have gotten a very great deal out of intelligent constructive discussion of the problems that come up from time to time." Bessie Guthrie, who led a group in Monroe County, New York, described the transformation of the mothers in her club into learners and thinkers: "Several women told me they just found themselves thinking about various things they do all week. This was apparently a very foreign process, that of thinking, and they [were] very much delighted with themselves."[56] Thinking was carried into daily life, rather than simply inhering in the text.

Group members themselves were instrumental in getting program organizers to structure the clubs to allow for the free play of ideas. Mrs. Walter Quinn's group, which was exceptionally articulate, lively, and long-lived, criticized the didacticism of the Cornell clubs: "If all the questions were not answered for us, if we could use some other answer than 'yes' or 'no' and were given an opportunity to answer in our own way perhaps the interest would be held instead of growing monotony. . . . They [members] like to think things out for themselves."[57] Apparently, this group did maneuver around this didacticism, for it continued meeting at least through 1940. But not all parents objected to didacticism; in fact, some parents requested that they be lectured to, rather than engage in discussion, so that they could more quickly gain access to the information. Perhaps these parents had more clear-cut reasons for attending groups and classes: They simply wanted to acquire information. For the longer-lasting child-study groups, however, it was learning to think critically about expert advice and their own child-rearing strategies that made the groups of value to their members.

The subject matter that mothers were exposed to in groups, however, certainly fostered a psychological approach to life. Historian Sol Cohen has postulated that language use reveals the extent to which individuals have incorporated therapeutic concepts into their worldviews.[58] Whether they resisted particular forms of advice or not, the vocabulary in child-study groups suggests that mothers were imbibing a therapeutic point of view. Mothers used phrases such as "personality," "self-expression," "repression," and "psychological weaning" in speaking about their children and themselves. A leader of a Minnesota Home Bureau group remarked that members had developed a "psychological attitude" toward the situations they encountered and toward other people.[59] The use of the language of psychology is indicative both of the infiltration of psychological concepts into everyday life and of mothers' growing acceptance of responsibility for the emotional well-being of their families.

Mothers were often encouraged by parent educators to seek out professionals—pediatricians and psychiatrists—for help in caring for their children. Even the elite women of the Mothers' Club of Cambridge needed to be told in 1921 that children required yearly physical examinations. In 1933, a Minnesota mother was urged by study group members to consult a doctor about her child's physical malformation and was pleased to find that surgery could correct her child's problem. And group leaders of the Minnesota Home Bureau reported that many mothers who had never taken their children to clinics or dentists had begun to do so.[60]

But mothers were unwilling or unable to use physicians for the entire range of childhood problems. A PTA group from Scranton, New York, read a book on the "tired child" that urged mothers to take such children to the doctor, but the mothers decided that they would prefer to solve such problems on their own. A group secretary queried the Cornell staff: "If a child is not normal for his years aren't there ways a parent can be taught to help the child? All our books say see a psychiatrist. So many parents can't afford that."[61] Finances were clearly an issue in mothers' readiness to consult professionals, but in addition, members objected to the notion that they were unable to handle everyday children's problems without expert help.

Child-study club mothers were cognizant of the increasing emphasis in the medical profession on distinguishing normal from abnormal child development.[62] Professionals urged mothers with "abnormal" children to seek expert assistance. Child guidance professionals quickly extended the definition of "abnormal" during the 1920s to include "tired" children, "dawdlers," "bed-wetters," and fledgling juvenile delinquents. But study group mothers were slower than the experts to extend the definition of abnormal to such everyday childhood problems. Only when the problem was clearly beyond the group's purview—a clear physical malformation, for instance—did they encourage their fellow member to seek professional advice.

The consensus of child-study mothers seemed to be that almost all children—even the worst behaved—were normal and that all mothers were coping with similar problems. A poem recited at a dinner sponsored by the African-American mothers active in the Child Study Association embodies this philosophy:

Mothers' Problems
If a mother has a problem
With her John or Joan—
If she cannot solve this problem
Need a mother groan?

Take her to a study meeting—
There she will be shown
That every other Mother's problem
Is very like her own!

A Minnesota mother testified that the child development project had shown her that "the problems in child development that puzzled and harassed us [were] but the natural growth of the child." Mothers from numerous groups confessed that they had worried about their children but realized as a result of group participation that they were normal.[63] The description of the human life cycle as a sequence of psychosocial stages was also an integral component of the child-study platform. Again, however, the idea that children passed through stages, such as adolescence, was generally invoked by members to quiet parental fears and anxieties. The most troubling teenage or preschool behavior was treated as just a stage the child was passing through.

The records of child-study groups associated with Cornell University and the Minnesota Institute of Child Welfare reveal women engaged in evaluating knowledge in the light of their individual and collective experiences as mothers. A study of lay leaders of parent education groups in New York, many of them associated with the Home Bureau, recorded that although warned by professionals to avoid discussion of personal problems and to bring in examples from the book instead, leaders "often stray from the path professional workers map out for them to follow. *They are forced to do so* [emphasis mine]. Parent groups in general demand an 'experience' meeting and it is all but impossible for the lay leader to keep the discussion on a wholly impersonal plane."[64] Leaders were compelled to stray beyond textbook material because the mothers at the meetings knew the texts did not provide all the answers and that they were more likely to receive help if they aired their problems with other mothers. Although child development professionals during this period displayed little respect for mothers' "nonobjective" knowledge about children, mothers themselves insisted on taking their own experiences and other mothers' common sense as a starting point in constructing an informed philosophy of motherhood.

Chapter 6 Democracy Begins at Home:
The Practice and Politics of Parenting
in the 1930s and 1940s

Published without fanfare in 1938, *Babies Are Human Beings,* by C. Anderson and Mary M. Aldrich, signaled an approach to childhood that returned to the implicit message of G. Stanley Hall: Teach parents about the nature of children's growth and development so that they can evolve appropriate guidance strategies. Acknowledging that at some point children must be taught to conform to the adult world, the Aldriches nonetheless encouraged parents to be more discerning in their attempts to induce conformity: "But if in our management we can learn to be less rigid, to take our cues from the baby himself as he pursues his developmental course, and to urge conformity upon him at periods when he is ready to accept, we will be collaborating with growth and his compromise will be on a more reasonable and satisfying basis."[1] The message that parents should take their cues from their babies in raising them, rather than trying to impose regimentation, would shortly become the dominant ideology within the child development community, and more successful popularizers, such as Arnold Gesell and Benjamin Spock, would package these ideas for the book-buying public.

Changes in the approach to baby's training were just one of the ways in which the parent education movement was modifying its theories of childhood, women, and the family during the 1930s and 1940s. War followed the economic crisis, and children, gender roles, and the family were subject to ideological scrutiny. Child psychologists returned to the theme of development in children's growth and encouraged parental flexibility rather than regimentation. By this time, the impact of psychoanalysis on the profession was profound and educators had come to believe that parents' emotional health was more significant than the acquisition of information in their children's well-being. The cataclysmic economic and political changes led educators to broaden their vision of the family beyond the exclusive mother-child dyad, to include fathers and society at large. Responding to political and economic forces and ideologies, alterations in the research emphases of professional child scientists, and the changing priorities of women who had been participating in study clubs for many years, educators reconfigured the subject material of parents' classes.

FROM TRAINING CHILDREN TO ADJUSTING PARENTS: PARENT EDUCATION IN THE 1930S

Although the parent education movement did not gain significant momentum until the 1920s, by the 1930s it was experiencing a crisis of self-definition. The catastrophe of the Depression threw into question the scientific utopianism of the 1920s. No longer did superior child training seem to be the solution to social problems. According to educator Helen Witmer, the child psychology that had held attraction for parents during an era of prosperity had far less appeal in an unraveling economy.[2]

But sociologists, educators, and psychologists who saw the family as a locus of stability in the midst of an increasingly fractured society delivered a persuasive message. Family life could represent an oasis in the midst of social and economic turbulence, though it would not remain unscathed. The Child Study Association rationalized concentrating on the family during this period: "It represents the most integrated unit in our world of distracted and sundered groups, the most promising symbol, despite its difficulties, of greatly needed unification in our lives." In their study of Middletown families during the 1930s, Robert and Helen Lynd remarked, "Each family seems to wish wistfully that the depression had not happened to *it,* while at the same time feeling that the depression has in a vague general way 'been good for family life.'" Social commentator Louis Adamic noted that although many families were shattered by the destruction of the economy, others ended up "more closely integrated than they had been before the depression," for they were forced to pull together to meet the problems it created.[3] The rhetoric about the family as a unit performing invaluable social and emotional functions may have been strengthened during the Depression. Early twentieth-century commentators had heralded the advent of the democratic family as a replacement for the patriarchal family of the past.[4] The democratic conception of family life however presupposed an ethos of comradeship between parents and children and husbands and wives, which was difficult to maintain in a society that was still divided into separate spheres of activity for mothers and fathers. During the late 1920s, commentators began protesting the absence of the father from family life and his single-minded pursuit of professional success. The premise of the new psychology was that active and engaged husbands were essential to the happiness and emotional adjustment of wives and children. Perhaps the prosperity of the 1920s also gave fathers the luxury to expand the range of their activities beyond the role of breadwinner. Curiously, the social problems generated by the Depression may also have served to promote greater involvement by fathers in family life.

During the Depression, the father's sphere of activity, once predicated on his breadwinning, became increasingly uncertain. Men who were attached to this conception of themselves sometimes left their families, despondent about their inability to find work. But unemployed husbands who remained at home with wives and children had to find ways of surmounting a sense of meaninglessness. Some fathers took advantage of the time at home to forge stronger ties with their children. A Middletown journalist was perhaps being idealistic when he suggested that "more families are now acquainted with their constituent members than at any time since the log-cabin days of America." His account suggested that father was more likely to help Johnny with his homework in the evening.[5] Such a rosy picture of family life was probably unwarranted, but the close proximity in which family members lived during periods of unemployment could generate both intimacy and friction. No longer could mothers and children sequester themselves from the social and political realities that shaped family life; nor could fathers ignore the sustaining role of the family during a period of social change.

Sociologists speculated that "adaptable" families were most capable of withstanding the Depression—and that included husbands who could tolerate working wives or who were willing to pitch in with household chores. But despite what was often a necessary flexibility in roles for women and men, the era contributed to a growing consensus that the married woman's place was in the home. Ideologies of motherhood together with economics turned the tide of public opinion against employed mothers, although the numbers of married women workers continued to rise, primarily in response to economic necessity.[6]

Employed wives were made to feel guilty about having work when so many men were standing in the unemployment lines. Glen Elder interviewed adults who had been raised during the Depression and found that when economic circumstances forced parents into nontraditional gender roles, children viewed the changes as problematic. The children also perceived unemployed fathers as suffering a loss of authority in the home, in relation to both their children and their wives. Sociologists Samuel Stouffer and Paul Lazarsfeld observed: "In the process of damaging the stereotype of 'father,' the Depression may have altered the stereotype of "family."[7] While the male role as breadwinner was increasingly under siege and women wage workers encountered discrimination and public disapproval, women's work in the home went on quietly as before, perhaps gaining increased significance in family life, meanwhile, as masculine economic authority eroded.[8]

The role of children in the family was also being reconceptualized by parent educators, some of whom were backing away from their single-minded 1920s preoccupation with the socialization of young children. As early as 1927, adult educator Eduard Lindeman had suggested that an implicit danger lay in focusing on the needs of children at the expense of parents: "It appears that the so-called 'age of the child' has run its course. Adults are . . beginning to make claims on their own behalf. . . . If sound and happy children are to be produced through the sacrifice of parents, the family will, patently, become an unbalanced institution."[9] In the 1930s, devoting exclusive attention to young children seemed especially inappropriate, given the havoc being wrought in adult lives. In response, parent educators widened the scope of their programs to include broader familial concerns. Study programs that had been termed child development projects or child-study clubs were recast as "family relationships" projects and "family life groups."[10] The family was no longer envisioned as a self-enclosed unit but as a web of relationships with ties to the larger community.

Changes in the content of parent education coincided with the increasing institutionalization of the movement. The National Council on Parent Education was incorporated in 1930, with sponsorship by the Spelman Foundation, to coordinate parent education initiatives nationwide. In 1933, the federally sponsored Works Progress Administration Emergency Nursery School Program inaugurated a nationwide network of nursery schools with parent education classes, to provide jobs for unemployed teachers and ensure that the children of the poor received nutritious meals and health care. The 1930 White House Conference on Children was a landmark event that established a separate committee on parent education and put children's mental hygiene on the national agenda.[11] By the 1930s, the child welfare institutes at the Universities of Minnesota, Iowa, and California had achieved national prominence. The Home Bureau child-study groups, first initiated in the 1920s, burgeoned in the early 1930s.

Conferences, reports, and publications in profusion emerged from the parent education community of the 1930s. Because parent education itself was not a discipline but drew on contributions from a variety of disciplines, such as psychiatry, social work, education, medicine, psychology, and biology—all of which were themselves undergoing transformations—the movement's goals became increasingly obscure. Educators hoped to carve out a separate niche for parent education by characterizing the study of "family life" as a multidisciplinary enterprise, even if its content was unclear. The director of the National Council of Parent Education attempted to map out the terrain of parent education by distinguishing it from other fields of study: "Parent ed is coming to be thought of as education in family life, marriage and parenthood, a type of educational activity separate and different from child development research on the one hand and nursery education on the other."[12]

Meanwhile, child development as a research specialty was gaining in focus and prestige. Fewer researchers appeared interested in putting their scholarship in the service of reform efforts, such as parent education. The history of *Parents' Magazine,* which began publication in 1926 and achieved astounding popularity almost from its founding, reflects the emerging rift between parent educators and child developmentalists. Lawrence Frank, whose philanthropic efforts supported *Parents'* during its early years, attempted to provide for the formal participation of child welfare research institutes in the new magazine, in the hope that popularization and academic excellence could be combined. The two proved to be incompatible, however, and the researchers increasingly distanced themselves from the new magazine.[13]

The divorce between research and educational efforts lent uncertainty to the parent education enterprise, and a scientific basis for the work seemed to be slipping out of the grasp of its proponents. The uncertainty is vividly revealed in a 1932 report for the Parental Advisory Department of the Detroit Public

Schools, which defined parent education as "anything which makes one a better parent."[14] But the question of what made for a 'better parent' had not been answered. Parent educators questioned both the methodology of parent education and definitions of good parenting. They noted the disjunction between their progressive theory of education, which was premised on the notion that students should interact with academic subject material on the basis of their real-life experiences, and their practice, which was often didactic. A 1930 report of the National Council of Parent Education spoke to this phenomenon: "There is still a dominant tendency in parent education, contrary to advanced theory, to *tell* parents what is 'right,' 'wrong,' 'good,' 'bad,' etc."[15] Part of the problem was that the "right" methods of child training in the 1920s were no longer considered to be correct in the 1930s. In the 1920s there had been a broad professional consensus about the validity of behaviorist methods of child training, but by the 1930s child developmentalists were much less sure which styles of parenting were most likely to produce healthy children.

The simple-minded scientism of behaviorism was also being undermined by new concepts about reality being promulgated by physicists, biologists, and engineers that emphasized relativity and randomness. As historian Hamilton Cravens has posited: "Theories of nature predicated on polarities yielded to those stressing interrelatedness." Thus Eduard Lindeman would contend at the 1930 conference of the National Council of Parent Education: "Objectivity and subjectivity are not the absolutely separable units of fact which we once thought them to be; objectivity, which in the statement of the most rigorous of so-called scientific laws, is always interfused and mixed with some degree of subjectivity. Truth, again, is of the situation, not external to human need or purpose." Parent educators across the spectrum agreed that they had been too quick to tell parents what to do during the 1920s, but some still tried to pin the blame on parents. One educator characterized the situation this way: "One of the things they [parents] tell you in despair—I thought two years ago, three years ago, you told us this; is not this what you said?—because they can not get flexible now about moving into new areas of experimentation."[16] Thus the inflexibility of parents rather than the dogmatism of experts was the problem.

The rapid succession of theories of child development induced educators to wonder whether what they really hoped was that parents would assimilate *facts* about children. Whether they admitted it or not, that had been the strong tendency up through the mid-1930s. Parent educators of the 1910s and 1920s had followed in the footsteps of progressive reformers who had faith in the power of factual information to resolve social problems, but as one explanation of child behavior succeeded another, such an approach seemed impractical at best. Educators also noted that the impressive number of facts amassed by reformers and researchers had done little to alleviate the social and economic disarray of the 1930s. More and more parent educators were conceding, "It is more important that parents learn how to learn than it is that they assimilate bits of subject matter."[17] Helen Witmer expressed the view that educators were laboring in the context of a shift in paradigm: "It was the previous assumption that parents were ignorant of the latest scientific discoveries but were well-intentioned and teachable by didactic methods. Under the influence of the new psychology [psychoanalysis] that assumption was modified."[18]

What were now termed parents' groups (although the vast majority of members were still women) consciously oriented themselves toward fulfilling the emotional needs of the members themselves. Mental hygienists postulated that the purging of fears, anxieties, and frustrations would allow individuals to achieve a more harmonious fit with their group. The clinical perspective subtly undermined the conventional structure of the child-study group, which had been predicated on the assumption that education consisted of the conjunction of textual information with the experiences of parents in their everyday lives.

But clinicians insisted that matters were far more complicated than parent educators of the past had believed. The assumption of psychoanalysis was that the fundamental sources of human behavior were unconscious and could therefore be discerned only with expert assistance. Although mothers in child-study groups regularly offered much "inexpert" advice to each other, parent educators were increasingly worried that laypersons were ill equipped to offer other parents psychological advice. Psychiatrists were also critical of parent education, arguing that the peculiar conflicts and intensity of the mother-child relationship would undermine any educational benefits to be derived from groups, lectures, or reading prescriptive literature.[19]

The psychoanalytic perspective led parent educators to question the usefulness of the child-study groups as then conceptualized. Some educators suggested that individual psychiatric consultations might be more useful to troubled parents.[20] Organizations traditionally oriented toward parent education, such as the Child Study Association of America and Chicago's Association for Family Living, instituted clinical consultation services for parents during this period. But the growing clinical orientation of the parent education movement detracted from the consolation and strength that child-study groups had provided for mothers, which had its source in the belief that they could learn from the experience of other mothers and that the problems of mothering were related to the intrinsic difficulty of caring for children, rather than to the emotional difficulties of individual parents.

For less clinically oriented practitioners, the very concept of parent education was called into question by the Depression. One such individual asserted at a parent education conference: "People must feel security, economic, before they can adjust—wages, unemployment insurance. Make people economically secure first, then adjust human relationships." The idea that a family's basic human needs must be met before their psychic needs could be attended to clearly posed a moral quandary for some educators; however, most found ways to justify their work by arguing that strong families were especially needed during a period of economic and social dislocation.[21] Rather than seeking to alter the social system, such courses were designed to help individuals adjust to the social and economic conditions they were confronting.

Despite the state of confusion regarding the appropriate content and methods for parent education during the 1930s, the Home Bureau child-study groups proved to be vital and long-lasting educational institutions. The study group records disclose the processes by which the adult women incorporated psychiatric models for understanding individual and familial values into their conception of themselves and their families. In the 1930s the psychiatric concept of "adjustment" was commonly used to describe a person's psychological health. In his popular text *The Normal Mind,* William Burnham theorized, "The common aim of education and mental hygiene is adjustment. . . . We refer to the evolution of the physical organism as adjustment. We think of normal living as adjustment to one's environment, physical and social."[22] Achieving such normalcy was especially trying in the context of the economic crises of the period, but theorists of adjustment contended that good mental hygiene would enable individuals to cope with whatever situations confronted them. For women the concept of adjustment also encompassed the ability to achieve satisfaction in their prescribed role as wives and mothers.

Fred Matthews, who has chronicled the history of mental hygiene in the 1920s and 1930s, defines "good adjustment" as "acting to win the approval of a postulated community whose norms, once revised along hygienic lines, would be universal and unquestioned."[23] According to him, applied psychology had the potential to promote smooth interpersonal relationships, undercut the competitiveness and aggression so prized in the Victorian era, and mold individuals suited to life in twentieth-century capitalist bureaucracy.[24] But the mental hygiene movement actually drew on two streams of Enlightenment thought, as Theresa Richardson points out: "one, a positivistic rationalism

directed toward controlling social change from positions of authority according
to ideals of order and efficiency; the other a broad based humanism directed
toward perfecting the human condition according to equalitarian principles."
Parent educators applied the twin concepts of mental hygiene—social adjustment and individualism—to the situation of mothers in families. In child-
study groups, women sought to achieve a balance between unremitting devotion to their families and their own need for self-expression both within and
outside of the family.[25]

The function of the "therapeutic approach" was to help the modern mother
to adjust to a changing world. The therapeutic ethos, while lending support to
women's emerging individualism within the context of the family, did not
throw into question the existing social structure based on traditional gender
roles. A 1930s poll for the *Ladies' Home Journal* illuminates the contradictions
implicit in the struggle to form more egalitarian personal relationships within
the traditional family unit. The study showed that a majority of women opposed the use of the word "obey" in marriage vows, advocated equal decision-
making capabilities for husband and wife, and thought that unemployed husbands should do housework. But 90 percent of the women also believed that
married women should abandon careers if their husbands wished them to stay
in the home, a view that leaves intact the notion of a separate and subordinate
sphere for women.[26]

A veiled hostility toward the male role in the family is discernible in parent
education texts. The female college graduates interviewed by researchers at the
Merrill-Palmer School of Homemaking described their spouses as "naive, ego-
centric, spoiled children in their roles as husband and father." According to the
study, men forestalled women's efforts to improve family life: "Wives are continually seeking help on child care and training, sex adjustment, personal
compatibility problems, and the like, while their efforts are resisted by their
husbands." In a sense, the mental hygiene philosophy privileged the traditional
preoccupation of women with relationships and disparaged the masculine
propensity to avoid openly discussing and seeking assistance for family problems. According to historian Elizabeth Lunbeck, who has researched the impact
of psychiatric thinking on American society, "Women appear to have been
better versed in the conventions of self-disclosure on which the psychiatric
analysis of marriage depended, more willing to engage with professionals in a
dialogue about their emotional needs and desires." Mothers may also have
gained some leverage from the ideology of family democracy that permeated
the family life literature, which maligned dictatorial authority. For instance, a

nonfictional account of family life commonly used in parent education classes, *There's No Place Like Home,* by James Lee Ellenwood, contains a chapter entitled "Are You a Dictator?" that cites only examples of male dictatorial behavior.[27]

The curricula of family life groups contained critiques from an explicitly feminist perspective of the division of labor within the family, but the material was often rejected by club members if it did not positively acknowledge their roles as wives and mothers. Members were sympathetic to readings that disparaged dictatorial husbands, as well as to those which spoke of the necessity for homemakers to develop their identity as individuals, without neglecting their responsibilities as wives and mothers. Both the forms of self-disclosure encouraged in the clubs and the emerging therapeutic ethos conveyed in the readings and discussions could provide women with tools for examining the psychodynamics of family life and the power differential that underlay those dynamics. Therapeutic language could provide women with useful artillery in their struggle to become equal partners with their spouses. But the therapeutic approach also opened the door to discontent when women confronted psychic needs that could not be met in their family lives.[28]

"ARE FATHERS PARENTS?": GENDER AND FAMILY LIFE COURSES

Family life courses were intended to address issues of concern to the entire family, but educators took into consideration that their primary constituency was women. Sociologists, who had pioneered in the study of family relationships, took as their starting point the breakdown of the traditional patriarchal family. Acknowledging that gender roles were in a state of flux, influential sociologists such as Ernest Groves and William Fielding Ogburn posited that the democratic family was more able than the hierarchical family to cope with the vicissitudes of modern life. They entended that the dislocations in the family were generated by the tensions women felt between the mandates of individualism inculcated by society and the requirement for subservience of the traditional marriage. In their text *American Marriage and Family Relationships* (1938) Groves and Ogburn hypothesized: "The modern wife cannot be trained to enjoy self-expression and to maintain personality and at the same time be asked by marriage to enter upon a program of constant self-effacement."[29] Experts in family relationships maintained that if marriage was to adapt to modern conditions, women must be allowed to partake of some of the benefits of individualism.

Family life courses attempted to reconcile the competing claims of individuality and community within the family. Educators did not propose that the family be radically restructured or that mothers eschew their domestic and familial responsibilities. But they recommended that fathers become more engaged in family life and that mothers maintain their individuality, because democratic family life depended on the involvement and self-realization of each member of the family.

In the process of studying the broader network of family relationships, child-study groups inaugurated discussions of marital relationships. Group members encouraged one another to demand more emotional involvement from their husbands. Study group leaders, in emphasizing democracy in family relationships, advocated resolving problems through a "family council." Ada Hart Arlitt described the democratic family as an organization that allows the individual to "develop in line with his own interests and his individual capacities." When each parent had an equal voice in the family, familial conflict could result. A reporter for the Minnesota Home Bureau suggested that the growing propensity for the mother to assert her point of view had resulted in "more thrashing out of problems—less peace at any price."[30] Rather than putting the onus for the family's emotional well-being solely on mothers, the new philosophy held all family members responsible for the maintenance of sound family relationships.

At the turn of the century, members of the Child Study Association had regarded fathers' absence from the home as a not necessarily regrettable fact of life, but by the 1920s women were complaining audibly about their spouses' lack of involvement in family life. By the 1930s the absentee father had become a recurrent theme of the parent education movement. At the 1930 White House Conference on Child Health and Protection, Sidonie Gruenberg protested: "From being an active participant in all the significant activities in the home the father has been steadily converted into a provider." Cornell sponsored a panel discussion entitled "Are Fathers Parents?" which was no doubt designed both to provoke and to prod. A joke told in a child-study group exemplifies the concern with the absent father: "The father was a traveling man only home on Sunday and the small child went crying home to his mother 'That man who is here on Sundays spanked me!'"[31] It is doubtful that men were substantially more preoccupied with their roles as providers during this period than earlier, because late nineteenth-century mothers had also commented on the phenomenon of absentee fathers. What is clear is that by the 1930s both mothers and professionals were increasingly pressuring fathers to participate in the emotional life of the family.

Since the 1920s, parent educators had made a sustained effort to include fathers under the rubric of "parents" in their programs, through both the organization of fathers' groups and what were termed "mixed" parents' groups. Even though these efforts did not yield substantial results, some fathers' groups were established—and took on quite a different character from that of mothers' groups. The California parent education program attempted to institute the "home project" method, through which fathers would test the validity of child development concepts in their interactions with children. The project was unsuccessful, though, because of "the scanty contact between the fathers and their children." Many of the fathers who participated in parent education programs were upper-middle-class professionals whose careers undoubtedly absorbed a great deal of their time. Certainly, if even fathers who were interested enough in parenting to attend classes had only "scanty" contact with their children, minimal father-child interaction must have been as much of a problem as child-study mothers had made it out to be.

When fathers did attend classes, their approaches to children's problems were quite different from those of their female counterparts. Educator Herbert Stolz commented on a fathers' group that was studying adolescence: "Both the age of the children considered and the customary male viewpoint tended to focus attention upon community participation in the solution of the problems of youth."[32] Unlike many mothers, who were willing to accept personal responsibility for the psychological well-being of their children, fathers placed greater responsibility for their children's problems on society as a whole.

When parent education classes included both men and women, gender differences manifested themselves in both educational styles and the content of the classes. Herbert Stolz, who directed the California parent education program and worked with men in both mixed and all-male settings, reflected on some of the barriers to male participation in mixed parents' groups: "The great majority of men shift most of their responsibility for training their children upon the mothers and tend to resent any effort to persuade them to help carry the load. Moreover, the resentment is enhanced when the group leader and the mothers in a mixed meeting appear to conspire against the titular head of the family. In discussing problems of child raising in a mixed group all but a few men feel as necessary as their wives would feel in a discussion of the day's events on the stock market."[33] The backing mothers gained for their child-rearing strategies and point of view in child-study groups could disrupt the traditional pattern of male authority in the family. Parents' groups were intended to lessen the gap between fathers and mothers, but the gap was sometimes too wide.

Several parents' groups for couples in New York modified the conventional structure of the child-study group to reflect male perspectives. Unlike their female counterparts, many men found that mere discussions of family problems were not enough to hold their interest. Fathers proposed that the group visit model kitchens sponsored by the Home Bureau, and decided to have the club engage in "shop nights," during which men made furniture and toys, and women made Christmas decorations. In another "married couples' group" in New York, described as a "keen live group of young people," the female members of the group were willing to rely on books and their own experiences as the subject matter for the course, whereas the men were eager to invite experts to speak to the group.[34]

Although men were often hesitant to become involved in discussions of family life, child study's purported reliance on scientific techniques held some appeal for them. Traditional gender ideologies associated fathers with rationality, mothers with emotion. Some men appreciated mothers' efforts to bring "rational" methods to child training. A mother who was purchasing a child-care book asserted: "My husband wants me to have one, so he can read it too. He thinks the club should be for fathers also." For some women, though, participation in child study represented a critical act of independence and had the potential to bolster their authority in the home by attaching their child-rearing decisions to an objective standard of expertise.[35]

Insisting that it was difficult to put child-study precepts into practice without their husbands' cooperation, mothers commonly protested about fathers' absence from parent education classes. Their complaints were buttressed by studies reporting that men were much less likely than women to avail themselves of child development expertise. A survey of American families conducted in 1930 found that 45.8 percent of the mothers interviewed had at some point attended a child-study or PTA meeting, as opposed to only 13.2 percent of the fathers. Mothers were also more likely than fathers to have read articles on child care in newspapers and magazines—73.9 percent of mothers as compared to 36.7 percent of fathers.[36]

Mothers who assiduously read books and attended classes and lectures to better themselves as parents were clearly bothered by these discrepancies. A Minnesota Home Bureau leader reported, "Our one regret is that the men do not get it. Some of the husbands devour all the material and talk the lesson over with their wives, others are indifferent. All of the women wish men could come to meetings." In response to a query about whether she would like to attend a parents' meeting, one Nashville mother complained, "Fathers and mothers need help, but mothers shouldn't be asked to go to meetings. Whatever is given should be for fathers as well as mothers." The women's complaints about the lack of a masculine presence in parent education classes suggests an implicit awareness that expert knowledge was helping further differentiate "modern mothers" from their more traditional, authoritarian, perhaps even patriarchal, spouses. Mothers obviously felt, moreover, that the challenges of child rearing were more than they could handle on their own.[37]

Parent educators were in the forefront of attempts to bring fathers into the mainstream of family life. The psychological literature underscored the idea that fathers' absence imperiled family life, and in particular children's sex role development. The United Parents Association of New York urged the disbanding of mothers' clubs and their conversion into parents' associations, "it being possible to trace many defects in personality development to the aloof attitude of the father towards the child's problems." Of course, one of the educators' motivations for bringing fathers into family life was fear of increasing maternal influence in the home, but women themselves were apparently expecting more emotional responsiveness from their marital partners. According to Groves and Ogburn, "Not only do women demand more of life; they also demand more of their husbands."[38]

The child-rearing literature went beyond asking men to be available to their children to aid in their emotional and sexual adjustment; fathers were exhorted to alter their patterns of interaction with children. The traditional patriarchal father remained a distant figure who demanded implicit obedience; the modern father celebrated by parent educators returned from work to romp as a "pal" with his children. In his study of the history of fatherhood Robert L. Griswold remarks, "Not surprisingly, the idea of fathers as buddies clashed with traditional views of patriarchal authority. . . . The modern middle-class father was now seen as a kindly, nurturing democrat who shared rather than monopolized power."[39] But the ideal father was perhaps an even greater distortion of reality than the ideal mother, who at least received a constant barrage of information and encouragement.

The role of the father—both as an ideal and as a reality—was frequently discussed in child-study groups. During a meeting on the topic "What Is the Role of the Father?" group members conceded that father should "become acquainted with his children" by periodically taking responsibility for baths, meals, and bedtimes. Yet they did not go as far as some of the professionals and imagine that all fathers could be "pals" with their children: women objected that it was beyond the capacities of some men to get down on their knees and play with kids. Most agreed, however, that it was time for fathers to do more than make money and administer punishment.[40]

From the professional point of view, a fatherly influence in the family was needed to offset maternal intensity. Excessive maternal control had made children dependent on their mothers and had alienated them from their fathers. In discussing the lack of paternal involvement in child rearing, a group from Erie County, New York, agreed that a father should be regarded as more than a "pocketbook" or "furnace tender." They also agreed with some professionals that mothers thwarted fathers' attempts to be closer to their children. The desire to maintain maternal control was reflected in the deliberations at another club meeting, where some members insisted that they were perfectly happy to handle their children's discipline without their husbands' help.[41]

Strikingly absent from these discussions is any analysis of the division of labor in the family. Within the family, mothers often dealt with problems that arose from differences related to gender and power, but they did not assume that addressing the problems meant changing the basic structure of the family—and indeed few were willing to challenge it openly.[42]

Women clearly valued the opportunity to participate in an exclusively female organization and cherished their evenings away from husbands and children. Mrs. Walter Quinn, who led such a study group in New York, acknowledged: "We certainly do enjoy ourselves at what the men call our 'hen parties' (no men or children allowed). The fathers stay at home with the children on child-study nights."[43] Women from Middletown, New York, met together but for the first couple of years included their husbands only at the group's social gatherings. Once they had developed the requisite leadership skills, though, they felt confident enough to invite the husbands to some meetings to get the "fathers' viewpoints": "This year no one had the courage to lead a meeting with men present but now everyone seems to have gained confidence and I think we can show our husbands that we really do accomplish a lot."[44]

In theory clubwomen recognized that it was desirable for mothers to develop interests outside the family. But it was often difficult, practically speaking, for mothers to pursue their interests, even activities related to family life, such as parent education. Study group leader Delia Huston wrote: "Thinking and studying about family life makes one see beneath the surface into the deeper meaning of one's family relationships—even at the very time the family is interfering with the freedom of the precious work and study hours."[45] It is paradoxical that in this case study group participation served to introduce a woman to the pleasures of work and study and also caused her to view her family as an impediment to the pursuit of these pleasures.

Even though mothers insisted that participation in the group contributed to their ability to perform their role in the family, some husbands viewed all women's activities outside the home as a challenge to masculine domination. A cautionary tale was told in a Cornell group about a mother with several children who had put them to bed and left them in the care of their father while she went off to her meeting. On her return home, she found that the father had displayed his resentment by leaving the children alone in the house. When she next attempted to go to a club meeting, the father stayed home for the first time in several weeks to make sure the mother did not leave the house, because "women's place is in the home." Not many such dramatic stories about interaction with husbands made their way into meeting minutes. The leader noted, though, that after the incident was recounted, few of the women with younger children continued to attend the group meetings. The leader's implication was that their confidence in their husbands' ability to care for the children had been shaken.[46]

Men worried about the impact of study clubs on their wives may have inferred correctly that their wives' introduction to the philosophy of mental hygiene could make them more reflective about their lives and circumstances. Elizabeth Lunbeck theorizes that "men rightly perceived women's talk as a challenge to the undisputed authority they imagined themselves commanding within the household."[47] Mothers' problems, worries, joys, and frustrations had been the real subject matter of child-study groups throughout their history. When mothers talked about children's fears and inhibitions, they often found themselves discussing their own fears, anxieties, and dilemmas or felt inspired to share memories of their earliest childhood experiences. A Cornell mother confessed that as a child she had lived in fear that her father would commit suicide and so hid his razor every day before leaving for school. According to the secretary of this group, "It is very easy to get the group to talk about their own thoughts and feelings."[48] The confessional nature of some of the meetings reveals a commonly held belief that talking about traumas would help restore inner harmony. In fact, such talk could easily lead to greater dissatisfaction by bringing to light the dilemmas at the core of women's lives as wives and homemakers that the group lacked the resources to resolve.

The child-study group's penchant for delving into members' life experiences probably spurred administrative efforts to come up with courses centering on the perceived needs and interests of the members themselves. These courses also reflected the 1930s preoccupation with self-improvement manifested in such best-selling texts as Dale Carnegie's *How To Win Friends and Influence People.* Self-improvement emerged as a major theme in study groups during the mid- to late 1930s.[49] Family life projects at Cornell and the University of Minnesota sponsored courses with such titles as "The Homemaker Herself" and "About Ourselves," which were eagerly adopted by clubwomen.

Mothers' needs were increasingly brought to the fore. Magazine articles and books decried the old-fashioned self-sacrificing mother as dominating her children and hindering their independence. And quite apart from the negative effects on children of maternal overindulgence, it was destructive for the mother, too. Educators alluded to the "empty nest syndrome" that afflicted many women after their children had grown. In a Cornell group the point was reinforced with vigilance: "*Don't neglect yourself* as a member of the family. . . . Some mothers . . . when the children are grown they find themselves lacking; the husband and family having progressed. As you go along *train yourself for later life.*" Mothers were encouraged to pursue personal agendas and allow other family members to take care of themselves. According to a mother with the Minnesota Home Bureau: "This lesson helped me realise that the most serious problem is myself. I have allowed my family to depend on me too much. My family will hereafter receive suggestions and be urged to work things out for themselves." A group from Sandy Creek, New York, decided that the way to handle children who behaved disrespectfully was to leave the house or pretend to be sick so that children could see what it was like to take care of themselves.[50]

The groups were designed, in part, to counter frustration in the homemaker and to help her adjust to her situation as a wife and mother; thus, the subject of the homemaker's happiness or lack thereof was an ever-present theme. An Orange County, New York, group explored the topic "The Human Quest," but the meeting really centered on the homemaker and her happiness. One of the mothers asked if the homemaker should act happy if she really wasn't. Although the group's response to her question was not recorded, the prevailing philosophy in family life groups was that happiness was a maternal responsibility. At a Niagara County, New York, group meeting on the topic of keeping mentally fit, it was proposed that "unhappiness is a sign of maladjustment." A member of a group from Orange County, New York, gave a talk called "Understanding Yourself," in which she urged that wives should remain cheerful in dealings with their husbands and "not complain but be as loving as before married."[51] Individuality was not to be achieved through a sacrifice of the marital relationship.

The amount of time devoted to discussions of the homemaker's happiness suggests that it was not an ideal easily achieved by child-study mothers. A group of university women from Syracuse, New York, discussed "the question of frustration in the mother, its cause, effects, and possible cure." Advice about dealing with unhappiness was an amalgam of positive thinking and hard-headed realism. A long-lasting and intimate Hilton, New York, group sponsored a course on "personality," and members listed things that made them "go to pieces." One of the members asked the group how she should cope with her own "scars of childhood." The members advised her to "face facts" and "solve problems." But the questioner sighed and said that "we are too hurried in our lives with our families not to make mistakes."[52] Although the groups provided homemakers with the opportunity to express their fears and worries, other club members usually urged them to get on with their lives, to make the best of what they had, to "adjust" themselves to their situations.

Because by this time many of the women in both the New York and Minnesota Home Bureau clubs were approaching middle age, home economics faculty developed courses for homemakers specifically pertaining to this period in their lives. Several groups studied "Problems of the Middle Years," to confront the issue of careers for women whose children had grown; other groups considered "The Health Problems of Women Over Forty." The syllabi for the courses included such titles as "Careers After Forty," "Life Begins at Forty," and "I Love Life at Seventy." Women also requested and were provided with study materials and speakers on menopause, although very little of the subject matter made its way into meeting minutes. The records suggest, however, that the readings helped put to rest some misconceptions that women had about menopause. A Buffalo group's discussion served to counter some members' belief that menopause caused insanity in a normal person. According to the secretary: "The women in the group who have reached the menopause feel that they have been greatly aided by the discussion and have lost many of their fears concerning it. The rest of us feel that when it comes to us we can meet it calmly." At another meeting members wondered if doctors were able to help women who were "suffering" through menopause. Sessions on menopause often generated discussions about possibilities for women who were past childbearing age. At one such meeting a member displayed a newspaper clipping urging that schools be opened to offer middle-aged women job training. What to do with one's life once the children no longer needed one's constant attention was in fact a favorite topic of conversation.[53]

Notwithstanding concern in the groups about women's roles, only occasionally did clubwomen grapple with feminist issues head on. Over the course of five years, the South Alabama, New York, group periodically discussed the question of sexual equality. In 1935, they debated whether it was better for children when the mother or father is "superior." Although they conceded that children would benefit from having a superior mother, they also thought that if the wife looked down on her husband there was "bound to be trouble." In 1940 the group considered the topic "It's a Man's World and Why" and examined the ways in which New York State law discriminated against women in relation to property and child custody. Mrs. Leo Mack's group from Monroe, New York, also held extensive discussions about women's rights. One meeting centered on whether the winning of suffrage had benefited women. The group admitted that the vote had helped alleviate legal injustices against women and had undermined the symbolic basis of male authority. But more important to group members than the right to vote itself was the greater creativity that they believed attention to women's rights had fostered in their home life. Club members appreciated both the developments in household technology and the various educational opportunities and organizational activities related to twentieth-century homemaking.[54]

This group also subjected women's role as mothers to scrutiny, conceding that although women were no longer exclusively "childbearers," it was best for women to remain in the home after marriage. The group also debated whether wives should receive a salary, and while some members argued that a salary would enhance the homemaker's sense of self and afford her access to her own money, others contended that wages would relegate the wife to the status of a servant. Both sides agreed, however, that under the present circumstances, wives should consider their husband's salary as their own.[55]

Child-study group mothers were far from radical when it came to their attitudes toward gender. They tended to be uncomfortable with divorce and could be critical of mothers who did not live up to their standards of maternal and wifely responsibility. The mental hygiene approach, though, with its emphasis on the needs of the individual, gave mothers license to consider how their familial roles impinged on their ability to fulfill personal goals. They also gained rhetorical tools to elicit increased respect from the family for their requirements as individuals.

The emphasis on adult mental hygiene did not suit all the women who signed up for family life groups, however. A Monroe County group examining the topic "Keeping Mentally Fit" questioned the emphasis in the materials assigned: "The answer that the better we understand ourselves, the better we can understand our children, does not furnish the majority with sufficient reasons for the perusal of this particular book." This group was also more resistant to the mental hygiene precepts promoted in the courses than were the majority of study group women. Mrs. Palmer cited a sentence from a group text: "The adult who comes into most frequent conflict with the adolescent is an adult who has not fully grown up—is immature." According to Palmer, "This drew fire from the group and was not well received!"[56] These women rejected the notion that the construction of their individual personalities was relevant to their children's development. They had come to study groups hoping to learn techniques for dealing with children's behavior and were not interested in engaging in dissections of parental psychology.

Resistance to the mental hygiene point of view emerged in other contexts as well. The idea that one's external appearance reflects one's inner sense of self came up in a Genesee County group session. One of the members quipped that "she hoped her body didn't express her." Regarding the importance of appearance, the Clinton, New York, study club vigorously objected to the psychological profiles based on body types that were then in vogue, flatly stating: "We also disagree quite firmly with Mr. Groves as to his rather arbitrary typing of individuals. Some of us are *not* nervous because we happen to be thin or placid and calm because we are fat." Another group of women from rural New York disagreed with the mental hygienists' posing the extrovert as the ideal personality type: "If with right environment everyone could be an extrovert—would it be well? We decided it would not." The phrase "we decided it would not" shows once again the important role played by the club as a community: the women came to a collective agreement about the validity of their reading material. The group from Ulster County, New York, did not reject all aspects of the mental hygiene philosophy, but they felt free to arrive at these critical assessments in the company of other "inexpert" women.[57]

The pursuit of mental hygiene and individual adjustment remained at the core of the family life group discussions, but the issues raised by the Depression also inevitably found their way into the meetings, although unemployment is rarely mentioned in meeting minutes. In many areas of the country, group membership faltered, because of illness, family problems, or lack of reliable transportation. In 1931 a group leader from Oneida County, New York, complained to headquarters that her members could not afford to purchase the lesson materials; at least six of the mothers in the group had husbands who had been employed only part-time through the winter. Numerous groups appear to have lost momentum as a result of personal and economic crises in their families. Georgie Watkins wrote to Margaret Wylie in 1931 about her Monroe County group: "One woman lost her child to a brain tumor, and with the unemployment situation and their personal depression they have allowed themselves to become so harassed."[58]

The Depression manifested itself in less obvious ways as well. The in-law problem was widely discussed, because families were often thrown together for financial reasons during the 1930s. In general, groups corroborated the sociological view that living with in-laws was problematic, although some mothers thought that the problems had been exaggerated. Minnesota Home Bureau chapters raised the issue of children who, for economic reasons, were not receiving adequate medical and dental attention, and the mothers in the groups worked to garner improved care for their children during the crisis.[59]

The next step for many child-study mothers was becoming involved in public work to alleviate some of the problems that concerned them. According to a reporter for the Minnesota Home Bureau: "Not all women are satisfied with just a study project. They want to take things into their own hands." Some mothers were inspired to start local PTA chapters. Members of Minnesota Home Bureau clubs established child health and immunization days in their communities, lobbied for improved recreational facilities for children, and campaigned to include books on vocational and sex education in school libraries. Other groups established playschools, local libraries, and day-care centers. This description of a meeting in a rural New York suburb illustrates the kinds of social activities that club members were involved in: "The meeting began with complaints of the closing of the branch library a few doors away; that led to planning a petition for reopening it. One group member was concerned about traffic accidents at a corner near the school, and proposed petitioning the city council to declare one of the streets a one-way street." Some clubs made the leap beyond child-related advocacy. Members of a Coldwater, New York, group, who by 1936 had been studying children for three years, decided that they were ready to move on to the study of civics and current events. And an Oneida County, New York, group speculated in 1939: "Could a group like ours help in cleaning up rotten politics?" Although I found no evidence that child-study groups contributed to a rise in female political agitation, coteries of small-town and rural women throughout the country were no doubt motivated to work for improvements in their towns and communities as a result of their participation in study groups.[60]

MOTHERHOOD IN WARTIME

The Depression was soon overshadowed by the crisis of World War II, an event which, like the Depression, illuminated both the changes and continuities in women's lives. War often has the effect of catapulting some women into non-traditional sex roles, but wartime rhetoric often relies on stereotypical notions of the civic responsibilities of men and women. In a radio broadcast from New York's Baby Institute in 1944, pediatrician Edith Jackson pronounced: "In a world at war, mothers still sing to their babies. The proper care and training, the development of our children, is as essential to true and final victory as the warfare on our fighting fronts." Jackson's belief that child rearing represented the pinnacle of women's patriotic responsibilities was widely held. In one of the many articles of the period detailing the dangers in mothers' working, Henry Zucker insisted: "A mother's greatest patriotic contribution lies in her responsibility to her children." And another commentator intoned: "If they carry out their pregnancies successfully, this is the most patriotic job they can do."[61] Although mothers with older children were urged to work, the official policy of the Manpower Commission was that mothers of small children should continue to be full-time mothers. While the number of working wives rose tremendously during the war years, approximately two thirds of adult women continued to be full-time homemakers.[62] Many mothers with young children continued to identify with the homemaker's role, yet their conception of it was continually being altered by the pervasiveness of a therapeutic ethos that focused on the attainment of individual satisfaction.

The patriotic responsibility of motherhood was no less subject to public scrutiny and ideologies arising out of the wartime experience than was women's wage work during the same period. Homemakers were bombarded with theories of optimal family life that embodied the political ideologies of the period, which historian Sonya Michel has termed the "discourse of the democratic family." Popular child-rearing works challenged parents to adopt democratic child-rearing strategies, using powerful political terminology to reinforce concepts of the ideal American family held by progressive thinkers since the turn of the century. The 1940 White House Conference on Children, in characterizing the family as the "threshold of democracy" and enjoining mothers to participate in the task of raising democratic citizens, mirrored and modified the rhetoric of republican motherhood of the revolutionary era.[63]

According to the ideology, the democratic family provided a favorable environment for the personality development of all its members and employed nonauthoritarian discipline and decision making. Experts warned of the dangers to the family and the polity posed by "authoritarian" personalities and speculated about the child-rearing practices likely to produce such personalities. Robert Dalton, head of Child Development and Family Life at Cornell University, contended: "If we want citizens who are able to share freely the responsibilities and privileges of a democratic society it is incumbent upon us to determine the kind of character structure which will enable the individual to exercise most fully the energies which are his."[64] Of course, once social scientists had decided what the most desirable "character structure" should be, mothers would be expected to mold their child-rearing strategies to the cultural mandate.

The application of the concept of democracy to family life was by no means an ideological innovation; it had its roots in the nineteenth century, when more child-centered theories of child rearing took hold in America. Both in the nineteenth century and in its 1940s context, the concept was most influential with the native urban middle class, but it took on heightened meaning in the context of the battle between democracy and fascism. Social scientists speculated on the authoritarian child-rearing patterns that had engendered a German populace susceptible to the temptations of fascism and argued that democratic child-rearing practices were essential to the maintenance of democracy.[65] This idea made for great media headlines, highlighting the superiority of American child-rearing practices and reinforcing the patriotic responsibilities of American mothers. In an article entitled "How *Not* to Raise Our Children," Harriet Eager Davis characterized German parenting practices as "socially destructive" and contrasted them with "our American progressive methods," which were "sound and mature."[66]

The discourse of the democratic family provided a critique of behaviorist child-rearing practices that up until the late 1930s achieved both popular and professional legitimation. Of course, the new thinking had not yet filtered down to many pediatricians, who continued to instruct mothers in the practices recommended by the behaviorists. As sociologist Alfred Baldwin astutely noted in a study comparing democratic child-rearing practices with behaviorist practices, "It often seems that by the time a theory has been put into actual practice by parents, it is no longer accepted."[67] But mothers who continued to rely on scheduled feedings and who avoided picking up the baby when it cried, to avoid spoiling him, were increasingly subject to criticism.

Studies appeared throughout the 1940s suggesting that behaviorist parenting strategies were more damaging than beneficial to children. Nursery school teacher Dorothy Baruch described the upper-middle-class children at her school as victims of "certain frustrating cultural impositions." According to Baruch, "Almost all their mothers have tried hard to learn the 'correct' methods of child rearing and have attempted to carry them out to the letter of the law." It was the mothers who had most closely followed the advice of experts, she maintained, whose children were the most maladjusted. They exhibited behavior problems that she believed grew out of "deprivation of cuddling experiences; rigid feeding schedules; early toilet training, usually starting under the age of 6 months; and the parental policy of letting the baby 'cry it out.'" Another study more explicitly linked the differences in parental practices to class and concluded that working-class children "do not meet as many frustrations as do the middle-class children." The researchers W. Allison Davis and Robert J. Havighurst studied the parenting practices of middle- and lower-class white and African-American parents and discovered that class was a more significant factor than race in determining child-rearing methods: middle-class parents were more apt to regulate their children's habits and play. For a brief time, working-class parents, who had previously been dismissed as uneducated and neglectful in their child-rearing practices, appeared to have an edge over those middle-class parents who continued dutifully to follow the recommendations of the behaviorists. It seems ironic that during this period those parents most out of touch with "scientific" parenting techniques were judged to have the best adjusted children—the opposite of what parent educators had intended.[68]

In the new child-rearing literature, mothers were urged to gently encourage children's development rather than to impose systematic regimentation. The baby book gurus of the 1940s, Arnold Gesell and Frances Ilg, promoted the new developmentalist point of view in their popular text, *Infant and Child in the Culture of Today.* The text's pivotal concept was "growth," a process that the authors argued was antithetical to dictatorial parental training: "The concept of growth has much in common with the ideology of democracy." According to the theory, children's psychosocial development was guided by inherent biological mechanisms that were impervious to parental training; indeed, embedded in the very notion of parental training were the seeds of fascism: "If parents and teachers begin with the assumption that they can make over and mold a child into a preconceived pattern, they are bound to become autocratic." The notion of individual differences was an important component in the philosophy of democratic child rearing. Children might be different in their rates of growth, their personalities, their upbringings, or their cultures. Recognizing that human beings are different and yet equal was the goal for parents in relation to their children as it was for citizens in relation to each other. In a manual on parent education for preschool teachers, Edith Norton stressed this point: "In a democratic society the goal is not to make all people think and act in the same way, like and dislike the same things. Equal, not identical, is the ideal. Genuine acceptance of differences without prejudice and criticism is basically important in any kind of good human relations." From Gesell's point of view, parents must be aware early on of children's uniqueness and develop techniques of child rearing that allowed them to grow up to be the individuals they were meant to be.[69]

Gesell was part of a larger movement within the child development community to promote feeding on demand, as opposed to the scheduled feedings advocated by the behaviorists. According to *Infant and Child in the Culture of Today,* scheduled feedings were more appropriate for an authoritarian political regime: "A totalitarian type of culture would place the first and last premium upon the extrinsic cultural pattern; it would have little patience with self-demands."[70] This point was reiterated by Gesell at the White House Conference on Children in a Democracy in 1940: "Strict adherence to regimen (for its own sake) in the habit training period, and unreasonable demands of parents (just to establish their authoritative position) in the next years, lead only to the child's rebellion against all authority."[71] Parents wishing to produce children who neither slavishly followed the dictates of authorities nor acted out their aggression in the form of juvenile delinquency were enjoined to adopt democratic child-rearing practices.

Professionals of many different persuasions found common ground in their advocacy of more child-centered parenting practices. Gesell and his colleagues at the Yale Clinic of Child Development were not psychoanalytically inclined, yet much of their specific advice to parents about the treatment of young children was not much different from the recommendations of psychoanalysts. While Gesell and his fellow researchers were less likely than their psychoanalytic counterparts to attribute childhood problems to parental behaviors, both groups agreed that early childhood should be a time of relatively relaxed guidance and that parents should attempt to meet, rather than regulate, children's physical and emotional needs. Psychoanalyst John Dollard and his colleagues at the Yale Institute for Human Relations published an enormously influential book in 1939 entitled *Frustration and Aggression.* They contended that "aggression is always a consequence of frustration" and connected the frustration of young children with most personal and social ills. This concept had immediate ramifications for child care, because early toilet training and scheduled feedings were seen as major sources of frustration in young children, which had the potential for producing aggressive adults.[72]

With the exception of the Gesell group—which believed that children's temperaments were primarily due to their genetic inheritance—most experts conceded the centrality of mothering in producing happy and productive, or unhappy and maladjusted, citizens. According to psychologist David Levy, whose book *Maternal Overprotection* (1943) received widespread attention, "The play of social responses between mothers and children would then represent the foundation of social life, and its investigation the pivotal attack on the problem of social behavior." Thus societal problems were in no small part a product of faulty mothering. The key problem, according to Levy, was mothers' "overprotection" of their children, which was linked to women's "unconscious hostility" toward their role as females. This hostility could be manifested by either career or stay-at-home mothers, who either overprotected *or* rejected and neglected their children. Since the hostility was unconscious, few mothers could conclude that they were without it.[73]

Whether or not they were full-time homemakers, mothers were subjected to vigorous attacks during the 1940s for their presumed failure at the job of mothering. Experts harped on the entire spectrum of negative maternal behaviors. Philip Wylie coined the term "momism" in his best-selling book *A Generation of Vipers,* and army psychiatrist Edward A. Strecker also used the expression in magazine articles and his influential account of shell-shocked GI's, *Their Mothers' Sons.* Blaming mothers for GIs' cracking under the strain of war, Strecker defined "mom" as "the woman who has failed in the elementary mother function of weaning her offspring emotionally as well as physically." Many commentators worried about the effects of the so-called matriarchal family, which resulted from father's absence from the family, whether owing to wartime exigencies or to the all-consuming task of breadwinning. According to Strecker, momism was the result of a "social system veering toward matriarchy."[74]

While Strecker and Levy were primarily concerned with the excessive power and influence of mothers, others feared the impact on the family of mothers' working and blamed the increased rates of juvenile delinquency on this development. In an article on "latchkey children" Henry Zucker claimed: "The house key tied around the neck is the symbol of cold meals, of a child neglected and shorn of the security of a mother's love and affection." Only the mother could be a proper caretaker, according to Zucker, who worried that grandmothers and neighbors could do "irreparable damage" to children by being either "oversolicitous" or neglectful.[75] Powerful studies of the emotional damage inflicted on institutionalized children bolstered the case for mothers' profound impact on the development of children. Psychologists Anna Freud and Dorothy Burlingham's studies of children who had been separated from their parents during wartime reinforced the importance of the mother-child bond, as did Renée Spitz's studies of hospitalized children.[76]

Mothers were charged with maintaining a harmonious emotional atmosphere in the home, with ensuring that family members had the security necessary to offset the strains of war. They were expected to provide children with emotional shields to withstand tumultuous times. One commentator noted: "Stable children take war in their stride when properly guided." And she told a story of a mother who wondered how she should calm her five-year-old daughter, who was terrified of the war. The mother was told: "Her present state may be *intensified* by knowledge of real dangers . . . but it is not *caused* by these things. If she were given greater security at home, her terror would decrease." Most experts maintained that parents should be honest with their children about the war and its ramifications, but insisted that emotionally healthy homes would produce children who could handle the terror and insecurity of war.[77]

Mothers were also enjoined to rear tolerant children who would be able to transcend the racial and ethnic biases of their parents' generation. American biases were glaringly at odds with the ideals of American democracy, and seemed even more threatening when juxtaposed to the racial hatreds that had spawned the war in Europe. Teaching that children are born without prejudice, popular personalities such as Pearl Buck and Hodding Carter urged parents to encourage their children to make friends from diverse backgrounds, and progressive educators advocated the adoption of intercultural education in the public schools that would integrate materials on non-European peoples into the curriculum.[78]

Parent educators also insisted that children should not be taught to hate either the enemy or American citizens of Japanese or German origin. In 1944, the PTA resolved to assist Japanese-Americans, both in relocation camps and in resettling once they were allowed to leave. One of the association's goals was to "create public understanding of the problems of Japanese-Americans." At the same convention the group proclaimed "the necessity of doing away with race prejudices and racial discrimination and of providing equal rights and opportunities for all American citizens regardless of race, color, and creed."[79] In an article entitled "Democracy Before Five!" C. Madeline Dixon remonstrated with the readers of *Parents' Magazine,* "Regardless of our narrow prejudices, if we win this war, we are going to find ourselves living in a world which not only demands wider tolerances but deeper understandings and sharper appreciations. We are sidestepping responsibility if we don't fairly outstrip ourselves in doing away with our own motheaten prejudices before our children get to the point of calling our bluffs." The solution: teaching children to play with and respect other children as individuals rather than as members of particular racial or ethnic groups.[80] Parent educators meant well in attempting to teach parents the importance of raising children without prejudice, but it is far from clear that parents were able or willing to put these ideals into practice.

"WAR AND MOTHERHOOD ARE ANTITHETICAL": MOTHERS' STUDY CLUBS IN THE 1940S

Many mothers' study clubs continued to meet throughout the 1940s; others were forced to disband due to mothers' employment, wartime migrations, or a surfeit of both home- and war-related responsibilities. Because so many of its members were engaged in war work, the League of Mothers' Clubs discontinued its activities in 1943, and many Home Bureaus concentrated on more timely activities, such as making nutritious meals with sparse rations. Parent education continued to flourish in a variety of settings, however. Nineteen states sponsored parent education programs in the 1940s, either through their state Department of Education or in conjunction with the Agricultural Extension Service. In 1943, both the Army and the Navy committed themselves to making available to servicemen's wives the parent education materials produced by Chicago's Association for Family Living. The Chicago Association, which had been sponsoring parents' groups since the 1920s, continued to expand during the 1940s, sponsoring 405 different parents' groups in 1945. The PTA more than doubled its membership during the 1940s, attaining a total membership of more than six million by 1950. Home economics courses in family life and parenting flourished at universities and in high schools, and classes for expectant parents were inaugurated in connection with hospitals and maternity center associations. Child guidance and family service agencies competed for the attention of parents with troublesome children. Radio broadcasts, magazine articles, and newspaper columns on child rearing continued to provide a wealth of information to inquiring parents.[81]

The Cornell Family Life groups continued to meet and left significant documents of their activities for the war years. Although in many states home economics extension was limited to more practical functions during the war, such as nutrition and gardening, the Cornell College of Home Economics 1944 annual report stated: "The significance of maintaining mental health has brought into focus the value of continued extension teaching in child care and in adolescent and family psychology. As casualties increase and anxieties enter more homes, programs guided by the family life department become more essential."[82] In more than two hundred study groups in forty-eight counties of New York, the members contemplated the essential questions of women, children, and family life.[83] The minutes of these meetings underscore the centrality of marriage and motherhood in many women's lives during the 1940s, despite the expansion of career opportunities that accompanied the wartime emergency. The records also reveal the possibilities and limitations that the democratic philosophy of family life held for many mothers. Although mothers were generally positive about the possibility of democracy in the marital relationship, they were less wholeheartedly enthusiastic about its potential ramifications for the relationships of mothers and children.

The mothers who belonged to child-study clubs were a self-selected group of women whose identities were heavily contingent on their child-rearing responsibilities, rather than their roles as wage workers or even as patriotic citizens. For many of these women, motherhood stood in opposition to the aims of war and the demands of the marketplace. In discussing their program for the coming year just before the war, one group's spokesperson told a speaker, "We don't want to go into war too much this year. . . . War and motherhood are antithetical." Another group complained that they were reluctant to have more children "as long as they were to be used as cannon fodder." Historian D'Ann Campbell believes that farm women were "especially dovish" during this period, and indeed rural study club women found that their identities as child rearers and nurturers fit uneasily with the warlike fervor that dominated the national agenda.[84]

The Cornell mothers, their identities firmly ensconced in motherhood, were disquieted by the increasing numbers of mothers of young children who were entering the workforce. In this they were not alone. In 1943, the PTA's War Committee suggested that before being allowed to engage in war work, mothers should receive "clearance" indicating that they had acquired appropriate child care, and the committee opposed the entry into the workforce of mothers with children under fourteen.[85] Even the female leaders of the U.S. Children's Bureau refused to publicly sanction wage work for mothers of young children and were pessimistic about the consequences of government-sponsored child-care services.[86]

The suggestion that children could be adequately cared for by individuals other than their mother was disconcerting to women who had built their adult identities around motherhood. The Bennett Study Club unanimously assented: "*No* one *can* possibly take the place of a mother in the home."[87] The report of the Greece Child Study Club revealed that for most members, motherhood implied a full-time commitment to child rearing when they discussed whether mothers could work and be successful parents: "Most agreed 'no,' at least while children are younger. After that . . . some thot [*sic*] mother could work. She could then be a successful *parent,* but [according to a few] not necessarily a successful mother."[88] Other women made more personal attacks on working mothers. Indeed, the secretary of the Lockport club recorded in 1943, "The members were all disgusted and alarmed over the fact that war working mothers have so little regard for their children and all wished that something could be done about it."[89]

That this stance was not representative of all the Cornell clubs is indicated by reports referring to members who have taken war jobs. The disjunction may have reflected class differences, as well as ideological differences and differences in the ages of children of mothers who worked. A leader of a rural study club in St. Lawrence County admitted that it was difficult to keep the club going owing to war conditions, including the "scarcity of help and everyone trying to raise a large garden. One active member is attending summer school and will be teaching in September, making four members who are teaching. Several more have moved to industrial centers to work."[90] Women who chose to stay in the home could also profit from wartime opportunities. A group of mothers from suburban Nassau County wrote to Cornell that they wished to read about the influence of heredity and environment on the rearing of children because they were providing child care for the children of working mothers.[91]

The government propaganda inducing women to take war jobs had an impact as the war progressed. Wartime propaganda conflicted, however, with much of the psychological literature, which underscored the dangers to children—maladjustment and juvenile delinquency—when mothers worked outside the home.[92]

With so many experts offering opinions on women's duties, maladjustments, and proclivities, it is not surprising that many clubwomen maintained their interest in studying the role of women in the modern world. Cornell continued to provide club members with feminist reading materials, as is reflected in the summaries of readings and discussions contained in many groups' meeting minutes, which included such statements as this: "Position of women was not always inferior to that of man. Rise of Christianity, as well as rise of capitalism, placed women in inferior position."[93] The material was sufficiently feminist that Cornell received a fair amount of correspondence complaining that some of the reading materials were downright subversive.

In contrast to discussions of feminism in the 1930s, which were not exactly pro-feminist but also not explicitly antifeminist, club deliberations during this period reveal a strong vein of defensiveness, perhaps in response to the assault on American motherhood being launched by experts. Not only did different club members and different clubs think differently about feminist issues, but individual clubwomen seemed to have been confused about their own feelings on the appropriate role of women in society. The secretary of the Bennett Study Club conveyed both defensiveness about her role as a mother and sophisticated, almost feminist, critique of experts' disquisitions about women. In her report to Cornell she noted first the statement of one member with whom she was in accord: "Instead of muddling in politics, sociology and ranting about our responsibilities to society why can't we be realists and recognize the need of mothers to train citizens, wage earners, etc.? *Hurrah!!!* My sentiments!" This was a fairly conventional response to literature advocating careers for women, but at the conclusion of the report, she suggested that what she found most troubling was the experts' penchant for telling women what they should be doing: "A great deal of modern psychology may be bunkum but a real service might be rendered if someone were to make the revolutionary discovery that in adult females there are individual differences. It is dangerous to generalize when education, environment, natural inclination, and previous condition of servitude affect women as well as men."[94]

In addition to suspecting that much of psychology was probably "bunkum," this woman also turned the experts' rhetoric on its head by recommending that the professionals apply the concept of "individual differences" in talking about women, rather than make sweeping analyses about the plight of women in general. Similar annoyance was exhibited at a group meeting where, during a discussion of "Special Problems of Homemakers During War," the chairwoman asserted: "It was presumptuous to tell us what problems we faced when we could each present our own."[95] Thus clubwomen did not merely defend their role as homemakers but tried to maintain some agency in defining that role.

Educational and class differences between women inevitably crept into the discussions of women's roles. One meeting held in Spencerport in 1944 was the scene of a "terrific verbal combat" over the plight of the modern mother. The group had read an article entitled "The Care and Feeding of Mothers," which postulated that "the only contented mothers were the uneducated women who have no outside interests." This statement aroused the ire both of the non-college-educated women in the group, who felt that they were being characterized as docile domestics, and of some college-educated women, who considered themselves "fairly well contented" in their roles as homemakers. At the same time, some were offended by a member's statement that a well-educated married women should not "be made to drudge over washtubs, dishes etc." It is intriguing that in this altercation, offense was taken at the notions both that uneducated women were content to pursue domesticity and that educated women should not have to do the tiresome chores of the typical homemaker.[96] The groups tended to disparage both women who were unduly submissive and women who were discontented with their lot as mothers. The Kingston Child Study Club criticized the wife who would "make her husband the center of her universe."[97] Yet clubwomen were also critical of women who complained about their status as housewives. When the leader of a New Paltz study club confessed to her fellow members that she felt "suppressed" and "submerged" in her role as mother and that she would not be compensated by having one of her children do great things in the world, one of the members wondered whether the complainer had "discarded her Bible" and surmised that her children would be damaged by her misguided attitude. This conversation demonstrates the competing value systems at work in club deliberations—one woman employing both feminist and psychological language to explain her dissatisfaction with her situation and another woman contending that the Bible was a reliable source of advice for dealing with discontent.[98]

If the meaning of motherhood was somewhat in contest, fatherhood appears to have been a less controversial theme during this period. Robert Griswold argues that the war brought fathers to the fore, at least ideologically, as both their enhanced role as breadwinners and their added wartime responsibilities made experts increasingly aware of fathers' impact on families. The extensive debate on whether fathers should be drafted focused attention on the psychological function of fatherhood. Experts insisted that fathers were essential to the well-being of the entire family and that their absence imperiled children's development and might lead to juvenile delinquency and family disorder.[99]

As men's responsibilities outside the home increased, clubwomen adjusted their expectations of fathers' participation in family life, simultaneously acknowledging the psychological significance of absentee fathers. In response to reading materials on the father's role in the family, one group noted: "It is difficult for father *now* to find time to give to children or settle problems with mother. This is due to long working hours and time given to civilian defense etc. This war will leave its mark on our homes."[100] The clubwomen of this era did not evince the frustration with the absent father that women of the 1920s and 1930s had. They forbore sometimes out of patriotism, but equally often out of principle. Several clubs, for instance, debated whether fathers should spend some time each day with their babies, but most members were hesitant to make it a requirement, both because of fathers' responsibilities and because "it would make him feel that it was a duty rather than a pleasure."[101] Whereas women's responsibilities to children were couched in terms of duty, men's interactions with their children were deemed a matter of pleasure. When asked whether they would like to see their husbands attend parenting classes, few women were enthusiastic, unlike their counterparts in the 1930s. The Small Fry Study Club gave a representative response: "Classes for fathers seem rather useless but a discussion with doctor, books and chance to handle baby [are] best."[102] On the subject of teamwork in the home, some thought men should participate in housework, but most felt that the husband's help with housework was "quite uncalled for except in an emergency or illness."[103] Women wished that their husbands would be involved in family life, but they appeared relatively unwilling to *make* them play a role. Between the 1930s and the 1940s, there was a marked shift in the attitudes of wives in the clubs. Whereas 1930s clubwomen had incessantly discussed their wishes to have husbands take a greater part in family life, to share both the blessings and burdens of parenting, mothers of the 1940s were more accepting of fathers' level of involvement with family life. Fathers were expected to make both financial and emotional contributions to family life, but these were to be made within the confines of a clearly defined masculine role. Despite the expanded opportunities for women in the workplace during the war, women's quest to have their male partners play a more equal part in child rearing appears to have been placed on the back burner.

But although women were willing to maintain the traditional division of labor in the home, they did not necessarily accept a gender hierarchy that assigned greater value to men and their responsibilities. The Bennett Study

Club, for instance, whose members insisted that mothers were irreplaceable as homemakers, contended that "we must train ourselves [and our men] to feel women's place today is just as important as men's." And they invoked a specific example of female devaluation to prove their point: "We should not permit boys to be called 'sissies,' thereby inferring girls are inferior in opening boys to ridicule as such."[104] Yet in their continued defense of the homemaking role as women's most valued and valid occupation, clubwomen promoted a version of equality that emphasized gender-based differentiation.

Most club members at least paid lip service to the concept that the marital relationship should be based on democracy, yet many were skeptical about democratic child-rearing practices, which they viewed as likely to upset the balance of power in the family. They were sympathetic to the developmentalist critique of behaviorism and agreed that affection and flexibility were essential aspects of the mother's repertoire. Women were also responsive to theories that underscored the mother's responsibility to instill a sense of emotional security in her children.

The majority of rural mothers did not fit easily, however, into the categories of either "developmental" or "traditional" mothers that sociologist Evelyn Millis Duvall employed in her survey of the views on child rearing held by Chicago mothers in parent education groups. Duvall discovered that middle- and upper-class white and Jewish mothers in groups were more likely than white working-class and African-American mothers to favor a developmental perspective, focusing on their children's "growth and development" rather than "specific behavioral conformities." The language used by developmentally in-clined mothers was imbued with the democratic child-rearing philosophy then in vogue. According to Duvall, "These mothers speak of their children as having rights of their own." One mother, whom Duvall held up as an exemplar of the developmental mother, described her philosophy in these terms: "If we call them and they are doing something, we don't expect them to drop what they are doing right that minute and come. Their activities are important, too, and they should be able to finish what they are doing. We try to respect the individual rights of the child." By contrast, "traditional" mothers were less interested in children's individual rights and modes of self-expression than in their acquisition of good habits and manners.[105]

That a simple class differentiation does not easily fit the situations of rural families has been noted by a range of scholars.[106] Study club mothers were usually middle-class according to standard criteria, such as income and educa-tion, but families from rural areas undoubtedly had what historian William

Tuttle has termed a distinct "ecological psychology" from that of urban families.[107] Thus the democratic philosophy of child rearing that clearly had appeal
for some urban middle-class mothers was seen as sadly impractical by many of
the Cornell mothers. Because rural mothers had so many duties and chores to
perform, strict disciplinary techniques were considered essential to the homemaker's efficiency.

Parent educators assumed that homemakers should adjust their household
routines to serve the needs of children, but mothers who did not possess the
model of the well-off middle-class family with one or two children found it
difficult to adhere to this mandate. In a study of the practices of parents with
preschool children, educator Gertrude Gilmore Lafore observed: "In many
cases, the parent seemed chiefly concerned with the performance of household
or other tasks. Much of the time the parent tried to continue these tasks even
though the child desired, demanded, or needed attention." She concluded that
many problems would be solved if the parent accepted the "legitimacy of the
child's incessant day-by-day demands."[108]

But putting the child first conflicted with the numerous other responsibilities that contended for mothers' attention. A study of Vermont farm
women conducted in 1946 revealed that mothers with children devoted approximately ten and a half hours of their work week to child care. Relatives and
others assisted with child care, and older children often supervised their
younger siblings.[109] Children fit into the lives of the busy rural homemaker
rather than the other way around.

This account of the Vermont homemaker may not be exactly typical of the
Cornell club member, although many lived in rural areas, kept large gardens,
and performed laborious household chores. Women with such busy lives as
homemakers leveled a major critique at the texts they read: they were impractical. In reviewing the book *Children in the Family* by Harold Anderson, club
mothers contended that the text was "too idealistic and not very practical. We
thought that the author had worked with children but had not the worry of
other household tribulations."[110] In keeping with this practicality, most
mothers found that they could not refrain from saying "don't" to their children;
they insisted that the many chores which competed for their attention did not
permit them the laxity promoted in the books. According to the Lockport
group, "We find that despite what the books say, we are forced to use the word
'don't' because a child moves so quickly that there isn't time to distract him."[111]
Similarly in a lesson on "learning vs. naughtiness," which questioned whether
children's propensity to explore and take things apart was part of the learning

process, the members of another group queried "how any mothers could stand by and see their work undone, and whether or not this was learning." One mother offered as an example a child who had taken a pile of freshly ironed napkins and heaped them on the floor.[112]

Another problem with the prescriptive literature was that it proposed high standards for women both as mothers and as wives. The women of the Tonawanda Gahunda Study Club observed that in addition to mothering and homemaking, they must "be the vivacious, elated and charming wife to her husband as well as his counselor, right-hand man, comforter. WHEW!"[113] Performing the various emotional functions prescribed for women by the expert literature conflicted with the practical demands of physically caring for children and a household.

The Cornell mothers also sought to maintain their positions of authority in the family. According to the mandates of the democratic family, parents and children should be on an equal footing in decision making. Sidonie Gruenberg argued: "When democratic tendencies are in the ascendant, children's needs and wants are given as much consideration as those of their parents."[114] Some mothers, however, could not concede that children's wishes should be on a par with adult priorities in their households. The Mt. Morris Home Bureau unit announced its response to a series on democratic child rearing: "Majority believed that there is too much democracy in the home compared to previous years."[115] Another group accepted a certain amount of democracy as beneficial, but warned against the dangers of granting too much power to the family's younger members: "A family should adjust, modify, or arrange its living at least on a fifty-fifty basis to meet a child's needs or demands—not to the extent, however, that the child 'rules the roost.'"[116] Unwilling to relinquish their authority either to experts or to their own children, mothers in a Henrietta group warned against the dangers of too much democracy, asserting that "We also decided that to abolish a young dictator from the family we must be dictators to do it."[117] Although their presence in a child-study group indicated that the Cornell mothers were becoming increasingly child-centered, they felt ambivalence about it and a concomitant resistance toward complete transfer of adult authority to children.

Some groups seem to have accepted, at least superficially, the predominant developmentalist approach of discipline, which downplayed the importance of punishment. A Clarence Center group defined discipline as "the way in which the person who is in control understands the child's inner problems at various stages of this growth and the relationship which exists between that person and the child." Some group members claimed that they were now more likely to employ reasoning than corporal punishment with their children, at least in part thanks to their participation in child-study groups.[118]

Other groups were open about preferring their own disciplinary techniques, regardless of whether they received professional approval. The Churchville group expressed exasperation at the textbook discussion of discipline: "The textbook resumes brought out disapproval of practically every conceivable form of discipline so our first natural reaction was to ask how *can* one discipline a child?" They decided as a group that practices disapproved of by the textbook writer, such as slapping or withdrawing privileges, could be used in moderation. They did, however, concede that it was more important to avoid inculcating fears and neurosis in a child than to have a "perfect child."[119]

Some groups were more stubborn in their adherence to traditional disciplinary techniques over "recommended" methods. In discussing the problem of a mother whose older child was jealous of the baby, one group offered these solutions: "Put the child in a barrel every time he hits the baby. Someone else suggested packing his things and sending him to a relative or a friend for a few days. Make him think you didn't want him around if he didn't want the baby." After listening to a lecture by an expert who insisted that parents should try to find out why children bite, rather than to punish them, the Spencerport club rebutted, "The general consensus of opinion was then, as now, 'The only way to cure biting is for the masher to bite back!' "[120] Apparently an array of disciplinary tactics were discussed in the clubs that were not sanctioned by the books.

Clubwomen also discussed the special requirements of childhood in times when the nation was at war and examined the studies of Burlingham and Freud on the impact of children's separation from their mothers and the dangers of "matriarchy" in a society where men were absorbed with war work. Perhaps of most pressing importance for these mothers was fostering a sense of security in their children in perilous times, a maternal duty that was urged on them in countless ways by the experts. But how to establish that security was another question. A summary of a discussion on this question suggests that the dilemma received substantial group time: "As is usual the discussion led around to debating the pt. whether we must protect our children from the pressure of war times—or teach them to be self-reliant and have faith in the future that it will work out well for us." The Oakfield mothers' club wondered whether it was even possible to give children a feeling of security in such dangerous times, suggesting that they did not share the belief in maternal omnipotence expressed by many of the experts.[121]

Club mothers tended be rather negative about war in general and they seem to have been receptive to the notion that they bore a responsibility as mothers for rearing children who would help create a more peaceful world. Such statements as "Mothers have tried to teach children that war is unnecessary—it's a sign of human stupidity and arrogance—must teach them better" and "If we hold to our own prejudices we encourage a warlike spirit" are common in club records.[122]

The Cornell mothers were disconcertingly candid in expressing their views on the subject of prejudice. They were undoubtedly more enlightened than many of their neighbors, given their exposure to progressive thinking on racial relations at least in their study club programs. But there was, as they put it, a large "lag" between their ideas and their feelings. In the minutes, every statement of an ideal in regard to racial differences is followed by the reality of club members' prejudices. One club questioned, for instance: "How can we overcome race hatred if we still feel we are better than the foreign born?" And the deliberations of another group reflected the literature on the one hand and their own prejudices on the other: "Need to teach tolerance of other races tho [sic] some felt that we don't want children to associate too closely with foreign stock." In a discussion of African-Americans, one group noted that "Colored people . . . have come very much to the fore since the war. . . . Colored people should have all advantages but should be segregated."[123] Many mentioned that they were not willing to allow their child to bring an African-American or immigrant child to play. As with many other concepts that the Cornell mothers read about and discussed, they could not easily change their practices and value systems, even when they recognized the validity of an idea in theory. Prejudice was too deeply ingrained in their attitudes and social structure for an occasional reading or discussion to transform them.

Perhaps in regard to racial tolerance, the "books" maintained a standard that mothers felt they could not, or would not, live up to, and in this case, as in many others, mothers employed the collective opinion of the group as a rationale for resisting expert advice. Sara Ruddick has hypothesized that one of the primary tasks of mothering is to raise children who are socially acceptable to the mother's peer group, a task that can lead mothers into making inauthentic choices—choices that may conflict with the injunction to nurture their children's growth.[124] Thus mothers might resist applying expert advice to their family lives that could make them or their children less than socially acceptable.

Club mothers generally pieced together elements of expert advice with elements of traditional values about marriage and motherhood that they were unwilling to relinquish. A report from a 1930 meeting of the Sound Avenue child-study club reveals the ambiguities that accompanied this process: "One mother, at a certain point in the discussion, quoted, half in fun, the much-abused 'Spare the rod and spoil the child,' adding, 'That's in the book.' (We have had quite a bit of fun about things being or not being 'in the book.') 'Oh, but that's in the old Book,' some made answer, and to that another said, 'I guess you have to mix the two!'"[125] The aphorism "spare the rod and spoil the child," though not from the Bible, undoubtedly had its roots in the Old Testament proverbs that speak of the dangers to children's spiritual well-being of "sparing the rod." This mother characterized the Bible as a "book"—a socially sanctioned source of authority—that might contend with secular books on child rearing. The quoted exchange also gives some idea of the diversity of perspectives represented; within the clubs some might look to the Bible as the most authoritative source of advice on child rearing, some were more favorably inclined to the "newer" books proffered by professional child developmentalists, and finally, some were willing to draw on both these competing sources of authority in shaping their ideas about the treatment of children. In the clubs women could sort out these diverse perspectives in a community of their peers and clarify their thoughts about children and their own role as wives and mothers.[126]

Reading the minutes of child-study clubs brings to mind two phenomena of more recent times: the feminist consciousness-raising groups of the 1960s and 1970s, and the ubiquitous self-help groups of the 1980s and 1990s. Child-study groups did not yet engage in the feminist discourse that would become popular in the 1970s to analyze male-dominated society, although a subtler brand of "consciousness-raising" appears to have been in operation. As in the consciousness-raising groups, in the child-study groups shared experiences could yield collective insights, which might then serve to either challenge or further disseminate expert advice.

Like today's self-help groups, the clubs provided women with a network of support to make changes in their familial and personal situations. Child-study groups offered a balance between adjustment and change; change was to be made within the context of the standard social structure. In this sense, the child-study group was less than revolutionary. To the extent that groups clad women's concerns in therapeutic language, they obscured the sociostructural inequality of the traditional family and its negative consequences for women.

But therapeutic language could also offer a means of furthering women's autonomy in the family and demanding greater personal accountability from spouses. Child-study groups could be an instrument to support the status quo, yet they also helped mothers to cope with the exigencies of their lives and to develop themselves as individuals, who were also mothers and wives.

Chapter 7 Dear Doctor: The Impact of the Baby Book on Post–World War II Mothers

The May 16, 1955, cover of *Newsweek* depicted a melancholy two-year-old with her elbows resting on a stack of books by noted authorities on children, including Arnold Gesell, Benjamin Spock, and the nineteenth-century pediatrician L. Emmett Holt. The featured article was "Bringing Up Baby on Books," and the subtitle queried, "Was Grandmother Right?" Were parents in danger of relinquishing their common sense to the experts? In 1956, another journalist spoke of his generation's propensity to use books to rear their children: "Where our parents walked thump-thump and carried a big club (on the whole that is) we walk dainty-dainty and carry a big book."[1] The baby book was here to stay. In fact, read in private by countless suburban mothers, it came to supplant the child-study club, where a whole array of books had provided a springboard for freewheeling discussions of everyday life with children.

Yet the ubiquity of baby books during this period should not lead us to assume that mothers accepted their content without reservation. Although the reading material could be both informative and reassuring, some texts exacerbated women's anxieties about their abilities as parents. As in the past, women were irritated when experts made statements that they thought contradicted good common sense. Many mothers who started out trying to raise babies "by the book" eventually learned to regard the books as accessories to the knowledge about children they themselves had gleaned from experience, tradition, and the vast body of ideas known as common sense.

The demographic phenomenon of the "baby boom" surely contributed to the heightened appeal of child-care manuals during this period. Greater numbers of Americans of all classes were marrying at a younger age and having larger families than their predecessors. The typical woman walking down the aisle in the 1950s had grown up in a family with only two children, but unlike her mother, she aspired to have three, four, or even more children. Postwar families were more mobile than those of the preceding generation and often looked to the expanding suburbs rather than to urban areas as a likely place to rear their children.[2] The gap between native white working-class and middle-class Americans was closing as more families were able to acquire the material goods previously associated with middle-class status. The generous provisions for veterans following World War II gave some previously working-class couples the opportunity to achieve the middle-class American "dream" of a home of their own and, in some instances, a college-educated breadwinner.[3]

Despite the fact that more mothers continued to enter the workforce in the 1950s, many women who could afford to do so remained at home until their children were of school age. Many white families had achieved prosperity and subscribed to the predominant view that mothers should devote themselves exclusively to the task of raising preschoolers. Child mortality had substantially decreased, in spite of the terrifying polio epidemic of the 1940s and 1950s. Middle-class mothers increasingly devoted themselves to raising, as historian Brett Harvey has put it, "*perfect* children—with unblemished bodies, high intelligence, and 'normal' personalities."[4] Mothers faced a series of obstacles, however, in their quest to be the perfect parents of perfect children, not the least of which was the isolation that many women complained of during this period.

The postwar economy scattered many American families in search of work and housing. The government's commitment to a large peacetime army led to the necessity for numerous young families to make do with constant mobility and absentee fathers.[5] Transience contributed to a feeling of loneliness among many homemakers. According to a 1957 study of women's child-rearing behavior, the major problem of contemporary mothers was "related to cultural isolation." A mother quoted in the study underscored this theme: "I think almost anything the children do is going to isolate me. . . . I may not leave this house for six or eight weeks at a time, even to go out for a social evening, and I think just being around the children so much irritates me, and for that reason they're irritated and for that reason we all get wound up and nervous." Many women lamented that their mothers and grandmothers were not available to lend assistance in their new homes. Confined to the home, with scant adult companionship, middle-class mothers turned to women's magazines and baby books for company, advice, and reassurance as they labored to rear their children.[6]

Not only were middle-class mothers of the 1950s liable to be geographically separated from their families of origin, but they often had to cast aside adult identities as students or employees when they had children. One woman related the transition in her identity from working woman to mother in a letter to Dr. Spock: "I had worked [as a registered nurse] until three months before David was born. It was therefore rather a blow to find myself suddenly tied to a small, demanding creature who was my only companion and who seemed to resist all my efforts to make him comfortable. My loneliness and sense of inadequacy were severe." The mass media, particularly television, romanticized the nuclear family unit, displaying images of patient, charming, and devoted stay-at-home mothers and sympathetic fathers who returned from work to participate fully in both family fun and discipline of children. Women were expected to reach the ultimate in feminine self-fulfillment through bearing and rearing children, yet the gap between the ideal represented in such television shows as *Leave It to Beaver* and *Father Knows Best* and real life made it even more difficult for women to cope with the tumultuous feelings that often accompanied the transition to full-time motherhood.[7]

Pediatricians and child-care experts increasingly met the needs of many mothers for assistance and advice—providing a one-on-one relationship marked by inequality and deference (on the mothers' part) rather than by the mutuality that characterized the discussions of mothers in groups. The tendency to defer to expertise in discussions of children was commented on by one critic of this phenomenon: "Listen to any group of women swapping stories about their children. Instead of the 'I find,' 'My mother said,' 'I feel,' 'Our family does,' that would have punctuated such a discussion 25 years ago, you hear: 'My pediatrician says,' 'My children's nursery school teacher believes,' 'Dr.

So and So claims.'"[8] Raising baby by the book was no longer a joke but a way of life, at least according to the popular media, which were disposed to take trends among educated New Yorkers as indicative of the life of the nation as a whole.

Although women were having children in larger numbers and in closer succession than their mothers and grandmothers had, parenting advice demanded that mothers attend more closely to the needs of each child. Mothers were expected to adjust their schedules—whether for feeding or toilet training—to children, rather than the other way around. According to the advice offered by such popular figures as Spock, Gesell, and others, children should be allowed to "express" themselves, and much of what might have been considered misbehavior or even sin in an earlier era was now characterized as "age-appropriate" behavior. The two-year-old who dismantled the family home, for instance, was now an "explorer" whose energies should be redirected instead of a little devil who should be punished. Aggressive behavior, tantrums, and crying were normal aspects of the growth process rather than indications of faulty character formation. Contrary to the strictures of early nineteenth-century parenting literature, the job of parents was not to "break the will" or to avoid spoiling their charges at all costs but to encourage children's growth through all their developmental stages. Of course, this injunction stood in contrast to traditional authoritarian approaches to child rearing and the behaviorist approach of the 1920s, which were both still being transmitted to young mothers by many family members, neighbors, and pediatricians as "common sense."

The contrast between traditional authoritarian approaches to parenting and the increasingly child-centered approach promulgated by 1950s advice-givers is graphically illustrated in a letter from a grandfather to Benjamin Spock regarding the difference in perspectives on children between his daughter on the one hand and himself and his wife on the other. His daughter and her children were coming for an extended visit, and the grandparents were worried that their newly acquired antiques might be in danger with a twenty-two-month-old baby wandering around the house. The grandmother recommended that the daughter teach the child the meaning of the word "no" before visiting. Her daughter responded: "She knows and understands the meaning of 'no,' but it doesn't make a bit of difference to her! I can pull her out of my kitchen cabinet, etc., a hundred times a day, but she still goes the next day! I use the so-called 'distraction' technique—it doesn't seem to work with her. And one doesn't *beat* an infant into obedience." In his letter to Spock, the grandfather explained the divergence between his and his daughter's philosophies of parenting: "By thus narrowing the possibilities for guidance, it seems to us that the baby's destiny is pretty much in her own hands, and we do not subscribe to such laissez-faire methods of child-rearing. Nor do [we] go along with the idea that corporal punishment (or corporal management) is synonymous with *beating*."[9] The "child-proofing" of the family home was an indispensable tactic for those who sought to substitute child-centered parenting for the authoritarian discipline of an earlier age.

Clearly, differences in child-rearing philosophies could cause rifts between young mothers and their parents. Just as women could point to books to justify their child-rearing preferences to their spouses, they could also use them to distinguish themselves, as modern mothers, from their parents' generation. Some mothers resented the strictness of their own upbringings and valued the emotional expressiveness that the experts were championing. A follower of Spock confided, "My mother was too strict, so I've never tried to imitate her methods." Repression (meaning prohibitions on the expression of negative emotions), authoritarianism, and corporal punishment were associated with the "old-fashioned" family of the past. One mother spoke for many when she disparaged the lack of emotional expressiveness that characterized her own childhood and voiced her intention to raise her children differently: "I myself was raised in an 'old-fashioned' family which allowed us children no expression of our feelings."[10] "Modern" mothers of the 1950s appreciated emotional expressiveness, sought to avoid corporal punishment, and tried to foster their children's development, with the assistance of baby books, pediatricians, and like-minded women.

Some mothers viewed medical expertise as an ally in their struggle to dispose of the traditional medical remedies that their relatives were foisting on them. A third-generation Italian woman maintained that Spock's book aided her in her efforts to resist her mother and grandmother's child-care recommendations (which she called "ethnic old wives' tales"), including such unsanitary practices as wiping babies' faces with their wet diapers to improve their complexions. Speaking for herself and the other young mothers with whom she conversed, she exclaimed, about Spock's influence, "We had an expert on our side!" Conflating science with common sense, a mother from Bangor, Maine, also aligned herself with the doctors in opposition to her relatives: "I have raised him following my doctor's advice and using my own good common sense and ignoring all of the unasked for advice received from other sources [in-laws]," who "insist that the doctors are all completely incompetent." In this case, common sense itself was a source of contention, given that both the relatives and the mother felt themselves to be in possession of it. For many mothers of the 1950s, then, common sense could be equated with the wisdom of medical experts, rather than with familial traditions.[11]

Many mothers incorporated expert knowledge of child development into their ideals of good parenting as they strove to enact the romanticized vision of family life popularized in the media. Yet as in the past, the psychologists' concept of good motherhood did not hold equal appeal for all women. Child-centered parenting is *time-consuming,* because it requires a high degree of supervision and attention to the needs and emotions of individual children. In the last chapter we saw that busy farm mothers of the 1940s spent relatively little time actively caring for their children; the supervision of children was carried out simultaneously with the numerous household chores. Yet middle-class mothers of the 1950s were supposed to be acutely attuned to all their youngsters at all times. Overly conscientious mothers were left exhausted and irritable by their unremitting efforts to satisfy the needs of several young children, a situation that could lead to familial conflict and personal turmoil. Unfortunately, many mothers learned only through the practice of mothering that it was possible go overboard. They then took a critical look at the theories in circulation and devised strategies for coping with their youngsters that also took into account their own perspective as parents. In fact, when they corresponded with Spock, for example, about the difficulty of actually putting the prescribed practices into practice, he revised his advice to suit the requirements of his audience.[12]

A great many mothers expressed their thoughts about raising children, along with their feelings of isolation, anxiety, desperation, and joy, in letters to popular child-care experts Benjamin Spock, Louise Bates Ames, and Frances Ilg. Arnold Gesell seems to have received less mail in response to his baby books than his colleagues Ames and Ilg. Both were collaborators with Gesell at the Yale Clinic of Child Development, but from 1951 to 1973 the two women also jointly wrote the newspaper column "Parents Ask," which was syndicated in as many as sixty-five newspapers at a time, including the *Boston Globe,* the *Washington Post,* the *Philadelphia Bulletin,* and the *Los Angeles Times,* and had a circulation of approximately nine and a half million.[13] Ames and Ilg invited parents' letters and wrote a detailed personal response to each correspondent, even if they did not print the letter. The columnists were both single mothers of grown daughters.

The letters to Spock consist primarily of responses to a series of child-care articles called "Talks with Mothers," written for the *Ladies' Home Journal* during the 1950s and 1960s, and letters parents wrote to praise or criticize his well-known manual *Baby and Child Care.* Gesell and Spock did not always answer letters from parents, and when they did, their responses were cursory. Spock invited letters from parents for use in his *Journal* articles; however, he publicly confessed that he would not be able to provide personal responses. When he did respond, his standard recommendation to a writer with a problem—whether it was a five-year-old bed wetter or a husband who was sexually abusing his young child—was to seek professional help.[14]

The letters expand our knowledge of mothers' reactions to the prescriptive literature and illuminate the mindset and circumstances of the readers of child-care advice. No monolithic voice emerges from the letters; still, whether a reader was convinced or dismayed by a child-rearing tract, her response usually echoed themes found in other letters. The documents reveal much about the experiences of white, native-born women, many of whom were new mothers who were unsure of their maternal abilities. Regardless of whether they had received formal education, the writers were generally *readers,* who consulted multiple sources of information about children. The fact that many of these women sought assistance from a distant expert suggests that this was a more troubled group than a representative sample of mothers might be.

Many of the letter writers seemed unduly unnerved by common problems in child training, and their expressions of fear, frustration, and guilt were often overwhelmingly disproportionate to the problem being discussed. In some cases anxiety, isolation, and stress combined to produce despair, disorientation, and uncontrolled anger toward children. More commonly, however, mothers managed to withstand their children's growing pains and became more confident about their abilities as mothers with succeeding children.

In their letters many mothers represented themselves as experts. The letters are packed with the kinds of details about children's physical and psychological development that one expects in a medical chart. Mothers offered their favorite remedies for children's physical and emotional problems to the experts for consideration. Spock published several of these letters, including one describing the differences in development between twins—remarking among other things on the "gross motor skills" of one twin and the manual dexterity of the other. The writer concluded, "It is a most interesting and rewarding life for a mother to understand and appreciate individual children."[15] Like many dedicated professionals, most women complained about their working conditions without seeking to relinquish the work itself. But before we turn our attention to the voices of mothers speaking to child-care experts, we shall examine the dominant ideologies of motherhood to which these women were responding, as well as the lives, work, and intellectual influences, and motivations of the experts to whom they wrote.

"DOING WHAT COMES NATURALLY": IDEOLOGIES OF MOTHERHOOD IN THE 1950S

The numerous mothers' clubs and classes of the 1920s and 1930s had dwindled by the 1950s. The earlier mothers' clubs had often been composed of longtime relatives and friends, but many mothers of the 1950s lived in new suburban developments, at a distance from the families and friends that they had grown up with. In the insulated middle-class family, mothers often sought the emotional sustenance from their husbands that their mothers might have received from female relatives, neighbors, and friends. Classes for expectant parents—including both mothers and fathers—mushroomed, but these were relatively short-term sessions conducted by physicians and nurses and were limited to prenatal and early infant care. Role differentiation by gender was at an all-time high, yet the role of a husband and father was ideally supposed to encompass more than breadwinning. He was to contribute the primary emotional support for his wife in the raising of children and making of a home.

The premise of most popular culture was that women's fulfillment should come from being loving and devoted wives and mothers, rather than individuals in their own right. Drawing on popularized Freudian psychology, such as that represented in the 1947 bestseller *Modern Woman: The Lost Sex* by Ferdinand Lundberg and Marynia F. Farnham, many writers insisted that women's psychological adjustment depended on a happy heterosexual relationship and children. Women who did not achieve these ends were likely to be "thwarted," frustrated, or suffering from "penis envy." Choosing to remain single was suspect, perhaps even un-American; feminists were deemed to be sadly maladjusted caricatures of men. In her introduction to *Life* magazine's special issue on women in 1956, Catherine Marshall declared that women had strong "urges and instinctive needs" to experience heterosexual romance and bear children. "When women do *not* have the deep satisfaction of these experiences," Marshall contended, "their troubles begin." She went on to speculate that women's present-day difficulties might have been caused by their earlier preoccupation with their "rights."[16] Of course, these messages contradicted strongly the cultural emphasis on *individual* self-fulfillment that many women had received in college or in the workplace before marriage, and even in the mass media, which continued to celebrate the achievements of career women, even while they valorized homemaking. Authors such as Farnham and Lundberg regarded these contrasting messages as imperiling the mental health of American women by preventing them from devoting themselves wholeheartedly to the sphere in which they could best express their intrinsic female natures.[17]

According to most prescriptions, the ideal family included a contented stay-at-home mom, who had no misgivings about devoting herself wholeheartedly to her children's needs. It was not so much her knowledge of child rearing that made her the perfect mother as her serene and wholesome personality. Parent education in the 1950s had changed considerably since its inception in the 1920s, when the mastery of scientific knowledge was assumed to be the key to having happy, healthy, and productive children. Within the professional community, a new paradigm for rearing children had emerged, which a panel of experts with the Midcentury White House Conference on Children and Youth termed naturalism, meaning that a mother's natural instincts toward her child were the best guide to good parenting. Of course, it would be up to the experts to determine what these instincts were and to pathologize women who did not exhibit them.[18]

Education, once deemed essential to the proper practice of parenting, was now viewed as irrelevant by many professionals. Benjamin Spock admitted as much in an article for the *Ladies' Home Journal,* "Can Motherhood Be Taught?": "Home influences during a girl's early upbringing are usually more important [than education]—particularly her mother's basic feeling about motherhood." He was not convinced that parent education was of much value to parents; it was liable to make them feel "guilty," whereas his goal was to make them more "comfortable." He was concerned about the problems of warning parents "about the unfortunate outcomes of minor, common behavior problems." But Spock seemed to be unaware that in practice child-study clubs did not necessarily reinforce the injunctions of much of the professional literature—or that a baby book read in isolation could be more injurious than beneficial to self-confidence.[19]

In keeping with the resolutely upbeat tempo of the times, writers of the late 1940s and 1950s stressed that mothering should be easy, pleasurable, and fun. Earlier writers had characterized motherhood as an intellectual enterprise, worthy of the talents of a Radcliffe graduate. The experts of the 1950s contended that a woman didn't need to be a college graduate to be a good mother; indeed, any simpleton could do the job, as long as she was in tune with her "natural" instincts. Famous pediatrician and psychoanalyst D. W. Winnicott patronizingly reassured mothers in his *Mother and Child: A Primer of First*

Relationships: "You do not have to be clever and you do not even have to think if you do not want to. You may have been hopeless in arithmetic at school; or perhaps all your friends got scholarships but you couldn't stand the sight of a history book and so failed and left school early. Or you may be really clever. But all this does not matter, and it hasn't anything to do with whether or not you are a good mother. If a child can play with a doll, you can be an ordinary devoted mother." Winnicott was seemingly unaware of the contradiction inherent in handing women a primer on motherhood and then telling them that they didn't have to "think" to do the job right. Mothers were instructed to indulge their natural instincts toward children, with instincts generally being defined as spontaneous responses to children's demands for food, attention, and affection. By interpreting these maternal behaviors as instincts, Winnicott and others trivialized the thinking involved in the countless decisions mothers must make on a daily basis about how to treat their children and sought to promote their own recommended methods in contradistinction to the supposedly "artificial" behaviorist child-rearing methods of the past.[20]

Formal education might not be a prerequisite for being a good mother, but the conditions required for adequate mothering, according to the literature, made it nearly impossible to avoid permanently damaging a child's psyche. A mother had to get her child off to a good start by delivering calm, caring, and continuous nurturing, beginning with the infant's first days of life. The expectation that the emotionally adjusted mother would suffer no doubts about her profession but commit herself cheerfully to the care of her husband and children intensified the feelings of inadequacy of mothers who were less than fully satisfied with their situation. Mothers who were discontented with full-time homemaking, who had grown up in troubled homes, whose own mothers had felt unfulfilled, or whose marital relationship was less than ideal posed a risk to their children's psychological development. According to one mother who wrote to advice-giver Louise Bates Ames about her disenchantment with the Freudian approach to parenting, "The theory tends to create the feeling that since the causes are so deeply rooted there is no chance of ever really changing them and the child is blighted for life."[21]

These weighty complexes and maladjustments required one-on-one expert consultations. Parents outside the mainstream middle class were possibly even more alienated by the psychoanalytic orientation of parent education than they had been by the message of child development in the 1920s, which had at least included concrete suggestions for training children. Getting at the root of why you were an "overprotective" mother might take years of expensive psychoanalysis; by then, your children could already be adults with their own complexes to get rid of.

During the 1940s many psychologists had analyzed the damage that "unnatural" mothers could do to their children. In defining the "natural" mother of the 1950s, experts were less negative, although they continued to employ the concepts of maternal rejection and overprotection bandied about by psychoanalytic popularizers of the 1940s. A woman's basic feeling about her maternal role was the key to her success as a mother. Psychologists and pediatricians maintained that ambivalence about motherhood or even pregnancy could have dire consequences for children. (One expert even argued that such ambivalence could cause miscarriages.)[22]

Prominent psychologist John Bowlby's research into "maternal deprivation" provided ammunition to those who argued that good mothering was the key to an emotionally healthy childhood. Bowlby had been commissioned to study the plight of English and American infants who were institutionalized during World War II. Discovering that these children had serious developmental problems, he argued in the popularized version of his research, *Child Care and the Growth of Love* (1953), that infants must have an early attachment to a nurturing individual. Bowlby, however, then extrapolated from his knowledge of the impact of institutionalization on young children to a larger social context to claim that children could be deprived in "normal" families if their mothers worked outside the home or were otherwise unconsciously "rejecting." He contended, "The absolute need of infants and toddlers for the continuous care of their mothers will be borne in on all who read this book." Children without the enduring care of their mothers may turn to juvenile delinquency, according to Bowlby. Fathers bear little responsibility for children's emotional well-being in Bowlby's account: "Little will be said of the father-child relation; his value as the economic and emotional support of the mother will be assumed."[23] Motherhood was seen as a defining aspect of female identity; those who did not embrace it could permanently damage their children's psychic well-being.

While many writers proclaimed the joy and fulfillment that women found in their maternal roles, other authors cast homemaking in a more negative light, detailing the exhaustion, frustration, and loneliness that too often accompanied this demanding job. As we have seen in previous chapters, certain critics asserted that traditional gender roles impeded women's ability to attain the individualism essential for a healthy psyche.[24] Some questioned whether the American commitment to individualism applied to women, who were expected to give themselves over entirely to the nurture of others. Sidonie Gruenberg and her daughter Hilda Sidney Krech insisted that contemporary women's goals did not include "complete self-abnegation" and maintained that women should find ways to combine outside activities, whether paid or unpaid, with marriage and motherhood.[25] Although mainstream culture continued to valorize "self-realization," self-realization for women was for the most part couched in terms of their assistance to other family members in *their* quest for self-fulfillment. This clearly mixed message left some women flailing, as they sought to reconcile personal ambitions with maternal responsibilities.[26]

Although some continued to wonder whether higher education made women unfit for their motherly duties, others worried about women's increasing propensity to discontinue their educations to take up marriage and motherhood. Most champions of women's education argued that women should not be *limited* to marriage and motherhood but still insisted that the latter should take precedence over careers.[27] Growing numbers of married women with school-age children were entering the workforce during this period, but few were able to pursue the professional careers that they had envisioned as young women.[28] The modern mother's dilemma was that her education and life before motherhood had often inadequately prepared her either for life as a full-time mother *or* for a full-time career.

As Betty Friedan eloquently demonstrated in her groundbreaking *Feminine Mystique,* many women achieved no easy rapprochement with their roles as mothers during this era. Despite the relentlessly cheery tone of his baby book, even Benjamin Spock admitted in 1951, "Anyone who works with parents . . . finds mothers who are resentful, either frankly or covertly, about their role as housekeeper and child rearer." The February 1956 cover article in the *Ladies' Home Journal* featured the "The Plight of the Young Mother" as a matter deserving national attention. The journal issue denounced the long working hours and isolation of the average mother and expressed indignation at society's devaluation of the homemaker's job. Certainly many young and idealistic women and men embarked optimistically on the enterprise of raising large, happy families. Yet numerous young mothers found the experience a severe test of their emotional stamina.[29]

Lacking a supportive female community within which they could discuss the day-to-day frustrations of dealing with children, and still confronting a barrage of professional advice, mothers found their interactions with children taking on a peculiar intensity. Poet and essayist Adrienne Rich, who gave birth to her children during the "family-centered, consumer-oriented, Freudian-American world of the 1950s," wrote in her diary of the "murderous alternation between bitter resentment and raw-edged nerves, and blissful gratification and tenderness" that accompanied her experience of motherhood.[30] Seemingly petty problems with children were magnified by the homemaker's isolation and the inescapable critical commentary of the experts. Interestingly, the writers to whom mothers responded most readily were those less likely to engage in the "mother-blaming" rhetoric. Even if some of the parenting strategies advocated by experts such as Benjamin Spock, Louise Bates Ames, and Frances Ilg might be vetoed by mothers, these writers tended to inspire mothers' confidence because they appeared to be optimistic about mothers' abilities to be good and effective parents.

MODERN BIBLES FOR MODERN TIMES: THE BABY BOOK GURUS OF THE 1940S AND 1950S

The names of Arnold Gesell, Louise Bates Ames, and Frances Ilg have been overshadowed by that of the legendary author of *Baby and Child Care,* Dr. Spock. Yet the impact of these first three on American parents and educators has outlasted the period of their greatest renown, the 1940s and 1950s. I have already discussed the Gesell group's contribution to the "discourse of the democratic family," their philosophy of "growth," and their promotion of self-demand feeding. Perhaps more important, they popularized the stage theory of childhood development, which lingers on in everyday talk of the behavior one expects of children at various ages. Paperbacks by Ames and Ilg detailing the behaviors to be expected of the one-year-old, the two-year-old, and so on, still have a place in the child-care section of most bookstores. The trio also made major contributions to pediatrics and education, including the construction of developmental tests to gauge the normalcy of infants, and school-readiness tests, some of which are still in use today.[31]

A student of G. Stanley Hall, Arnold Gesell began his working life as a teacher and later a principal in Wisconsin before earning a Ph.D. in psychology from Clark University in 1906. Gesell seems to have acquired from Hall a faith in the power of nature to foster children's development. He was hired as assistant professor of education in 1911 by Yale University, where he pursued a medical degree and instituted the Yale Clinic of Child Development as a diagnostic and advisory facility for children with developmental problems. He was hired simultaneously by the state of Connecticut as the nation's first school psychologist in 1915; in this work he joined his interest in the diagnosis of developmental problems with his advocacy of educational provisions for children with special needs. Early in his career, Gesell was something of a reformer and believed in the efficacy of preschools and public health measures in improving children's health. Like many of his contemporaries, Gesell flirted with behaviorism in the 1920s; one of his first publications described human psychology as a "bundle of habits, complexes, and conditioned reflexes."[32]

Gesell's research on the problems of the developmentally impaired eventually led him to his study of the normal child, for which he is best known. Using Yale's nursery school and research clinic, he embarked on extensive research to ascertain the physical, emotional, and intellectual milestones along the road of children's development. In the course of his studies, he found himself abandoning his environmentalist orientation and returning to the ideas of his mentor Hall. The studies, setting forth Gesell's own maturationist theory of growth, resulted in 1940 in the publication of his popular *First Five Years of Life*. In numerous additional works he pursued his preoccupation with defining the boundaries of normal childhood growth and development. His texts served both to inform pediatricians about developmental norms and to provide parents with guidance on whether their children were developing normally.[33]

Gesell's colleague Louise Bates Ames received a master's degree in psychology from the University of Maine in 1933. Her master's thesis was based on a behavioral analysis of her own infant daughter, using motion pictures as documentation, a procedure she would incorporate into her work at the Yale Clinic. Ames would make herself indispensable as Gesell's assistant, and on completing her doctoral studies in 1936, she was appointed an instructor at Yale. Ames collaborated with Gesell on some of his most famous works, including *Infant and Child in the Culture of Today* (1943) and *The Child from Five to Ten* (1946). Shortly after Gesell retired in 1948, Yale appointed child psychologist Milton Senn as the new director of the clinic. Senn disparaged what he considered to be the sloppy work of his predecessors. As a result, Ames, along with Frances Ilg and their associate Janet Learned, left Yale to found the Gesell Institute of Child Development. Gesell had been queried several times about the possibility of writing a popular newspaper column for parents, a possibility he consistently rejected. Ames and Ilg were more amenable to this suggestion, however, and in 1951 launched the widely syndicated newspaper column "Child Behavior" that would later become "Parents Ask." Louise Bates Ames continued an active program of research and writing at the Gesell Institute until her death in 1996.[34]

Frances Ilg joined the Yale Clinic of Child Development as a pediatrician newly trained at Cornell who had completed a residency at the New England

Hospital for Women and Children in Boston. She worked at the clinic as a research assistant from 1933 to 1936 before taking a year's leave to work with children's health in Sweden. She returned to the clinic as assistant professor of child development, a position she maintained until 1947, when she was appointed research associate at the Yale University School of Medicine. Ilg became the director of the Gesell Institute of Child Development, which she and Ames founded in 1950. She researched and helped write many of the works for which Arnold Gesell is most famous, including *Infant and Child in the Culture of Today, The First Five Years of Life,* and *The Child from Five to Ten.* While in Sweden, Ilg adopted a daughter, of whom she has said, "My perceptions were greatly sharpened by living with a child from day to day and growing up with her. She became an intimate part of the work and of the books. She and the books grew up together."[35]

Gesell, Ilg, and Ames were a united team of researchers who staunchly defended their hereditarian point of view and remained relatively impervious to developments in the field that were unrelated to their own research. Because of their unrelenting focus on the role of genetics in determining children's growth, their seeming disregard for environmental influences on children, their questionable research methods, and their failure to interact with other child developmentalists, they were considered to be iconoclastic and were dismissed by many of their peers, yet their impact on parents and pediatricians is indisputable.[36]

AGES AND STAGES: THE GESELL GROUP CHARTS THE PROGRESS OF NORMAL DEVELOPMENT

Gesell and his colleagues argued that most children's problems were biologically based and that parental interventions had only a minor impact on children's behavior. The Gesell books had the effect of alleviating the overwhelming sense of responsibility with which many mothers had been imbued. One journalist characterized Gesell's impact on parents in these terms: "He has allayed a good deal of anxiety and provided the reassurance many uneasy parents need that they have spawned—not kicking, biting, head-thumping, no-no-ing tantrum-prone, discipline-resistant little monsters—but reasonably representative infants and children who in their own developmental time will calm down before they bust out all over again."[37] The Gesell baby is not always reasonable or easily controlled; the child has a will, temperament, and genetic constitution of its own, with which parents cannot tamper at will. If the Gesell approach alleviated parental responsibility it also implicitly favored a child-centered approach to child rearing, for much unruly behavior was characterized as age-appropriate and therefore requiring parental understanding rather than correction. In a parents' discussion outline for the Gesell group's popular film *Life With Baby,* for instance, the audience was informed: "Parents often punish their children for behavior that is entirely normal—but the parents who understand the stages of growth are able to guide the child and enjoy him because they know that some very troublesome phases are simply natural stages of development."[38] According to the Gesell research, then, behavior once defined as being far enough beyond the bounds to merit punishment was now defined as normal and thus not necessarily punishable.

Gesell's early texts were not as calculated to appeal to a popular audience as were Spock's; indeed, many wished that Gesell would repackage his ideas so that he would be more accessible to the masses, a job that Ames and Ilg would take on in later years. In striking contrast to the opening line of Spock's *Baby and Child Care,* "You know more than you think you do," which immediately draws the mother into the text through a direct appeal to her, the first sentence of *The First Five Years of Life* purports to be a factual statement: "In a biological sense the span of human infancy extends from the zero hour of birth to the middle twenties."[39] In charting the stages of behavior, Gesell appealed to a mass audience's desire for simplification, but he did not present himself in the role of paternalistic adviser.

The normalization of age-specific behaviors in Gesell's books was viewed with suspicion by some within the child development community who feared that the norms would lead to parental anxiety when children did not exhibit behavior that was age-appropriate according to the experts' definitions. Milton Senn, who directed the Yale clinic after Gesell's retirement, devoted an article in a 1955 issue of the *Woman's Home Companion* to denouncing the effect of his predecessor's theories on American parents. Senn claimed that he was besieged by worried mothers, each of them complaining that "her child's behavior appears to differ from the 'normal' behavior listed for his age in certain books," specifically those of the Gesell group.[40] The books did, however, reassure parents, many of whom may not have had the chance to observe the progress of "normal" childhood development, that most children would outgrow their troubling behavior sooner or later. One mother confided to Ames and Ilg, "There are definite times when every parent is puzzled—in fact there are moments when you aren't at all sure that your darling isn't a little bit 'off'— these are the times when the 'books' are a beautiful, luxurious comfort!"

Numerous complaints came, though, from parents who objected to the implied permissiveness of the Gesellian theories. And the question remained how representative the group's definitions of normalcy were. One individual offered a telling critique in response to a journalistic account of the Gesell group's work: "Gesell gives us data on children who have been brought up in a culture that is too meddlesome and too emotional. Will someone please give us some data on children who have been guided with a light hand?"[41]

From a scientific point of view, the research on which Gesell based his writings was seriously flawed; it relied on unrepresentative samples of white middle-class children and made unjustifiable claims on the basis of limited data. Many scholars find Gesell's characterization of the various stages of child development almost laughable because of their stereotypical descriptions of children's behavior at different ages. Such prose as "THREE has a conforming mind. FOUR has a lively mind. THREE is assentive; FOUR assertive" may be appealing to a popular audience but is appallingly reductive.[42] Nonetheless, there was apparently enough truth in the group's characterization of the typical behaviors of white middle-class children that many parents and preschool teachers responded—and continue to respond—favorably.

Ames and Ilg, in their popularization of Gesell's work, campaigned against what they regarded as the parent blaming of the Freudians and hypothesized that most children's behavior could be attributed to either their developmental stage or their basic genetic makeup.[43] In keeping with their hereditarian point of view, Ames and Ilg also were proponents of William Sheldon's theory of constitutional psychology, which correlated personality with differing body types (ectomorph, mesomorph, and endomorph), even after his findings were discredited.[44]

Psychoanalysts were concerned that the Gesell group's exclusive attention to heredity might cause parents to ignore their own contributions to childhood behavior problems (and might also cut down on visits to child psychologists). Even colleagues such as Margaret Mead and Benjamin Spock with whom the Gesell group had at one point been closely aligned would later object that the group went too far in downplaying the parents' formative role.[45] But many parents found the Gesell theories of child development a welcome respite. The Gesell group did not seek to alter mothers' personalities or to suggest the need for psychotherapy or radical changes in their parenting practices. Their aims were more modest: to educate mothers about the various behaviors they might encounter as they raised their children.

As they carved out careers in the parental advice industry for themselves,

Ames and Ilg also took a fairly progressive approach to gender roles. They did not support Bowlby's theory that an immediate and enduring attachment with a maternal figure was necessary for children's adjustment, and they were equally uncomfortable with theories of maternal rejection or overprotection. Like many child developmentalists today, they recognized that mothers are not the only influential actors in the parent-child encounter: "Nearly all mothers try hard to make their relationship with their children as perfect as possible. Some try too hard. For the relationship depends not just on the mother alone but on the child as well, and often failure in this relationship is due, not to the mother's ineptness, but to the kind of child she is dealing with."[46] Unlike many of their peers, they considered autism and other serious psychological or developmental problems to be primarily physical in origin rather than precipitated by bad mothering.[47]

Ames and Ilg also did not hedge when it came to the question of mothers and careers but stated quite flatly that the choice to work outside the home depended on the character of the individual mother. In fact, they defended working mothers from their critics: "These women are not lazy. They are not slackers. They are not unnatural mothers." Their belief in the inherent individuality of each person led them to posit that there was no one path in life for women or men.[48] Their concept of individuality also contributed to their relatively relaxed approach to children who did not conform to traditional gender roles. When panic-stricken parents wrote about boy children who enjoyed playing with dolls and girls who would not wear dresses, they urged parents to tolerate the unconventional behavior, not only because ridicule and punishment were likely to be more problematic than helpful but because there was probably little that a parent could do to make a boy child more "manly" if his inclinations led him in a different direction.[49] Children would develop appropriate sex-role identities in their own time. The child-centered parenting strategies that Ames and Ilg promoted were in congruence with mainstream professional opinion, yet they did not hesitate to express points of view distinctly at odds with those of their colleagues in the field.

"YOU KNOW MORE THAN YOU THINK YOU DO": THE APPEAL OF BABY AND CHILD CARE

Most Americans are familiar with the career of Benjamin Spock as a pediatrician and political activist. His name has become indelibly associated with the baby boomer generation, and his manual, *The Commonsense Book of Baby and*

Child Care (often shortened to *Baby and Child Care*) was a mainstay of many middle-class homes. Spock was primarily a disseminator of information who conveyed the research of other scholars to parents in a palatable and chatty form. He encouraged a relatively relaxed approach to child rearing and, like the Gesell group, advocated that parents discard the rigidity of behaviorist child-rearing prescriptions. Spock championed the idea that parenting should be both fun and easy, a message that was meant to restore parental self-confidence but that in fact could be frustrating to those who found parenting more of a struggle than a satisfaction. Unlike the Gesell group, Spock enjoyed a fair amount of support from the professional community of child developmentalists for his efforts, although he was criticized, by those with whom he worked closely, for his simplistic approach to research and teaching.[50]

Born in 1903 in New Haven, Connecticut, into a stern but loving Protestant family, Spock followed in his father's footsteps by attending Yale as an undergraduate. He obtained his degree in medicine from Columbia, pursued advanced degrees in both pediatrics and psychiatry, and received five years of psychoanalytic training in the early 1930s. He maintained a private practice in New York City from 1933 until the publication of his baby manual. In accordance with the tenets of John B. Watson and L. Emmett Holt, which were widely held by pediatricians of the time, Spock and his wife fed their first child, born in the 1930s, according to a schedule and avoided picking him up when he cried. Following his years of psychoanalytic training, however, Spock began to question the advisability of frustrating the infant's needs, and his second child, born in 1944, received the more flexible combination of scheduled feedings and feedings on demand that Spock recommended in *Baby and Child Care,* published two years later. Spock's philosophy of child care evolved both from his psychoanalytic training and from his increasing interest in the progressive educational philosophy of his mentor Caroline Zachary and John Dewey.[51]

In his dual training as a pediatrician and psychoanalyst, Spock was somewhat of an anomaly, given that few pediatricians seemed interested in psychoanalysis and few analysts cared about applying their ideas to mundane matters of child rearing. Although he had considered a career as a psychoanalyst, he experienced only failure with the three patients whom he analyzed. Thus he moved increasingly in the direction of pediatrics, where he thought that his psychoanalytic insights might help him to develop more adequate responses to parents' questions about feeding, toilet training, and disciplinary problems. He was influenced by a prominent group of New York intellectuals, all of whom were profoundly affected by psychoanalytic theory in the 1930s, including anthropologist Margaret Mead and psychologist Erik Erickson. Indeed, Spock describes his early pediatrics practice as comprising largely the families of psychiatrists, social workers, educators, and others who were concerned that they receive "psychologically correct" advice on matters of rearing children (one of whom was Mead's daughter, Catherine Bateson). Spock's growing reputation as a psychologically oriented pediatrician resulted in a query from Doubleday about the possibility of his writing an inexpensive child-rearing manual based on psychoanalytic theory, a challenge that he accepted.[52]

Initially priced at just twenty-five cents a copy, Spock's comprehensive guide to baby's physical and emotional care, *Baby and Child Care,* sold three-quarters of a million copies during its first year of publication. Spock explains that his book emanated from both theory and his ten years of practice as a pediatrician; he has never mentioned that his experience as a parent was influential in the formation of his ideas. His wife at the time, Jane Cheney Spock, insisted that she had a larger role in shaping the book's content than her husband acknowledged, and it is possible that her contributions may have derived from her experiences with their children. Spock did admit, however, to making use of his patients' insights into and observations about children's behavior, claiming, "Every time a mother told me something even slightly different from my previous concepts, I revised my ideas accordingly." Spock's success was undoubtedly related to his responsiveness to his audience: he was constantly revising his book to take into account his readers' criticisms and suggestions.[53]

In 1954, Spock began writing an extremely popular monthly column for the *Ladies' Home Journal,* which would introduce new readers to his writings, thereby contributing to the growing popularity of *Baby and Child Care.* The column also afforded him the opportunity to engage in exchanges with mothers that would help him continue to tailor his advice to his audience. In 1962, Spock was fired by new editors who did not care for his left-wing politics. He began writing instead for *Redbook,* a less stodgy magazine than the *Journal.*[54] Throughout these years, Spock taught at the Mayo Clinic, the University of Pittsburgh, and Western Reserve University. Spock had a second career, however, which would both enhance his name recognition and increase his symbolic association with the baby boomer generation. Beginning with his support for presidential candidates Adlai Stevenson and John F. Kennedy, Spock became involved in liberal politics and was a highly visible opponent of the war in Vietnam in 1968. Spockian "permissiveness" was blamed for the protests and unconventionality of many of the baby boomers; his radical, antimilitaristic political views led his critics to underscore the connections between progressive politics and advocacy of nonauthoritarian parenting styles. The politics of child rearing and the politics of the nation had rarely been so clearly linked in the popular imagination.[55]

It is probably no accident that the cheap, homespun compendium of information, advice, and reassurance won Spock thousands of ardent admirers during the postwar period. The book combined extensive information on many of the most common childhood illnesses with information about children's care and development and was widely distributed by doctors and nurses to American mothers. Publication of the manual in 1946 serendipitously coincided with the beginning of the baby boom, and successive editions took advantage of the surge in the birth rate.[56]

Women whose husband's jobs took them away from their families of origin, especially servicemen's wives, appear to have been especially appreciative of Spock's book. One woman living on an army base in Mississippi implied that *Baby and Child Care* was a substitute for her own mother, "I think your book is wonderful. Especially for a new mother away from home who doesn't have her mother to run to every time something new arises."[57] Some of these mothers had had little experience with infants before having their own children. A California mother confided in Spock, "Many young mothers, particularly like myself who have never been around a small child before our own children, are very thankful for a reliable source like your book to refer to when a problem arises."[58]

Many middle-class mothers would have liked to receive the counsel of their physicians, but actual doctors could be offputting, expensive, and inaccessible. Consequently, the information in Spock's book detailing the diagnosis and treatment of children's minor illnesses and behavior problems could be a lifesaver. The empowerment that a child-rearing manual delivered was apparent in one testimonial: "That book to a mother was knowledge—confidence—you could lean on it and know what you were doing. It saved Doctors so many unnecessary trips and so many bills that they probably never would have collected."[59]

Spock believed that mothers had been harmed by the experts' many injunctions and wished to restore their faith in their own "common sense." In a magazine article, he admitted, "I wanted to write to a mother in a way that would *reassure* her. I didn't want to scold and lecture her." Spock's strategy for achieving this reassurance was to insist that mothers already had at their disposal most of the knowledge needed to raise children; hence he began his book with the line mentioned earlier: "You know more than you think you do." He assured mothers that raising a baby was easy if they had faith in their natural feminine instincts and trust in their doctors: "Bringing up your child won't be a complicated job if you take it easy, trust your own instincts, and follow the directions that the doctor gives you." Of course, what was a woman to do if her "instincts" told her one thing and her doctor another? Indeed, if mothers truly relied on their "instincts" or on maternal practices sanctioned by tradition, there would be no need for the pediatrician's child-rearing advice—surely not the outcome Spock intended. The underlying message was that Spock (with the assistance of a personal pediatrician) could reassure mothers about their capacity to accomplish everything the experts required: the readers of *Baby and Child Care* could be ideal parents.[60] That Spock did not, in fact, inspire the desired confidence in mothers is suggested by a journalist's characterization of the manual as one that "many mothers clutch like a pacifier."[61]

In applying psychoanalysis to his book, Spock diluted and distorted Freud's theories, especially with regard to the role of instincts in the infant's life. The Spockian infant harbors few of the dark impulses attributed by Freud to young human beings; instincts are instead bathed in a benevolent light. Spock, for instance, characterizes aggression as a natural impulse that is easily dealt with by the good mother, who knows how to take hair-pulling and biting in stride, realizing that in time children's aggressive behavior will be channeled into more socially acceptable activities, such as making a living. Spock's characterization of instincts may have been designed to assuage the anxieties of mothers who would be disturbed by Freud's dimmer view of human impulses. Whereas Freud depicted the infant as ruled by unconscious, irrational drives, Spock described the baby's natural instincts and impulses as eminently reasonable. Nonetheless, Spock feared that psychic damage would occur if mothers too consistently thwarted their children's natural impulses. Thus Spock's characterization of the baby as "reasonable" was in part a rhetorical ploy designed to secure mothers' compliance with his child-rearing strategies by appealing to—rather than disturbing—his audience.[62]

It may be misleading to characterize Spock's advice to parents as permissive, for he was always an advocate of firm and consistent discipline. His advice can certainly be defined as child-centered, though, in the sense that parents were urged to tailor their child-rearing strategies to the nature and needs of their children. Spock implied that if mothers were sufficiently in tune with these, they would find ways to secure compliance through cooperation and manipulation rather than traditional authoritarian discipline. In keeping with this goal, one of Spock's admitted aims was to tell mothers, ostensibly on the basis of scientific knowledge, what children are like and what behavioral changes they go through as they develop.

His contention was that with a loving home and security children develop without much trouble. The Spockian child is not a schemer or a troublemaker, out to drive his mother to distraction. Unlike the Gesellian baby, who can be quite "unreasonable" depending on its age or nature, the infant Spock characterizes is rational and considerate: "Your baby is born to be a reasonable, friendly human being. If you treat him nicely, he won't take advantage of you"—advice that was hardly reassuring to mothers whose children were rarely reasonable or friendly.[63] The Spockian baby acquires the habits of grown-up living with ease, because he wants to: "But each child wants, himself, to eat at sensible hours, and later to learn good table manners. . . . In all these habits he will fit into the family's way of doing things sooner or later without much effort on your part." With such reassurance, it is not surprising that some mothers would be frustrated when their child failed to behave accordingly. A mother writing to Spock conveyed just this sentiment, "I read your book on child care and was thoroughly disgusted with it. . . . You made it sound so easy. All you had to do was feed your baby burp her good and lay her back down and the little angel would go rite [sic] to sleep."[64] On the other hand, many mothers were soothed by Spock's depiction of parenting as a natural and easy activity, which allowed them to relax and trust their own "common sense" as a reliable guide.

Spock's psychoanalytic orientation influenced the form in which he addressed the mothers for whom the book was intended. His desire to convey the message that motherhood was natural and instinctual distinguished his book from earlier behaviorist child-rearing manuals that portrayed motherhood as a learned activity.[65] Spock hoped that his book would provide mothers with a cathartic experience by verbalizing for them the anxieties, fears, and frustrations that accompanied child rearing but that might otherwise go unacknowledged. In fact, Spock worried that these anxieties might contribute to the maternal "pathologies" that his psychoanalyst friends were dissecting. He hoped instead to lessen the intensity of common maternal anxieties by acknowledging their legitimacy. In a letter to a colleague, Spock articulated his therapeutic intent: "I am always looking for chances to express their [mothers'] probable feelings, especially the less admirable ones—irritation at the child, anxieties, suppressed irritation at the know it all experts, anger when the child rejects carefully prepared foods." Thus, unlike the objective, scientific tone that some earlier child-rearing manuals strove for, Spock's simple language and appeals to common maternal emotions inspired a devoted following among parents grateful to have their complicated emotions legitimated. A friend of Spock's described mothers' reactions to his lectures: "It's a revelation to see audience reactions to him. The women strain toward him, they're happy, they seem to be saying, 'Tell me more! Tell me again that I'm not so bad! Reassure me that it won't be awful if I get angry with my child! Tell me! Tell me!' "[66] Perhaps Spock hoped to play the perfect parent, like the psychoanalyst, and have his reader achieve the transference that accompanies a good therapeutic relationship. If indeed that occurred, many readers, like the father who equated writing to Spock with writing to God or some other supernatural power, seem not to have worked through the transference.[67]

In fact, Spock achieved his aim to disguise the therapeutic underpinnings of his baby book, his desire to seem an advocate of "common sense" rather than science. Indeed, he was viewed as the voice of common sense in the midst of an inchoate dialogue of experts. One journalist claimed that "Spockism . . . gives to the modern mother, paddling frantically about in a dark pool of Freudian implications, torn between the embattled forces of Discipline and Permissiveness, dazed by the potential perils of rejection, affection, early weaning, late toilet-training and chronic thumb-sucking, traumatized by the fear of causing a trauma and helplessly stuck with the suspicion that a little psychiatric orientation is a burdensome thing—to her Spockism gives surcease from anxiety, relief from guilt."[68]

It was in keeping with his reassuring tone that Spock did not overtly blame mothers for rejecting, neglecting, or overprotecting their children. Rather than directly criticize mothers who worked outside the home, he implied that women who truly cared about young children would stay at home with them: "The younger the child the more necessary it is for him to have a steady, loving person taking care of him. In most cases, the mother is the best one to give him this sense of 'belonging.' . . . If a mother realizes clearly how vital this kind of care is to a small child, it may make it easier for her to decide that the extra money she might earn, or the satisfaction she might receive from an outside job, is not so important after all."[69] Spock's attitudes toward working mothers were also influenced by his understanding of gender differences. Buying into a popular psychoanalytic line of thinking, Spock supported the notion that "woman's creativeness has a direct, soul-satisfying outlet in the bearing and rearing of children" that may prevent her from achieving the "highest levels of creativity in other fields."[70] Thus, while Spock soft-peddled his psychoanalytic understanding of women, as he did everything else, he basically viewed them as caretakers who should orient their lives toward nurturing children.

Working mothers were only one of a category of women not addressed in Dr. Spock's writings. Writing to a colleague in India about his work with rural parents at the Mayo Clinic in Minnesota, Spock inquired whether her clients were as unaware as his patients of the psychiatric implications of parenting: "I guess what I am asking is whether you are able to count on an awareness that what a parent does to his children has an influence one way or the other, and a belief that science has a contribution to make to understanding children. These are two assumptions that we can make, at least in American cities, and which we count on for our therapeutic efforts. . . . In Minnesota I found that some people from rural America have no such beliefs and I was then helpless, not only in advising but even in getting a history."[71] Thus, despite the important role that common sense ostensibly played in Spock's baby book, in his actual work with parents he hoped that they would be more attuned to "science" than to tradition.

Spock was even more forthright about his concerns about the mothers who attended his family clinic at Western Reserve in the 1950s, 95 percent of whom were young African-American women and many of whom were recent migrants from the South. He confessed to the well-known child psychologist Urie Bronfenbrenner his exasperation with their failure to follow "doctor's orders" in regard to child training: "I have to confess that they are frustrating for the medical students and me. They don't seem to expect or want medical advice on infant feeding, weaning, toilet training, sleep arrangements, sleep problems. In fact they silently but firmly refuse to take advice which is pressed on them." In an article about the same clinic in 1961, John Kennell claimed that although African-American mothers would accept advice about formula and immunization for newborns, later advice fell on deaf ears. When doctors recommend, for instance, that a mother provide children with their own bedrooms, "the mother fails to take the advice because she already knows that her sister plans to visit." Similarly, when the doctor urged the mother not to give the baby a bottle every time the baby whimpered, the mother was more concerned about protecting her neighbors from the sound of her baby's crying. Mothers tended to disregard doctor's advice that conflicted with their cultural or personal values, especially if such advice did not appear to be essential to ensuring their children's physical survival. These mothers acted in accord with Spock's purported belief that they should rely on their own common sense in rearing their children. Their response was not what Spock was accustomed to, though, and he claimed that "it leaves a physician who has gotten his gratification from rescuing anxious parents feeling out of work and unwanted."[72] The audience that responded to the phrase "you know more than you think you do" was thus one Spock knew well: middle-class mothers who were insecure about their parenting practices and looking for advice and reassurance from a masculine authority figure. African-American mothers knew more than Spock knew they did. They knew that Dr. Spock was not writing for them.[73]

The perception that Spock purveyed the kind of child-rearing advice appropriate for a white audience was publicly expressed in 1971, when African-American voices were more likely to be represented in mainstream discourse than in the fifties. In a *New York Times* article, "Wanted: A Dr. Spock for Black Mothers," Joanne Dann recorded the reactions of some African-American mothers when questioned about Dr. Spock. "Dr. Spock? He's for rich kids. He can't help my children. He doesn't know my child," responded one mother. Another frequent refrain was, "Nobody knows my child as well as I do," a concept that experts would agree with in principle. African-American mothers were apt to consult their aunts and grandmothers for advice, who presumably were more likely than white pediatricians to have a knowledge of their children's situations. But by 1971 Dann and African-American pediatrician James Comer feared that changing family patterns within the African-American community had weakened the extended family upon which mothers had relied. According to Dann, African-American mothers sought a "black Dr. Spock" for the same reasons that white women had turned to Benjamin Spock: to buttress the endangered extended family structure.[74]

Gesell, Ames, Ilg, and Spock all sought to alleviate the insecurities that many young mothers expressed about the rearing of children, Spock by insisting that children are basically easy to manage and "want" to grow up, and the Gesell group by explaining that tantrums, balkiness, and difficulties were more a matter of nature than of nurture. Seeking to overturn the behaviorist dogma of the past that had lingered on in both pediatrics and parental practices, these advice-givers all focused on development and growth, rather than regulation and training. Gesell, Ames, and Ilg distinguished themselves from the Freudians and did not take take part in the discussions on the overprotective or "rejecting" mother, wishing instead merely to inform mothers about "normal" children's development and thereby provide the reassurance that most children's behavior was not too far off the course. Spock assumed that most women *wanted* and had the capacity to be good mothers. While he was much more interested in parental influences on children than was the Gesell group, he assumed that he was likely to help mothers more by praising than by blaming them.

MOTHERS' LETTERS TO THE EXPERTS: "WE PROBABLY MADE EVERY MISTAKE POSSIBLE"

The pervasive message of earlier experts, which Spock, Ames, Ilg, and Gesell sought to correct—that mothers were to blame for all their children's psychic ills—was one that contemporary experts continued to emphasize, albeit in more nuanced language. Kay D'Amico, a mother in the 1950s, remembers her fear about the consequences of her actions toward her baby: "I had the idea that every little thing I did could have this terrific impact on this tender little psyche."[75] Whatever negative behavior their children exhibited, mothers questioned what they might have done, or failed to do, to cause the problem. The mothers who wrote to child-care experts during the 1950s judged themselves harshly, often seeking in vain to find the source of their children's troublesome behavior in their own conduct as mothers. To some extent, they had incorporated enough of the philosophy of scientific utopianism to believe that proper child management could alleviate their intrinsic difficulties even in a culture that denied women the community assistance in raising children that had been available in other eras and milieus. Yet many of the letters quietly questioned the correctness of expert explanations for childhood problems.

By this time, the pediatrician was regarded by many mothers as the ultimate adviser on matters that had once been the province of women—when to toilet train, how to feed a young infant, how to handle a child who would not sleep through the night. Pediatricians themselves, however, were not always in agreement about the "best" methods of raising young children. One mother switched from a pediatrician who encouraged relaxed toilet-training to a more old-fashioned doctor when her baby was twenty-eight months old and still not completely trained. The new doctor was appalled that the child was not yet toilet trained and advised that the mother spank the child whenever he had a messy diaper. The mother admitted that she did not like to spank the child but appeared unwilling to go against the "orders" of her doctor.[76] Caught between changing streams of advice, parents wondered whether they had given their child enough security and love or whether they had spoiled and overindulged them. A couple with a fussy three-month old wrote to Ames, "Knowing absolutely nothing about babies, we probably made every mistake possible," because they had made the "mistake" of picking the baby up when it cried.[77] Apparently they were unaware that their actions were, in fact, in keeping with the prevailing professional recommendations for the treatment of very young babies.

Doubts about recent expertise may have been cloaked in expressions of deference to professional wisdom, but the sway psychiatrists and pediatricians exercised over mass culture could not quiet the misgivings mothers felt about professional advice as they sought to make sense of their children's behavior.[78] The letter writers were, for example, aware of the prevailing psychological stance that many of children's problems were related to women's ambivalence about motherhood. Yet in their letters women contended that although they offered their children as much love and security as was within their power, those did not stave off troublesome behavior. Describing a three-year-old daughter whose tantrums were out of hand, a mother defended herself at the outset from experts who might attribute the problem to maternal rejection: "No child was ever so wanted and so happily received! . . . Have we failed so miserably as parents? We just can't shrug off her attitude—we feel there must be a reason."[79] In their response and in their professional writings, Ames and Ilg did not accept the explanation of maternal rejection as a common cause of childhood problems. They insisted that the reason for the tantrums lay in the child's basic personality structure and her age and stage, a response that must have been comforting to a mother who had assumed that she would be blamed.

Many of the problems discussed in child-study groups of the 1920s and 1930s similarly preoccupied 1950s mothers: temper tantrums, toilet-training, sleeping problems, and thumb-sucking, to name a few. In the 1920s, thumb-sucking had been regarded as a bad habit that needed to be eradicated, while in the 1950s it was regarded as a troublesome symptom of insecurity that required understanding, if not professional intervention. In *The Complete Book of Mothercraft* (1952), put together by a team of twenty-five experts, including Spock and Gesell, the authors claimed that a child sucks his thumb "when he feels that he is not loved enough, not safe enough, not good enough."[80] Writing about her seven-year-old son who continued to suck his thumb, a mother confessed, "I keep wondering if he feels insecure and what I can do to help him. We love him very much and have given him all the affection and care that is in our power." Mothers were aware that they were being held responsible for children's insecurity, but accepting that responsibility would mean that they had somehow failed to "love" or properly care for their children. Another mother with a six-year-old thumb-sucker also gathered that the suckers were not given enough love: "I have read all the material I could find on the subject, and it informs me that the cause is that the child feels unwanted. If ever a child received attention and love and affection, mine does. I will be quite frank and admit I work in an office and my mother keeps him while I work—now, before and after school." As a working mother, this woman anticipated criticisms that her child must be "neglected" but defended herself against them. In her response Ames supported the writer's belief that a child whose mother worked outside the home could be much loved.[81] Some writers also anticipated that they might be considered emotionally troubled themselves or "tense" because they had failed to train their children adequately. A parent seeking help with a four-year-old who was not yet toilet-trained predicted, "No doubt you must feel that I am tense about this and have transferred my feelings to my child."[82]

Some writers anticipated critiques of themselves or defended themselves at the outset; other writers readily accepted responsibility for their children's problems. In discussing her five-year-old boy's willfulness and negativity, a mother acknowledged, "Being slow and particular at my work and not a good manager, I think many of our boys wants were not satisfied and went overboard [*sic*] on others. Even when small I spanked him and was rough with him." Notice that the mother takes responsibility both for failing to fulfill her children's desires and for overindulging them. She was remorseful about the mistakes she had made and worried about passing her own behavior traits on to her child: "With the personality I have and the shameful mistakes I have made, how can we raise our boy to become a better person?" The letter goes into detail about how to deal with particular problems, such as what to do when her son won't eat his dinner or get dressed. Should they reason with him, make him sit on a chair in the corner, act "firm but friendly"? "A person reads so much and gets so undecided," she admitted, implying that the competing messages of the various baby books hardly assuaged her sense of inadequacy as a mother.[83]

A letter to Dr. Spock from a guilt-ridden mother gives some idea of the angst over maternal behavior that many suffered. After the mother had corrected her four-and-a-half-year-old son, he angrily asserted that he didn't like her "as a boss" and wished she would leave the house. The mother pretended to leave the house, carrying the three-year-old. When she returned seconds later, her son was screaming, "Mommy!" with tears running down his face. The woman confessed to Spock that she was "too ashamed to discuss it with my husband or Doctor or anyone I know, really. I think I shall always feel a twinge of guilt and remorse for needlessly causing my child one minute of terror."[84] Her shame and inability to forgive herself suggests the degree to which the phantom "good mother" haunted many ordinary mothers, who made mistakes, lost their tempers, and agonized over the choices they had made.

The language that mothers used in analyzing both their own and their children's behavior reveals the continuing prominence of psychological concepts in their thinking about everyday interactions with their children. They may not have agreed that their child was wetting his bed because he was unloved or unwanted, but for the most part they accepted that children should receive large doses of love and affection and experience a minimum of frustration and tension. As we have seen, however, messages about how to rear psychologically healthy children were more likely to be heard by white middle-class women. Women who had not initially read the literature were dismayed when they discovered that their child-rearing practices were now considered pathological. A mother from the mountains of Pennsylvania wrote to Spock in despair about her recent reading:

> I didn't read many books on child care as I had been around children quite a lot. Now I read that the most important years in forming the personality are the first two. For our first child a girl and usually a very good baby we would let her cry herself to sleep sometimes 15–20 min because we thought we would spoil her. I can even remmer [sic] evenings when she was playing in the play pen quietly, that I often wanted to pick her up but didn't think I should since she was contented. We didn't often have baby sitters but we didn't hold and rock her much and she usually had her bottle propped and as she got older I made her listen, altho [sic] you usually didn't have much trouble making her listen, if I would slap her hand once she would usually stop and I always made her take a nap in the afternoon. . . . All the articles I read lately have me worrying that maybe she doesn't know we love her and maybe this could be because of the way we took care of her the first 2 yr. . . . Is there anything to do that can make up for not being as close to her altho she seemed contented most of the time.

The mother's concern that she would spoil her baby by picking her up harks back to expert advice from an earlier era, probably passed down to her orally by relatives rather than through books. The mother also feared the psychic damage that might result from her perceived failure to assure her child of her love for her. Perhaps most important, however, is the mother's own perception of the child as a "good baby" who "seemed contented most of the time." Her doubts were awakened by her reading of advice columns rather than by her own worries about her daughter.[85]

"LOVING REASON *DOES* SOMETIMES FAIL"

Some correspondents contested expert prescriptions explicitly, on the basis of mothering principles they had garnered from religion, community, family, and experience.[86] In a study conducted in 1978, researchers discovered that the most common objections to child-rearing texts were that they were "not practical enough," "not specific enough," and "too permissive," criticisms that seem to characterize mothers' reactions to baby books in the earlier period as well.[87] Perhaps the most frequent criticism was that experts made mothering seem too easy and that they saw no need for discipline or punishment. Mothers rarely conformed to the letter of the advice and mediated between theory and practice on a daily basis. In fact, studies of mothers' child-rearing practices during this era found that the majority of mothers could be characterized as neither permissive nor strict; most belonged somewhere in the middle. Similarly, researchers found that the largest percentage of mothers were wholly committed neither to feeding infants on demand nor to scheduling feedings but rather combined the two methods.[88] Mothers pragmatically sought solutions that combined the needs for regularity and for flexibility. Some mothers believed— or learned from experience—that child-centered parenting was liable to produce unmanageable children who were unable to cope in the adult world.

It was in the arena of punishment and discipline that experts and mothers diverged most dramatically. Like Gesell, Spock was not convinced of the benefits of punishment, arguing, "People who have specialized in child care feel that it [punishment] is seldom required." The large majority of mothers, however, persisted in believing that successful parenting required occasional judicious application of punishment. A mother from Sarasota, Florida, wrote to both Spock and Ames and Ilg within a year and a half. In her first letter she thanked Ames and Ilg for their many sensible recommendations but expressed one reservation: "You don't deal enough in the situation where the child *must* be punished in some way. . . . Imagine that sympathy—talks—ignoring it— have failed. . . . In other words does punishment in any form exist in your theories? I wonder if even you were to avoid it successfully—is this perfectly managed childhood a good preparation for life anyway? Loving reason *does* sometimes fail except in the laboratories." Writing to Spock the next year, this same woman threw up her hands in exasperation at expert advice: "Modern educational and psychological theories are nothing but unscientific theories, a lot of them. They have yet to be proved, and after the devastating theories didn't work on my first child, I refused, as far as I can, to offer up my second child for more experiments."[89] This mother objected to the advice on grounds that it was impractical; after all, mothers don't raise children in laboratories, and the strategies that might work in controlled conditions did not always succeed in the more tumultuous arena of the home. But—no doubt partly because of the rapidity with which child-care precepts were overturned and replaced with new ones—the writer also perceived that the advice was not properly "scientific" and had yet to be proved effective. Like many mothers, she was less willing to accept the professional wisdom docilely after experience with her first child.

By 1957 even Spock would admit that parents of the 1950s were too permissive and that he was planning to rewrite his baby book to reinforce the importance of firm discipline in rearing children, in part as a result of his correspondence with mothers. He conceded that he had been reacting in his earlier book to the rigidity of behaviorist child-rearing prescriptions and had perhaps failed to underscore the need for an authoritative parental presence in the home. In response to his revised stance, one mother wrote to Spock acknowledging that the indirect methods of disciplining children advocated by *Baby and Child Care* had caused her nothing but problems and that her younger children had been raised with a more "no-nonsense" approach: "I realize that your approach to discipline has changed considerably since the Spock Bible of 1947. Probably the infinite attempts to distract, substitute other activities, consult the child— eventually a blow up of exhaustion and a guilty conscience are just my foolishness, although our three younger children have had much less nonsense and I've learned something by the experience."[90] Other mothers also asserted that their practical experience with children had led them to be more critical in their responses to the professional literature and that they had raised later children with a firmer hand than baby books counseled.

Another group of mothers challenged the experts on the grounds of principle rather than of practicality. These mothers held views of child rearing that differed starkly from those sanctioned by the professional community. The indulgent approach to raising children was anathema to mothers who believed in strong discipline to prepare children for an unforgiving world and who rejected the notion that their job as parents was to avoid "frustrating" their children's needs. They did not advocate self-expression as a value in its own right but insisted that particular forms of self-expression were not acceptable. In response to a "Parents Ask" column that had explained that it was normal for children of certain ages to voice hostility toward their parents, an Ohio mother responded vehemently: "The day will *never* come when either one of them would so much as dare to retort with 'I hate you!', much less walk away from either me or my husband when being reprimanded, muttering under her breath 'I hate her!' The trouble with what you call normal children these days is parents, and doctors such as yourselves who write such obnoxious columns."[91] Such individuals disputed not only the advice about how to handle children but the experts' judgments about what constituted *normal* behavior.

Parents with a different conception of child rearing than that fostered by the dominant ideology felt under siege from the constant stream of advice urging them to shape their parenting to the needs of children. Their belief that children would be best prepared for the adult world if they confronted its realities at an early age was a minority view in the pages of the prescriptive literature. They contested the emphases of the parenting literature on lessening children's frustrations and enhancing their security. A mother of eight grown children informed Spock about her philosophy of child rearing:

> Won't you please tell the mothers of to-day's children that the Lord never intended parents to be burnt offerings to the children they brought in the world and that they can't give their children a "sense of security" by keeping them in cotton-wool—safe from the cruel world, which, when he gets out in it won't give a hooray about his complexes and frustrations. The helpless, pampered children of to-day have about as much chance of success in that world as the proverbial snowball has of getting through—you know where! I am so fed up on parents who let their children become little monsters, because they are afraid of the results of allowing them to be "frustrated" that I long to overcome those frustrations by the outmoded hairbrush.

Most of the letter writers were educated women who had been exposed to the tenets of psychology, as their vocabulary reveals. The mother cited above employs such phrases as "sense of security," "complexes," and "frustrations." Her modern sensibility is also implicit in her insinuation that she longs to, but would not actually, use the "outmoded hairbrush." She makes a religious reference to the "Lord," but her major complaint is more secular: child-centered parenting fails to prepare children for the world they must live in. As an afterthought, the writer gave a brief resume of her qualifications, "I had no degree in psychology and my family grew up long before your books and articles appeared, so I learned child-training the hard way—by doing it." As evidence for the validity of her own parental practices she offered the example of her eight grown children, all of them apparently happy and productive citizens.[92] Although few writers asked Spock whether he was in fact responsible for raising his own children, many of the letters implied that the author was lacking in practical experience.

A more renowned mother, the popular writer Taylor Caldwell, was disturbed by the sentimentalization of childhood, which she thought the psychological literature promoted. After being tormented by other children when she was growing up, she was disinclined to accept the benign interpretation of children's behavior that Spock and other writers offered. In recounting some of the exploits of the little harassers, she claimed, "It was not a search for 'security,' for the brats came from loving and wealthy families who adored them." Having converted to the Catholic church, Caldwell found a better explanation for children's behavior than that in the psychological literature: "The Church teaches that man is born naturally inclined to evil, averse to good. . . . It takes many, many years of stern discipline, spiritual instruction, punishment, severity tempered with affection, unremitting civilizing efforts, to convert the child-beast to a human being. If these things are not done—à la John Dewey—the beast remains a beast, becomes a delinquent, or worse."[93]

Caldwell was not the only mother for whom the Bible counted as a major reference guide in the rearing of children. In general, people with a strong religious affiliation will develop child-rearing values that at least partially derive from their communities of belief. African-American mothers, for instance, have historically called on both the Bible and the church as major sources of socialization for their children. Na'im Akbar noted in a speech given in 1975 that African-American mothers "didn't know nothin' 'bout Dr. Spock, but they did know the Bible—'raise up a child in the way he should go and when he is old he will not depart from it.'" Similarly, a study of lower-income mothers, including African-American, Hispanic, and Caucasian women, found that the only significant factor correlated with "adequacy" (as compared to neglect) in a mother was church attendance. Although churches often incorporate psychological conceptions of human nature into their religious teachings, they may also have alternative explanations for behavior that compete with the psychological point of view.[94]

MOTHERS AT THEIR WITS' END

Some mothers found solace and assistance at church, but other women had difficulty finding social support for parenting. Young middle-class mothers who did not have enough extra cash to hire help or to send young children to nursery schools often tried to raise their babies "by the book," but they resorted to screaming, spanking, nagging, and other "undesirable" behaviors when the textbook remedies failed to have an effect.[95] Not surprisingly, a profusion of letters detailing the exasperating conduct of one-and-a half- to three-year-old children highlight the difficulties of raising children of this age, especially when there is more than one youngster to care for. One mother wrote to Spock about her trials with the youngest of her three boys, who was twenty-one months old: "I realize all babies are curious, and are into alot [*sic*]. But this one seems to go day and night. He is motor driven or something. His will is stronger than mine. He is a rebel, he is defiant. . . . I have tried to reason with him by interesting him in something else. Nothing doing. I now spank him also when he does something wrong. He is constantly playing or doing something dangerous to himself." Despite her zealous attempts to watch over him, he had already gotten electric shocks and bruised and cut himself in the process of his explorations. On top of his daytime activities, the baby refused to sleep at night and required endless attention from both parents before he would settle down. Her doctor said that the baby was intelligent and active: "He says it's healthy. For the baby, yes, but how about me and my husband?" Many other mothers, too, continued to resort to spanking, after reasoning with or trying to distract their child, even knowing that it was not the approved method.[96]

Plenty of mothers wrote about mobile, willful children who were difficult to keep up with, and another group of letters described problem children who were overly attached to their mothers. Writing about her nineteen-month-old daughter, "who refuses to go to sleep, stay asleep or leave mommy for a minute," a mother admitted that she was "ready to collapse." She began the letter by stating that her problem had started when she "spoiled" her daughter as an infant by refusing to let her "cry it out" when she had colic. Like many of the writers, this mother provides environmental details that help explain her situation, especially the dearth of physical and emotional support: "My husband is away most of the time and cannot help me as much as I would like, and both our families live too far away to come over and help." She also insinuates that part of the problem may be that she cares *too* much: "It is because I want her to be so happy that I am so distraught and incompetent." As this mother implied when she expressed her acute desire to make her child happy, the stakes of motherhood are high, especially in a culture that considers happiness to be the birthright of every child. Baby books provided mothers with strategies for achieving the elusive "happy childhood," but the pressure-cooker atmosphere of some homes, where isolated mothers anxiously sought to ensure their children's happiness, had severe psychic consequences for women, as Friedan and other writers have amply demonstrated. This mother confided that she was "so nervous I literally itch all over and have a hang dog expression." Another baby like this one, she feared, would make her "take the gas pipe."[97]

Unfortunately, such desperate feelings were not uncommon in the correspondence with Spock. A former kindergarten teacher had not expected motherhood to be terribly hard; however, with a four-year-old son, a two-year-old daughter, and a third child on the way, and her husband pursuing his Ph.D., she found herself at her wits' end. Her major complaint concerned her four-year-old son, whom she described as "balky, whiny, always demanding, often crying, complaining, rarely pleasant." "Ours is a viscious [*sic*] circle," she contended, "Davey and I both fighting for control. . . . Surely there must be something for troubled mothers as AA is for drinkers to call SOS when they need help." The depth of her distress is evident: "It's gotten to the point where I dislike the child most of the time and wish I could get rid of him somehow." What is striking about these letters is the sense of helplessness that women experienced in relation to their young children, the feeling that children had the upper hand. Suggesting that they are "fighting for control" with a toddler, and that their child's "will is stronger than mine," these mothers appear to be unable to control their own lives or their children's.[98]

The feeling of inadequacy expressed in these letters was reiterated in the popular literature, which portrayed women as "insecure" in their roles as wives, mothers, and individuals in society. The 1956 *Life* magazine issue on women introduced a series of articles on "Her Position, Her Inadequacies, Her Heritage and Her Prospects." Strangely, the image of the "inadequate" and vulnerable American woman coexisted with the image of the domineering matriarchal female out to strip men—and especially her sons—of their masculinity. According to an article in the same issue by Robert Coughlan, the growing rates of divorce and juvenile delinquency were due to women who "rob men of their masculine egos."[99]

"SIMPLY A SILENT PARTNER"

The mobility of the postwar generation contributed to heightened expectations that husbands and wives would fulfill each other's emotional needs and that children would fulfill them for both. In the women's magazines of the period, both motherhood and heterosexual romance were glorified, and women increasingly looked to their spouses for emotional gratification. One of the most popular women's magazines of the period, *McCall's*, touted the "togetherness" of the new family, where women and men found fulfillment, "not as women alone or men alone, isolated from one another, but as a family sharing a common experience." Women were seeking their husband's assistance in raising children, and the parenting literature continued to underscore the importance of a fatherly presence in the home. Some popular commentators, however, viewed the emphasis on father's role in the family as yet another onus on the overworked breadwinner. One journalist elaborated: "This human beast of burden, now as adept at diaper-changing as his wife is at explaining the international situation, receives periodic warnings from the child-care experts about neglecting his portion of child care."[100] In fact, studies revealed that the vast majority of fathers participated minimally in routine child care, though they might interact with children or participate in decision making with their wives about children's discipline and futures. At the same time, as Robert Griswold tellingly remarks: "The message to fathers in the decade of family togetherness and backyard barbecues could hardly be clearer. Men's commitment to and involvement with their children had a decisive impact on personality development and social order. But not all fathers, sociologists included, were so committed."[101] This disjunction between the prescriptive ideal and the reality of fathers' participation in family life could produce unforeseen conflict.

That wives considered their husbands partners in rearing—if not in caring for—their children is attested to by female letter writers' common use of the pronoun "we" in discussing their dilemmas with children. In addition, a fair number of fathers wrote letters to the experts about their worries regarding children's behavior. Many women reported that their husbands were actively involved, at least as young parents, in making decisions about how to raise their children. One woman wrote to Spock in 1958 regarding the problems she and her husband, both schoolteachers, were having with their children: "My husband and I are young and full of shining goals and ideals. We strive to do what is 'right'—and usually get a good deal of satisfaction from our work—*at school.* At home we have the same feelings of insecurity and bewilderment *any* parents of a 4-yr. old and an 18-mo. old baby have." Other women spoke of spouses who were so enthralled with Spock's book that they were quoting it back to their wives when difficulties arose with the children. For the most part, the letter writers accepted the expert prescription that on coming home from work fathers should play with and give attention to their children, especially boys, who were likely to become "sissies" without their father's guidance. Aware that fatherly attention to a male child was a therapeutic mandate, a mother who wondered how to handle her "wild" three-and-a-half-year-old son explained: "My husband plays with the boys before they go to bed, and so Jonny is not lacking in attention from his parents."[102]

Mothers could use the psychological messages of baby books, with their expert backing, to challenge their husbands' parenting principles and practices. When women complained about their husbands, it was generally to say that the men were uninterested in their children, too strict and authoritarian, or apt to dismiss their wives' concerns about the children as unimportant. One mother, who was seemingly vexed by the experts' emphasis on *mothers,* asked Spock to "*please write for fathers too*" because she could not "fight the battle alone" of trying to teach her child socially acceptable manners. Her arguments with her husband about how they must train their child had been fruitless, and she looked for expert confirmation of her views to gain his support. Another mother wrote to Spock about her young daughter's nightmares, which she and her husband had decided were due to his harsh disciplinary measures. Together they decided that he must refrain from scolding her, and the nightmares ceased. In this instance, it is likely that the mother's readings of Spock and other writers on fears and punishment had provided her with rhetorical weapons to combat her husband's treatment of their daughter.[103]

The expectation that a father would play some role in the life of the family could be disappointing, if not devastating, however, for those whose spouses rarely interacted with their children. A young mother with two small children and another on the way complained to Spock: "My husband is the 'working' type. We live well, but he comes home tired. He never roughhouses, or tells them stories—lunches in the park, trips to kiddieland, pony rides—he never goes with us. . . . He loves them dearly, but is simply a silent partner. I feel as though the load is all on my shoulders at times. Being pregnant I have been turning into a 'screamer' which I loathe." Writer Adrienne Rich longed for her husband to return from work "when for an hour or two at least the circle drawn around mother and children would grow looser, the intensity between us slacken, because there was another adult in the house."[104] But for some mothers, their husband's return from work did not signify an end to their isolation as mothers.

Dominating spouses could also take a toll on women and on their attempts to exert control over their children. This predicament was vividly illustrated in a letter to Ames and Ilg. The writer suggested that her husband's authoritarian attitude toward her had undermined her effectiveness as a parent: "My husband has incessantly countermanded my instructions to them and insists upon using and reusing an ordering tone with everything he wants me to do. I feel that my children must now regard me on their level and so are heedless of my wishes." The problem had reached such a point that she felt "increasingly sure" that she should leave her husband and children.[105] Although fairly rigidly defined gender roles prevailed in the 1950s, the companionate marriage was a more alluring ideal than ever. Women's quest for equality had not garnered them substantial public power, but as we have seen, many asserted themselves in the private realm. Most women expected to be treated with respect by their husbands for the work that they performed in the home; when their expectations were not met, their discontent manifested itself.

There was trouble as well when husbands and wives had substantially different perspectives on matters of child rearing and discipline. Writers of child-care literature always insisted on the importance of parents' presenting a united front in regard to disciplinary measures; but the writers overlooked the likelihood that if their audience consisted mostly of mothers, the new ideas about children were generally not reaching fathers directly and that the up-to-date methods in the baby books might conflict with paternal ideas. Parent educator Orville Brim alluded to the possibility that wives' new knowledge could "produce interpersonal friction, resentment, and hostility between husband and wife," which could be detrimental to children. A serviceman's wife who had had her baby while her husband was away claimed that her child was "perfect" until her father returned home from the service. The mother complained that her husband's endless criticisms of the child had contributed to the baby's nervousness and tendency to cry at night. According to the letter writer, "There are thousands of us young service wives who are torn between husband and child. . . . By the way he thinks it's 'all poppycock'—to raise a child by the book."[106] In her letter the mother implied not only that she differed from her husband in her approach to child rearing but that she felt caught between her interest in her child's well-being and her relationship with her husband.

This conflict was exacerbated when a woman had to contend with her husband's overtly abusive behavior toward their children. Some fathers favored stronger disciplinary tactics than their wives did, which could turn to violence. Writing to Spock about her four-year-old daughter, who was not yet toilet trained, a mother admitted that her "problem is more with my husband than with my daughter," because he beat the child when she wet her training pants "until she has welts on her body."[107] In such cases the doctors rarely if ever suggested the option of divorce. The heterosexual partnership was to be protected at all costs. Therefore, despite the apparent child-centeredness of the 1950s, many children who were victims of physical and sexual abuse were sacrificed upon the altar of family "togetherness."

"LORD, DELIVER ME FROM MOMISM"

Even with the assistance of a supportive spouse—that is, one who might come home from work to play with the children—mothers struggled to find time for *themselves,* a nearly impossible task with even two or three youngsters. Both popular and professional literature had espoused the importance of individual self-expression, but the demands of motherhood were often in conflict with this aim. Several authors, including Spock, wrote of the need for the young home-maker to venture outside the home and avail herself of adult companionship. In an article entitled "Mothers Need a Break," Spock argued that in primitive societies women were not deprived of adult companionship as a result of caring for children. Even apartment dwellers in the earlier decades of the century, he observed, had the opportunity to commune with other women at area parks, while their children played. But the suburban homemaker was likely to stay indoors attending to her housework and supervising her children. Spock suggested that both the community and the mother herself seek solutions to the problem—the community by providing spaces for mothers and children at local shopping centers, the mothers by participating in clubs and classes. Interestingly, however, most mothers appear to have discounted the idea that social solutions could solve what they viewed as primarily personal problems. From that perspective, several mothers pointed out the difficulties associated with giving themselves a "break," perhaps most important of which was finding and affording a babysitter. A mother of three preschoolers wrote amusingly about another problem: "You are a dear for trying to figure out 'a break' for us mothers. . . . But 'as I see it' the problem is not just finding a sitter and getting out. It is about what to do about the mountain of work that accumulates in the half-day at the Y or supermarket club. . . . It seems easier to an exhausted mother to stay home and battle the engulfing tides than to 'escape' only to return to a more hopeless Herculean stable." The above mother doubtless had high expectations for herself and believed that she must conform to the image of the put-together housewife portrayed in the women's magazines and television. Before going out she had to "wash and set hair, press dress, pull on girdle (the worst hazard to me), find a pair of run-less stockings, leave instructions for babysitter, make sure nipples are in bottles, baby is taken care of in every way so he will be good for babysitter, etc. etc."[108] Unwilling to present herself in public as anything less than perfect, this woman chose to reserve outings for very special occasions.

Not all women set such high standards for themselves as housekeepers, although few of the correspondents were willing to stint when it came to motherhood. That did not mean, however, that they felt that they must give all their time to children, and a fair number of working mothers were featured in the popular media, although (probably being too busy) few of them wrote to child-care experts. Even mothers who did not work for wages outside the home, meanwhile, sought time and space to fill personal needs that could not be met by children or husbands. A nursing school graduate wrote to Spock about the difficulty of maintaining a sense of self while raising children: "I am willing to give generously of my time and energy to my children, but not to the point of hindering my own self-development. . . . They say 'The family that plays together stays together,' but Lord, deliver me from 'Momism.' . . . We all want our children to be happy, and as a strong advocate of freedom of expression, I sometimes find 'freedom' incompatible with 'family togetherness.'" This mother implicitly recognized that conflicting cultural messages were being given to women—they should give generously of their time to children yet avoid the overprotective "momism."[109] At the same time the writer used the term "momism" to make a case for pursuing her own self-development.

This theme was also touched on in a letter from a mother who was exasperated with her three children's apparent inability to entertain themselves: "Can the fact that I am never at a loss for something to do, and find a lot of pleasure in filling my few spare hours with activities very fulfilling to me personally, somehow be having a reverse [sic] effect on the children who resent the fact that my every moment isn't spent with them and doing for them? . . . I am devoted to my children and worship the ground they walk on, and I do my best to always 'be there' when they need me . . . but I am not cut out to be a human doormat, I do crave a certain amount of personal privacy, and I do need moments when I can just 'sit' and watch an ant crawl up the table leg without having an audience of three standing around each with a specific demand that has to be fulfilled at that very moment." As some of the experts realized, women were not necessarily eager to abandon motherhood but were seeking some way to reconcile their own needs with those of their children. According to educational reformer Althea Hottel, "Almost without exception, women consider marriage, homemaking, and child rearing as major goals and responsibilities," but they are also motivated "to use all of their abilities and energies throughout their lives."[110]

MOTHERHOOD IS MY MOST VALUED CAREER

There is no doubt that many women of the fifties embarked upon their roles as wives and mothers with optimism, believing that in raising large numbers of children and maintaining a happy home they would find meaning, pleasure, and sustenance. They had had drummed into them the idea that women were meant for motherhood, and they were barred from expressing their talents in arenas other than child rearing. Raising children and making a home can indeed offer women—and men—a respite from the demands of the competitive, impersonal, and mechanistic society in which we live. Parenting is also an intellectually and emotionally challenging occupation that requires serious reflection, especially in a society that sends competing messages about the best way to raise children and insists that children require highly individualized forms of nurture.

The letters to child-care experts give convincing evidence of the passion with which many mothers regarded this "career" and their desire to learn anything that might make them better mothers. Mothers did gain in self-confidence as they raised their children, but more often from the experience itself than from books. After an article by Spock was published in *Redbook* in 1974 regarding some misgivings he had about his earlier manual, one mother admitted that she had been too quick to use Spock in her younger days: "I was so eager to do everything you said when my babies were little—not because I weighed what you said and thought you were right, but just because you were a doctor and therefore an expert." As an older, more experienced mother, she claimed, "I rarely use your book now and I know I would do a lot differently if I had another child."[111] Another mother, writing to Ames and Ilg, claimed that she learned more from other mothers than from the books she obviously read: "The best help I have had in bringing up my children has not come from reading books and articles, although they are a good guide, but from observing a neighbor of mine who has the utmost patience and understanding towards children."[112]

Through both the practice of caring for children and networks of maternal assistance, mothers developed a repertoire of child-care tactics on which they relied. Spock discovered the strength of mothers' convictions about certain unconventional child-rearing practices when he sent out a call in the *Journal* for women's opinions about the use of the pacifier in 1954.[113] Professionals disapproved of pacifiers, which they thought were unsanitary and encouraged habits that could lead to thumb-sucking. Spock had not even mentioned the use of the pacifier in his child-rearing manual, and the *Complete Guide to Mothercraft* had similarly neglected to discuss this popular means of quieting infants. He received a voluminous response from mothers, many of whom had made use of the pacifier despite public criticism of the practice. Mothers expressed gratitude about being asked to offer their opinions on a subject about which they were knowledgeable. The tone of the following response was fairly representative: "Ever since the birth of my second girl I've wanted to get up on a soap-box and shout about my experiences with a pacifier. Of course, I never expected to have such a distinguished audience."[114] Mothers were used to expressing their opinions about such matters to each other but their views were seldom solicited by professionals. In their correspondence, women confessed that their use of the pacifier was prompted by the realities of trying to cope with crying and sleepless babies. One mother praised the "miraculous pacifier," which she had turned to in her desperate search for some way to calm her infant: "It came about during the dark hours of the night while I sat with a howling baby. It was a time for trying anything, a time when one has understanding for the unbalanced parent who abuses a child to quiet him." After witnessing African-American women using pacifiers with their babies, a white mother from Florida purchased one to comfort her first-born child. "What a difference—he took it like a duck to water," she exclaimed.[115] In such cases, mothers determined pragmatically what worked and did not work for them, regardless of professional sanctions. To Spock's credit, he decided that he would lend his support to those who found the pacifier useful for quieting fussy infants.

Mothers often conveyed their ideas about children's behaviors and child-rearing techniques to the experts and sometimes their ideas made their way into print. Mothers had ideas about how teasing works, how to handle bullying neighborhood children, how to manage large families, strategies for traveling with a child, and how to cure diaper rash. These mothers saw themselves as students who were collecting information about how to rear children, through both their reading and their experiences. A Texas woman expressed her passion for learning about motherhood most eloquently in a letter to Spock: "Marriage and motherhood is my vocation in life—my most valued career. I bend over backwards (figuratively, of course) to give each of our children love, appreciation, and understanding. But even so, I am a student. I'm learning and I don't know all the answers." Another mother writing to Ames and Ilg conveyed a combination of caring, thoughtfulness, angst, and a sense of identification as a student mother: "I burn with the passion of self-improvement. . . . I would do anything to help our children learn all they must know to become happy, useful adults. My great desire—part of this improvement plan—is to become a more ideal mother—more relaxed, patient, calm-voiced, less demanding."[116] As we have seen, this passion could sometimes translate into distress or fear of making mistakes during a baby's earliest years that, according to some experts, could have ramifications for him as an adult. And with few other available outlets for their passions, mothers were often doomed to disappointment in their efforts to be "perfect" parents.

Some letters exhibit a disconcerting degree of despair, but more are reminiscent of Erma Bombeck's humorous accounts of family life, with the anger and frustration veiled by self-denigrating wit. A Connecticut woman claimed that child psychology had done nothing to alleviate her exasperation with her children: "I have tried using psychology with them, understanding each phase and stage they are going through and disciplining them accordingly. But it seems as though I invariably wind up hollering my head off like some kind of a crazy woman which accomplishes nothing at all but a headache for me." In her discussion of "housewife humor," Friedan explains how women's ability to make light of a sometimes desperate situation may actually have deflected needed political change. At the same time, humor acts as a coping mechanism and as a form of covert resistance for the marginalized. In the example just cited, humor allows the mother to express her hostility toward the experts, and Spock in particular, for persuading her to use child-rearing tactics that result in "nothing but a headache" for her.[117]

The psychologists' conceptions of good mothering that permeated popular culture surely affected how many mothers viewed their jobs as caretakers. But even amid the cultural conformity of the 1950s, a more multifaceted discourse about child rearing existed than we might expect, in private conversations, correspondence, and the occasional magazine article that struck a discordant note—or even within the professional community itself. In their daily interactions with children, mothers strove to make manifest their own conception of good motherhood, one informed by, but not determined by, the culture of expertise.

Conclusion

"Gorilla Saves Tot in Brookfield Zoo Ape Pit" was the headline of the August 17, 1996, *Chicago Tribune*. Substantial attention was paid to the local story in the national press as well. The elaborated subtitle may explain some of the hoopla surrounding the event: "Maternal Feelings Prevail at the Tropic World Exhibit, When a Mother Ape Carries an Injured 3-Year-Old Boy to Safety." After the toddler had fallen more than fifteen feet into a pit containing seven gorillas, a female ape (Binti), with her own baby clinging to her back, lumbered over to the boy, cradled him in her arms, carried him to a doorway and laid him gingerly at the feet of waiting paramedics. The phrase "Maternal Feelings Prevail" evokes a sense of both the naturalness and the timelessness of maternal sentiments, transcending even species. Readers who followed the article to its conclusion, however, discovered that there was more to the story. The zookeeper attributed Binti's actions to the behavioral-enrichment training she had received to teach her how to be a mom. Binti's own mother had rejected her, and she was raised by humans. The trainers used dolls to teach Binti the parenting skills she had never acquired as a young gorilla. Apparently, the maternal instinct is not infallible, even in nonhuman species. Whether we learn to parent from our mothers or our doctors or though actively caring for children, good parenting is largely a learned behavior.[1]

More mothers than ever work outside the home, and feminists have done much to dispel the notion that parenting must be performed by women. Yet in spite of these social changes, we hold to the notion of the mother-child bond as an exclusive, enduring, inherently meaningful, and *essential* aspect of our humanity, perhaps because we have few other human relationships that can compete with the intimacy and permanency we associate with the bond. Marriages are unstable; fathers are more likely than mothers to fail to maintain relationships with their children. We live increasingly transient lives. But regardless of place of residence, mothers are likely to remain a constant presence in their children's lives. Most mothers have played the primary role in caring for children's physical selves during early life, when they are most physically vulnerable. The intimacy between mother and child that is fostered by the mother's diapering, bathing, feeding, and soothing her baby can be deep and enduring. Fathers have been less likely to engage in physical care, although they may become involved in playing with children, disciplining them, and introducing them to the wonders of the outside world. The distinctions between these types of parenting pertain to gender roles rather than biology. Perhaps it is understandable that we are reluctant to dilute the intimacy of mother-child relationships by expanding our notion of who is able to mother. Yet, as history shows us, we have all had to pay a price for assigning sole responsibility for children to mothers.

Mothers have been thwarted in their ability to express themselves outside the home and to attain political and economic equality. They have also been subject to relentless criticisms from both society and their own children for failing to embody the perfect mother as depicted in the prescriptive literature. Our therapeutic ethos leads us to attribute many of life's traumas to our experiences in the family and especially with our mothers. It is impossible for most mothers to fulfill the demands their children make of them. When a forty-year-old friend of mine told her colleagues that her mother was coming to visit, most of them expressed sympathy. Only her Indian-born colleague said of the visit, "That's really nice." We have made mothers the scapegoats for a society that fails to support families and children.

Following the feminist heyday of the 1960s and 1970s, we seem to be entering a period when, despite—or maybe because of—the fluctuating family constellation in modern society, we wish to retain a nostalgic notion of the mother-child relationship as the key to children's well-being, the fulfillment of women's identity, and our future as a society. In the introduction to a book published in 1995, *Motherhood: From 1920 to the Present Day*, which is based largely on oral interviews, the author contends that the maternal instinct is "as natural, 'timeless and immutable' as ever."[2] Abundant examples of the continuing importance of this symbol are to be found in daytime television commercials. A commercial for Pampers, for instance, displays a mother bending lovingly over her infant, with the voice-over saying, "Nothing's closer to your baby except you."[3] Pooh-poohing the egalitarian rhetoric of feminists who insist that parenting should be shared equally by both sexes, the prominent child-care expert Penelope Leach argues that we are ignoring the developmental needs of children if we support measures such as day care that allow people other than mothers to care for young children. Leach maintains in her best-selling book *Children First* that only women can be *mothers:* "The obvious biological differences between females and males do not only ensure that their adult experience of parenthood is different, but that they arrive there by divergent developmental paths." Biology, Leach tacitly implies, determines that men cannot be mothers.[4] Pediatrician T. Berry Brazelton echoes Leach: "Mommies and daddies are different, whether we like it or not," he instructed a young couple on his television show.[5]

Women themselves evince a desire to preserve their image as primary caretakers, even while their roles are undergoing change in other arenas. Much has been made in feminist scholarship of men's unwillingness to participate in child care or housework now that the majority of mothers with small children work for wages. But relatively few feminists have acknowledged women's desires to maintain a central—if not *the* central—role in the raising of their children. According to Martha McMahon, many women describe becoming a mother as a "moral transformation" that symbolizes "connectedness" and say it is central to their identity as women. Whereas in previous decades, as we have seen, many women strove to gain a sense of individuality and felt constrained by their responsibilities to others, today many women seek to reclaim the sense of connectedness that motherhood embodies. Fearing the loss of such traditional feminine values in a society that is beginning to champion professional success as a legitimate goal for women, many women are unwilling to substitute values traditionally viewed as masculine for the maternal values with which many have been raised and which are reinforced by the practice of mothering.[6]

Journalist Sherrye Henry recently set out, through a series of focus interviews and telephone surveys, to discover the sources of women's resistance to feminism and "equality." Among the many provocative findings was Henry's discovery that most women saw motherhood as the best part of being a woman and insisted that women should put children first in their lives. Although they appreciated that men were doing more to help them in bringing up children, they were "not prepared to relinquish the role of primary parent," whether or not they were working outside the home. Even a self-described feminist claimed, "A man cannot be a mother in my opinion. A child really deserves to have the kind of a relationship with a mother being the mother, not the man being the mother."[7] Political theorist Susan Moller Okin and other feminist scholars have argued compellingly that mothers who care for children while their male spouses work for wages are the victims of an unjust family system, which leaves them economically vulnerable. Yet many women and men remain committed to retaining a modified form of the traditional nuclear family. This means, in some cases, that women with financial resources take time off from high-powered careers to care for small children or work part-time during their children's early years, thus leaving their spouses in positions of financial superiority and reinforcing, for the next generation, the patterns of gendered parenting to which we have become accustomed.[8]

Even as they further the message that mothers must be taught to mother, such popular experts as Brazelton, Leach, and psychologist David Elkind continue to reinforce patterns of gendered parenting as natural. The experts seem confident that they know what is naturally best for children and that it is their responsibility to instruct mothers about how to ensure their children's well-being. The messages are not so very different from Spock's earlier injunction to trust your instincts and follow the directions the doctor gives you, counsel that continues to have a good deal of appeal. A commercial aired during Brazelton's television show *What Every Baby Knows* shows a woman confidently claiming, "At first you read all the books . . . but eventually you get over it." Of course, if viewers had gotten over it, why would they be watching a show purporting to give them answers to all their questions about babies? The appeal of the message is that women can consult expertise without relinquishing their own judgment. But it is by no means clear that a woman watching a television show alone with her baby will be able to sort out for herself how to use childcare advice. For that, she must turn to a network of other mothers who have raised or are raising children, if she is lucky enough to have one.[9]

Each of the experts mentioned earlier—Brazelton, Leach, and Elkind—has a television show. Brazelton, an older man, is the best known of the group and has been billed as the successor to Dr. Spock. Perhaps because she is a woman,

Leach appears to be the most comfortable of the three with openly disputing feminist challenges to the traditional family structure. But all three continue to privilege the female role in parenting.[10]

Brazelton's show usually includes several married couples who discuss their parenting problems with Brazelton and each other, although the wives generally lead the conversations. A common topic is what happens when mom must leave a young infant, to enter the work force. During the course of many interchanges, Brazelton gently suggests that even though alternative care may not endanger baby's development, the mother suffers from the loss of connection with her infant. Directing his question to a woman who was going back to work six weeks after having twins, without any particular prompting from the mother, Brazelton queries: "Do you feel you never had a chance to consolidate your relationship with the twins?" Although fathers will sometimes confess that they miss their babies when they are away at work, most of the conversations center around the sense of loss that mothers feel when they leave their babies in the care of others.[11]

Brazelton's tone of voice is therapeutic, reassuring, and he generally seems to take parents' perspectives seriously. But he seeks to steer them gently into accepting explanations of children's behavior that fit into his theories of children's development. For instance, when a mother tried to explain her child's preference for its father on the basis of temperamental factors, Brazelton asked her whether her attempt to understand the situation wasn't a rationalization. The mother had failed to accept Brazelton's assessment of the behavior, based primarily on notions of gender differences.[12]

Brazelton's show is followed in my area by *Kids These Days,* focusing on children between six and twelve, with host Dana Fleming (also a mother). David Elkind is the designated expert, although the show also features experts on more specific topics. The formats of *Kids These Days* and the Brazelton show are similar in their involvement of parents, but on the former show only women are present, a set-up that makes it appear as if fathers have no role in the rearing of school-aged children.

The mothers pelt Elkind with questions about the subject of the day, to which he responds with ready answers. On occasion, however, the mothers instruct Elkind. When the day's topic was children's cliques, one of the mothers on the show remarked that her eight-year-old daughter was already being pressured to join a clique. Elkind responded that this was quite unusual behavior for eight-year-olds, at which point several other mothers interjected that their eight-year-olds were also experiencing such pressures. Then Elkind rapidly integrated this new information into one of his favorite formulations: This is just one more example of how children are growing up too fast today. Clearly, even if mothers do not often receive credit for their observations about children, they continue to play a critical role in informing experts about the real lives of children.[13]

Of course, neither these programs, nor most of the parenting books available, address the needs of poor parents, who must struggle to provide their children with the bare essentials. Few single mothers are featured on the shows; most of the participants have spouses who appear to play some role in helping to bring up the children. The parents surrounding the experts on the television shows are mostly middle-class; when African-Americans appear, they too seem to be relatively well-off. These are intensive parents; whether or not they work outside the home, they manage to find the financial and emotional resources to cater to the multifarious needs of their children. And of course, the parents seek private solutions to what could be seen as public problems: locating a good nanny, instead of striving to obtain government-sponsored child care; making do financially during the three months of unpaid maternity leave, instead of working politically for guaranteed paid parental leave, which exists in many other countries. At best, we relegate single mothers to welfare so that their children can receive paid medical care, housing, and food, instead of insisting that these necessities should not be dependent on employment or marital status.[14]

Learning to care *well* for children is not inscribed in female genetic coding. We learn to care for children in the context of the families and the communities in which we live. And as we can readily see, experts cannot solve the problems that beset American mothers and their families. For too long, experts have failed to listen to the voices of those who care for children. We propagate gender inequality when we set apart those who produce information about children from the people who raise them and when we consign the primary responsibility for children to the politically and economically disempowered. Although we may have to sacrifice some of our most nostalgic ideas about the unbroken bond between mother and child, if we want to live in a society that knows how to care for children and their mothers, maternal practices and discourse about children should become the concern of all citizens.

Notes

ABBREVIATIONS FOR MANUSCRIPT COLLECTIONS CITED

AAUW   American Association of University Women Archives, 1881–1976, microfilm collection (Sanford, N.C.: Microfilming Corp. of America, 1980)

BS   Benjamin Spock Papers, Syracuse University Library Archives, Syracuse, N.Y.

CSA   Child Study Association of America Papers, Social Welfare History Archives, University of Minnesota, Minneapolis, Minn.

LBA   Louise Bates Ames Papers, Library of Congress, Manuscript Division, Washington, D.C.

LSRM   Laura Spelman Rockefeller Memorial Papers, Rockefeller Archives, North Tarrytown, N.Y.

MW   Margaret Wylie Papers, Cornell University Library, Division of Rare and Manuscript Collections, Ithaca, N.Y.

UM   University of Minnesota Institute of Child Welfare Papers, University of Minnesota Archives, Minneapolis, Minn.

UNH   United Neighborhood House Papers, Social Welfare History Archives, University of Minnesota, Minneapolis, Minn.

INTRODUCTION

1. Arlene Eisenberg, *What to Expect When You're Expecting* (New York: Workman, 1991).
2. Seba Smith, "Anxious Mothers," *The Mother's Assistant* 2 (December 1842): 17.
3. Margaret Mead, "The Impact of Culture on Personality Development in the United States Today," in *Proceedings of the Midcentury White House Conference on Children and Youth,* ed. Edward A. Richards (Raleigh, N.C.: Health Publications Institute, 1951), 84.
4. Christopher Lasch, *Haven in a Heartless World: The Family Besieged* (New York: Basic Books, 1977). See Diane E. Eyer, *Mother-Infant Bonding: A Scientific Fiction* (New Haven: Yale University Press, 1992).
5. Clifford Geertz, "Common Sense as a Cultural System," in Geertz, *Local Knowledge: Further Essays in Interpretive Anthropology* (New York: Basic Books, 1983), 75. See also Peter L. Berger and Thomas Luckman, *The Social Construction of Reality: A Treatise in the Sociology of Knowledge* (Garden City, N.Y.: Doubleday, 1966).
6. See Eyer, *Mother-Infant Bonding,* for a full-blown analysis of how theories of child development reflect social anxieties. On the impact of the concept of the "invention of childhood" on history and psychology, see Emily Cahan, Jay Mechling, Brian Sutton-Smith, and Sheldon H. White, "The Elusive Historical Child: Ways of Knowing the Child in History and Psychology," in *Children in Time and Place: Developmental and Historical Perspectives,* ed. Glen H. Elder, Jr., John Modell, and Ross D. Parke (New York: Cambridge University Press, 1993), 192–223. On the invention of motherhood, see, for instance, Shari L. Thurer, *The Myths of Motherhood: How Culture Reinvents the Good Mother* (New York: Penguin, 1994).
7. According to Clifford Geertz, "ideology" is marginal in societies where there is little social change but more pronounced when existing institutions and maxims are being questioned. See Geertz, "Ideology as a Cultural System," in Geertz, *The Interpretation of Cultures* (New York: Basic Books, 1973), 218. Theresa R. Richardson, *The Century of the Child: The Mental Hygiene Movement and Social Policy in the United States and Canada* (Albany: State University of New York Press, 1989), 186–91; Cathy Urwin and Elaine Sharland, "From Bodies to Minds in Childcare Literature: Advice to Parents in Inter-War Britain," in *In the Name of the Child: Health and Welfare,* ed. Roger Cooter (London: Routledge, 1992), 174–99.
8. The most influential of the earlier works include Barbara Ehrenreich and Deirdre English, *For Her Own Good: 150 Years of the Experts' Advice to Women* (Garden City, N.Y.: Doubleday, 1979), and Sheila M. Rothman, *Woman's Proper Place: A History of Changing Ideals and Practices, 1870 to the Present* (New York: Basic Books, 1978). An important exception to the top-down orientation of the studies mentioned is an earlier work, Nancy Pottisham Weiss, "Mother, the Invention of Necessity: Dr. Benjamin Spock's *Baby and Child Care,*" *American Quarterly* 5 (Winter 1977): 519–46. Steven L. Schlossman's work also provides significant information on parent education as a social movement in "Before Home Start: Notes Toward a History of Parent Education in America, 1897–1929," *Harvard Educational Review* 61 (August 1976): 436–67, and "Philanthropy and the Gospel of Child Development," *History of Education Quarterly* 21 (Fall 1981): 275–99. Works that address women as consumers of child development expertise include Molly Ladd-Taylor's *Mother-*

Work: Women, Child Welfare, and the State, 1890–1930 (Urbana: University of Illinois Press, 1994), and *Raising a Baby the Government Way: Mothers' Letters to the Children's Bureau, 1915–1932* (New Brunswick, N.J.: Rutgers University Press, 1986); Margo Horn, *Before It's Too Late: The Child Guidance Movement in the United States, 1922–1945* (Philadelphia: Temple University Press, 1993); Linda Gordon, *Heroes of Their Own Lives: The Politics and History of Family Violence: Boston, 1880–1960* (New York: Penguin, 1989); Kathleen W. Jones, "Sentiment and Science: The Late Nineteenth-Century Pediatrician as Mother's Advisor," *Journal of Social History* (Fall 1983): 79–96; Rima D. Apple, *Mothers and Medicine: A Social History of Infant Feeding, 1890–1950* (Madison: University of Wisconsin Press, 1987); and Martha McMahon, *Engendering Motherhood: Identity and Self-Transformation in Women's Lives* (New York: Guilford Press, 1995), 5.

9. Judith Leavitt, *Brought to Bed: Child-Bearing in America, 1750–1950* (New York: Oxford University Press, 1986); Apple, *Mothers and Medicine,* 18.

10. Evelyn Nakano Glenn, "Social Constructions of Mothering: A Thematic Overview," in *Mothering: Ideology, Experience, and Agency,* ed. Evelyn Nakano Glenn, Grace Chang, and Linda Rennie Forcey (New York: Routledge, 1994), 3.

11. Sara Ruddick, "Thinking Mothers/Conceiving Birth," in *Representations of Motherhood,* ed. Donna Bassin, Margaret Honey, and Meryle Mahrer Kaplan (New Haven: Yale University Press, 1994), 33; Ruddick, *Maternal Thinking: Toward a Politics of Peace* (New York: Ballantine Books, 1989), 13. See also Vrinda Dalmiya and Linda Alcoff, "Are 'Old Wives' Tales' Justified?" in *Feminist Epistemologies,* ed. Linda Alcoff and Elizabeth Potter (New York: Routledge, 1993), 217–44.

12. For instance, Katherine Arnup, in *Education for Motherhood: Advice for Mothers in Twentieth-Century Canada* (Toronto: University of Toronto, 1994), made use of both written sources (primarily professional reports and correspondence) and oral histories of Canadian mothers and reports "virtually *no* evidence of resistance to child-rearing advice" (132)—a dubious finding, given the great diversity of the Canadian population.

Another study of British mothers, which was based on personal testimonies of women who had already raised children, came to the conclusion that "the vast majority of women bringing up their children between the wars and well into the 1950s and accepted their role as wife and mother intuitively, and dedicated their lives to their husbands and families, with pride and contentment" (Vivien Devlin, *Motherhood: From 1920 to the Present Day* [Edinburgh: Polygon, 1995], 5). Again, this seems to be an enormous generalization for such a large and diverse a population. More probing studies that benefit from oral histories include Susan Cotts Watkins and Angela D. Danzi, "Women's Gossip and Social Change: Childbirth and Fertility Control Among Italian and Jewish Women in the United States, 1920–1940," *Gender and Society* 9 (August 1995): 469–91; Jacquelyn Litt, "Mothering, Medicalization, and Jewish Identity," *Gender and Society* 10 (April 1996): 185–98; and Neil Cowan and Ruth Schwartz Cowan, *Our Parents' Lives: The Americanization of Eastern European Jews* (New York: Basic Books, 1989).

13. Robyn Muncy, *Creating a Female Dominion in American Reform, 1890–1935* (New York: Oxford University Press, 1991); Richard A. Meckel, *Save the Babies: American Public Health Reform and the Prevention of Infant Mortality, 1850–1929* (Baltimore: Johns Hop-

kins University Press, 1990); Judy Barrett Litoff, *American Midwives, 1860 to the Present* (Westport, Conn.: Greenwood Press, 1978).

14. "The Children's Charter," in *White House Conference on Child Health and Protection: Addresses and Abstracts of Committee Reports* (New York: Century, 1931), 45; Helen Leland Witmer and Ruth Kotinsky, *Personality in the Making: The Fact-Finding Report of the Midcentury White House Conference on Children and Youth* (New York: Harper & Row, 1952).

15. See Burton Bledstein, *The Culture of Professionalism: The Middle Class and the Development of Higher Education in America* (New York: Norton, 1976), and Magali Sarfatti Larson, *The Rise of Professionalism* (Berkeley: University of California Press, 1977).

16. See Ladd-Taylor, *Mother-Work,* 116–18, for an analysis of wages for housework during this period. Arnup notes that mothers were regulated by those who were not mothers in *Education for Motherhood,* 42.

17. See Schlossman, "Philanthropy." On scientific utopianism, see Fred Matthews, "The Utopia of Human Relations: The Conflict-Free Family in American Social Thought, 1930–1960," *Journal of the History of the Behavioral Sciences* 24 (October 1988): 343–62.

18. See Nancy Chodorow, *The Reproduction of Mothering: Psychoanalysis and the Sociology of Gender* (Berkeley: University of California Press, 1979), and Sara Ruddick, *Maternal Thinking: Toward a Politics of Peace* (Boston: Beacon Press, 1989).

CHAPTER 1

1. Stephanie Coontz explodes the myth of the model family in *The Way We Never Were: American Families and the Nostalgia Trap* (New York: HarperCollins, 1992).

2. Quoted in Sylvia D. Hoffert, *Private Matters: American Attitudes Toward Childbearing and Infant Nurture in the Urban North, 1800–1860* (Urbana: University of Illinois Press, 1989), 142.

3. Laurel Thatcher Ulrich, *Good Wives: Image and Reality in the Lives of Women in Northern New England, 1650–1750* (New York: Knopf, 1980), 157. See also Tamara Hareven, "Historical Changes in Children's Networks in the Family and the Community," in *Children's Social Networks and Social Supports,* ed. Deborah Belle (New York: Wiley, 1989), 15–36.

4. Steven Mintz and Susan Kellogg, *Domestic Revolutions: A Social History of American Family Life* (New York: Free Press, 1988), 51.

5. See, for instance, Nancy F. Cott, *The Bonds of Womanhood: "Woman's Sphere" in New England, 1780–1835* (New Haven: Yale University Press, 1977), 84–85; Ruth H. Bloch, "American Feminine Ideals in Transition: The Rise of the Moral Mother, 1785–1815," *Feminist Studies* 4 (June 1978): 101–26; Anne L. Kuhn, *The Mother's Role in Childhood Education* (New Haven: Yale University Press, 1947); Barbara Welter, "The Cult of True Womanhood: 1820–1860," *American Quarterly* 18 (Summer 1966): 151–74; Hoffert, *Private Matters;* Bernard Wishy, *The Child and the Republic: The Dawn of Modern American Child Nurture* (Philadelphia: University of Pennsylvania Press, 1968), 4; Mintz and Kellogg, *Domestic Revolutions;* Peter Gregg Slater, *Children in the New England Mind: In Death and in Life* (Hamden, Conn.: Archon Books, 1977).

6. Karen Halttunen, *Confidence Men and Painted Women: A Study of Middle-Class Culture in*

America, 1830–1870 (New Haven: Yale University Press, 1982), 35; Richard D. Brown, *Knowledge Is Power: The Diffusion of Information in Early America, 1700–1865* (New York: Oxford University Press, 1989), 295. Harvey J. Graff notes in *Conflicting Paths: Growing Up in America* (Cambridge: Harvard University Press, 1995) that nineteenth-century children encountered many transitions in their lives.

7. Wishy, *The Child and the Republic,* 4. Cathy N. Davidson, "Antebellum Reading and the Ironies of Technological Innovation," in *Reading in America,* ed. Davidson (Baltimore: Johns Hopkins University Press, 1989), 80–200; Carl F. Kaestle, "Studying the History of Literacy," in *Literacy in the United States: Readers and Reading Since 1880,* ed. Kaestle et al. (New Haven: Yale University Press, 1991), 25; John K. Folger and Charles B. Nam, *Education of the American Population* (Washington, D.C.: Government Printing Office, 1967), 113–14; Brown, *Knowledge Is Power,* 12.

8. T. J. Jackson Lears, *No Place of Grace: Antimodernism and the Transformation of American Culture, 1880–1920* (New York: Pantheon Books, 1981), 15. See Londa Schiebinger, *The Mind Has No Sex? Women in the Origins of Modern Science* (Cambridge: Harvard University Press, 1989), for a discussion of the emergence of a scientific justification for what she terms complementary sex roles. See also Tamara K. Hareven, "Historical Changes in Children's Networks," and Marilyn Dell Brady, "The New Model Middle-Class Family (1815–1930)," in *American Families: A Research Guide and Historical Handbook,* ed. Joseph M. Hawes and Elizabeth I. Nybakken (Westport, Conn.: Greenwood Press, 1991), 85.

9. See Christopher Lasch, *Haven in a Heartless World: The Family Besieged* (New York: Basic Books, 1977).

10. Slater, *Children in the New England Mind,* 129–31; Steven L. Schlossman, *Love and the American Delinquent: The Theory and Practice of "Progressive" Juvenile Justice, 1825–1920* (Chicago: University of Chicago Press, 1977), 50; Linda Pollock, *Forgotten Children: Parent-Child Relations from 1500 to 1900* (London: Cambridge University Press, 1983), 106.

11. Karin Calvert, *Children in the House* (Boston: Northeastern University Press, 1992), 37, 47. See also Jane C. Nylander, *Our Own Snug Fireside: Images of the New England Home, 1760–1860* (New York: Knopf, 1993), 32–34.

12. Richard A. Meckel, *Save the Babies: American Public Health Reform and the Prevention of Infant Mortality, 1850–1929* (Baltimore: Johns Hopkins University Press, 1990), 1. Meckel acknowledges that it is extremely difficult to estimate infant mortality rates for the nineteenth century but that approximately 15–20 percent of infants born in the United States during the second half of the nineteenth century died before their first birthday.

13. William Buchan, *Advice to Mothers* (Philadelphia: John Bioren, 1804), 85, 2; Meckel, *Save the Babies,* 23. Buchan's text went through nineteen editions. He stated as one of its aims to "teach them [mothers] how to prevent diseases that are almost always the consequences of mismanagement," 3. On Buchan, see Sir Leslie Stephen and Sir Sidney Lee, eds., *The Dictionary of National Biography,* vol. 3 (London: Oxford University Press, 1973), 180–81.

14. Michel Foucault, "The Politics of Health in the Eighteenth Century," in Foucault,

Power/Knowledge: Selected Interviews and Other Writings, 1972–1977, trans. Colin Gordon (New York: Pantheon Books, 1980), 173.

15. William P. Dewees, *Treatise on the Physical and Medical Treatment of Children* (Philadelphia: Carey & LEA, 1825), xiii.

16. John Locke, "Some Thoughts Concerning Education," in *The Educational Writings of John Locke,* ed. John William Adamson (Cambridge: Cambridge University Press, 1922), 23, 42, 46; John Cleverley and D. C. Phillips, *Visions of Childhood: Influential Models from Locke to Spock* (New York: Teachers College Press, 1986). In *John Locke and the Problem of Depravity* (New York: Clarendon Press, 1988), W. M. Spellman argues that Locke never wholly abandoned the notion of depravity and was not particularly optimistic about the power of education to offset it.

17. Locke, "Some Thoughts Concerning Education," 46; Anne Bradstreet, "In Anne's Hand," in *The Complete Works of Anne Bradstreet,* ed. Joseph R. McElrath, Jr., and Allan P. Robb (Boston: Twayne, 1981), 196. See also Ross W. Beales, "Anne Bradstreet and Her Children," in *Regulated Children/Liberated Children,* ed. Barbara Finkelstein (New York: Psychohistory Press, 1979), 19.

18. Linda Pollock, *A Lasting Relationship* (Hanover, N.H.: University Press of New England, 1987), 179, quoting from Benjamin B. Wisner, *The Memoirs of the Late Mrs. S. Huntington* (Glasgow: William Collins, 1828).

19. Jean-Jacques Rousseau, *Emile: or, On Education,* trans. Allan Bloom (New York: Basic Books, 1979), 37; C. John Sommerville, *The Rise and Fall of Childhood* (Beverly Hills, Calif.: Sage, 1982), 149.

20. Rousseau, *Emile,* 37–38; Barbara Beatty, *Preschool Education in America: The Culture of Young Children from the Colonial Era to the Present* (New Haven: Yale University Press, 1995), 12.

21. William Cadogan, "An Essay on Nursing," in *The Child,* ed. William Kessen (New York: Wiley, 1965), 9. Marylynn Salmon points to the importance of breast-feeding in the early modern period in "The Cultural Significance of Breastfeeding and Infant Care in Early Modern England and America," *Journal of Social History* 28 (Winter 1994): 247–69.

22. Buchan, *Advice to Mothers,* 15, 164, 166, 94.

23. On the regulated child, see Finkelstein, *Regulated Children/Liberated Children.* See also Daniel T. Rodgers, "Socializing Middle-Class Children: Institutions, Fables, and Work Values in 19th-Century America," in *Growing Up in America,* ed. Joseph Hawes and N. Ray Hiner (Urbana: University of Illinois Press, 1985), 119–32; Beatty, *Preschool Education in America,* 9. In *The Protestant Temperament: Patterns of Child-Rearing, Religious Experience, and the Self in Early America* (New York: Knopf, 1977) Philip Greven reminds us that child-rearing beliefs and practices have varied throughout American history. Philip Slater argues that "a real choice [in child-rearing theories] did exist for the literate classes of New England by the end of the early national period" (*Children in the New England Mind,* 152).

24. Cott, *Bonds of Womanhood,* 94; Linda K. Kerber, *Women of the Republic* (Chapel Hill: University of North Carolina Press, 1980), 283.

25. See, for instance, Bloch, "American Feminine Ideals in Transition"; Kuhn, *The Mother's Role in Childhood Education;* Welter, "The Cult of True Womanhood"; Hoffert, *Private*

Matters; John Demos, "The Changing Faces of Fatherhood," in *Past, Present, and Personal: The Family and the Life Course in American History* (New York: Oxford University Press, 1986), 45; Mary P. Ryan, *The Empire of the Mother: American Writing About Domesticity, 1830–1860, Women and History,* vols. 2 and 3 (Summer/Fall 1982), 56; C. John Sommerville, *The Discovery of Childhood in Puritan England* (Atlanta: University of Georgia Press, 1992), 100.

26. T. S. Arthur, *The Mother* (Philadelphia: Anners, 1846), 17, 92; L. H. Sigourney, *Letters to Mothers* (Hartford, Conn.: Hudson and Skinner, 1838), 12.

27. *The Maternal Physician* (New York: Arno Press, 1972 [1811]), 7, 33.

28. Mrs. Barwell, *Infant Treatment with Directions to Mothers for Self-Management Before, During, and After Pregnancy* (New York: James Mowatt, 1844), ix, 101.

29. "Review of *Thoughts on Domestic Education, The Result of Experience,*" *Ladies Magazine* 2 (August 1829): 386; Kimberley Tolley, "Science for Ladies, Classics for Gentlemen: A Comparative Analysis of Scientific Subjects in the Curriculum of Boys' and Girls' Secondary Schools in the United States, 1794–1850," paper presented at History of Education Society Conference, October 21, 1995, Minneapolis, Minn.; Cott, *Bonds of Womanhood,* 89. Margaret W. Rossiter's superlative study *Women Scientists in America: Struggles and Strategies to 1940* (Baltimore: Johns Hopkins University Press, 1982) documents the systematic exclusion of women from the sciences.

30. Lydia Maria Child, *The Mother's Book* (New York: Arno Press, 1972 [1831]); Catherine Beecher, *Treatise on Domestic Economy* (Boston: Marsh, Capen, Lyon, and Webb, 1841), ix.

31. Child, *Mother's Book,* 29.

32. Warren I. Susman, "'Personality' and the Making of Twentieth-Century Culture," in Susman, *Culture as History: The Transformation of American Society in the Twentieth Century* (New York: Pantheon Books, 1973), 271; Pollock, *Forgotten Children,* 269; Sigourney, *Letters to Mothers,* 27–28.

33. Richard A. Meckel, "Educating a Ministry of Mothers: Evangelical Maternal Associations, 1815–1860," *Journal of the Early Republic* 2 (Winter 1982): 410, 406.

34. *Sabbath School Visitant and Juvenile Magazine* (1 August 1829), 270, quoted in Mary P. Ryan, *Cradle of the Middle Class: The Family in Oneida County, New York, 1790–1865* (Cambridge: Cambridge University Press, 1981), 105; Meckel, "Educating a Ministry of Mothers," 406.

35. Harvey Newcomb, "Maternal Associations," *Mother's Assistant* 2 (January 1842): 6; Newcomb, *Newcomb's Manual for Maternal Associations* (Boston: Massachusetts Sabbath School Society, 1840), 10.

36. Newcomb, *Newcomb's Manual,* 11, 38, 40, 49.

37. Meckel, "Educating a Ministry of Mothers."

38. Meckel, "Educating a Ministry of Mothers," 415–23; Mary P. Ryan, "A Woman's Awakening: Evangelical Religion and the Families of Utica, 1800–1840," *American Quarterly* 30 (Winter 1978): 61.

39. Newcomb, *Newcomb's Manual,* 31; Ryan quotes the association's constitution in "A Woman's Awakening," 90.

40. "Fretting and Scolding," *Mother's Assistant* 5 (November 1845): 128. Robert Sunley, in his

essay, "Early 19th-Century American Literature on Child Rearing," in *Childhood in Contemporary Cultures,* ed. Margaret Mead and Martha Wolfenstein (Chicago: University of Chicago Press, 1955), states that "breaking the will" was a key concern of members of maternal associations, 160.

41. See Newcomb, *Newcomb's Manual* and "Marlboro Maternal Association Constitution," 27 May 1836, Old Sturbridge Village Library; "19th Annual Report of the Maternal Association of High Street Church, Providence, Rhode Island," *Mother's Assistant* (1855), 205.

42. F. Prochaska, "A Mother's Country: Mothers' Meetings and Family Welfare in Britain, 1850–1950," *History* 74 (October 1989): 380.

43. First Congregational Church, North Mission (Chicago), Minute Book, September 1865; October 1865; September 1869; May 1867; October 1868, Chicago Historical Society. Hannah Root Hubbard's minutes of mothers' meetings are in the Minute Book, records of the First Congregational Church, North Mission (Chicago), at the Chicago Historical Society.

44. Ann Douglas, *The Feminization of American Culture* (New York: Avon Books, 1977), 245–46. See Susan Juster, *Disorderly Women: Sexual Politics and Evangelicalism in Revolutionary New England* (Ithaca: Cornell University Press, 1994), for a discussion of the use of language in creating evangelical communities, 33.

45. First Congregational Church Minute Book, May 1871.

46. First Congregational Church Minute Book, April 1865; August 1865.

47. First Congregational Church Minute Book, April 1882.

48. Horace Bushnell, *Views of Christian Nurture* (Hartford, Conn., 1847); Wishy, *The Child and the Republic,* 22–23.

49. Anne Firor Scott, *Natural Allies: Women's Associations in American History* (Urbana: University of Illinois Press, 1993), 125. Scott's reconstruction of the history of the Mothers' Club of Cambridge is extremely helpful.

50. Mothers' Discussion Club Papers, 6 December 1949, box 2, folder 13, "Fiftieth Anniversary Party," Schlesinger Library, Radcliffe College, Cambridge, 4.

51. Stella Scott Gilman, *Mothers in Council* (New York: Harper & Brothers, 1884), 3.

52. Paper by Mrs. Arthur Pope and Winifred Whiting, December 1944, box 1, vol. 6, Mothers' Study Club Papers, Schlesinger Library.

53. Mothers' Study Club Papers, 12 March 1884, box 1, minute book, vol. 1, Schlesinger Library.

54. See Wishy, *The Child and the Republic,* for an illuminating discussion of Abbott's text; Gilman, *Mothers in Council,* 16–18; Jacob Abbott, *Gentle Measures in the Management and Training of the Young* (New York: Harper & Brothers, 1871).

55. Paper by Mrs. Crothers, 30 November 1904, box 1, Cambridge Mothers' Club Papers, Schlesinger Library.

56. Paper by Mrs. Crothers, 30 November 1904, box 1, Cambridge Mothers' Club Papers, Schlesinger Library; Crothers, "25 Years After," 13 April 1928, box 1, Cambridge Mothers' Club Papers, Schlesinger Library, 13.

57. Mrs. Crothers, "25 Years After," 14.

58. Robert Owen opened the first infant school in New Lanark, Scotland, in 1816. See Dean

May and Maris A. Vinovskis, "A Ray of Millennial Light: Early Education and Social Reform in the Infant School Movement in Massachusetts, 1826–1840," in *Family and Kin in Urban Communities, 1700–1930,* ed. Tamara Hareven (New York: New Viewpoints, 1977), 63.

59. Caroline Winterer, "Avoiding a 'Hothouse System of Education': Nineteenth-Century Early Childhood Education from the Infant Schools to the Kindergarten," *History of Education Quarterly* 32 (Fall 1992): 290–92; May and Vinovskis, "A Ray of Millennial Light," 64–68.

60. "Infant Schools," *Ladies' Magazine* 3 (May 1830): 224.

61. William Russell, *Address on Infant Schools* (Boston: Hiram Tupper, 1829), 8–9.

62. Beatty, *Preschool Education in America,* 24.

63. Russell, *Address on Infant Schools,* 4; Beatty, *Preschool Education in America,* 29.

64. On the age of children attending primary schools, see Carl F. Kaestle and Maris A. Vinovskis, *Education and Social Change in Nineteenth-Century Massachusetts* (Cambridge: Cambridge University Press, 1980), 51. One of the first texts to discuss the dangers of early schooling was Amariah Brigham's *Remarks on the Influence of Mental Cultivation and Mental Excitement upon Health* (Hartford, Conn.: Huntington, 1832). See also Winterer, "Avoiding a 'Hothouse System of Education,'" 289–314, and Beatty, *Preschool Education in America,* 29.

65. Beatty, *Preschool Education in America,* 38; Beatty, "Child Gardening: The Training of Young Children in American Schools," in *American Teachers: Histories of a Profession at Work,* ed. Donald Warren (New York: Macmillan, 1989), 66.

66. Kate Douglas Wiggin, *Children's Rights: A Book of Nursery Logic* (Boston: Houghton Mifflin, 1894). See also Beatty, *Preschool Education in America,* 44–45, 96, and Michael Steven Shapiro, *Child's Garden: The Kindergarten Movement from Froebel to Dewey* (University Park: Pennsylvania State University Press, 1983), 23.

67. Beatty, *Preschool Education in America,* 41–42; Shapiro, *Child's Garden,* 20–23.

68. Elizabeth Harrison, *A Study of Child Nature from the Kindergarten Standpoint* (New York: Garland, 1987 [1895]), 12, 9.

69. Elizabeth Harrison, "The Scope and Results of Mothers' Classes," in *Addresses and Proceedings of the National Educational Association* (Washington, D.C.: National Education Association, 1903): 401–3.

70. Beatty, *Preschool Education in America,* 90. See also Ross, *G. Stanley Hall.*

71. "The Chicago Conference of Mothers, An Epoch in the History of Education," *Kindergarten Magazine* 7 (November 1894): 212.

72. "The Chicago Conference of Mothers," 220–21.

73. Leila Zenderland, "Education, Evangelism, and the Origins of Clinical Psychology: The Child-Study Legacy," *Journal of the History of the Behavioral Sciences* 24 (April 1988). The most important and comprehensive study of Hall's life and thought is still Dorothy Ross's *G. Stanley Hall: The Psychologist as Prophet* (Chicago: University of Chicago Press, 1972). On Freud's visit to America, see Ross, 386–412.

74. Ross, *G. Stanley Hall,* xiii; Schlossman, "Philanthropy and the Gospel of Child Development," 276–77.

75. G. Stanley Hall, *Life and Confessions of a Psychologist* (New York: Appleton, 1923), 380.

76. Ross, *G. Stanley Hall,* 283–84; "Fourth Congress of the Illinois Society for Child-Study," *Pedagogical Seminary* 8 (July 1897): 299.

77. Zenderland, "Education, Evangelism," 156. Heather Munro Prescott, "'A Doctor of Their Own': The Emergence of Adolescence Medicine as a Clinical Sub-Specialty, 1904–1980," (Ph.d. diss., Cornell University, 1992), 46–47. On the significance of Hall's findings in the light of more recent work on child development, see Sheldon H. White, "Child Study at Clark University: 1894–1904," *Journal of the History of the Behavioral Sciences* 26 (April 1990): 131–50, and Sheldon H. White, "G. Stanley Hall: From Philosophy to Developmental Psychology," *Developmental Psychology* 28 (January 1992): 25–34.

78. William T. Preyer, *The Mind of the Child* (New York: Appleton, 1890); Sara Wiltse, "A Preliminary Sketch of the History of Child Study in America," *Pedagogical Seminary* 3 (October 1894): 196, 208–9; Millicent W. Shinn, *The Biography of a Baby* (Boston: Houghton Mifflin, 1900).

79. Ross, *G. Stanley Hall,* 341–42.

CHAPTER 2

1. F. Scott Fitzgerald, "Imagination—and a Few Mothers," *Ladies' Home Journal* 40 (June 1923), reprinted in *The Ladies' Home Journal Treasury,* ed. John Mason Brown (New York, Simon and Schuster, 1956), 122.

2. On the women's club movement, see Karen Blair, *The Clubwoman as Feminist* (New York: Holmes & Meier, 1980); Theodora Penny Martin, *The Sound of Our Own Voices* (Boston: Beacon Press, 1987); and Anne Firor Scott, *Natural Allies: Women's Associations in American History* (Urbana: University of Illinois Press, 1991). On the political ramifications of women's club work, see Paula Baker, "The Domestication of Politics: Women and American Political Society, 1780–1920," *American Historical Review* 89 (June 1984): 620–47. On the womanly ideals of the nineteenth century, see Barbara Welter, "The Cult of True Womanhood, 1820–1860," *American Quarterly* 18 (Summer 1966): 151–74. In *Creating a Female Dominion in Progressive Reform* (New York: Oxford University Press, 1991), Robyn Muncy analyzes the roles of clubwomen and reformers in institutionalizing their work in "municipal housekeeping."

3. The development of the discipline of home economics was one outgrowth of that shift. See *Rethinking Women and Home Economics,* ed. Sarah Stage and Virginia Vincenti (Ithaca: Cornell University Press, 1997); Maxine L. Margolis, *Mothers and Such: Views of American Women and Why They Changed* (Berkeley: University of California Press, 1984), 124–47; John L. Rury, "Vocationalism for Home and Work: Women's Education in the United States," *History of Education Quarterly* 24 (Spring 1984): 21–45; Emma Seifrit Weigley, "It Might Have Been Euthenics: The Lake Placid Conferences and the Home Economics Movement," *American Quarterly* 26 (March 1974): 79–96; and Jane Bernard Powers, *The 'Girl' Question in Education: Vocational Education for Young Women in the Progressive Era* (London: Falmer Press, 1992).

4. Paula Baker, *The Moral Frameworks of Public Life: Gender, Politics, and the State in Rural New York, 1870–1930* (New York: Oxford University Press, 1991), 173.

5. Only the American Association of University Women (AAUW) remained an exclusively female organization throughout its history. Both the Child Study Association of America and the National Congress of Mothers were founded by women and retained primarily female constituencies, although male membership was more common after the 1920s.

6. Nathan Hale, *Freud and the Americans* (New York: Oxford University Press, 1971), 421. Following are some of the popular book-length texts discussed in child-study groups during the 1920s and 1930s (the authors include educators, psychologists, sociologists, and physicians, many of whom were involved in child welfare institutes and parent education programs): John B. Watson, *Psychological Care of Infant and Child* (New York: Norton, 1928); Elizabeth Cleveland, *Training the Toddler* (Philadelphia: Lippincott, 1925); Ernest R. Groves, *Wholesome Childhood* (Boston: Houghton Mifflin, 1924); Josephine C. Foster and John E. Anderson, *The Young Child and His Parents* (Minneapolis: University of Minnesota Press, 1927); Ada Hart Arlitt, *Psychology of Infancy and Early Childhood* (New York: McGraw-Hill, 1928); Arlitt, *The Child from One to Twelve: Psychology for Parents* (New York: McGraw-Hill, 1931); William H. Burnham, *The Normal Mind: An Introduction to Mental Hygiene* (New York; Appleton, 1924); Alice C. Brill and May Pardee Youtz, *Your Child and His Parents* (New York: Appleton, 1932); Angelo Patri, *The Problems of Childhood* (New York: Appleton, 1926); Michael Vincent O'Shea, *The Child: His Nature and His Needs; A Survey of Present-Day Knowledge Concerning Child Nature and the Promotion of Well-Being and Education of the Young* (New York: Children's Foundation, 1924); O'Shea, *Our Children* (Chicago: American Library Association, 1925); Edwin A. Kirkpatrick, *Fundamentals of Child Study* (New York: Macmillan, 1922); Benjamin C. Gruenberg, *Outlines of Child Study: A Manual for Parents and Teachers* (New York: Macmillan, 1924); Jessie C. Fenton, *A Practical Psychology of Babyhood* (Boston: Houghton Mifflin, 1926); Hector C. Cameron, *The Nervous Child* (Oxford: Oxford University Press, 1924); Max Seham and Grete Seham, *The Tired Child* (Philadelphia: Lippincott, 1926); Frances G. Wickes, *The Inner World of Childhood* (New York: Macmillan, 1925); Naomi N. Norsworthy and Mary T. Whitley, *The Psychology of Childhood* (New York: Macmillan, 1925); Bird T. Baldwin and Lorle I. Stecher, *The Psychology of the Preschool Child* (New York: Appleton, 1925); Douglas A. Thom, *Everyday Problems of the Everyday Child* (New York: Appleton, 1927).

7. According to Geraldine Joncich, *The Sane Positivist: A Biography of Edward T. Thorndike* (Middletown, Conn.: Wesleyan University Press, 1968), "Despite what are called recent 'perversions' in the direction of softness, American social institutions have steadfastly espoused habit formation," 410.

8. A study of the child-rearing literature of the 1920s and 1930s suggests that the works of Sigmund Freud had not yet been popularized. See A. Michael Sulman, "The Humanization of the American Child: Benjamin Spock as a Popularizer of Psychoanalytic Thought," in *Journal of the History of the Behavioral Sciences* 9 (July 1973): 258–65.

9. See Dorothy Ross, *G. Stanley Hall: The Psychologist as Prophet* (Chicago: University of Chicago Press, 1972), 124, and Herbert M. Kliebard, *The Struggle for the American Curriculum, 1893–1958* (Boston: Routledge & Kegan Paul, 1986), 160.

10. Paula Fass, *The Damned and the Beautiful: American Youth in the 1920s* (New York: Oxford University Press, 1977), 106; Christopher Lasch, *Haven in a Heartless World* (New York: Basic Books, 1977); Watson, *Psychological Care;* Fitzgerald, "Imagination—and a Few Mothers," 123.

11. Marcel C. LaFollette, *Making Science Our Own: Public Images of Science, 1910–1955* (Chicago: University of Chicago Press, 1990), 123.

12. John B. Watson, *Behaviorism* (New York: Norton, 1924), 103–4.

13. John B. Watson, *The Ways of Behaviorism* (New York: Harper & Brothers, 1928), 40; Dora Halperin, "The Changing Perceptions of the Nature of the Child in the Context of Early Childhood Education" (Ph.D. diss., Nova Scotia University, 1986); Maxine L. Margolis, *Mothers and Such,* 57.

14. See Lucille C. Birnbaum, "Behaviorism in the 1920s," *American Quarterly* 7 (Spring 1955): 15–30; John Dewey, *Democracy and Education* (New York: Macmillan, 1916), 55.

15. Fred Matthews, "The Utopia of Human Relations: The Conflict-Free Family in American Social Thought, 1930–1960," *Journal of the History of the Behavioral Sciences* 24 (October 1988): 343; Department of National Education Association, "Formulae and Technique in Behavior," *Child Welfare* 11 (July 1923): 465. See also Lillian Gilbreth's *The Home-Maker and Her Job* (New York: Appleton, 1927) and *Living with Our Children* (New York: Norton, 1928) on applying techniques of scientific management to the home.

16. American adapters of Freud stressed parental influence more than Freud himself did. See Hale, *Freud and the Americans.*

17. Mrs. C. H. Remington, "Department of Public Welfare," *Child Welfare Magazine* 17 (August 1924): 536; Dom Cavallo, "From Perfection to Habit: Moral Training in the American Kindergarten, 1860–1920," *History of Education Quarterly* 16 (Summer 1976): 154.

18. L. Emmett Holt, *The Care and Feeding of Infants* (New York: Appleton, 1896); Julia Wrigley, "Do Young Children Need Intellectual Stimulation? Experts' Advice to Parents, 1900–1985," *History of Education Quarterly* 29 (Spring 1989): 53.

19. William James, *Principles of Psychology,* vol. 1 (New York: Dover, 1950 [1890]), 127.

20. Cavallo, "From Perfection to Habit"; Edward Thorndike, *Notes on Child Study* (New York: Macmillan, 1901), 136; Thorndike, *Educational Psychology,* vol. 2 (New York: Teachers College Press, 1913), 22.

21. Watson, *The Ways of Behaviorism,* 47.

22. Martha Wolfenstein, "Fun Morality: An Analysis of Recent American Child-Training Literature," in *Childhood in Contemporary Cultures,* ed. Margaret Mead and Martha Wolfenstein (Chicago: University of Chicago Press, 1955), 169–71. Nancy Pottisham Weiss's articles are also essential for understanding this era in the history of child-care advice. See Weiss, "Mother, The Invention of Necessity: Dr. Benjamin Spock's *Baby and Child Care,*" *American Quarterly* 5 (Winter 1977): 519–46, and "The Mother-Child Dyad Revisited: Perceptions of Mothers and Children in Twentieth Century Child-Rearing Manuals," *Journal of Social Issues* 34 (November 1978): 29–45.

23. Watson, *Psychological Care,* 69–70.

24. Sidonie Matsner Gruenberg, autobiography in manuscript, Sidonie Matsner Gruenberg and Benjamin Gruenberg papers, Library of Congress, 112.

25. Watson, *Psychological Care*, 69. On page 73, Watson also suggests that women resisted Dr. Emmett Holt's injunction to stop rocking the baby to sleep, saying, "It is doubtful if mothers could have given it up if home economics had not demanded it."

26. Unlike the other two organizations, the Child Study Association of America did not have a legislative agenda.

27. Molly Ladd-Taylor, *Mother-Work: Women, Child Welfare, and the State, 1890–1930* (Urbana: University of Illinois Press, 1994), 3. See also Seth Koven and Sonya Michel, "Womanly Duties: Maternalist Politics and the Origin of Welfare States in France, Germany, Great Britain, and the United States, 1880–1920," *American Historical Review* 95 (October 1990): 1076–1108. Linda Gordon also suggests that the terms "maternalist" and "feminist" are not so easily distinguishable, in "Putting Children First: Women, Maternalism, and Welfare in the Early Twentieth Century," in *U.S. History as Women's History: New Feminist Essays,* ed. Linda K. Kerber, Alice Kessler-Harris, and Kathryn Kish Sklar (Chapel Hill: University of North Carolina Press, 1995), 68.

28. For an in-depth discussion of the ideals of domesticity in relation to college-educated women at the turn of the century, see Roberta Fort, *Collegiate Women: Domesticity and Career in Turn-of-the-Century America* (New York: New York University Press, 1977). Ellen Carol Dubois, in "Outgrowing the Compact of the Fathers: Equal Rights, Woman Suffrage, and the United States Constitution, 1820–1878," *Journal of American History* 74 (December 1987): 837–62, analyzes the vacillation within the women's rights movement between the view of women as individuals deserving of equal rights and essentialist arguments in which women's differences were valorized, in an attempt to gain female political power.

29. Emily Cahan, "Science, Practice, and Gender Roles in Early American Child Psychology," in *Contemporary Constructions of the Child: Essays in Honor of William Kessen,* ed. Frank S. Kessel, Marc H. Bornstein, and Arnold J. Sameroff (Hillsdale, N.J.: Erlbaum, 1991), 231–33.

30. Robert R. Sears, "Your Ancients Revisited: A History of Child Development," in *Review of Child Development Research,* vol. 5, ed. E. Mavis Hetherington (Chicago: University of Chicago Press, 1975), 20; Lawrence K. Frank, "Future Policy of the Spelman Fund," 13 March 1929, Lawrence K. Frank Papers, National Library of Medicine, Bethesda, Md., 1. Steven L. Schlossman's work on parent education has been invaluable, especially "Philanthropy and the Gospel of Child Development," *History of Education Quarterly* 21 (Fall 1981): 275–99; "Before Home Start: Notes Toward a History of Parent Education in America," *Harvard Educational Review* 46 (August 1976): 436–67; and "The Formative Era in Parent Education: Overview and Interpretation," in *Parent Education and Public Policy,* ed. Ron Haskins and Diane Adams (Norwood, N.J.: Ablex, 1983), 7–38.

31. Roberta Wollons, "Women Educating Women: The Child Study Association of America as Women's Culture," in *Changing Education: Women as Radicals and Conservators,* ed. Joyce Antler and Sari Knopp Biklen (Albany: State University of New York Press, 1990), 55.

32. Sidonie Matsner Gruenberg, autobiography, 45. Wollons, "Women Educating Women," 56.

33. Society for the Study of Child Nature, minutes, 18 November 1890, microfilm no. 7,

Child Study Association Papers, Social Welfare History Archives, University of Minnesota, Minneapolis (hereafter referred to as CSA); Society for the Study of Child Nature, minutes, 17 December 1890, microfilm no. 7, CSA; Society for the Study of Child Nature, minutes, 4 February 1891, microfilm no. 7, CSA; Wollons, "Women Educating Women," 58.

34. Milton J. E. Senn, record of oral history interview with Margaret Mead, Child Development Archive, National Library of Medicine, 13.

35. Charles Darwin, *A Biographical Sketch of an Infant* (Philadelphia: Lippincott, 1971); William T. Preyer, *The Mind of the Child* (New York: Appleton, 1890).

36. Society for the Study of Child Nature, minutes, 21 January 1891, microfilm no. 7, CSA.

37. Martin, *The Sound of Our Own Voices,* 117–34; Society for the Study of Child Nature, minutes, 1890, supplement, box 5, CSA.

38. "Minutes of the Meetings of the Society for the Study of Child Nature, 1890," Chapter 13, n.d. (1914–18), box 1, folder 4, CSA.

39. Minutes, Chapter 13 (1914–18), 16 December (no year noted), box 1, folder 4, CSA; minutes, Chapter 13, 10 November 1922, box 1, folder 4, CSA; minutes, Chapter 13, 16 November 1923, box 1, folder 4, CSA.

40. "Minutes of the Meeting of the Society for the Study of Child Nature—1890," n.d., "Programs, Yearbooks," supplement, box 5, CSA; "Minutes of the Meeting of the Society for the Study of Child Nature—1890," 4 February 1891, microfilm no. 7, CSA.

41. See Wollons, "Women Educating Women."

42. "A History of the Child Study Association of America: Its Growth and Activities, 1928," box 25, no. 255, CSA, 1–2; Sidonie Matsner Gruenberg, autobiography, 71.

43. Sidonie Matsner Gruenberg, autobiography, 70, 92–93; Sidonie Matsner Gruenberg, *Your Child Today and Tomorrow* (Philadelphia: Lippincott, 1920).

44. Sidonie Matsner Gruenberg, *Your Child Today and Tomorrow,* 11; "The Purpose of the Federation for Child Study," 1913, CSA, 1.

45. Minutes, Chapter 13, 1914–18, 22 March 1916, box 1, folder 4, CSA; "Introduction to the Conference of the 40th Anniversary of the Child Study Association," 20 November 1928, box 5, supplement, CSA; Sidonie Matsner Gruenberg, autobiography, 131; minutes, Chapter 379, 11 July 1930, box 27, no. 379, CSA.

46. Bernard Wishy, *The Child and the Republic: The Dawn of Modern American Child Nurture* (Philadelphia: University of Pennsylvania Press, 1968), discusses the transition from clerical to clinical experts in child training. He also includes a brief portrait of the early CSA in this work. Wollons, "Women Educating Women," 62–63; William I. Thomas, *The Child in America: Behavior Problems and Programs* (New York: Knopf, 1928), 305, 307.

47. Christine Mary Shea, "The Ideology of Mental Health and the Emergence of the Therapeutic Liberal State: the American Mental Hygiene Movement, 1900–1930" (Ph.D. diss., University of Illinois at Urbana, 1980), 302; Sidonie Matsner Gruenberg to Bird Stein Gans, 10 April 1929, Sidonie Matsner Gruenberg and Benjamin Gruenberg papers, Library of Congress, Washington, D.C.

48. "Report, Federation for Child Study, 18 April 1923," CSA; series 3, box 27, no. 289, Laura

Spelman Rockefeller Memorial Archives, Rockefeller Archive Center, Tarrytown, N.Y. (hereafter referred to as LSRM), 5.

49. Schlossman, "The Formative Era," 17. For a discussion of the association's efforts to educate African-American mothers, see Chapter Four in this book.

50. "A Summary of Activities During the Year 1927–28," box 25, folder 255, CSA; Schlossman, "The Formative Era," 17.

51. Dorothy Canfield Fisher and Sidonie Matsner Gruenberg, *Our Children: A Handbook for Parents* (New York: Viking Press, 1932); Child Study Association of America, *Outlines of Child Study: A Manual for Parents and Teachers*, ed. Benjamin C. Gruenberg (New York: Macmillan, 1924). For publications of the CSA during the 1920s and 1930s, see also *Concerning Parents: A Symposium on Present Day Parenthood* (New York: New Republic, 1926); Child Study Association of America, *Guidance of Childhood and Youth*, ed. Benjamin C. Gruenberg (New York: Macmillan, 1926); Sidonie Matsner Gruenberg and Benjamin C. Gruenberg, *Parents, Children, and Money: Learning to Spend, Save, and Earn* (New York: Viking Press, 1933); Margaret Jacot Quilliard, *Child Study Discussion Records: Development—Methods—Techniques* (New York: Child Study Association of America, 1928); and "The Child Study Association of America, 1880–1933: A Chronicle of Growth," Supplement 5, 45th Anniversary, 1933, CSA.

52. Schlossman, "Philanthropy."

53. Elvena B. Tillman, "Alice Josephine McLellan Birney," in *Notable American Women, 1607–1950*, ed. Edward James (Cambridge: Harvard University Press, 1971), vol. 1, 147–48.

54. Quoted in Harry and Bonaro Overstreet, *Where Children Come First: A Study of the PTA Idea* (Chicago: National Congress of Parents and Teachers, 1949), 40–41.

55. Theda Skocpol, *Protecting Soldiers and Mothers: The Political Origins of Social Policy in the United States* (Cambridge: Belknap Press of Harvard University Press, 1992), 334. Skocpol's work contains much interesting information regarding the work of the congress, especially the campaigns for mothers' pensions. Overstreet, *Where Children Come First*, 148.

56. Quoted in Overstreet, *Where Children Come First*, 38.

57. David J. Rothman and Sheila M. Rothman, eds., *National Congress of Mothers: The First Conventions* (New York: Garland, 1987). See also Ladd-Taylor, *Mother-Work*, 43. This important work contains the first full evaluation of the National Congress of Mothers' ideology and activities.

58. Susan M. Reverby, *Ordered to Care: The Dilemma of American Nursing, 1850–1945* (Cambridge: Cambridge University Press, 1987), 42.

59. Susan Tiffin, *In Whose Best Interest: Child Welfare Reform in the Progressive Era* (Westport, Conn.: Greenwood Press, 1982), and Hamilton Cravens, "Child-Saving in the Age of Professionalism, 1915–1930," in *American Childhood: A Research Guide and Historical Handbook*, ed. Joseph Hawes and Ray Hiner (Westport, Conn.: Greenwood Press, 1985), 415–81. According to Anthony M. Platt, *The Child Savers: The Invention of Delinquency* (Chicago: University of Chicago Press, 1969), "In a rapidly changing and increasingly complex urban society, the child-saving philosophy represented a defense against 'foreign' ideologies and a proclamation of cherished values," 177.

60. Ellen Key, *The Century of the Child* (New York: Putnam, 1909), 3. In *The Grounding of Modern Feminism* (New Haven: Yale University Press, 1987), Nancy Cott analyses the conflicting definitions of "feminism" represented by individuals like Key, whom Charlotte Perkins Gilman termed a female feminist, and Gilman, who called herself a human feminist, 48–49.

61. G. Stanley Hall, "New Ideals of Motherhood Suggested by Child Study," in National Congress of Mothers, *The Child in Home, School, and State: Proceedings of the Annual Meeting* (Washington, D.C.: National Congress of Mothers, 1905), 19.

62. "Address by President Roosevelt," *Report of the National Congress of Mothers* (Washington, D.C.: National Congress of Mothers, 1905), 79–84; Preface, *Report of the Proceedings of the Second Annual Convention of the National Congress of Mothers, May 2–7, 1898* (New York: Garland, 1987 [1898]), 1–2. See also Gwendolyn Mink, "The Lady and the Tramp: Gender, Race, and the Origins of the American Welfare State," in *Women, the State, and Welfare,* ed. Linda Gordon (Madison: University of Wisconsin Press, 1990), 103.

63. In 1900 women constituted 36.8 percent of the college population. See Barbara Miller Solomon, *In the Company of Educated Women* (New Haven: Yale University Press, 1985), 63. Although there had been a gradual decline in the overall U.S. fertility rate throughout the nineteenth and early twentieth centuries, between 1870 and 1915 the contrast between the low fertility rate of the urban middle class and the high fertility rates of the farm and immigrant populations contributed to middle-class fears of "race suicide."

64. On divorce statistics, see Steven Mintz and Susan Kellogg, *Domestic Revolutions* (New York: Free Press, 1988), 109–10. For the theory of "cultural lag," see William Fielding Ogburn, *Social Change: With Respect to Culture and Original Nature* (New York: Huebsch, 1922), 200–201.

65. Mary Lowe Dickinson, "Response to Address of Welcome," in *The Work and Words of the National Congress of Mothers: First Annual Session, February 17–19, 1897* (New York: Garland, 1987 [1897]), 18; Ross, *G. Stanley Hall,* 287.

66. Mrs. Frederick Schoff, "The Mothers of the Nation," in National Congress of Mothers, *The Child in Home, School, and State,* 12.

67. Martha Sprague Mason, *Parents and Teachers* (Boston: Ginn, 1928), 282; minutes of thirty-second annual convention, Cleveland, Ohio, 27 April–5 May 1928, file 12, PTA Papers, University of Illinois at Chicago Circle Library (hereafter referred to as PTA); Ladd-Taylor, *Mother-Work,* 120.

68. Mason, *Parents and Teachers,* 116; Lawrence Cremin, *The Transformation of the School: Progressivism in American Education, 1876–1957* (New York: Knopf, 1961), viii. See also Lasch, *Haven in a Heartless World.* "Report of Child Hygiene Committee," 28 June 1926, vol. 8, PTA Minute Book, PTA, and Mason, *Parents and Teachers,* 130. On teachers' discomfort with activist parents, see Sara Lawrence Lightfoot, *Worlds Apart: Relationships Between Families and Schools* (New York: Basic Books, 1978).

69. Quoted in Julian E. Butterworth, *The Parent-Teacher Association and Its Work* (New York: Macmillan, 1928), 44.

70. Ladd-Taylor, *Mother-Work,* 70. See also Elmer S. Holbeck, "An Analysis of the Activities and Potentialities for Achievement of the Parent-Teacher Associations, with Recom-

mendations," *Teachers College Contributions to Education,* no. 601 (1934), and Butterworth, *The Parent-Teacher Association,* 1–2.

71. Carl N. Degler, *In Search of Human Nature: The Decline and Revival of Darwinism in American Social Thought* (New York: Oxford University Press, 1991), 144–45.

72. "Review of *Mental Hygiene of Childhood* by William Allen White," *Child Welfare Magazine* 12 (August 1919): 341; Schlossman, "Philanthropy," 276.

73. Julia Wrigley explores the denigration of parents in early childhood education in "Children's Caregivers and Ideologies of Parental Inadequacy," in *Circles of Care: Work and Identity in Women's Lives,* ed. Emily K. Abel and Margaret K. Nelson (Albany: State University of New York, 1990), 290–312; Douglas Thom, "Child Management," *Child Welfare Magazine* 20 (December 1925): 247; Michael Vincent O'Shea, "Problems for Investigation and Discussion," *Child Welfare Magazine* 19 (April 1925): 414.

74. Ada Hart Arlitt, "Parent Education," in National Congress of Parents and Teachers, *Proceedings of the Thirty-Fifth Annual Meeting* (Hot Springs, Ark.: National Congress of Parents and Teachers, 1931), 168–69.

75. An informal study conducted by the AAUW in 1932 revealed that the PTA hosted far more study groups than any other organization. See "Survey of Parent Education, March 1932," reel 94, American Association of University Women Microfilms, Brandeis University (hereafter referred to as AAUW); Arlitt, "Parent Education," 169.

76. Grace Crum, "The Study Circle," *Child Welfare Magazine* 21 (November 1926): 144; and Crum, "Study Program III," *Child Welfare Magazine* 21 (March 1927): 348.

77. Mary E. Woolley, "The American Association of University Women," *Journal of the American Association of University Women* 24 (June 1931): 170–72.

78. Marion Talbot, *The Education of Women* (Chicago: University of Chicago Press, 1910), 8.

79. On Emily Talbot and the origins of child study in the AAUW, see Marion Talbot, "Beginnings of Child Study," *Journal of the American Association of University Women* 32 (January 1939): 87–91. See also Richard J. Storr, "Marion Talbot," in *Notable American Women,* vol. 3, ed. Edward T. James et al. (Cambridge: Harvard University Press, 1971), 423–24.

80. Marion Talbot, "The History, Aims and Methods of the Association of Collegiate Alumnae," 1893, reel 1, AAUW, 6. Millicent W. Shinn, *The Biography of a Baby* (Boston: Houghton Mifflin, 1900); Shinn, "Study of Development of Children," *Publications of the Association of Collegiate Alumnae,* series 3, no. 6 (1903): 48–60; "The Baby's Mind: A Study for College Women," *Journal of the AAUW* 34 (October 1940): 36–37.

81. Quoted in Solomon, *Company of Educated Women,* 84.

82. Mary Roberts Smith, "Shall the College Curriculum Be Modified for Women?" *Publications of the Association for Collegiate Alumnae,* series 3, no. 1 (1898): 2, 9, 11. For valuable discussions of attitudes toward working mothers at the turn of the century, see Lynn Y. Weiner, *From Working Girl to Working Mother* (Chapel Hill: University of North Carolina Press, 1985), and Margolis, *Mothers and Such.* Lynn Gordon discusses the debate on marriage versus career that characterized the experience of second-generation college women in *Gender and Higher Education in the Progressive Era* (New Haven: Yale University Press, 1990).

83. Talbot, *The Education of Women,* 243–44.

84. Ruth W. Tryon, *AAUW, 1881–1949* (Washington: American Association of University Women, 1950), 4; Esther Loring Richards, "Evolving Educational Policies in A.A.U.W.," *Journal of the American Association of University Women* 28 (June 1935): 223–28; "Report of the Committee on Educational Policies, American Association of University Women—1922 National Convention, Kansas City, Missouri," reel 95, AAUW, 1. For biographical information on Woolley, see Rosalind Rosenberg, *Beyond Separate Spheres: Intellectual Roots of Modern Feminism* (New Haven: Yale University Press, 1982), 62, 66; and Elizabeth Scarborough and Laurel Fuomoto, *Untold Lives: The First Generation of American Women Psychologists* (New York: Columbia University Press, 1989), 199–201.

85. "Report of the Committee on Educational Policies, AAUW 1922 National Convention," reel 95, AAUW, 1–2; minutes of the first business session of the convention, 15 April 1922, reel 32, AAUW, 18–19.

86. Frances Fenton Bernard, "Report of the Committee on Educational Policies," AAUW 1923 National Convention, July 16–21, Portland, Ore., reel 7, AAUW, 1; Ruby Takanishi, "Lois Hayden Meek Stolz: An American Child Development Pioneer," 1978, oral history, Schlesinger Library, Radcliffe College, Cambridge, 14, 21. On changing views toward single women, see Estelle B. Freedman, "Separatism as Strategy: Female Institution-Building and American Feminism, 1870–1930," *Feminist Studies* 5 (Fall 1979): 512–29, and Estelle B. Freedman, "The New Woman: Changing Views of Women in the 1920s," *Journal of American History* 61 (September 1974): 372–93.

87. Barbara Solomon, "Education, Work, Family, and Public Commitment," 152; "Motions Passed at Convention, Portland, July 16–21, 1923," *Journal of the American Association of University Women* 16 (October 1923): 100–101.

88. Ada Comstock, "An Interpretation of the National Education Program," proceedings 5th national convention and 41st general meeting, AAUW, 30 March–2 April, 1927, Washington, D.C., reel 7, AAUW, 19; Schlossman, "Philanthropy"; Lawrence K. Frank, interview with Aurelia Henry Reinhardt, president, AAUW, 24 November 1923, series 3, box 26, no. 268, LSRM.

89. Lawrence K. Frank, memo of interview with Frances Fenton Bernard, educational secretary, AAUW, 3 December 1923, series 3, box 26, no. 268, LSRM. Tryon, *AAUW,* 24.

90. Takanishi, "Lois Hayden Meek Stolz," 1–2, 13.

91. Frances Fenton Bernard, "Progress of the Educational Program," *Journal of the American Association of University Women* 17 (1924): 3; "Our Educational Program (Including the Report of the Educational Secretary)," 1 April 1925, AAUW 1925 National Convention, 8–11 April, Indianapolis, Ind., reel 71, AAUW, 1; Lawrence K. Frank to Frances Fenton Bernard, 11 April 1924, series 3, box 26, no. 268, LSRM; "What the Branches Are Doing," *Journal of the AAUW* 27 (June 1934): 251–53; Harriet Ahlers Houdlette, "Child Development Study Groups as a Basis for Community Action," *Journal of the AAUW* 29 (June 1936): 247–49.

92. "Report of the Executive and Educational Secretary of the AAUW to the Spelman Fund, October 20, 1929, to June 1, 1931," reel 144, AAUW, 15; Lois Hayden Meek, "Manual for Study Group Leaders in Preschool, Elementary and Adolescent Education," 1929, reel 94, AAUW; Elizabeth Moore Manwell, "Guidance Material for Study Groups: The

Social Development of the Child," ed. Kathryn McHale Walsh, 1932, reel 95, AAUW; Takanishi, "Lois Hayden Meek Stolz," 30.

93. Lois Hayden Meek to Lawrence K. Frank, 16 April 1927, reel 95, AAUW; Marion Talbot, *The History of the American Association of University Women* (Boston: Houghton Mifflin, 1931), 404. See also Lois Hayden Meek, "Progress During Five Years," *Journal of the American Association of University Women* 22 (June 1929): 204, and "Treasurer's Biennial Report," *Journal of the American Association of University Women* 29 (October, 1935): 61.

94. Patricia Woodward Cautley, *AAUW Members Look at College Education: An Interim Report* (Washington, D.C.: American Association of University Women, 1948), 5.

95. "Conference of Educational Chairmen, AAUW," 11 April 1925, AAUW 1925 National Convention, 8–11 April, Indianapolis, Ind., reel 7, AAUW, 187.

96. Ladd-Taylor, *Mother-Work.*

97. For a very thorough and cogent discussion of the development of maternalist discourse in the United States and other industrial countries, see Koven and Michel, "Womanly Duties." For more on "relational feminism," see Karen Offen, "Defining Feminism: A Comparative Historical Approach," *Signs* 14 (Autumn 1988): 119–57.

98. Evelyn Nakano Glenn makes the point in "Social Constructions of Motherhood: A Thematic Overview," in *Mothering: Ideology, Experience, and Agency,* ed. Evelyn Nakano Glenn, Grace Chang, and Linda Rennie Forcey (New York: Routledge, 1994), 18, that mothers of all classes "have also asserted the validity of their own knowledge and skill in the face of messages that they are inadequate mothers" and that mothers' "everyday activities" may be seen as "resistance."

CHAPTER 3

1. In writing this chapter and the book, I benefited greatly from Paula Fass's insightful study of the phenomenon of the generation gap in the 1920s, *The Damned and the Beautiful: American Youth in the 1920s* (New York: Oxford University Press, 1977). Fass, who has studied the increase in journalistic accounts of the youth problem in the 1920s, notes that the word "youth" emerged as a separate listing in the *New York Times Index* in 1920, 379. Marjorie Swett, "Progressive Parents—Their Tragedy," *New Republic* 40 (19 November 1924): 296.

2. Radio talk by Mrs. Howard S. Gans, 22 June 1923, series 3, box 27, no. 289, LSRM.

3. "Report of Activities Carried On Under Spelman Fund Appropriation Number 72," attached to letter to Anna Blauvelt from Ada Hart Arlitt, 21 March 1933, series 3, box 44, no. 457, LSRM; Robert S. Lynd and Helen Merrell Lynd, *Middletown* (New York: Harcourt Brace Jovanovich, 1956), 133.

4. Lynd and Lynd, *Middletown,* 133; report of the Home Problems Conference held at Merrill-Palmer School, Detroit, 18–20 April 1927, series 3, box 33, no. 354, LSRM, 11. See also "The Revolution in Manners and Morals," in Frederick Lewis Allen's contemporary survey of the period, *Only Yesterday: An Informal History of the Nineteen-Twenties* (New York: Harper & Brothers, 1931), 88–122.

5. Quoted in Leonard Covello, *The Social Background of the Italo-American School Child* (Leiden, Netherlands: Brill, 1967 [1944]), 315.

6. Sydney Stahl Weinberg also notes in *The World of Our Mothers: The Lives of Jewish Immigrant Women* (Chapel Hill: University of North Carolina Press, 1988) that "the strains of immigration thus exacerbated the 'generation gap' of modern society," 118. See also Department of the Interior, Bureau of Education, "An Americanization Program," bulletin no. 30 (Washington, D.C.: Government Printing Office, 1923); Mina Carson, *Settlement Folk: Social Thought and the American Settlement Movement, 1885–1930* (Chicago: University of Chicago Press, 1990); Sophonisba P. Breckinridge, *New Homes for Old* (New York: Harper & Brothers, 1921).

7. Elizabeth A. Woodward, "Where Home and Kindergarten May Join Forces," *League of Mothers' Clubs Bulletin* (April 1926): 1, in United Neighborhood House Papers, Social Welfare History Archives, University of Minnesota, Minneapolis (hereafter referred to as UNH); "Report of Henry Street Mothers' Club," *League of Mothers' Clubs Bulletin,* 13 November 1925, box 65, legal folder 25, UNH.

8. Covello, *Italo-American School Child,* 324; Maxine Schwartz Seller, *Immigrant Women* (Philadelphia: Temple University Press, 1981). Linda Gordon does an excellent job of spelling out the tensions between reformers and an immigrant clientele accused of neglecting or abusing their children in *Heroes of Their Own Lives: The Politics and History of Family Violence* (New York: Penguin, 1988).

9. See Ruth Hutchinson Crocker, *Social Work and Social Order: The Settlement Movement in Two Industrial Cities* (Urbana: University of Illinois Press, 1992); George Sanchez, *"Go After the Women": Americanization and the Mexican Immigrant Woman, 1915–1929* (Stanford: Stanford Center for Chicano Research, 1984); Baby Hygiene Association, 8th annual report, 1917, Massachusetts State House Library, Boston, 25; "Children's Bureau on the Care of Infants," *School and Society* 8 (24 August 1918): 226.

10. Elizabeth Ewen, *Immigrant Women in the Land of Dollars: Life and Culture on the Lower East Side* (New York: Monthly Review Press, 1985), 16, 85, 94. See also Breckinridge, *New Homes for Old,* 150–51.

11. See John Higham, *Strangers in the Land: Patterns of American Nativism, 1860–1925* (New York: Atheneum, 1963).

12. Marie Leff-Caldwell, "Taking Mother into Camp," *Woman's Home Companion* 47 (March 1920): 29; Frances Kellor, "What Is Americanization?" in *Immigration and Americanization,* ed. Philip Davis (Boston: Ginn, 1920), 624.

13. Gwendolyn Mink, "The Lady and the Tramp: Gender, Race, and the Origins of the American Welfare State," in *Women, the State, and Welfare,* ed. Linda Gordon (Madison: University of Wisconsin Press, 1990), 98. See also Werner Sollors, *Beyond Ethnicity: Consent and Descent in American Culture* (New York: Oxford University Press, 1986).

14. Carl Degler, *In Search of Human Nature: The Decline and Revival of Darwinism in American Social Thought* (New York: Oxford University Press), 139–40.

15. Grace Caldwell, "Play School for Habit Training: A Report of the Experiment Years, 1922–1946," North Bennet Street Industrial School Papers, box 102, vol. 79, Schlesinger Library, Radcliffe College, 11.

16. Breckinridge, *New Homes for Old,* 50; Woodward, "Where Home and Kindergarten May Join Forces," 1.

17. See, for instance, Virginia Yans-McLaughlin, *Family and Community: Italian Immigrants*

in Buffalo, 1880–1930 (Ithaca, N.Y.: Cornell University Press, 1977), 149, and Ewen, *Immigrant Women,* 85–87. On the ethos of collectivism in immigrant families, see John Bodnar, *The Transplanted: A History of Immigrants in Urban America* (Bloomington: Indiana University Press, 1985).

18. Ewen, *Immigrant Women,* 136.

19. See Maxine Seller, "The Education of the Immigrant Woman 1900–1935," *Journal of Urban History* 4 (May 1978): 307–30; Pearl Idelia Ellis, *Americanization Through Home-making* (Los Angeles: Wetzel, 1929); and Mary Antin, *The Promised Land* (Boston: Houghton & Mifflin, 1912), 187. For a more negative portrait of the Americanization efforts of social reformers, see Anzia Yezierska's story "The Free Vacation House," in *Hungry Hearts* (Boston: Houghton Mifflin, 1920), 97–113.

20. Michael M. Davis, Jr., *Immigrant Health and the Community* (Harper & Brothers: New York, 1921), 300; Carson, *Settlement Folk,* 85.

21. John Higham notes in *Strangers in the Land* that Americanization programs embodied both democratic and discriminatory elements, 235. Bessie Locke, "The Kindergarten, a Vital Americanizing Agency," *Child Welfare Magazine* 13 (February 1919): 147.

22. Mrs. Frederic Schoff, "Congress of Mothers and Parent-Teacher Bodies," address at National Americanization Conference, 1919, Davis, Calif., *Immigration and Americanization,* 739.

23. Molly Ladd-Taylor, *Mother-Work: Women, Child Welfare, and the State, 1890–1930* (Urbana: University of Illinois Press, 1994), 33.

24. John Langdon-Davies, "Education: Savage and Civilized," in *The New Generation: The Intimate Problems of Modern Parents and Children,* ed. V. F. Calverton and Samuel D. Schmalhausen (New York: Macaulay, 1930), 27. John Dewey also put forth a similar notion in *Democracy and Education* (New York: Macmillan, 1916), when he said that "Progressive communities . . . endeavor to shape the experience of the young so that instead of reproducing current habits, better habits shall be formed," 92.

25. John E. Anderson, *The Young Child in the Home* (New York: Appleton-Century, 1936), 287, 102.

26. Ladd-Taylor, *Mother-Work,* 33; Judy Barrett Litoff, *American Midwives, 1860 to the Present* (Westport, Conn.: Greenwood Press, 1978). Carolyn Leonard Carson provides interesting evidence about the propensity of African-American migrant mothers in Pittsburgh to make use of modern medicine in " 'And the Results Showed Promise' . . . Physicians, Childbirth, and Southern Black Migrant Women, 1916–1930: Pittsburgh as a Case Study," *Journal of American Ethnic History* 14 (Fall 1994): 32–64.

27. Neil M. Cowan and Ruth Schwartz Cowan, *Our Parents' Lives: The Americanization of Eastern European Jews* (New York: Basic Books, 1989), 202–3. Jacqueline Litt also makes a similar point—that medicalization was tied to Americanization for Jewish immigrants—in "Mothering, Medicalization, and Jewish Identity, 1928–1940," *Gender and Society* 10 (April 1996): 197.

28. Litt, "Mothering, Medicalization," 197.

29. Cowan and Cowan, *Our Parents' Lives,* 202–3.

30. Margaret Jarman Hagood, *Mothers of the South: Portraiture of the White Tenant Farm Woman* (New York: Norton, 1977), 137–38.

31. Cora May Trawick Court, "A Study of Parent Education in a City of the South, 1934," box 2, Cora May Trawick Court Papers, Schlesinger Library, 75.

32. African-American mothers may have been dubious about the kind of help available to them, but that did not mean that they did not need assistance. As one mother despondently remarked, "I don't see what will do any good. I wish somebody would start something to help us." See Court, "Parent Education," 74.

33. Tillie Olsen, "I Stand Here Ironing," in Olsen, *Tell Me a Riddle: A Collection* (Philadelphia: Lippincott, 1961), 75. Michigan State University American Studies graduate student Susan Dominguez drew my attention to the relevance of this story for parent education. Court, "Parent Education," 30.

34. Christopher Lasch, *Haven in a Heartless World* (New York: Basic Books, 1977), 13. On the reformist aspects of the kindergarten, see Marvin Lazerson, "Social Reform and Early Childhood Education: Some Historical Perspectives," in *As the Twig Is Bent: Readings in Early Childhood Education,* ed. Robert Anderson and Harold Shane (Boston: Houghton Mifflin, 1971), 26. For more on kindergarten activists and the reformation of the family, see Michael Shapiro, *Child's Garden: The Kindergarten Movement from Froebel to Dewey* (University Park: Pennsylvania State University Press, 1983); Ann Taylor Allen, "Let Us Live with Our Children: Kindergarten Movements in Germany and the United States, 1890–1914," *History of Education Quarterly* 28 (Spring 1988): 23–48; Marvin Lazerson, "Urban Reform and the Schools: Kindergartens in Massachusetts, 1870–1915," *History of Education Quarterly* 11 (Summer 1971): 115–42; Dom Cavallo, "From Perfection to Habit: Moral Training in the American Kindergarten, 1860–1920," *History of Education Quarterly* 16 (Summer 1976): 147–61; and Cavallo, "The Politics of Latency: Kindergarten Pedagogy, 1860–1930," in *Regulated Children/Liberated Children,* ed. Barbara Finkelstein (New York: Psychohistory Press, 1979), 158–83; and Barbara Beatty, "A Vocation from on High: Pre-School Advocacy and Teaching as an Occupation for Women in Nineteenth-Century Boston" (Ed.D. diss., Harvard Graduate School of Education, Boston, 1981). On social control and the Sunday school movement, see Paul Boyer, *Urban Masses and Moral Order in America, 1820–1920* (Cambridge: Harvard University Press, 1978).

35. Women's Education Association, 51st annual report, 1923, Eliot-Pearson Child-Study Papers, Tufts University Archives, Medford, Mass.; Robert Melvin Tank, "Young Children, Families, and Society in America Since the 1920s: The Evolution of Health, Education, and Child Care Programs for the Preschool Child" (Ph.D. diss., University of Michigan, 1980), 292, 258. The Ruggles Street Nursery School and the Play School for Habit Training were two philanthropic nursery schools in Boston which served primarily immigrant families in the 1920s. The papers of both schools illustrate the extent to which the goal of Americanization combined with the social-scientific aims of the nursery school. Both sets of papers are at the Radcliffe's Schlesinger Library; papers pertaining to Eliot's school are also housed at Tufts with the Eliot-Pearson papers. The Abigail Adams Eliot manuscript collection contains information relevant to the Ruggles Street Nursery School. The papers of the Play School are included in the North Bennet Street Industrial School collection.

36. Sydney A. Halpern, *American Pediatrics* (Berkeley: University of California Press, 1988), 85; William J. Breen, *Uncle Sam at Home: Civilian Mobilization, Wartime Federalism, and*

the Council of National Defense, 1917–1919 (Westport, Conn: Greenwood Press, 1984), 127–28; Alisa Klaus, "Women's Organizations and the Infant Health Movement in France and the United States, 1890–1920," in Lady Bountiful Revisited: Women, Philanthropy, and Power, ed. Kathleen D. McCarthy (New Brunswick, N.J.: Rutgers University Press, 1990), 157–73; Marilyn Irvin Holt, Linoleum, Better Babies and the Modern Farm Woman, 1890–1930 (Albuquerque: University of New Mexico Press, 1995), 114.

37. Halpern, American Pediatrics, 85, 98. For a detailed account of the infant-health movement see Richard A. Meckel, Save the Babies: American Public Health Reform and the Prevention of Infant Mortality, 1850–1929 (Baltimore: Johns Hopkins University Press, 1990).

38. Meckel, Save the Babies.

39. Meckel, Save the Babies, 144–45.

40. Sara Josephine Baker, "Talks with Mothers," New York Milk Committee, 1913, New York Academy of Medicine Manuscript Collection, 3. Ellen Ross, Love and Toil: Motherhood in Outcast London, 1870–1918 (New York: Oxford University Press, 1993), 203.

41. Baker, "Talks With Mothers," 4. For more on Baker's work, see Meckel, Save the Babies, 143–45.

42. Esther G. Barrows, Neighbors All: A Settlement Notebook (Boston: Houghton Mifflin, 1929), 151.

43. Alice Hamilton, "Hull House Within and Without," in 100 Years at Hull House, ed. Mary Lynn McCree Bryan and Allen F. Davis (Bloomington: Indiana University Press, 1990), 109.

44. Phillip Youtz, "Report on the Teachers College Conference on Household Engineering," in report of the Home Problems Conference held at Merrill-Palmer School, Detroit, 18–20 April 1927, series 3, box 33, no. 354, LSRM, 15; John E. Anderson, Young Child in the Home (New York: Appleton-Century, 1936) 287, 102.

45. Margaret J. Quilliard, Child Study Discussion Records: Development-Methods-Techniques (New York: Child Study Association of America, 1928), 57; Gordon, Heroes of Their Own Lives, 139. Settle's survey appears in Court, "Parent Education," 71.

46. Marie Belle Fowler, "Parent Education in the Nursery School," in University of the State of New York, State Education Department, Child Development and Parental Education, Report of Work in Child Development and Parental Education Supported by Grant from the Spelman Fund to the State Education Department (Albany: University of the State of New York, 1933), 21; "Albany, Report 1932–33," series 3, box 26, no. 265, LSRM, 6; Stella Crossley, "Confessions of an Amateur Mother," Children: The Magazine for Parents 2 (March 1927): 28.

47. Sidonie Matsner Gruenberg, autobiography in manuscript, Library of Congress, 112.

48. Martha McMahon's Engendering Motherhood: Identity and Self-Transformation in Women's Lives (New York: Guilford Press, 1995) has sparked my thinking on the metaphor of the mother-child bond, although our conclusions are somewhat different.

49. May Peabody, "Organized Discussion," Child Welfare Magazine 24 (October 1929): 89.

50. Abigail Adams Eliot to Ella Harris, 16 October 1923, Eliot-Pearson Papers, Tufts University Archives.

51. Abigail A. Eliot, "The Demand for Nursery Schools," Childhood Education 2 (1926):

477–78. See also Hamilton Cravens, *The Triumph of Evolution: American Scientists and the Heredity-Environment Controversy, 1900–1940* (Philadelphia: University of Pennsylvania Press, 1978), for an analysis of the discussion of heredity versus environment in the scientific community. Cravens's work suggests that the compromise solution embraced by Eliot was the predominant point of view held by scientists during this period. See Cravens's *Before Head Start: The Iowa Station and America's Children* (Chapel Hill: University of North Carolina Press, 1993) for an account of the Iowa Station's pioneering role in investigating questions of heredity and environment in intelligence.

52. Edward L. Thorndike, Elsie O. Grebman, J. Warren Tilton, and Ella Woodward, *Adult Learning* (New York: Macmillan, 1928), 177–78.

53. Paula S. Fass, *Outside In: Minorities and the Transformation of American Education* (New York: Oxford University Press, 1989), 59.

54. "Report of University of Georgia, College of Agriculture, Child Development and Parent Education, 19 January 1929," series 3, box 44, no. 461, LSRM.

55. Josephine C. Foster and Marion L. Mattson, *Nursery-School Education* (New York: Appleton-Century, 1939), 310.

56. Maria Lambin Rogers, *A Contribution to the Theory and Practise of Parents' Associations* (New York: United Parents' Association, 1931), 42.

57. Elizabeth McFadden, "Dey's All Got Debbils!" *Children: The Magazine for Parents* 3 (October 1929): 22–24.

58. Nancy Underhill, report 6, December 1929, at Neighborhood House, Margaret Wylie Papers, Division of Rare and Manuscript Collections, Cornell University Library, Ithaca, N.Y. (hereafter referred to as MW).

59. Quilliard, *Child Study Discussion Records,* 72.

60. "Albany, report, 1932–33," series 3, box 26, no. 265, LSRM, 7; Arnold, "A History of the Organization of Negro Groups in Cincinnati," attached to letter to Lawrence K. Frank from Ada Hart Arlitt, 27 November 1929, series 3, box 44, no. 456, LSRM; Rogers, *A Contribution to the Theory and Practise,* 31.

61. Betty Trager, "What the Henry Street Settlement Means to Me," circa 1949, box 40, folder 20, UNH.

62. Press Release from United Neighborhood Houses, 16 November 1926, box 65, folder 30, UNH.

63. Albert Joseph Kennedy, *Social Settlements in New York City, Their Activities, Policies, and Administration* (New York: Columbia University Press, 1935), 106, 109, 121, 124.

64. *The League of Mothers' Clubs Bulletin* (1927), LMC, box 49, folder 512, UNH; "Inventories," *League of Mothers' Clubs Bulletin* (April 1927), box 66, folder 31, UNH; "Informal Educational Experiments in Learning by Doing," "United Neighborhood Houses, Spring Conference, 24 May 1938," box 75, scrapbook 19, UNH.

65. Mrs. Gilbert's Speech, 29 March, 1943, box 53, folder 46, UNH, 6.

66. See, for instance, Amos Griswold Warner, *American Charities and Social Work* (New Haven: Yale University Press, 1925), 104; "The League of Mothers' Clubs" (1926), box 49, no. 512, UNH, 3–4.

67. Alma C. Guillet, "Report of Homemaking Supervisor, 1927," box 66, folder 31, UNH; quoted in Lillian D. Wald, *The House on Henry Street* (New York: Henry Holt, 1915), 179.

68. "Mothers in Home-Making," *League of Mothers' Clubs Bulletin* (January 1927), box 66, legal folder 31, UNH.

69. "Mrs. Gilbert's Speech, 29 March, 1943," box 53, folder 46, UNH, 3; press release, 16 November 1926, box 65, folder 30, UNH; "Program of Mothers' Club, Stuyvesant Neighborhood House," n.d. (1925–26?), box 65, legal folder 26, UNH.

70. *League of Mothers' Clubs Bulletin* (November 1924), legal folder 23, UNH; "League of Mothers' Clubs Speaker's Bureau," 5 May 1931, box 68, legal folder 47, UNH. See Louise A. Mayo, *The Ambivalent Image: Nineteenth-Century America's Perception of the Jew* (London: Associated Universities Press, 1988), 148; June Sochen, *Consecrate Every Day: The Public Lives of Jewish American Women 1880–1980* (Albany: State University of New York Press, 1981), 45.

71. Report of the Executive Committee Meeting, 10 November 1930, box 68, no. 46, UNH; League of Mothers' Clubs Report of Preliminary Executive Committee Meeting, 26 November 1930, box 68, no. 46, UNH; Report of Executive Committee Meeting, 9 February 1931, box 68, no. 46, UNH.

72. "Mrs. Gilbert's Speech," 29 March 1943, box 53, folder 46, UNH, 4; "League of Mothers' Clubs Committee on Health Education, 1926–27," 17 May 1927, UNH; "Reports of League of Mothers' Clubs, 1938–39," box 49, no. 523, UNH.

73. "Miss Josephine Schain Speaks," *League of Mothers' Clubs Bulletin* (October 1924), legal folder 23, UNH.

74. Cheryl Lynn Greenberg, *"Or Does It Explode?": Black Harlem in the Great Depression* (New York: Oxford University Press, 1991).

75. Cynthia Neverdon-Morton, "African American Women and Adult Education in the South, 1895–1925," in *Education of the African American Adult: An Historical Overview,* ed. Harvey G. Neufeldt and Leo McGee (Westport, Conn.: Greenwood Press, 1990): 163–78, has reconstructed the history of these groups; Wilson Jeremiah Moses, *The Golden Age of Black Nationalism,* 117, 108; Anne Meis Knupfer, " 'Prevented from Mingling Easily and Generally with the Rest,' African-American Settlements in Chicago, 1900–1920," unpublished paper delivered at American Educational Research Association Meeting, San Francisco, April 1995.

76. Dorothy Salem, *To Better Our World: Black Women in Organized Reform, 1890–1920* (Brooklyn, N.Y.: Carlson, 1990), 79–80; Camilla Weems, "Supervising Rural Schools," *Spelman Messenger* (November 1915): 6, quoted in Neverdon-Morton, "African-American Women and Adult Education in the South"; Eileen Boris, "The Power of Motherhood: Black and White Women Redefine the 'Political,' " in *Mothers of a New World: Maternalist Politics and the Origins of Welfare States,* ed. Seth Koven and Sonya Michel (New York: Routledge, 1993), 225.

77. Anderson, *Young Child in the Home,* 292. See also the records of the National Parent-Teacher Association at the University of Illinois at Chicago for historical accounts of the National Congress of Colored Parents and Teachers. More research on this organization is sorely needed.

78. Greenberg, *"Or Does It Explode?"* 58–59.

79. See Moses, *Black Nationalism, 1850–1925* (New York: Oxford University Press, 1978), 103; Salem, *To Better Our World;* Boris, "The Power of Motherhood"; Stephanie J. Shaw,

"Black Club Women and the Creation of the National Association of Colored Women," in *"We Specialize in the Wholly Impossible": A Reader in Black Women's History,* ed. Darlene Clark Hine et al. (Brooklyn, N.Y.: Carlson, 1995), 443–47.

80. Moses, *Black Nationalism,* 131.

81. Ernest Burgess, "Family Relations and Personality Adjustment," in *Papers on Parent Education Presented at the Biennial Conference* (Washington, D.C.: National Council of Parent Education, 1930), 43. See also E. Franklin Frazier, *The Negro Family in Chicago* (Chicago: University of Chicago Press, 1932); W. E. B. DuBois, *The Philadelphia Negro: A Social Study* (Philadelphia: University of Pennsylvania Press, 1899); T. J. Woofter, Jr., *Negro Problems in Cities* (New York: Doubleday, Doran, 1928); and Louise Kennedy, *The Negro Peasant Turns Cityward: Effects of Recent Migrations to Northern Centers* (New York: Columbia University Press, 1930).

82. Margaret Quilliard to Leonard Blumgart, 29 May 1930, box 40, no. 419, CSA.

83. Margaret Quilliard to Mrs. Fifield, 13 October 1930, box 42, folder 449, CSA; "Inter-Community Child Study Committee," 11 June 1931, box 41, folder 438, CSA, 1; "Inter-Community Child Study Committee," 3.

84. Janice E. Hale-Benson, *Black Children: Their Roots, Culture, and Learning Styles* (Baltimore: Johns Hopkins University Press, 1982), 126. See also Wilma King, *Stolen Childhood: Slave Youth in Nineteenth-Century America* (Bloomington: Indiana University Press, 1995), for a discussion of the importance of obedience and respect for adults in slave families.

85. For overviews of African-American adult education programs that included components of parent education, especially in Harlem, see Judith Weisenfeld, "The Harlem YWCA and the Secular City, 1904–1945," *Journal of Women's History* 6 (Fall 1994): 62–78; V. P. Franklin, "Education for Life: Adult Education Programs for African-Americans in Northern Cities, 1900–1942," 113–34, and Lillian S. Williams, "Black Communities and Adult Education: YMCA, YWCA, and Fraternal Organizations," 135–62, both in *Education of the African-American Adult,* ed. Harvey G. Neufeldt and Leo McGee (Westport, Conn.: Greenwood Press, 1990).

86. Biographical data on Smith was obtained from *Who's Who in Colored America, 1928–1929,* ed. Joseph J. Boris (New York: Who's Who in Colored America, 1929), 338; "First Meeting of Harlem Committee for Furthering Child Study," 5 December 1928, box 42, no. 454, CSA, 1.

87. "Report of the North Harlem Child Study Committee," 16 October 1933, box 43, folder 456, CSA; "Negro Mass Meeting, 28 May 1929," box 42, no. 455, CSA, 1–2.

88. "Negro Mass Meeting," 2.

89. The actual figure given by Joe William Trotter, Jr., is 23.9 percent, in "Blacks in the Urban North: The 'Underclass Question' in Historical Perspective," in *The "Underclass Debate": Views from History,* ed. Michael B. Katz (Princeton, N.J.: Princeton University Press, 1993), 74.

90. "Negro Mass Meeting," 5. See also Degler, *In Search of Human Nature.*

91. It is likely that this study was the one conducted by Ira de Augustine Reid for the New York Urban League in 1927, which surveyed 2,400 African-American families in Harlem and found that two thirds of wives and mothers were employed outside the home. See

Reid, New York Urban League, "Twenty-Four Hundred Negro Families in Harlem," report, May 1927, microfilm Sc R3612, Schomburg Archives, 20 (reference in Greenberg, *"Or Does It Explode?,"* 22).

92. "Negro Mass Meeting," 5–8.

93. "First Meeting of Harlem Committee," 2; "Negro Mass Meeting," 6; "First Meeting of Harlem Committee," 4.

94. "Negro Mass Meeting," 6.

95. Jean Grossman to Margaret Quilliard, 7 June 1929, box 42, folder 455, CSA.

96. See Greenberg, *"Or Does It Explode?"* for a description and analysis of the impact of the Depression on Harlem.

97. "Speaking Points for Child Study Committee," attached to letter from Hortense R. Tate to Margaret Quilliard, November 1932, box 42, folder 450, CSA.

98. "Report of the North Harlem Child Study Committee," 1.

99. Estella Carr to Margaret Quilliard, 1 May 1929, box 41, file 444, CSA.

100. "Excerpts from the Minutes of the Advisory Board of the Child Study Group," 31 January 1933, box 41, no. 444, CSA. On the focus on mother's pensions rather than day nurseries in the white women's movement, see Sonya Michel, "The Limits of Maternalism: Policies Toward American Wage-Earning Mothers During the Progressive Era," in *Mothers of a New World,* 277–320.

101. Hale-Benson, *Black Children,* 136; "Montclair Child Study Group, 1930," box 42, folder 451, CSA; "Findings from the Child Study Group, 13 March 1930," Montclair, N.J., 1930–33, box 42, folder 448, CSA; "Montclair Child Study Group, 1930."

102. Meeting minutes, Brooklyn group, 17 November 1931, box 42, folder 455, CSA; "Bulletin of the Inter-Community Child Study Committee," no. 7, January 1935, box 41, no. 442, CSA, 2.

103. Mrs. Keron A. Battle to Margaret Quilliard, 19 October 1931, box 42, no. 454, CSA; Charlotte Atwood to Margaret Quilliard, 17 February 1932, box 43, no. 459, CSA. Sharon Harley has documented the public activism of Washington, D.C., female African-American educators in "Beyond the Classroom: The Organizational Lives of Black Female Educators in the District of Columbia, 1890–1930," *Journal of Negro Education* 51 (1982): 475–86.

104. Margaret Quilliard to Anne F. Smith, 24 June 1932, box 42, no. 446, CSA.

105. "Summary of Questionnaires Filled Out by Members of P.S. 90 Group," box 43, folder 456, CSA; "Negro Mass Meeting," box 42, no. 455, CSA; "Statements Made by Members of Study Groups at Englewood and Montclair, 1930–31," box 42, no. 451, CSA.

106. "Inter-Community Child Study Committee, 1933," box 41, no. 438, CSA.

107. Margaret Quilliard to Sidonie M. Gruenberg, 25 June 1931, attached to "Inter-Community Child Study Committee," 11 June 1931, box 41, no. 438, CSA; "Inter-Community Child Study Committee," 2.

108. Moses, *Black Nationalism,* 131; "Specific Characteristics of Negroes," March 1931, box 41, no. 438, CSA.

109. See Federal Writers Project, "The Depression in Harlem," in *Hitting Home: The Great Depression in Town and Country,* ed. Bernard Sternsher (Chicago: Quadrangle Books, 1970), 105–22.

110. Lawrence K. Frank, "Future Policy of the Spelman Fund," 13 March 1929, Lawrence K. Frank Papers, National Library of Medicine, 1.

111. Elizabeth Dyer, "Report of Work Being Carried On by the School of Household Administration Under the Grant of the Spelman Fund for the Year 1929–1930," series 3, box 44, no. 456, LSRM; "Child Study Fellowship Program," 19 March 1930, series 3.5, box 29, no. 312, LSRM.

112. Ada Hart Arlitt to Dorothea Davis, 15 May 1928, series 3, box 44, no. 456, LSRM.

113. Janet Arnold, "Organization of Negro Groups," attached to letter to Lawrence K. Frank from Ada Hart Arlitt dated 27 November 1929, series 3, box 44, no. 456, LSRM, 12.

114. Arnold, "Organization of Negro Groups," 7–8.

115. Elizabeth Dyer, "Report of Work Being Carried On," 5–6.

116. Dyer, "Report of Work Being Carried On," 1.

117. Dyer, "Report of Work Being Carried On," 2.

118. Ada Hart Arlitt to Beardsley Ruml, 16 December 1930, series 3, box 44, no. 456, LSRM.

119. "Activities Carried On Under Spelman Fund"; "Report of Mrs. Foster—Negro Parent Education Leader," attached to letter from Ada Hart Arlitt to Anna Blauvelt, 21 March 1933, series 3, box 44, no. 457, LSRM, 1–4.

120. Ada Hart Arlitt to Beardsley Ruml, 10 January 1931, series 3, box 44, no. 457, LSRM.

121. "Activities Carried On Under Spelman Fund."

122. Ada H. Arlitt, "On the Need for Caution in Establishing Race Norms," *Journal of Applied Psychology* 5 (June 1921): 182–83; Degler, *In Search of Human Nature,* 172–73.

CHAPTER 4

1. Guy Montrose Whipple, ed., *Twenty-eighth Yearbook of the National Society for the Study of Education: Preschool and Parental Education* (Bloomington, Ill.: National Society for the Study of Education, 1929), 7.

2. Eduard C. Lindeman, "Sociological Backgrounds of Family Life," in White House Conference on Child Health and Protection, *Parent Education: Types, Content, Method* (New York: Century, 1932), 3.

3. Accounts of the various statewide parent education programs in the 1920s include Hamilton Cravens, "Child-Saving in the Age of Professionalism, 1915–1930," in *American Childhood: A Research Guide and Historical Handbook,* ed. Joseph Hawes and Ray Hiner (Westport, Conn.: Greenwood Press, 1985); Dorothy Bradbury, *Pioneering in Child Welfare: A History of the Iowa Child Welfare Research Station* (Iowa City: State University of Iowa Press, 1933); Edith A. Davis and Esther McGinnis, *Parent Education: A Survey of the Program* (Westport, Conn.: Greenwood Press, 1939); Gertrude Laws, *Parent Education in California* (Sacramento: California State Printing Office, 1937); and University of the State of New York, State Education Department, Child Developmental and Parental Education, *Report of Work in Child Development and Parental Education Supported by Grant from the Spelman Fund to the State Education Department* (Albany: University of the State of New York, 1933). The Laura Spelman Rockefeller Memorial Archives at the Rockefeller Archive Center in Tarrytown, N.Y., contain information about the numerous programs for parent education in the 1920s.

4. See Cravens, "Child-Saving."

5. Hamilton Cravens, *Before Head Start: The Iowa Station and America's Children* (Chapel Hill: University of North Carolina Press, 1993).

6. For discussions of the relation between popular and professional demands in the establishment of the professions of pediatrics and child psychology, see Sydney Halpern, *American Pediatrics: The Social Dynamics of Professionalism, 1880–1980* (Berkeley: University of California Press, 1988), and Margot Horn, *Before It's Too Late: The Child Guidance Movement in the United States, 1922–1945* (Philadelphia: Temple University Press, 1989).

7. Bradbury, *Pioneering in Child Welfare*, 3; Cravens, *Before Head Start*, 7.

8. Bradbury, *Pioneering in Child Welfare*, 7.

9. Bradbury, *Pioneering in Child Welfare*, 7; Cora Bussey Hillis to Dr. George E. Vincent, 15 November 1920, series 3, box 40, no. 416, LSRM.

10. Molly Ladd-Taylor, *Mother-Work: Women, Child Welfare, and the State, 1890–1930* (Urbana: University of Illinois Press, 1994), 6, 18–19.

11. Cravens, *Before Head Start*, 11.

12. Bradbury, *Pioneering in Child Welfare*, 15.

13. Bradbury, *Pioneering in Child Welfare*, 24–25, 48; Cravens, "Child-Saving," 435–36; Carl N. Degler, *In Search of Human Nature: The Decline and Revival of Darwinism in American Social Thought* (New York: Oxford University Press, 1991), 145. See especially Degler's chapter in this text, "The Uncoupling of Behavior from Nature," for an extremely useful discussion of the movement away from eugenics in the social scientific community.

14. Cora Bussey Hillis to Dr. Bird T. Baldwin, 6 June 1923, series 3, box 40, no. 417, LSRM; Barbara Beatty, *Preschool Education in America: The Culture of Young Children from the Colonial Era to the Present* (New Haven: Yale University Press, 1995), 157.

15. Cravens, *Before Head Start*, 51.

16. "Conference on Research in Child Development, Iowa Child Welfare Research Station," 23–25 October 1925, series 3, box 36, no. 278, LSRM.

17. Cravens, "Child-Saving," 445; Lawrence K. Frank, memo of interview with Dean Anna Richardson of School of Home Economics at Iowa State Agricultural College, 2 March 1925, series 3, box 32, no. 341, LSRM; Cravens, *Before Head Start*, 53–55; "Progress Report, Iowa, 18 November 1929," series 3, box 40, no. 424, LSRM.

18. Margaret H. Strong, *History of the California Congress of Parents and Teachers, Inc., 1900–1944* (San Diego: California Congress of Parents and Teachers, 1945), 39–40.

19. Flyer for Assembly Bill 161, the Child Welfare Research Station Bill, "Save the Children Physically, Mentally, Morally," n.d., series 3, box 43, no. 452, LSRM; Cravens, "Child-Saving," 445–46.

20. "Set-Up of Proposed Parent Education Program of California," n.d., series 3, box 27, no. 280, LSRM, 4–5; Laws, *Parent Education in California*, 2.

21. "Set-Up," 1; Cravens, "Child-Saving," 446–47.

22. Memo concerning conference with Lawrence K. Frank of LSRM and Richard A. Bolt, attached to letter from Bolt to Frank, 21 July 1925, series 3, box 43, no. 452, LSRM.

23. Ethel Richardson to Lawrence K. Frank, 7 April 1927, series 3, box 43, no. 452, LSRM.

24. "An Experiment in Parent Education Carried On by Direction of the Superintendent of

Public Instruction of the State of California," 15 December 1927, series 3, box 27, no. 280, LSRM, 11–12; Strong, *History of the California Congress*, 39–42.

25. Cravens, "Child-Saving," 443.

26. Cravens, "Child-Saving," 443; Wylie B. McNeal to Dean Kelly, 20 February 1925, series 3, box 45, no. 465, LSRM; memo about Lawrence K. Frank and Dorothea Dixon's interview with Harold E. Anderson, 17 October 1927, series 3, box 45, no. 466, LSRM; Davis and McGinnis, *Parent Education*, 95.

27. John E. Anderson, "The Parent Education Program at the University of Minnesota," in National Congress of Parents and Teachers, *Parent Education: The First Yearbook* (Washington, D.C.: National Congress of Parents and Teachers, 1930), 71; Davis and McGinnis, *Parent Education*, 93.

28. Davis and McGinnis, *Parent Education*, 96, 107, 141; 1930 report on child development projects conducted by Institute of Child Welfare, University of Minnesota Institute of Child Welfare Papers, University of Minnesota Archives (hereafter referred to as UM), 5–7; 1932 report on child development projects conducted by Institute of Child Welfare, UM, 1.

29. 1937 report on child development, UM, 3, 11.

30. Milton J. Senn, oral history interview with George Stoddard, National Library of Medicine, Bethesda, Md., 6.

31. Ellen Fitzpatrick, *Endless Crusade: Women Social Scientists and Progressive Reform* (New York: Oxford University Press, 1990), 217. See also Robyn Muncy, *Creating a Female Dominion in American Reform, 1890–1935* (New York: Oxford University Press, 1991), and Ellen Condliffe Lagemann, *Private Power for the Public Good* (Middletown, Conn.: Wesleyan University Press, 1983). Robert R. Sears, "Your Ancients Revisited: A History of Child Development," *Review of Child Development Research*, vol. 5, ed. E. Mavis Hetherington (Chicago: University of Chicago Press, 1975), 4.

32. Cited in Cora Winchell, "Home Economics at the Crossroads," *Journal of Home Economics* 18 (October 1926): 554; Ellen Richards, "Opening Address to the Denver Meeting of the American Home Economics Association, 1909," *Journal of Home Economics* 1 (October 1909): 321–22. Valuable accounts of the home economics movement in relation to gender issues and women's education include Joyce Antler, "Culture, Service, and Work: Changing Ideas of Higher Education for Women," *The Undergraduate Woman: Issues in Educational Equity*, ed. Pamela J. Perun (Lexington, Mass.: Lexington Books, 1982), 15–41; Maxine L. Margolis, *Mothers and Such: Views of American Women and Why They Changed* (Berkeley: University of California Press, 1984), 124–47; John L. Rury, "Vocationalism for Home and Work: Women's Education in the United States," *History of Education Quarterly* 24 (Spring 1984): 21–45; Margaret Rossiter, *Women Scientists in America* (Baltimore: Johns Hopkins University Press, 1982); Barbara Miller Solomon, *In the Company of Educated Women* (New Haven: Yale University Press, 1985); Emma Seifrit Weigley, "It Might Have Been Euthenics: The Lake Placid Conferences and the Home Economics Movement," *American Quarterly* 26 (March 1974): 79–96.

33. Rury, "Vocationalism for Home and Work," 26. In her study, *The 'Girl' Question in Education: Vocational Education for Young Women in the Progressive Era* (London: Falmer

Press, 1992), Jane Bernard Powers has noted, "Home economics is both traditional and feminist, it contains continuities and contradictions," 4.

34. Elizabeth C. Jenkins, "The College Course in Home Economics," *Journal of Home Economics* 9 (July 1917): 305.

35. Jenkins, "The College Course," 309, 311; Katherine Blunt, "President's Address: The Unity of the American Home Economics Association," *Journal of Home Economics* 18 (October 1926): 552.

36. Edna Noble White to Lawrence K. Frank, 25 January 1925, series 3, box 32, no. 349, LSRM.

37. Emily Cahan, "Science, Practice, and Gender Roles in Early American Child Psychology," in *Contemporary Constructions of the Child: Essays in Honor of William Kessen,* ed. Frank S. Kessel, Marc H. Bornstein, and Arnold J. Sameroff (Hillsdale, N.J.: Erlbaum, 1991), 231–33.

38. I am indebted to Steven L. Schlossman, "Philanthropy and the Gospel of Child Development," *History of Education Quarterly* 21 (Fall 1981): 275–99, for this terminology. See also Schlossman's essay, "Before Home Start: Notes Toward a History of Parent Education in America," *Harvard Educational Review* 46 (August 1976): 436–67; Cravens, "Child-Saving"; and Christine Mary Shea's dissertation, "The Ideology of Mental Health and the Emergence of the Therapeutic Liberal State: The American Mental Hygiene Movement, 1900–1930" (Ph.D. diss., University of Illinois at Urbana, 1980), 294–96; Lawrence K. Frank to Mrs. Clifford Walker, 6 June 1924, series 3, box 44, no. 458, LSRM.

39. "Progress Report, American Home Economics Association, 15 November 1929," series 3, box 26, no. 274, LSRM; American Home Economics Association, *Home Economists: Portraits and Brief Biographies of the Men and Women Prominent in the Home Economics Movement in the United States* (Baltimore: American Home Economics Association, 1929), 60. One of Richardson's tasks was to provide an account of the extent to which child development had infiltrated the high school and college curriculum. The results of her research were published in Anna Euretta Richardson, *Child Development and Parental Education in Home Economics: A Survey of Schools and Colleges* (Baltimore: American Home Economics Association, 1928).

40. Genevieve Fisher to R. M. Hughes, 25 November 1929, series 3, box 32, no. 341, LSRM; memo by Lawrence K. Frank, re: American Home Economics Association, 15 March 1925, series 3, box 26, no. 273, LSRM.

41. "How Can Colleges Prepare Their Students for Marriage and Parenthood?" *Journal of Home Economics* 22 (March 1930): 175.

42. Lawrence K. Frank to Anna E. Richardson, 26 March 1927, series 3, box 26, no. 274, LSRM; the alleged remark by Baldwin was reported in Lawrence K. Frank's memo of interview with Dean Anna Richardson of School of Home Economics at Iowa, 2 March 1925, series 3, box 32, no. 341, LSRM; Harold Jones to Lawrence K. Frank, 28 September 1928, series 3, box 43, no. 452, LSRM.

43. Confidential report of the Home Economics Conference in Albany, 21 November 1929, box 2, folder 2, Cornell College of Home Economics Archives, Division of Rare and Manuscript Collections, Cornell University Library, Ithaca, N.Y.

44. Cora Marguerite Winchell, *Home Economics for Public School Administrators* (New York: Teachers College Press, 1931), 2.

45. Alma L. Binzel, "Education's Responsibility for Parenthood," *Child Welfare Magazine* 18 (February 1924): 247.

46. Phillip Youtz, "Report of the Teachers College Conference on Household Engineering" at the Home Problems Conference held at Merrill-Palmer School, Detroit, 18–20 April 1927, series 3, box 33, no. 354, LSRM, 35; Columbia University, Teachers College, *Homemaking as a Center for Research; Report of the Teachers College Conferences on Homemaking, March 2–April 20, 1927* (New York: Teachers College Press, 1927), 83.

47. Donald B. Marti, *Women of the Grange: Mutuality and Sisterhood in Rural America, 1866–1920* (Westport, Conn.: Greenwood Press, 1991), 73–86; quoted in Morris Bishop, *A History of Cornell* (Ithaca, N.Y.: Cornell University Press, 1962), 380; "Testimonials—Re: Farmers' Wives," n.d., box 24, folder 48, papers of the Cornell College of Home Economics; Bishop, *A History of Cornell,* 380.

48. Ethel Bushnell Waring, "History That Led Up to the College of Home Economics and to the Department of Family Life in 1925," box 1, Ethel Bushnell Waring Papers, Division of Rare and Manuscript Collections, Cornell University Library, 2; Bishop, *A History of Cornell,* 480.

49. For biographical information on Wylie, see Mary Ford et al., "Margaret Wylie," in *Necrology of Cornell Faculty, 1963–1964* (Ithaca, N.Y.: Cornell University Press), 41–42.

50. Marilyn Irvin Holt, *Linoleum, Better Babies, and the Modern Farm Woman, 1890–1930* (Albuquerque: University of New Mexico Press, 1995), 63.

51. New York State College of Home Economics at Cornell University, 16th annual report, Ithaca, N.Y., 1941, 20; Eugene T. Stromberg, "Influence of the Central Rural School on Community Organization," *Cornell Agricultural Experiment Station Bulletin* 699 (June 1938); W. A. Anderson, "Population Trends in New York State, 1900 to 1950," *Rural Sociology Publication* 47 (April 1956): 64–65.

52. W. A. Anderson finds that only 5 percent of Home Bureau members had fewer than eight years of education, in "Farm Women in the Home Bureau: A Study in Cortland County, New York, 1939," *Cornell University Agriculture Experiment Station Bulletin, Department of Rural Sociology* 3 (October 1941): 3. On the average educational level of adult females in New York, see *Sixteenth Census of the US: 1940 Population, vol. 3, part 5: New York-Oregon* (Washington, D.C.: Government Printing Office, 1943); Child Guidance Series questionnaires, Suffolk County, N.Y., 1928–29, MW.

53. W. A. Anderson, "Farm Women in the Home Bureau," 3. See also W. A. Anderson and Hans H. Plambeck, "The Social Participation of Farm Families," *Cornell University Agricultural Experiment Station, Department of Rural Sociology* 8 (March 1943): 13–14. On the New York farm woman, see Kathleen R. Babbitt, "The Productive Farm Woman and the Extension Home Economist in New York State, 1920–1940," *Agricultural History* 67 (Spring 1993): 83–101, and Holt, *Linoleum, Better Babies and the Modern Farm Woman,* 50.

54. Mrs. Will Arsup to Home Bureau, n.d., 1933–40, Oswego County Home Demonstration Agent, N.Y., MW.

55. "Memo, Extension Education," n.d., box 24, folder 11, papers of the Cornell College of Home Economics.

56. Jennie Bernhard to Margaret Wylie, 21 September 1943, in Bennett Study Club Records, Kenmore, Buffalo County, N.Y., MW; Mrs. Walter Quinn to Margaret Wylie, 17 November 1933, Madison County, N.Y., MW.

CHAPTER 5

1. Mrs. Crothers, "25 Years After," 13 March 1928, Mothers' Club of Cambridge papers, box 1, Schlesinger Library, Radcliffe College, Cambridge; Richard Meckel, *Save the Babies: American Public Health Reform and the Prevention of Infant Mortality* (Baltimore: Johns Hopkins University Press), 94. Christina Hardyment, *Dream Babies: Three Centuries of Good Advice on Child Care* (New York: Harper & Row, 1983), remarks: "If improved obstetrics, enlightened infant care, and the reduction of diseases such as small pox had not slashed the infant mortality rate, parents would have been less interested in reading about how the philosophers thought they should handle children," 14.

2. Early accounts of women's reception of child development expertise whose authors assume that prescriptive advice had a great influence on mothers' behavior include Barbara Ehrenreich and Deirdre English, *For Her Own Good: 150 Years of the Experts' Advice to Women* (Garden City, N.Y.: Doubleday, 1979), and Sheila Rothman, *Woman's Proper Place: A History of Changing Ideals and Practices, 1870 to the Present* (New York: Basic Books, 1978). In his "Advice to Historians on Advice to Mothers," *Journal of Social History* 9 (Fall 1975): 44–63, Jay Mechling warns historians not to suppose that prescriptive advice can tell us anything about mothers' actual child-rearing practices.

3. For a demographic profile of the Cornell groups, see Chapter Four.

4. Paul Lichterman, "Self-Help Reading as a Thin Culture," *Media, Culture and Society* 14 (1992): 422.

5. On "interpretive communities," see Stanley Fish, *Is There a Text in This Class? The Authority of Interpretive Communities* (Cambridge: Harvard University Press, 1980), and Janice Radway, *Reading the Romance: Women, Patriarchy, and Popular Literature* (Chapel Hill: University of North Carolina Press, 1984).

6. Through some representatives of a Charlotte, Michigan, mothers' club that began meeting in the late 1930s, I have learned of other mothers' clubs in the state that continue to meet. Michigan sponsored its own federation of child-study clubs, which was not attached to a national organization.

7. Chapter 378 minutes, 19 January 1931, 1930–31, box 26, no. 270, CSA; Chapter 128 minutes, 7 December 1926, box 26, no 268, CSA; Chapter 372 minutes, 26 January 1931, box 26, no. 273, CSA.

8. Chapter 371 minutes, 28 January 1931, box 26, folder 272, CSA; John B. Watson, *Psychological Care of Infant and Child* (New York: Norton, 1928), 66; Mary Cover Jones, "Conditioning and Reconditioning—An Experimental Study in Child Behavior," *Proceedings of the National Education Association* 62 (1924): 585–90; Hamilton Child Study Club report, 12 November 1935, MW. See also Peter N. Stearns and Timothy Haggerty,

"The Role of Fear: Transitions in American Emotional Standards for Children, 1850–1950," *American Historical Review* 96 (February 1991): 63–94, for a discussion of the changing approaches to children's fears in American psychology.

9. Chapter 376 minutes, 16 February 1931, box 27, no. 277, CSA; Chapter 371 minutes, 28 January 1931, box 26, no. 272, CSA.

10. Oakfield Child Study Club notebook, n.d., Genesee County, N.Y., 1929–30, MW.

11. *Federation for the Study of Child Nature Bulletin* 2 (2), "Child Study Groups—Habit Formation," 6; Mrs. Max West, *Infant Care* (Washington, D.C.: Government Printing Office, 1914), 57; Martha May Eliot, *Infant Care* (Washington, D.C.: Government Printing Office, 1929), 57.

12. Oakfield-Batavia report, n.d., 1928–29, Genesee County, N.Y., MW.

13. Helen Storey, "The First Conference on Parenthood," *Child Welfare Magazine* 21 (January 1926): 301–2; Katherine Brookman, "To All Parents Everywhere—An Appeal to Loosen the Apron Strings," *Child Welfare Magazine* 21 (March 1926): 389.

14. Webster Child Study Club report, 16 November 1939, Monroe County, N.Y., MW.

15. Sidonie Matsner Gruenberg, autobiography in manuscript, Library of Congress, 103; Margaret J. Quilliard, *Child Study Discussion Records* (New York: Child Study Association of America, 1928), 49; 1933 Report on Child Development Projects, Institute of Child Welfare, UM, 7.

16. 1930 Report on Child Development Projects, Institute of Child Welfare, UM; PTA School #65 Child Study Club report, 30 April 1930, Buffalo, Erie County, N.Y., MW.

17. Watson's views on maternal sentimentality are spelled out in his chapter "Too Much Mother Love" in *Psychological Care*. Watson was not alone, however, in focusing on the dangers of oversentimentality. See also Sidonie Matsner Gruenberg, autobiography; Southold Home Bureau Child Study Club notebook, 14 May 1930, Suffolk County, N.Y., MW.

18. Playlets for Mary Jemison Child Study Club, "A Sleeping Situation," 1934–36, Perry, Wyoming County, N.Y., MW.

19. Child Study Club report, 14 May 1929, Laura Gannett Smith, East Concord, N.Y., MW.

20. Jo Sharkey to Sidonie Matsner Gruenberg, 2 March 1931, Benjamin and Sidonie Matsner Gruenberg Papers, Library of Congress.

21. Playlets for Mary Jemison Child Study Club, "Situations in Eating, Feeding, Self, Training, etc.," Perry, Wyoming County, N.Y., MW.

22. Webster Family Life report, 12 February 1940, Monroe County, N.Y., MW.

23. Nancy Pottisham Weiss, "The Mother-Child Dyad Revisited: Perceptions of Mothers and Children in Twentieth Century Child-Rearing Manuals," *Journal of Social Issues* 34 (November 1978): 32.

24. Child Study Club report, n.d. (1931), Bessie Guthrie, Monroe County, N.Y., MW.

25. Naples Child Study Club report, 12 April 1932, Ontario County, N.Y., MW; Webster Child Study Club report, 16 March 1936, Monroe County, N.Y., MW.

26. "Report of Progress in Parent Education in California," 1 October–15 December 1926, series 3, box 27, no. 280, LSRM, 4. See, for example, Douglas A. Thom, *Everyday Problems of the Everyday Child* (New York: Appleton, 1927), in which he describes the

"cuff" and "unpleasant medications" which could be used to correct thumb-sucking, 107.

27. Milton J. E. Senn, "Insights on the Child Development Movement in the United States," *Monographs of the Society for Research in Child Development* 40 (August 1975): 28.

28. Sandy Creek Child Study Club report, 13 March 1934, Oswego County, N.Y., MW.

29. Watson, *Psychological Care*, 7; minutes of the meeting of the Society for the Study of Child Nature, 1890, n.d., supplement, box 5, CSA; Katherine Arnup, *Education for Motherhood: Advice for Mothers in Twentieth-Century Canada* (Toronto: University of Toronto Press, 1994), 39.

30. Chapter 379 minutes, box 26, folder 280, CSA; Sandy Creek Child Study Club report, n.d., folder for 1933–38, Oswego County, N.Y., MW.

31. Grace Crum, "Study Guide Based on *The Drifting Home* by Ernest Groves," *Child Welfare* 24 (September 1929): 32.

32. Syracuse—Salem Hyde Unit family life report, 3 April 1940, Syracuse (N.Y.) city report of unit meetings in Home Bureau units, MW; Hamilton Child Study Club report, 16 November 1932, Monroe County, N.Y., MW.

33. Paper by Mrs. Crothers, 30 November 1924, Mothers' Club of Cambridge, box 1, Schlesinger Library.

34. Sara Ruddick, "Maternal Thinking," in *Rethinking the Family: Some Feminist Questions*, ed. Barrie Thorne with Marilyn Yalom (New York: Longman, 1982), 81; Linda Gordon, *Heroes of Their Own Lives* (New York: Penguin Books, 1988), 139.

35. See Hamilton Cravens, *The Triumph of Evolution: American Scientists and the Heredity-Environment Controversy, 1900–1940* (Philadelphia: University of Pennsylvania Press, 1978); Chapter 375 minutes, 5 November 1930, box 27, folder 276, CSA.

36. John E. Anderson, *The Young Child in the Home* (New York: Appleton-Century, 1936), 218.

37. Chapter 371 minutes, 5 January 1931, CSA; Chapter 128 minutes, 1 December 1926, box 26, no. 268, CSA; Chapter 375 minutes, 29 October 1930, 1930–31, box 27, no. 276, CSA; Child Study Club report, 27 October 1937, Channing County–Elmira County, N.Y., MW.

38. Gordon, *Heroes of Their Own Lives*, 179; Report on Child Development and Parent Education in Rochester, 1 July 1931, series 3, box 39, no. 404, LSRM; Child Study Club report, n.d., 1930–32, Yates County, N.Y., MW.

39. Middletown Child Study Club report, 4 December 1935, Orange County, N.Y., MW; Minutes, 14 December 1931, box 27, no. 281, CSA; Middletown Child Study Club report, 4 December 1935, Orange County, N.Y., MW.

40. Sandy Creek Child Study Club report, 13 March 1934, Oswego County, N.Y., MW; 1933 Report on Child Development Projects, UM; Stearns and Haggerty, "The Role of Fear," 67.

41. Child Study Club report, 18 March 1930, box 8, small red volume, MW; Child Study Club report, 25 March 1930, box 8, small red volume, MW; Hilton Child Study Club report, 13 April 1931, Monroe County, N.Y., MW; Naples Child Study Club report, 26 January 1932, Ontario County, N.Y., MW.

42. Middletown Child Study Club report, 24 November 1939, Orange County, N.Y., MW.

43. School #65 PTA Child Study Club report, 6 January 1932, Buffalo, Erie County, N.Y., MW.

44. Coldwater Child Study Club report, 13 April 1936, Monroe County, N.Y., MW.

45. The most comprehensive account of the nursery school movement during this time is Barbara Beatty's *Preschool Education in America: The Culture of Young Children from the Colonial Era to the Present* (New Haven: Yale University Press, 1995).

46. "Report of Nursery School Committee," 27 January 1926, Chicago Woman's Club Papers, 1925–26, box 29, Chicago Historical Society, Chicago, Ill.; Chapter 378 minutes, 21 November 1930, box 27, no. 278, CSA.

47. W. Webster Child Study Club report, n.d. 1931, "Child Guidance," Monroe County, N.Y., MW; DeKalb Junction Child Study Club report, 25 April 1933, St. Lawrence County, N.Y., MW; Hilton Child Study Club report, 13 April 1931, Monroe County, N.Y., MW; Monroe Child Study Club report, 15 May 1935, Orange County, N.Y., MW; quoted in Margaret K. Nelson, "Mothering Others' Children: The Experiences of Family Day-Care Providers," *Signs* 15 (Spring 1990): 599–600.

48. DeKalb Junction Child Study Club report, 3 March 1936, St. Lawrence County, N.Y., MW.

49. 1933 Report on Child Development Projects, Institute of Child Welfare, UM.

50. 1933 Report on Child Development Project, Institute of Child Welfare, UM, 8; 1939 Report on Child Development Project, Institute of Child Welfare, UM, 11; 1933 Report on Child Development Project, Institute of Child Welfare, UM, 8; Scranton Child Study Club report, 21 April 1930, Erie County, N.Y.; Hilton Child Study Club report, n.d., Monroe County, N.Y., MW.

51. O. Mannoni, *Freud* (New York: Vintage Books, 1971), 182; Nathan Hale, *Freud and the Americans* (New York: Oxford University Press, 1971), 421; Chapter 13 minutes, 15 December 1922, box 1, no. 5, CSA.

52. See Estelle B. Freedman, "The New Woman: Changing Views of Women in the 1920s," *Journal of American History* 61 (September 1974): 372–93; and Christina Simmons, "Companionate Marriage and the Lesbian Threat," *Frontiers* 4 (1979): 54–59.

53. Miriam Van Waters, "Who Is the Owner of This Child?" *New Republic* 47 (21 July 1926): 248; Quilliard, *Child Study Discussion Records,* 65; "First Meeting of Harlem Committee for Furthering Child Study," 5 December 1928, box 42, no. 454, CSA.

54. Hazel M. Cushing, "Parent Education as a Mode in Mental Hygiene," *Mental Hygiene* 4 (October 1933): 637; Sandy Creek Child Study Club report, 24 March 1936, Oswego County, N.Y., MW. In her study, Cushing discovered that most mothers claimed that the primary benefit of the study club was the assistance it gave them in solving their personal problems, 637.

55. Mrs. Ralph White to Family Life Department at Cornell University, 7 December 1937, Niagara County Child Study Club, N.Y., MW.

56. Rhoda Denison to Margaret Wylie, 10 July 1933, Church of the Master Group, Monroe County, N.Y., MW; Hilton Child Study Club report, n.d., Monroe County, N.Y., MW.

57. Hilton Child Study Club report, n.d. (1931?), Monroe County, N.Y., MW.

58. Sol Cohen, "The Mental Hygiene Movement, the Development of Personality and the School," *History of Education Quarterly* 23 (Summer 1983): 134.

59. 1933 Report on Child Development Project, Institute of Child Welfare, UM, 11.

60. 1933 Report on Child Development Project, Institute of Child Welfare, UM; 1930 Report on Child Development Project, Institute of Child Welfare, UM, 7.

61. Minutes of Mothers' Thursday Club, vol. 1, 31 March 1921, Mothers' Thursday Club Papers, Schlesinger Library; PTA School #65 Child Study Club report, 18 November 1931, Buffalo, Erie County, N.Y., MW; S. Alabama Child Study Club report, 11 December 1935, Genesee County, N.Y., MW.

62. John E. Anderson, "Child Development: An Historical Perspective," *Child Development* 2 (June 1956): 183.

63. "Mrs. Miller, for Inter-Community Conference Dinner, May 23, 1931," ICCSC, 1931, box 41, folder 430, CSA; 1938 Report on Child Development Projects, Minnesota Institute of Child Welfare, UM.

64. Mary Shirley, *Can Parents Educate One Another? A Study of Lay Leadership in New York State* (New York: National Council of Parent Education, 1938), 7.

CHAPTER 6

1. C. Anderson Aldrich and Mary M. Aldrich, *Babies Are Human Beings: An Interpretation of Growth* (New York: Macmillan, 1939), 22.

2. Helen L. Witmer, *The Field of Parent Education,* Parent Education Monograph no. 1 (New York: National Council of Parent Education, 1934), 16.

3. Christopher Lasch, *Haven in a Heartless World* (New York: Basic Books, 1977), 62; "Child Study Association Extension Report, 1934–37," series 3, box 27, no. 288, LSRM; Robert S. Lynd and Helen Merrell Lynd, *Middletown in Transition* (New York: Harcourt, Brace, 1937), 146; Louis Adamic, *My America, 1928–1938* (New York: Harper & Row, 1938), 283.

4. Sonya Michel's article, "American Women and the Discourse of the Democratic Family in World War II," in *Behind the Lines: Gender and the Two World Wars,* ed. Margaret Randolph Higonnet, Jane Jenson, Sonya Michel, and Margaret Collins Weitz (New Haven: Yale University Press, 1987), 155–67, and her Ph.D. dissertation, "Children's Interests, Mother's Rights," Brown University, 1986, are some of the first works to examine the discourse of the democratic family. Primary source materials on the democratic family include Ada Hart Arlitt, *Family Relationships* (New York: McGraw-Hill, 1942); Frances Ilg and Arnold Gesell, *Infant and Child in the Culture of Today* (New York: Harper & Brothers, 1943); Lemo Dennis Rockwood, *Living Together in the Family* (Washington, D.C.: American Home Economics Association, 1934); and Katherine DuPre Lumpkin, *Family: A Study of Member Roles* (Chapel Hill: University of North Carolina Press, 1933).

5. Lynd and Lynd, *Middletown in Transition,* 146.

6. See, for instance, Lumpkin, *Family,* 169, and Michel, "American Women," 156. On wives' employment, see Winifred D. Wandersee Bolin, "The Economics of Middle-Income Family Life: Working Women During the Great Depression," *Journal of American History* 65 (June 1978): 60.

7. Glen Elder, *Children of the Great Depression: Social Change in Life Experience* (Chicago:

University of Chicago Press, 1974), 77; Samuel A. Stouffer and Paul F. Lazarsfeld, *Research Memorandum on the Family in the Depression* (New York: Social Science Research Council, 1937), 113. Other studies of the family during the Depression include Robert Cooley Angell, *The Family Encounters the Depression* (New York: Charles Scribner's Sons, 1936), and Ruth Shonle Cavan and Katherine Howland Ranck, *The Family and the Depression* (Chicago: University of Chicago Press, 1938).

8. See Lois Scharf, *To Work and to Wed: Female Employment, Feminism, and the Great Depression* (Westport, Conn.: Greenwood Press, 1980), and Susan Ware, *Holding Their Own: American Women in the 1930s* (Boston: Twayne, 1982). On working women who relinquish careers for motherhood, see Margaret Collins, "Careers Unlimited," *Scribner's Magazine* 102 (October 1937): 45–48; Jane Allen, "You May Have My Job: A Feminist Discovers Her Home," *Forum* 87 (April 1932): 228–31; and Judith Lambert, "I Quit My Job: Mother Goes Back to the Kitchen," *Forum* 98 (July 1937): 9–15.

9. Eduard C. Lindeman, "Newer Currents of Thought on Parent Education," *New Republic* 51 (6 July 1927): 173.

10. "Trends in Teaching Child Development and Family Relationships in the High School, June 1933," American Home Economics Association, Child Development, 1932–34, series 3, box 26, no. 272, LSRM. For an example of a typical home economics text of the period, see Rockwood, *Living Together in the Family*.

11. On the WPA nursery schools, see Emily D. Cahan, *Past Caring: A History of U.S. Preschool Care and Education for the Poor, 1820–1965* (New York: National Center for Children in Poverty, Columbia University, 1989), and Barbara Beatty, *Preschool Education in America: The Culture of Young Children from the Colonial Era to the Present* (New Haven: Yale University Press, 1995). On the impact of the White House Conference, see Sol Cohen, "The Mental Hygiene Movement, the Development of Personality and the School: The Medicalization of American Education," *History of Education Quarterly* 23 (Summer 1983): 135.

12. Ralph P. Bridgman, director, National Council of Parent Education, to Catherine Hill Taylor, Spelman Fund, 30 September 1936, series 3, box 35, no. 371, LSRM.

13. Steven L. Schlossman has charted the history of *Parents' Magazine* and its relation to the child development movement in "The Perils of Popularization: The Founding of *Parents' Magazine*," *Monographs of the Society for Research in Child Development* 50 (4–5): 65–77.

14. "Parental Advisory Dept. of Detroit Public Schools, 1931–32," series 3, box 32, no. 338, LSRM.

15. National Council of Parent Education, 1931–34, annual report 1930, series 3, box 35, no. 370, LSRM.

16. See Hamilton Cravens, "Child-Saving in the Age of Professionalism," in *American Childhood: A Research Guide and Historical Handbook*, ed. Joseph Hawes and N. Ray Hiner (Westport, Conn.: Greenwood Press, 1985), for a discussion of this movement away from behaviorism in child psychology. Eduard C. Lindeman, "Family Relatedness: A Basic Consideration for Parent Education," *Papers on Parent Education Presented at the Biennial Conference* (Washington, D.C.: National Council of Parent Education, 1930), 65; University of the State of New York, State Education Department, Child Develop-

ment and Parent Education, *Report of Work in Child Development and Parental Education Supported by Grant from the Spelman Fund to the State Education Department* (Albany, New York: University of the State of New York, 1933), 19.

17. Eduard C. Lindeman and Flora Thurston, *Problems of Parent Educators* (New York: National Council of Parent Education, 1929), 68.

18. Margo Horn, *Before It's Too Late: The Child Guidance Movement in the United States, 1922–1945* (Philadelphia: Temple University Press), 135; Witmer, *The Field of Parent Education,* 8.

19. Fred Matthews, "The Utopia of Human Relations: The Conflict-Free Family in American Social Thought, 1930–1960," *Journal of the History of the Behavioral Sciences* 24 (October 1988): 343–62; Gertrude Laws, *Parent Education in California* (Sacramento: California State Printing Office, 1937), 8; Lawrence K. Frank, "The Beginnings of Family Life Education," *Merrill-Palmer Quarterly* 8 (1962): 223.

20. See, for instance, *Problems for Parent Educators* 2 (1930), 15.

21. "Parent Education Conference, French Lick Springs, 1932," Abigail Adams Eliot Papers, Schlesinger Library.

22. William Henry Burnham, *The Normal Mind* (New York: Appleton, 1924), 27.

23. Fred Matthews, "In Defense of Common Sense: Mental Hygiene as Ideology and Mentality in 20th Century America," in *Prospects: An Annual of American Cultural Studies,* vol. 4, ed. Jack Weal (New York: Well Franklin, 1979), 476. Elizabeth Lunbeck uses the phrase "psychiatric persuasion" to describe the psychiatric way of viewing the world, in *The Psychiatric Persuasion: Knowledge, Gender, and Power in Modern America* (Princeton, N.J.: Princeton University Press, 1994), 46.

24. See Matthews, "In Defense of Common Sense," 483; Michael Zuckerman, "Dr. Spock: The Confidence Man," in *The Family in History,* ed. Charles E. Rosenberg (Philadelphia: University of Pennsylvania Press, 1975), 179–207; John C. Burnham, "The New Psychology: From Narcissism to Social Control," in *Change and Continuity in Twentieth-Century America,* ed. John Braeman, Robert H. Bremner, and David Brody (Columbus: Ohio State University Press, 1969), 397–98. For an in-depth exploration of the concept of "adjustment" in relation to the discipline of psychology, see Donald S. Napoli, *Architects of Adjustment: The History of the Psychological Profession in the United States* (Port Washington, N.Y.: Kennikat Press, 1981).

25. Theresa R. Richardson, *The Century of the Child: The Mental Hygiene Movement and Social Policy in the United States and Canada* (Albany: State University of New York Press, 1989), 3–4; Wendy Simonds, *Women and Self-Help Culture: Reading Between the Lines* (New Brunswick, N.J.: Rutgers University Press, 1992), 5–6.

26. Elaine Tyler May, *Homeward Bound: American Families in the Cold War Era* (New York: Basic Books, 1988), 14, 16.

27. Robert G. Foster and Pauline Park Wilson, *Women After College* (New York: Columbia University Press, 1942), 236; Lunbeck, *The Psychiatric Persuasion,* 256; James Lee Ellenwood, *There's No Place Like Home* (New York: Charles Scribner, 1938), 133–40.

28. On the therapeutic ethos see Philip Rieff, *The Triumph of the Therapeutic* (New York: Harper & Row, 1965). See also T. J. Jackson Lears, "From Salvation to Self-Realization:

Advertising and the Therapeutic Roots of the Consumer Culture, 1880–1930," in *The Culture of Consumption,* ed. Richard Wightman Fox and T. J. Jackson Lears (New York: Pantheon Books, 1983), 3–38.

29. Ernest Rutherford Groves and William Fielding Ogburn, *American Marriage and Family Relationships* (New York: Henry Holt, 1928), 57.

30. Arlitt, *Family Relationships,* 165; 1938 Report of Child Development Project, University of Minnesota Institute of Child Welfare, UM, 14.

31. Sidonie Gruenberg, "Parent Education and Child Welfare," in White House Conference on Child Health and Protection, *Parent Education: Types, Content, Method* (New York: Century, 1932), 24; Monroe Family Life report, 11 October 1939, Orange County, N.Y., MW.

32. Report of Progress, 1 October–15 December 1926, California Program of Parent Education, series 3, box 27, no. 280, LSRM.

33. Herbert Stolz, M.D., "An Experiment in Parent Education, California, 1926–27," series 3, box 27, no. 280, LSRM, 4, 9.

34. Hilton Family Life report, 18 May 1938, Monroe County, N.Y., MW; Frances E. W. Searles to Blanche Hedrick, 1 October 1937, MW.

35. Loyalty Child Study Club report, 20 November 1929, Penn Yan–Yates County, N.Y., MW, 8; Robert L. Griswold, *Fatherhood in America: A History* (New York: Basic Books, 1993), 129–30.

36. John E. Anderson, *The Young Child in the Home: A Survey of Three Thousand American Families* (New York: Appleton-Century, 1936), 77, 82.

37. 1934 Report on Child Development Project, UM; Fanny Bulger to Sidonie Matsner Gruenberg, 27 May 1938, Program Advisory Service, 1938, box 30, no. 306, CSA; Cora Trawick Court, "Parent Education in Nashville," box 1, Cora Trawick Court Papers, Schlesinger Library, 56; Griswold, *Fatherhood in America,* 129.

38. Maria Lambin Rogers, *A Contribution to the Theory and Practice of Parents' Associations* (New York: United Parents' Association of New York, 1931), 39; Groves and Ogburn, *American Marriage and Family Relationships,* 30. On the importance of men's providing "sex role models" for their children, see Griswold, *Fatherhood in America,* 94. Griswold argues that parent educators ignored and thereby further displaced fathers from family life by inevitably addressing their classes to women. He overlooks the efforts of parent educators and clubwomen themselves to engage men in their classes and programs, however.

39. Griswold, *Fatherhood in America,* 99.

40. Clarence Center Child Study Club report, 10 March 1937, Erie County, N.Y., MW; Warwick Family Life report, 4 December 1939, Orange County, N.Y., MW.

41. Clarence Center Child Study Club report, 1 April 1935, Erie County, N.Y., MW; Clarence Center Child Study Club report, 10 March 1937, Erie County, MW.

42. In *The Century of the Child,* Theresa Richardson says (190), "The dilemma for reformers who wanted to solve crime, disease, poverty, delinquency, and war by way of mental hygiene was that they did not want to change any of the structures that had caused the problems. The effort was to make social institutions 'work better' without altering their basic character."

43. Hilton Child Study Club report, 9 May 1933, Monroe County, N.Y., MW.

44. Dorothy Barnes to Blanche Hedrick, 13 May 1939, Orange County, N.Y., MW.
45. Delia C. Huston to Blanche Hedrick, 12 April 1939, Home Bureau Unit Meetings, Orange County, N.Y., MW.
46. Barnard Child Study Club report, 11 November 1930, Monroe County, N.Y., MW.
47. Lunbeck, *The Psychiatric Persuasion,* 266.
48. Hilton Child Study Club report, 23 November 1933, Monroe County, N.Y., MW.
49. See Charles H. Hearn, *The American Dream in the Great Depression* (Westport, Conn.: Greenwood Press, 1977).
50. Hilton Family Life Study Club report, 21 March 1940, Monroe County, N.Y., MW; 1939 Report on Child Development Project, Minnesota Institute of Child Welfare, UM; Sandy Creek Child Study Club report, 8 May 1934, Oswego County, N.Y., MW.
51. Family life report, 13 January 1939, Home Bureau Unit Meetings, Orange County, N.Y., MW; Gasport family life report, 3 November 1938, Niagara County, N.Y., MW; family life report, 6 January 1939, Home Bureau Unit Meetings, Orange County, N.Y., MW.
52. Syracuse University Unit family life report, 23 January 1940, Syracuse City, MW; Hilton Family Life Study Group report, 21 March 1940, Monroe County, N.Y., MW.
53. Irondequoit Bay Family Life Study Club report, 2 November 1939, Monroe County, N.Y., MW; Riverside Family Life Study Club report, 24 March 1942, Erie County, N.Y., MW.
54. South Alabama Family Life Study Club report, 10 January 1939, Genesee County, N.Y., MW; Monroe Family Life Study Club report, 7 November 1939, Orange County, N.Y., MW.
55. Monroe Family Life Study Club report, 5 December 1939, Orange County, N.Y., MW; Monroe Family Life Study Club report, 15 November 1938, Orange County, N.Y., MW.
56. Webster Child Study Club report, 6 March 1933, Monroe County, N.Y., MW; Fairport family life report, n.d., Monroe County, N.Y., 1935–38, MW.
57. Clinton Child Study Club report, 21 November 1940, Oneida County, N.Y., MW; Kerhonksen Family Life Study Club report, 28 November 1938, Ulster County, N.Y., MW.
58. Child Study Club report, 1931, Home Demonstration Agent, Oneida County, N.Y., MW; Georgie Watkins to Margaret Wylie, 23 February 1931, Monroe County, N.Y., MW.
59. See, for instance, Sandy Creek Study Club report, 24 April 1934, Oswego County, N.Y., MW, and University of Minnesota Institute of Child Welfare reports.
60. 1939 Report on Child Development Project, University of Minnesota Institute of Child Welfare, UM, 4; Mary Shirley, *Can Parents Educate One Another? A Study of Lay Leadership in New York State* (New York: National Council of Parent Education, 1938), 37; Norma Harmon to Margaret Wylie, 21 May 1936, Coldwater Group, Monroe County, N.Y., MW; family life report, 8 February 1939, Oneida County Home Bureau Unit Meetings, 1939–40, MW.
61. "The Baby Institute," 15 March 1944, Edith Banfield Jackson Papers, box 3, no. 44, Schlesinger Library; Henry L. Zucker, "Working Parents and Latchkey Children," in *Adolescents in Wartime,* ed. James H. S. Bossard and Eleanor S. Boll (Philadelphia: Annals of the American Academy of Political and Social Science: 1946): 43; George W. Kosmak, "Motherhood in Wartime," *Hygeia* 21 (December 1943): 867.

62. Lynn Y. Weiner, *From Working Girl to Working Mother: The Female Labor Force in the United States, 1820–1980* (Chapel Hill: University of North Carolina Press, 1985), 111; Michael C. C. Adams, *The Best War Ever: America and World War II* (Baltimore: Johns Hopkins University Press, 1994), 123; Sherna Berger Gluck, *Rosie the Riveter Revisited: Women, the War, and Social Change* (Boston: Twayne, 1987), 13; and Leila J. Rupp, *Survival in the Doldrums: The American Women's Rights Movement, 1945 to the 1960s* (New York: Oxford University Press, 1987), 97.

63. Michel, "American Women"; U.S. Children's Bureau, *White House Conference on Children in a Democracy: Final Report* (Washington: Government Printing Office, 1942).

64. Arnold Gesell and Frances Ilg, *Infant and Child in the Culture of Today* (New York: Harper & Row, 1943); Robert H. Dalton, "Developing Control for Democratic Living," *Journal of Home Economics* 39 (January 1947): 4.

65. Articles on this topic include James S. Plant, "Democracy Turns to the Family," *Journal of Home Economics* 34 (January 1942): 3; Alice V. Keliher, "Childhood and the Democratic Future," *National Education Association Journal* 37 (December 1948): 590; Karl Menninger et al., "The Roots of War in Human Nature," *Child Study* 20 (Spring 1943): 72–77, 91.

66. Harriet Eager Davis, "How *Not* to Raise Our Children," *Parents' Magazine* 20 (August 1945): 17.

67. Alfred L. Baldwin, "Socialization and the Parent-Child Relationship," *Child Development* 19 (September 1948): 127.

68. Dorothy Baruch, "Therapeutic Procedures as Part of the Educative Process," *Journal of Consulting Psychology* 4 (September–October 1940): 165–75; Martha C. Ericson, "Child-Rearing and Social Status," *American Journal of Sociology* 52 (November 1946): 191–92; W. Allison Davis and Robert J. Havighurst, "Social Class and Color Differences in Child Rearing," *American Sociological Review* 11 (December 1946): 698–710. A very useful discussion of these studies appears in William M. Tuttle, Jr., *"Daddy's Gone to War": The Second World War in the Lives of America's Children* (New York: Oxford University Press, 1993), 105–6. Evelyn Millis Duvall came to a somewhat different conclusion in "Conceptions of Parenthood," *American Journal of Sociology* 52 (November 1946): 193–203: she argues that middle-class mothers were more "developmental" than the "traditional" working-class mothers. In this case, however, Duvall surveyed mothers who were participants in parent education classes and were ostensibly more informed about the latest findings in child psychology.

69. Gesell and Ilg, *Infant and Child*, 10; Edith N. Norton, *Parent Education in the Nursery School* (Washington, D.C.: Association for Childhood Education International, 1949), 6.

70. Gesell and Ilg, *Infant and Child*, 58.

71. "White House Conference on Children in a Democracy, Points Suggested for Discussion at Group Meeting," 18 January 1940, Children in a Democracy, vols. 6–10, box 56, Arnold Gesell Papers, Library of Congress.

72. John Dollard et al., *Frustration and Aggression* (New Haven: Yale University Press, 1939), 1, 60–64.

73. David M. Levy, *Maternal Overprotection* (New York: Columbia University Press, 1943), 4.

74. Edward A. Strecker, "What's Wrong with American Mothers?" *Saturday Evening Post* 219 (26 October 1946): 14–15. See also Edward A. Strecker, *Their Mothers' Sons: A Psychiatrist Examines an American Problem* (Philadelphia: Lippincott, 1946), and Philip Wylie, *Generation of Vipers* (New York: Holt, Rinehart and Winston, 1955 [1942]). On the pathologization of motherhood, see Barbara Ehrenreich and Deirdre English, *For Her Own Good: 150 Years of the Experts' Advice to Women* (Garden City, N.Y.: Doubleday, 1979). On the debate about drafting fathers, see Griswold, *Fatherhood in America,* 167–72.

75. Zucker, "Working Parents and Latchkey Children," 43, 46.

76. Diane E. Eyer, *Mother-Infant Bonding: A Scientific Fiction* (New Haven: Yale University Press, 1992), 60, 64–5; Anna Freud and Dorothy Burlingham, *War and Children* (New York: Medical War Books, 1943). See also Freud and Burlingham, *Infants Without Families: The Case For and Against Residential Nurseries* (New York: Medical War Books, 1944); Renée A. Spitz, "Hospitalism: An Inquiry into the Genesis of Psychiatric Conditions in Early Childhood," *Psychoanalytic Study of the Child* 1 (1945): 53–75.

77. Eleanor S. Boll, "The Child," in *The American Family in World War II* (Philadelphia: The American Academy of Political and Social Science, 1943), 70. See also Karen Anderson, *Wartime Women: Sex Roles, Family Relations, and the Status of Women During World War II* (Westport, Conn.: Greenwood Press, 1981), 84; and Tuttle, *"Daddy's Gone to War,"* 109.

78. Pearl S. Buck, "Do You Want Your Children to Be Tolerant?" *Better Homes and Gardens* 25 (February 1947): 33, 132–35; Hodding Carter, "How to Stop the Hate Mongers in Your Home Town," *Better Homes and Gardens* 26 (November 1947): 45, 180, 182. Other articles on teaching children about racial and religious tolerance include Florence Mary Fitch, "Teaching Children Religious Tolerance," *Parents' Magazine* 21 (June 1946): 42–43, 101–4; Rhoda W. Bacmeister, "The World We Want for Our Children," *Parents' Magazine* 18 (November 1946): 17, 120–24; and M. F. Ashley Montagu, "Democracy, Education, and Race," *School and Society* 59 (1 April 1944): 227–29. On intercultural education see Sherry L. Field, "Intercultural Education and Negro History During the Second World War," *Journal of the Midwest History of Education Society* 22 (1995): 75–85.

79. "Report of the Committee to Cooperate with War Relocation Authority in Establishing PTA's," 22 May 1944–26 May 1944, 1944 Convention Appendices 1–35, National Congress of Parents and Teachers, vol. 25, PTA Papers, University of Illinois at Chicago Circle Manuscript Collections, 77.

80. C. Madeline Dixon, "Democracy Before Five!" *Parents' Magazine* 17 (August 1942): 25, 32. On intercultural education, see Tuttle, *"Daddy's Gone to War,"* chaps. 7 and 10.

81. Ellen C. Lombard, "Supervision of Parent Education as a Function of State Departments of Education," bulletin no. 1940, issue 6 (Washington: Government Printing Office, 1942); Board Meeting, 11 December 1943, box 4, file 3, Association for Family Living Papers, University of Illinois at Chicago Circle Manuscript Collections; *Association for Family Living Newsletter* (May 1945): 1, box 4, folder 12, Association for Family Living;

"National PTA Membership Figures, 1910 to Present," obtained from National Congress of Parents and Teachers Public Relations Department, Washington, D.C.

82. Flora Rose, *A Growing College: Home Economics at Cornell University* (New York: Cornell College of Home Economics, 1969), 183.

83. Data come from "Extension Work in New York in Agriculture and Home Economics," *Cornell Extension Bulletin,* bulletin no. 443 (August 1940): 59–60.

84. Evelyn Millis Duvall, "The Young Mother Faces War," in *National Parent-Teacher* (September 1942): 5–6; Bennett Study Club report, 19 February 1941, Buffalo County, N.Y., MW; D'Ann Campbell, *Women at War with America* (Cambridge: Harvard University Press, 1984), 5.

85. Report of War Committee, Appendix 13, Meetings of Executive Committee and Board of Managers, 23–25 September 1943, National Congress of Parents and Teachers, vol. 24, PTA Papers, 140.

86. Howard Dratch, "The Politics of Child Care in the 1940s," *Science and Society* 38 (Summer 1974): 169.

87. Bennett Study Club report, 6 November 1940, Buffalo County, N.Y., MW.

88. Greece Child Study Club report, 25 January 1945, Monroe County, N.Y., MW.

89. Lockport Study Club report, 15 June 1943, Niagara County, N.Y., MW.

90. DeKalb Junction Child Study Club, 2 July 1943, St. Lawrence County, N.Y., MW.

91. Nassau County Family Life Study Club report, 30 March 1944, Nassau County, N.Y., MW.

92. Tuttle, *"Daddy's Gone to War,"* 69–90.

93. Ellenville-Kerhonksen-Accord Family Life Study Group, 21 April 1941, Ulster County, N.Y., MW.

94. Bennett Child Study Club, 16 November 1941, Buffalo County, N.Y., MW.

95. Kingston II Child Study Club report, 22 March 1945, Ulster County, N.Y., MW.

96. Spencerport Family Life Study Club report, 24 April 1944, Monroe County, N.Y., MW.

97. Kingston II Child Study Club report, 6 April 1944, Ulster County, N.Y., MW.

98. Unknown writer to Blanche Hedrick, 25 July 1940, New Paltz Family Life Study Club, Ulster County, N.Y., MW.

99. Griswold, *Fatherhood in America,* 162.

100. Kenmore Family Life Group report, 13 February 1942, Erie County, N.Y., MW.

101. Ithaca Family Life Study Club report, 9 September 1944, Tompkins County, N.Y., MW.

102. Small Fry Study Club, 27 October 1943, Henrietta, Monroe County, N.Y., MW.

103. Kensington II Family Life Study Club report, 10 February 1944, Buffalo County, N.Y., MW.

104. Bennett Study Club report, 19 February 1941, Buffalo County, N.Y., MW.

105. Duvall, "Conceptions of Parenthood," 195–200.

106. Marilyn Irvin Holt makes a good argument for this in *Linoleum, Better Babies and the Modern Farm Woman* (Albuquerque: University of New Mexico Press, 1995), 7.

107. Tuttle, *"Daddy's Gone to War,"* 95.

108. Gertrude Gilmore Lafore, *Practices of Parents in Dealing with Preschool Children* (New York: Teachers College, 1945), 131.

109. Marianne Muse, "Time Expenditures on Homemaking Activities," Agricultural Exper-

iment Station, University of Vermont and State Agricultural College, Burlington, Vt., bulletin no. 530 (June 1946): 27.

110. Tonawanda Gahunda Family Life Study Club report, 25 February 1941, Genesee County, N.Y., MW. See Anderson, *Children in the Family.*

111. Lockport Child Study Club report, 20 February 1945, Mrs. Robert Shutes, Niagara County, N.Y., MW.

112. Williamsville Family Life Study Club, 10 April 1945, Erie County, N.Y., MW.

113. Tonawanda Gahunda Family Life Study Club report, 25 February 1941, Genesee County, N.Y., MW.

114. Sidonie Matsner Gruenberg, "Family Life—Then and Now," *Child Study* 16 (November 1938): 44.

115. Mt. Morris Home Bureau unit meeting report, 6 November 1941, Livingston County, N.Y., MW.

116. Oakfield Child Study Club report, 10 February 1944, Genesee County, N.Y., MW.

117. Henrietta Child Study Club report, 17 February 1942, Monroe County, N.Y., MW.

118. Clarence Center Family Life Group report, 27 October 1943, Erie County, N.Y., MW.

119. Churchville Family Life Study Club, 5 March 1941, Monroe County, N.Y., MW.

120. Henrietta Family Life Group report, 17 February 1942, Monroe County, N.Y., MW; Martha Anne Beckers to Anne Kuhn, 4 November 1943, Spencerport Family Life Group, Monroe County, N.Y., MW.

121. Kingston III Family Life Group report, 24 March 1942, MW; Oakfield Mothers' Club report, 10 December 1943, Genesee County, N.Y., MW.

122. Tonawanda Gahunda Family Life Study Group report, 4 June 1943, Genesee County, N.Y., MW.

123. Norwich Child Study Club report, 10 February 1941, Chenango County, N.Y., MW. University Heights Family Life Study Group report, 12 March 1943, Buffalo County, N.Y., MW; Tonawanda Gahunda Family Life Study Group report, 6 April 1943, Genesee County, N.Y., MW; Koenig Road Family Life Study Group report, 13 November 1945, Erie County, N.Y., MW.

124. Ruddick, *Maternal Thinking,* 103–23.

125. Sound Avenue Child Study Club Notebook, 10 January 1930, Suffolk County, N.Y., 1929–30, MW.

126. On the biblical roots of "sparing the rod," see Philip Greven, *Spare the Child: The Religious Roots of Punishment and the Psychological Impact of Physical Abuse* (New York: Random House, 1990), 48. He traces the aphorism "Spare the rod, spoil the child" to Samuel Butler's poem *Hudibras* (1664).

CHAPTER 7

1. "Bringing Up Baby on Books," *Newsweek* 45 (May 16, 1955): 65; Helen Puner, "Gesell's Children Grow Up," *Harper's Magazine* 212 (March 1956): 37–43.

2. Steven Mintz and Susan Kellogg, *Domestic Revolutions: A Social History of American Family Life* (New York: Free Press, 1988), 177–79; William L. O'Neill, *American High: The Years of Confidence, 1945–1960* (New York: Free Press, 1986), 40.

3. Arlene Skolnick, *Embattled Paradise: The American Family in an Age of Uncertainty* (New York: Basic Books, 1991), 53–59.

4. Brett Harvey, *The Fifties: A Woman's Oral History* (New York: Harper Perennial, 1993), 105.

5. John Modell, *Into One's Own: From Youth to Adulthood in the United States, 1920–1975* (Berkeley: University of California Press, 1989), 251; Skolnick, *Embattled Paradise*, 68.

6. Roberts R. Sears, Eleanor E. Maccoby, and Harry Levin, *Patterns of Child Rearing* (Evanston, Ill.: Row, Peterson, 1957), 49. In *The Fifties* (New York: Villard Books, 1993), David Halberstam argues that before television provided midday talk shows for women, "women's magazines provided the core reading material for the new young suburban wives," 590.

7. S. B. M. of Kansas City, Mo., to Benjamin Spock, 18 April 1960, series 1904–68, box 5, Benjamin Spock Papers, Syracuse University Library, Syracuse, N.Y. (hereafter referred to as BS). To protect the privacy of the letter writers, I will be using only their initials, place of residence, and date of letter. See also Harvey, *The Fifties*, 102.

8. Jane Whitbread, "Don't Let Experts Rule Your Children," *Coronet* 27 (February 1950): 47.

9. Mr. R. G. of Elgin, Ill., to Benjamin Spock, 11 May 1958, series 1904–68, box 4, BS.

10. V. V. of Frankfort, N.Y., to Julia Grant, 8 August 1996; C. W. of Madison, Wisc., to Benjamin Spock, 29 February 1960, series 1904–68, box 5, BS.

11. Mrs. P. B. of Bangor, Me., to Louise Bates Ames and Frances Ilg, 21 November 1957, box 12, Parents Ask Correspondence, Louise Bates Ames Papers, Library of Congress, Washington, D.C. (hereafter referred to as LBA).

12. M. B. of Gresham, Ore., to Louise Bates Ames and Frances Ilg, 30 May 1961, box 12, LBA.

13. Ernest Havemann, "The Age of Psychology in the U.S.," *Life* 42 (7 January 1957), 72.

14. See Benjamin Spock, "Spock Talks with Mothers," *Ladies' Home Journal* 71 (July 1954): 43, where he said, "There's no chance at all that I can answer any letter personally." In a personal telephone conversation (July 1993), Ames assured me that she felt it was her personal responsibility to respond to the letter writers. I am unaware whether Ilg was as vigilant as Ames in this respect. See also Nancy Pottisham Weiss, "Mother, the Invention of Necessity: Dr. Benjamin Spock's *Baby and Child Care*," in *Growing Up in America: Children in Historical Perspective*, ed. N. Ray Hiner and Joseph M. Hawes (Urbana: University of Illinois Press, 1985), 294. In a response to a letter writer who complained that her husband was "indulging in sex play" with her four-year-old daughter and said that she was thinking about divorce, Spock said, "I don't think that precipitate divorce is necessarily the next step." He also claimed that "a disposition of this kind means that a man has had his feelings mixed up by certain aspects of his upbringing," which can sometimes "be straightened out by psychoanalytic treatment." Other similar and equally problematic examples are present in the correspondence. See E. K. of Van Nuys, Calif., to Spock, 22 November 1960, series 1904–68, box 7, BS, and Spock to E. K., 6 December 1960, series 1904–68, box 7, BS.

15. E. K. H. of San Rafael, Calif., to Benjamin Spock, 6 September 1956, series 1904–68, box 3, BS.

16. Ferdinand Lundberg and Marynia F. Farnham, *Modern Woman: The Lost Sex* (New York:

Harper & Brothers, 1947); Mrs. Peter Marshall, "Introduction," *Life* (24 December 1956): 22.

17. See Lundberg and Farnham, *Modern Woman: The Lost Sex.* Joanne Meyerowitz has provided convincing evidence that, contrary to popular perceptions, women's magazines continued to celebrate career women in the 1950s in "Beyond the Feminine Mystique: A Reassessment of Postwar Mass Culture, 1946–1958," *Journal of American History* 79 (March 1993): 1455–82.

18. Helen Leland Witmer and Ruth Kotinsky, *Personality in the Making: The Fact-Finding Report of the Midcentury White House Conference on Children and Youth* (New York: Harper & Row, 1952), 102.

19. Benjamin Spock, "Can Motherhood Be Taught?" *Ladies' Home Journal* 76 (January 1958): 16; Benjamin Spock, "Communication in Parent Education," 1955, Parent Education 1955–65, series 1904–68, box 36, BS.

20. Martha Wolfenstein, "Fun Morality: An Analysis of Recent American Child Training Literature," *Childhood in Contemporary Cultures,* ed. Margaret Mead and Martha Wolfenstein (Chicago: University of Chicago Press, 1955), 168–78; D. W. Winnicott, M.D., *Mother and Child: A Primer of First Relationships* (New York: Basic Books, 1957), vii, cited in Barbara Ehrenreich and Deirdre English, *For Her Own Good: 150 Years of the Experts' Advice to Women* (Garden City, N.Y.: Doubleday, 1979), 224. See also Daniel R. Miller and Guy E. Swanson, *The Changing American Parent: A Study in the Detroit Area* (New York: Wiley, 1958), on defining "instincts" as acts of tenderness and indulgence; Witmer and Kotinsky, *Personality in the Making,* 102.

21. E. W. of Fitchburg, Mass., to Louise Bates Ames and Frances Ilg, 2 November 1953, box 8, LBA.

22. Elaine Tyler May, *Homeward Bound: American Families in the Cold War Era* (New York: Basic Books, 1988), 149.

23. John Bowlby, *Child Care and the Growth of Love* (Baltimore: Johns Hopkins University Press, 1953), 18, 16; Diane E. Eyer, *Mother-Infant Bonding: A Scientific Fiction* (New Haven: Yale University Press, 1992), 48–49.

24. Elaine Tyler May in *Homeward Bound* and Betty Friedan in *The Feminine Mystique* (New York: Dell, 1963) have focused mainly on the image of what Friedan calls the "happy housewife heroine" in their survey of the periodical literature. Joanne Meyerowitz attempts to revise this portrayal of women of the period in "Beyond the Feminine Mystique: A Reassessment of Postwar Mass Culture, 1946–1958," *Journal of American History* 79 (March 1993): 1455–82.

25. Sidonie M. Gruenberg and Hilda Sidney Krech, *The Many Lives of Modern Woman* (New York: Doubleday, 1952), 28, 31.

26. Warren I. Susman, "The Culture of Personality," in *Culture as History: The Transformation of American Society in the Twentieth Century* (New York: Pantheon, 1984), 276.

27. Althea K. Hottel, *How Fare American Women?* (Washington, D.C.: American Council on Education, 1955), v.

28. Eugenia Kaledin, *Mothers and More: American Women in the 1950s* (Boston: Twayne, 1984), 36–39.

29. Benjamin Spock, "What We Know About the Development of Healthy Personality in

Children," in *Proceedings of the Midcentury White House Conference on Children and Youth*, ed. Edward A. Richards (Raleigh, N.C.: Health Publications Institute, 1951), 69; Cover, *Ladies' Home Journal* 73 (February 1956).

30. Adrienne Rich, *Of Woman Born: Motherhood as Experience and Institution* (New York: Norton, 1976), 2.

31. Benjamin Spock, *The Commonsense Book of Baby and Child Care* (New York: Pocket Books, 1946); see also the third edition of *Gesell and Armtruda's Developmental Diagnosis*, ed. Hilda Knobloch and Benjamin Pasamanic (New York: Harper & Row, 1975).

32. For biographical details on Gesell, see his autobiographical essay, "Arnold Gesell," in *A History of Psychology in Autobiography*, vol. 4, ed. Edwin G. Boring (Worcester, Mass.: Clark University Press, 1952): 123–42; "Arnold Gesell, Obituary," in *American Journal of Psychiatry* 118 (December 1961): 574–76; "A Brief Sketch of the History of the Yale Clinic of Child Development," box 121, Yale Clinic History, 1923–51, Arnold Lucius Gesell Papers, Library of Congress, Washington, D.C.; Thomas K. Fagan, "Gesell: The First School Psychologist," Part 1, "The Road to Connecticut," *School Psychology Review* 16 (1987): 103–7; Fagan, "Gesell: The First School Psychologist," Part 2, "Practice and Significance," *School Psychology Review* 16 (1987): 399–409; and Arnold Gesell, *The Pre-School Child from the Standpoint of Public Hygiene and Education* (Boston: Houghton Mifflin, 1923), 9.

33. Arnold Gesell et al., *The First Five Years of Life: A Guide to the Study of the Preschool Child* (New York: Harper & Brothers, 1940).

34. Arnold Gesell and Frances L. Ilg in collaboration with Louise Bates Ames and Janet Learned, *Infant and Child in the Culture of Today* (New York: Harper & Brothers, 1943); Gesell and Ilg, in collaboration with Ames and Glenna E. Bullis, *The Child from Five to Ten* (New York: Harper & Brothers, 1946). On Ames's biography, see Gwendolyn Stevens and Sheldon Gardner, "Researcher as Celebrity: Louise Bates Ames," in *The Women of Psychology*, vol. 2: *Expansion and Refinement* (Cambridge, Mass.: Schenkman, 1982), 83–86. For Frances Ilg, see "Biographical Notes on Frances Ilg, M.D.," from the Hall Syndicate, 1 December 1951, box 3, LBA. See also "A Transcript of an Interview with Dr. Louise Bates Ames of the Gesell Institute of Human Development," conducted by Todd Russell on 1 February 1985, from the unprocessed portion of the collection, LBA, 5–6. I am grateful to librarian Michael J. Klein of the Manuscript Division of the Library of Congress for this reference.

35. See "Biographical Notes on Frances Ilg, M.D."

36. Ames claimed that critics of the group generally objected that group members did not pay enough attention to Freud, were oblivious to environmental factors, and did not respect children's individual differences, and moreover that Gesell's norms made parents anxious. See Ames, *Arnold Gesell—Themes of His Work* (New York: Human Sciences Press, 1989), 235.

37. Puner, "Gesell's Children Grow Up," 38.

38. "Life with Baby Discussion Outline," March of Time Correspondence, box 222, 1945–51, Arnold Lucius Gesell Papers, Library of Congress, 2.

39. Spock, *Baby and Child Care*, 3; Gesell, *The First Five Years of Life*, 3.

40. V. G. F. to Louise Bates Ames and Frances Ilg, 23 March 1953, box 8, LBA; Milton J. E.

Senn, "The Epoch Approach to Child Development," *Woman's Home Companion* 82 (November 1955): 41.

41. Mrs. Frederick G. Ely to *Harper's Magazine* 21 (May 1956): 10.

42. Senn, "The Epoch Approach," 42; Esther Thelen and Karen E. Adolph, "Arnold L. Gesell: The Paradox of Nature and Nurture," *Developmental Psychology* 28 (May 1992): 370; Arnold Gesell and Frances L. Ilg, *Child Development: An Introduction to the Study of Human Growth* (New York: Harpers, 1949), 224.

43. According to Sandra Scarr in *Mother Care/Other Care* (New York: Basic Books, 1984), "Gesell's child is good by nature and endowed with self-propelled maturation; he is largely unaffected by details of parental caregiving, as long as it is not abusive or neglectful," 63.

44. See chapter on "Physical Types, Sizes, Handedness, Vision," in Ames and Ilg, *Parents Ask* (New York: Harper & Brothers, 1962). See also William H. Sheldon, *Varieties of Temperament* (New York: Harper, 1942).

45. Margaret Mead to Frances Ilg, 25 February 1953, box 32, LBA. Mead wrote to Ilg, "The emphasis of the last few years on the potential damage that parents can do to children, the mistakes they can make and their consequences, has done so much harm—in some instances—that there is danger of a reaction in favor of less awareness of parental role." Ilg also wrote to Benjamin Spock, "You feel we are leaving out of consideration too many aspects of emotional development." Frances Ilg to Benjamin Spock, 5 March 1962, box 3, Benjamin Spock Papers, 1961–62, LBA.

46. Louise Bates Ames and Frances L. Ilg, *Child Behavior* (New York: Harper, 1955), 191. Even today's popular baby book writer T. Berry Brazelton and his colleague Bertrand G. Cramer recognize this concept in *The Earliest Relationship: Parents, Infants, and the Drama of Early Attachment* (Reading, Mass.: Addison-Wesley, 1990). In their analyses of several infant-parent relationships, however, they look at the *interactions* between babies with particular kinds of temperaments and mothers with different temperaments, an obvious elaboration, and improvement, on Ames and Ilg's analysis.

47. On Ilg and Ames's treatment of autism, see, for instance, *Parents Ask*, a compilation of their newspaper columns, 319–26. On the psychoanalytic approach of many Americans toward autism during the 1950s and 1960s, see Anne M Donnellan, ed., *Classic Readings in Autism,* 2–3, and Bruno Bettelheim's enormously influential *The Empty Fortress: Infantile Autism and the Birth of the Self* (New York: Free Press, 1967), in which he attributed autism to the parent's wish that the child should not exist, 125.

48. Ames and Ilg, *Parents Ask,* 101, 103–4.

49. See for instance Ames and Ilg, *Child Behavior,* 63, and *Parents Ask,* 222–25.

50. Lynn Z. Bloom's *Doctor Spock: Biography of a Conservative Radical* (Indianapolis: Bobbs Merrill, 1972) recounts the ambivalence and sometimes antipathy with which some of Spock's colleagues at Case Western Reserve and the University of Pittsburgh regarded his research and teaching.

51. Two major sources of Spock's biography include Benjamin Spock, *Spock on Spock: A Memoir of Growing Up with the Century* (New York: Pantheon, 1989), and Bloom, *Doctor Spock.* A much more telling and comprehensive biography of the baby book author is yet to be written, however. See also William Graebner, "The Unstable World of Benjamin

Spock: Social Engineering in a Democratic Culture, 1917–1950," *Journal of American History* 3 (December 1980): 612–29.

52. Carol Lawson, "At 88, an Undiminished Dr. Spock," *New York Times,* 141 (5 March 1992), C1. Other biographical information on Spock includes, Martha Weinman, "Now 'Dr. Spock' Goes to the White House," *New York Times Magazine* 109 (4 December 1960): 26, 121, and J. D. Ratcliff, "Meet Dr. Spock: Physician to 10 Million Babies," *Parents' Magazine* 33 (May 1958): 51, 78–80.

53. Spock, *Spock on Spock,* 133.

54. Spock, *Spock on Spock,* 135.

55. Bloom, *Doctor Spock.*

56. My interpretation of Spock's manual has been aided immensely by three particularly insightful analyses of his work: Weiss, "Mother, the Invention of Necessity"; Graebner, "The Unstable World of Benjamin Spock"; and Michael Zuckerman, "Dr. Spock: The Confidence Man," in *The Family in History,* ed. Charles Rosenberg (Philadelphia: University of Pennsylvania Press, 1975), 179–207.

57. Mrs. H. W. of Roela, Miss., to Benjamin Spock, 4 August 1954, box 2, BS.

58. Mrs. R. D. S. of Concord, Calif., to Benjamin Spock, 19 October 1954, box 2, BS. In a later study of readers of parental advice literature published in 1978, K. Alison Clarke-Stewart, "Popular Primers for Parents," *American Psychologist* 33 (April 1978), found that parents who consulted books for advice had very little contact with other parents or relatives and tended to be younger, better educated, and more worried about being good parents than those who did not consult such sources, 364.

59. Mrs. W. C. of Wakefield, Mass., to Benjamin Spock, 22 May 1968, box 1, BS.

60. "A Visit with Dr. Spock," *Look* 23 (21 July 1959): 24; Spock, *Baby and Child Care,* 3. Spock seemed to be aware that his use of the term "instincts" was commonsensical rather than scientific when, in a letter to parents, he defined instincts as "the manner in which you were brought up yourself." See Benjamin Spock to Mrs. G. T. of Binghamton, N.Y., 12 February 1958, box 23, 1990–, BS.

61. "A Visit with Dr. Spock," 24.

62. Spock, *Baby and Child Care,* 252.

63. See Graebner, "The Unstable World of Benjamin Spock," 612–29; Spock, *Spock on Spock,* 135; Benjamin Spock to B. M. J., 2 March 1954, series 1904–68, box 2, BS; Spock, *Baby and Child Care,* 19, 20. See also Zuckerman, "Dr. Spock."

64. Mrs. G. H. J. to Benjamin Spock, 1954, n.d., n.p., series 1904–68, box 2, BS.

65. See especially Nancy Pottisham Weiss on this topic, "The Mother-Child Dyad Revisited: Perceptions of Mothers and Children in Twentieth Century Child-Rearing Manuals," *Journal of Social Issues* 34 (Spring 1978): 29–45, and Zuckerman, "Dr. Spock."

66. Weinman, "Now 'Dr. Spock' Goes to the White House," 121.

67. J. B. of Brooklyn, N.Y., to Benjamin Spock, 15 November 1957, box 2, BS.

68. Weinman, "Now 'Dr. Spock' Goes to the White House," 121–22.

69. Spock, *Baby and Child Care,* 484.

70. Benjamin Spock, "The Difference Between the Sexes," *Ladies' Home Journal* 73 (September 1956): 31.

71. Benjamin Spock to Rose Chacko, 27 November 1957, box 3, BS.

72. Benjamin Spock to Urie Bronfenbrenner, 10 December 1957, series 1904–68, box 3, BS; John H. Kennell, M.D., "Experience with a Medical School Family Study," *Journal of Medical Education* 36 (December 1961): 1669.

73. Zena Smith Blau, "Exposure to Child-Rearing Experts: A Structural Interpretation of Class-Color Differences," *American Journal of Sociology* 69 (1964): 596–608, found large differences in the percentages of African-American mothers in Chicago maternity wards who had read Spock's book, even when class and education were controlled for. Although 48 percent of working-class white mothers had read the book, for instance, only 12 percent of working-class African-American mothers had read it; 77 percent of white middle-class mothers had read the book, while only 32 percent of African-American middle-class mothers had read it, 599.

74. Joanne Dann, "Wanted: A Dr. Spock for Black Mothers," *New York Times Magazine* 120 (18 April 1971): 78–84.

75. Quoted in Harvey, *The Fifties*, 108; J. L. G. to Louise Bates Ames and Frances Ilg, 24 November 1957, Parents Ask Correspondence, box 12, LBA.

76. Mrs. H. W. of Providence, R.I., to Louise Bates Ames and Frances Ilg, 22 November 1955, box 12, LBA.

77. Mr. and Mrs. G. F. B. of Franklin, Ohio, to Louise Bates Ames and Frances Ilg, 25 August 1955, box 10, Parents Ask Correspondence, LBA.

78. See Nathan G. Hale, Jr., *The Rise and Crisis of Psychoanalysis in the United States: Freud and the Americans, 1917–1985* (New York: Oxford University Press, 1995), for an account of the "popularization" of psychoanalysis during this period. See also Ellen Herman, *The Romance of American Psychology: Political Culture in the Age of Experts* (Berkeley: University of California Press, 1995), and Sydney A. Halpern, *American Pediatrics: The Social Dynamics of Professionalism, 1880–1980* (Berkeley: University of California Press, 1988).

79. L. V. G. to Louise Bates Ames and Frances Ilg, 23 August 1956, box 12, LBA.

80. *The Complete Book of Mothercraft, with Contributions from Twenty-Five Leading Specialists* (New York: Greystone Press, 1952), 377.

81. Mrs. J. B. of Philadelphia, Pa., to Louise Bates Ames and Frances Ilg, 27 September 1955, box 12, LBA; Mrs. W. E. A. of Jackson, Miss., to Louise Bates Ames and Frances Ilg, 26 November 1957, Parents Ask Correspondence, box 12, LBA; Louise Bates Ames to Mrs. W. E. A., 19 December 1957, Parents Ask Correspondence, box 12, LBA.

82. H. B. and L. B. of New York City to Louise Bates Ames and Frances Ilg, 13 June 1955, Parents Ask Correspondence, box 12, LBA.

83. Mrs. C. E. M. of North Manchester, Ind., to Louise Bates Ames and Frances Ilg, n.d., box 12, LBA.

84. Mrs. J. E. Wilson of Niles, Ohio, to Benjamin Spock, 11 May 1960, box 6, 1904–68, BS.

85. Mrs. S. K. of Wilkes Barre, Pa., to Benjamin Spock, 3 March 1960, box 6, BS. In a telephone interview conducted on 24 July 1996 with Mrs. S. K., I confirmed that my analysis of her situation was fairly accurate. The baby turned out fine, and in retrospect, Mrs. S. K. believed herself to have been "overly insecure" as a first-time mother. In Mirra Komarovsky's study *Blue-Collar Marriage* (New York: Random House, 1962), she claims that the working-class parents she researched evinced remarkably little awareness of psychological theories of childhood: "We, the interviewers, felt transported, as if by a

Wellsian time machine, into an older era, one of pre-Freudian innocence about human behavior," 78.

86. Jackson Lears, "A Matter of Taste: Corporate Cultural Hegemony in a Mass-Consumption Society," in *Recasting America: Culture and Politics in the Age of Cold War*, ed. Larry May (Chicago: University of Chicago Press, 1989), 48. In discussing the "mass consumption" ethos of the postwar era, Lears argues that "mediating institutions of family, community, or faith can prevent the individual's absorption by the all-encompassing system."

87. Clarke-Stewart, "Popular Primers," 367.

88. Goodwin Watson, "Some Personality Differences in Children Related to Strict or Permissive Parental Discipline," *Journal of Psychology* 44 (1957): 227–49. Watson found that he could not use the experiences of 53 percent of the respondents he surveyed because they did not fit into either of his two categories, 231. On unscheduled versus scheduled feedings, see Sears, Maccoby, and Levin, *Patterns of Child Rearing*, 78. Other studies include Daniel R. Miller and Guy E. Swanson, *The Changing American Parent: A Study in the Detroit Area* (New York: Wiley, 1958); Sylvia Brody, *Patterns of Mothering: Maternal Influences During Infancy* (New York: International Universities Press, 1956); John C. Glidewell, ed., *Parental Attitudes and Child Behavior* (Springfield, Ill.: Charles C. Thomas, 1961).

89. M. F. of Sarasota, Fla., to Louise Bates and Frances Ilg, 25 February 1957, box 12, LBA; M. F. of Sarasota, Fla., to Benjamin Spock, 6 July 1958, series 1904–68, box 4, BS. Wini Breines in *Young, White, and Miserable: Growing Up Female in the Fifties* (Boston: Beacon Press, 1992) notes that many "white, middle-class mothers in the 1950s were not yet Spockian permissive parents," 69.

90. Benjamin Spock, "Why I'm Rewriting My Baby Book," *Ladies' Home Journal* 74 (September 1957): 22; G. R. L. of Boston, Mass., to Benjamin Spock, 20 December 1960, box 7, BS.

91. B. E. H. of Steubenville, Ohio, to Louise Bates Ames and Frances Ilg, 18 January 1961, box 12, LBA.

92. Mrs. M. B. W. of St. Cloud, Fla., 3 March 1958, series 1990–, box 23, BS.

93. Taylor Caldwell of Buffalo, N.Y., to Benjamin Spock, 29 December 1959, series 1904–68, box 5, BS.

94. Janice E. Hale-Benson, *Black Children: Their Roots, Culture, and Learning Styles* (Baltimore: Johns Hopkins University Press, 1982), 52–53; Jeanne M. Giovanni and Andrew Billingsley, "Child Neglect Among the Poor: A Study of Parental Adequacy in Families of Three Ethnic Groups," *Child Welfare* 49 (1970): 471–76.

95. Ruth Schwartz Cowan, *More Work for Mother: The Ironies of Household Technology from the Open Hearth to the Microwave* (London: Free Association Books, 1989), 201; Kaledin, *Mothers and More*, 51.

96. Mrs. G. V. of Frankfort, N.Y., to Benjamin Spock, 8 August 1957, series 1904–68, box 3, BS.

97. Mrs. T. F. G. of Springfield, Pa., to Benjamin Spock, 14 August 1958, series 1904–68, box 4, BS.

98. C. W. of Madison, Wisc., to Benjamin Spock, 29 February 1960, series 1904–68, box 5, BS.

99. Robert Coughlan, "Changing Roles in Modern Marriage," *Life* 41 (24 December 1956): 113.

100. Quoted in Friedan, *Feminine Mystique,* 42–43; Cowan, *More Work for Mother,* 200. Cowan says that in the 1950s there was a "hullabaloo" about the "new husband" in the popular press. See also "The New American Domesticated Male," *Life* 36 (4 January 1954), 42–45; May, *Homeward Bound,* 146.

101. Robert L. Griswold, *Fatherhood in America: A History* (New York: HarperCollins, 1993), 194, 211.

102. Mrs. G. T. of Binghamton, N.Y., to Benjamin Spock, 6 February 1958, series 1990–, box 23, BS; Mrs. C. T. Weaver of Philadelphia, Pa., to Benjamin Spock, 22 July 1954, box 2, BS; Mrs. M. A. of University Heights, Ohio, to Spock, 30 November 1954, box 2, BS. On concerns about boys' becoming "sissies" in the 1950s, see May, *Homeward Bound,* 147.

103. Mrs. W. K. of Detroit, Mich., to Benjamin Spock, 17 July 1957, series 1904–68, box 3, BS; Mrs. J. H. B. of Sandwich, Mass., 5 November 1956, box 12, LBA. See Peter N. Stearns and Timothy Haggerty, "The Role of Fear: Transitions in American Emotional Standards for Children, 1850–1950," *American Historical Review* 96 (February 1991): 63–94, on the treatment of children's fears in the prescriptive literature of the period.

104. Mrs. K. B. of Wofford Heights, Calif., to Benjamin Spock, February 1960, box 5, BS; Rich, *Of Woman Born,* 4.

105. E. L. P. of Stoughton, Mass., to Louise Bates Ames and Frances Ilg, 21 November 1955, box 12, Parents Ask Correspondence, LBA.

106. Orville G. Brim, "The Causes of Parent Behavior," in *Parent Educators on the Job: Proceedings of the 12th Annual Institute for Workers in Parent Education* (New York: Child Study Association of America, 1959), 8; Mrs. R. A. Gritta of Long Beach, Calif., to Benjamin Spock, 26 June 1954, series 1904–68, box 2, BS.

107. K. S. of Greenville, Pa., to Benjamin Spock, 10 April 1959, series 1904–68, box 5, BS.

108. M. D. of North Wales, Pa., to Benjamin Spock, 12 February 1958, Redbook, series 1990–, box 23, BS.

109. V. K. M. of Pottowattomie (N.Y.?) to Benjamin Spock, 16 December 1956, series 1904–68, box 3, BS.

110. J. H. of Americus, Ga., to Benjamin Spock, 5 October 1959, series 1904–68, box 5, BS; Hottel, *How Fare American Women?,* 6.

111. P. G. of Milwaukee, Wisc., to Benjamin Spock, 19 February 1974, series 1990–, box 23, BS.

112. M. E. W. of Mt. Lebanon, Pa., to Louise Bates Ames and Frances Ilg, 11 December 1956, box 12, Parents Ask Correspondence, LBA.

113. Benjamin Spock, "Dr. Spock Talks with Mothers," *Ladies' Home Journal* 71 (July 1954): 43.

114. Mrs. R. J. N. of Minneapolis, Minn., to Benjamin Spock, 13 October 1954, series 1904–68, box 2, BS.

115. Mrs. A. K. of Elmira, N.Y., to Benjamin Spock, 20 July 1954, series 1904–68, box 2, BS.
116. Mrs. O. R. H. of Pampa, Tex., to Benjamin Spock, 31 December 1959, series 1904–68, box 5, BS; Mrs. H. F. of Houston, Tex., to Louise Bates Ames and Frances Ilg, 18 August 1957, Parents Ask Correspondence, box 12, LBA.
117. Friedan, *The Feminine Mystique,* 57.

CONCLUSION

1. Jeffrey Bils and Stacy Singer, "Gorilla Saves Tot at Brookfield Zoo," *Chicago Tribune* (August 17, 1996): A1.
2. Vivien Devlin, *Motherhood: From 1920 to the Present Day* (Edinburgh: Polygon, 1995), 11.
3. Pampers commercial, aired during *What Every Baby Knows, with Dr. T. Berry Brazelton,* on Lifetime Television for Women, 13 June 1996.
4. Penelope Leach, *Children First* (New York: Alfred A. Knopf, 1994), 37.
5. *What Every Baby Knows, with Dr. T. Berry Brazelton,* on Lifetime Television for Women, 14 October 1996.
6. Martha McMahon, *Engendering Motherhood: Identity and Self-Transformation in Women's Lives* (New York: Guilford Press, 1995), 268. See Arlie Hochschild on the problem of women's double day in *The Second Shift: Work, Parenting, and the Revolution at Home* (New York: Viking, 1989).
7. Sherrye Henry, *The Deep Divide: Why American Women Resist Equality* (New York: Macmillan, 1994), 141–44. I found Henry's formulations strikingly similar to those I had been hearing from my students over the past few years. The first chapter of Henry's book is entitled "I Enjoy Being a Girl," and I hear that sentiment more and more from my students. That is, they value the qualities associated with the word "feminine," although they do not see any necessary contradiction between being delicate, for instance, and being independent.
8. See Susan Moller Okin, *Justice, Gender, and the Family* (New York: Basic Books, 1995).
9. Benjamin Spock, *The Commonsense Book of Baby and Child Care* (New York: Pocket Books, 1946), 3; commercial for Luxe Detergent, aired during *What Every Baby Knows, with Dr. T. Berry Brazelton,* on Lifetime Television for Women, 13 June 1996.
10. I do not have access to the Leach show on my television. Therefore, I must confine my observations to the Brazelton and Elkind shows. My information on Leach is based on her written work.
11. *What Every Baby Knows, with Dr. T. Berry Brazelton,* Lifetime Television for Women, 13 June 1996.
12. *What Every Baby Knows, with Dr. T. Berry Brazelton,* Lifetime Television for Women, 15 October 1996.
13. *Kids These Days, with Dana Fleming,* Lifetime Television for Women, 1 August 1996.
14. See Julia Wrigley, *Other People's Children* (New York: Basic Books, 1995), on how parents seek private solutions to public problems.

Index